(W)ARCHIVES

Archival Imaginaries, War, and Contemporary Art

ARCHIVAL IMAGINARIES, WAR, and CONTEMPORARY ART

(W)ARCHIVES

Edited by DANIELA AGOSTINHO, SOLVEIG GADE, NANNA BONDE THYLSTRUP, and KRISTIN VEEL

Sternberg Press

CONTENTS

INTRODUCTION

(W)ARCHIVES
Materialities of War, Digital Archiving, and Artistic Engagements

Daniela Agostinho, Solveig Gade, Nanna Bonde Thylstrup, and Kristin Veel

This book explores the changing role of archives in contemporary war, the cultural and political impact of digitization upon the war-archive nexus, and the ways in which the artistic field has responded to these changes. *(W)archives* proposes that in order to understand the rationale of contemporary wars, we need to investigate the increasingly structuring role played by digitization and digital archives within warfare. At the same time, to grasp the changing role of archives in light of digitization, we need to explore the ways in which archives are deployed to an ever-greater extent as technologies of warfare, venues for dissent, and demands for accountability. The book further suggests that the space of artistic production constitutes a fruitful site from which to address and critically engage with the current (w)archival regime. *(W)archives* thus situates the archive as an epistemic structure of war in times of digitization, as well as a practice of critique, opposition, and sensorial-affective response to the consequences of historical and ongoing wars.

Historically, archives have served as technologies of warfare. Building on processes of intelligence gathering, surveillance, and reconnaissance, war archives have been instrumental in identifying an enemy's location, behavior, and anticipated future tactics and strategy. It is through these archival procedures that bodies, territories, and infrastructures come to be selected for targeting, injury, and destruction. In this sense, archives have always been "key technocultural forms" constituting "structures of enmity," as Kevin McSorley reminds us in his chapter in this book. Consequently, war archives have been well guarded by those entrusted with the right to interpret the information they contain. This archival gatekeeping echoes Jacques Derrida's reflections in his landmark 1995 book *Archive Fever: A Freudian Impression*, where he reminds us that the Greek noun *archive* initially referred to a house where official documents were filed and guarded by *archons* on whom was bestowed the authority and power to access and interpret the archive's contents.[1] Given this history of archives as locations intimately bound up with the issuing of laws, one might think that they are to be seen as only authoritative within theoretical approaches: as the origin "from which order is given,"[2] as a "totalizing assemblage,"[3] and even as an institution that lays down "the law of what can be said," as Michel Foucault puts it.[4] However, even given the totalizing, ordering will of archives, they are by no means static or stable institutions that are invulnerable to transformation.[5] As mid-twentieth-century post-structuralist thought and feminist, queer, postcolonial, and critical archival studies have shown, the archive as a technology, authoritative though it may be, is never immune to internal contradictions or external dissent.[6] In fact, in post-structuralist and theoretical terms, archives have always been regarded as dynamic and generative of knowledge. In *The Archaeology of Knowledge* (1969), Foucault characterizes archives as constituting a "web of which they [the holders of the archive] are not the masters."[7] In Derrida's feverish archives there is an "aggression and destruction drive," such that a number of internal attributes subvert archival order from within.[8] Rather than neutrally storing knowledge, archives produce what can be known through hermeneutic operations of selection, preservation, and modes of permitting (or denying) access, all of which add to archives' dynamism and knowledge-creating nature.[9]

(W)archives mobilizes and expands this extensive body of critical archival thinking to reflect on the changing role of archives as technologies of warfare under conditions of digitization. We take into account the archive as a site of authority and power, as well as inflections of that authority, to consider how current practices of data production, gathering, treatment, and distribution extend—but also profoundly transform—archival regimes of war. In today's connective, digital age, the analogue archives that constituted the source material for previous archive theories are increasingly giving way to ever-growing networked archives of data. Warfare today overlaps with the datafication of everyday life,

through which data is generated and recorded across permanently updating and reconfigurable archives that reach deep into the most intimate spaces and quotidian gestures. This is what Kevin McSorley terms "immanent digital archiving": practices of data collection that are integral to contemporary living, and within which much of embodied existence is premised on "being-archived," with racialized populations disproportionately exposed to its most dangerous effects. This immanent digital archiving, which in principle is always at work, everywhere and all the time, fundamentally challenges our understanding of archival time and space.

Not so long ago, growing possibilities for digital connectivity gave rise to the notion that we are all potential contributors to a global (w)archive, as we are able to access, upload, and share digital content on a greater scale and with increasing speed. Particularly in the wake of the Arab uprisings, these possibilities enabled widespread hope in the potential of the digital to create crowdsourced counter-archives that would more fully supplement and challenge the heavily guarded and opaque archives kept by those in power.[10] Palestinian artists Basel Abbas and Ruanne Abou-Rahme, in conversation with Tom Holert, refer to this act of producing and sharing subjective and horizontal archives in terms of a "living common archive" fueled by the multivocal desire for an "archival multitude."[11] At the same time, as they acknowledge, this archival multitude is necessarily entrenched in digital networks, and therefore subject to various sorts of capture. Most of the corporate social media platforms that have allowed a living common archive to take shape lodge this archival multitude in information economies that inflect their liberatory potential and render dissenting subjects and archives vulnerable to various forms of power and control.[12]

Indeed, over the years, numerous disclosures of information, including those by Edward Snowden, Reality Winner, and Brittany Kaiser, have raised public awareness that digital connectivity also creates the opportunity for asymmetrical access to and treatment of information, particularly in the form of blanket surveillance and the algorithmic misuse of data harvested from everyday digital engagements.[13] This immanent digital archiving further overlaps with an increasing investment in new forms of social network analysis, risk profiling, predictive analytics, machine learning, and artificial intelligence, all of which strengthen the military and police apparatus. Indeed, the datafication of everyday life is shaped partly by defense funding and military projects that become naturalized and integrated into infrastructures of digitally-connected living, with commercial and military regimes often overlapping with and informing one another. These overlaps make war rationalities ever more integral—even if inconspicuously so—to everyday life.[14]

Developments such as these, we argue, have fundamentally changed the materiality of warfare by enfolding the digital into it. In the 2010 preface to her book *Frames of War: When Is Life Grievable?*—written before these mutations became available to public scrutiny—Judith Butler reflected on the visual and discursive dimensions of war and their structuring role in warfare. Within this context, she urged readers to rethink the received terms of materialism in order to understand how cameras work as instruments of war, not only in their capacity to shape public perceptions of the reality of war, but also as actual weapons by virtue of the "operative images" through which violence is inflicted upon populations, for instance in drone warfare.[15] Here Butler issued a call to consider images as part of what she termed an "extended materiality" of war.[16] With *(W)archives* we take up and extend this call to consider how immanent digital archiving has become part of this even more extended materiality. In addition to pointing to how digital archiving has become integral to warfare, we wish to emphasize the very material effects of digital archiving, in order to push back against the idea (prevalent in military discourses) that current war destruction is more precise and less damaging as a result of the growing capacity to extract, process, and act upon information. We thus wish to counter the disappearance of the corporeality of war attempted by military reason, and instead to bring into view the materiality of conducting, experiencing, and living with and under digital warfare. *(W)archives* suggests that this extended materiality of war is composed not only of weapons, information, infrastructures, technologies, and images, but also of bodies, senses, gestures, memories, imaginations, structures of feeling, textures, intimacies, and natural environments. Finally, *(W)archives* emphasizes the materiality of artistic production by foregrounding the various media—from photography to film, sculpture, bodies, and movement—that artists have engaged with to account for the differentiated experiences of living with and under war.

The book shows that this new digital materiality of war reconfigures the "archival impulses" that have shaped artistic practices over the last decades.[17] In many ways, as Basel Abbas and Ruanne Abou-Rahme note, the interrogation of the archive to which artists have devoted themselves has come alive through the practices of the archival multitude, especially in the ways these new living archives challenge notions of authenticity and the document, and in how they push against the gaps and boundaries of archival regimes of war. At the same time, these digital transformations call for renewed artistic engagements with the challenges posed by the global (w)archive. Throughout this book, artistic practices emerge as potential sites from which to intervene in the epistemological gaps produced by datafied processes, to "make sensuous" what has been abstracted,[18] and to rearticulate the archival promise of witnessing and testimony. In doing so, artistic practices reconfigure what counts as an archive, and imagine new possibilities for social justice from within the aesthetic field.

(W)archives emerged from an international workshop on war, archives, and art organized by Solveig Gade and the Uncertain Archives research group (Daniela Agostinho, Nanna Bonde Thylstrup, and Kristin Veel) at the University of Copenhagen in August 2017, which included presentations by Susan Schuppli, Kevin McSorley, Anders Engberg-Pedersen, Anthony Downey, Mariam Ghani, Nisrine Boukhari, Louise Wolthers, and Sarah Tuck, and the performance of *Probable Title: Zero Probability* (2012) by Hito Steyerl and Rabih Mroué. In commissioning the content for this book, we were deeply inspired by the discussions that took shape during this two-day workshop, which brought together scholars, artists, curators, and cultural practitioners to think through the changing relationship between archiving, war, and artistic production. The contributions to this book explore many of the questions discussed at this event: How do we account for military violence when warfare is increasingly based not only on material acts, but also on imagined futures of wars, brought about by predictive data-driven technologies? How do we demand accountability when the perpetration of violence is diffused along

opaque chains of often automated and privatized commands, as in the case of drone warfare? How do we gauge the credibility of images that claim to represent war and conflict in an era when digital manipulation prevails, and when violent imagery is strategically used to an unprecedented extent to shape the perceptual fields of war-affected populations as well as global spectators? How do we make sense of operative images made by and intended for machines, rather than for the human eye? What is the role of the senses in apprehending and opposing war, at a time when sensing is technologized more than ever? Finally, how do we safely gather, store, and preserve vulnerable and contested information when today's war archives are dispersed across the unstable and uncertain archives of social media?

Guiding the workshop and this book is the conviction that different knowledges and epistemic practices are required to apprehend the mutations of war; that we can look to earlier vocabularies, concepts, and practices to make sense of current developments; and that the contemporary moment calls for sustained critical engagement to offer an account of war that goes beyond its available framings. Such a sustained critical engagement demands new epistemic alliances in order to more capaciously register, respond to, and oppose war. The book thus brings together scholarly and practice-based essays, interviews, roundtable conversations, and visual and written contributions from artists renowned for their long-term work on archives and warfare. In this way, multiple ways to conceive of archives in relation to war come together to problematize different archival usages and potentials. In addition, the book puts different regions and contexts into conversation, including contexts where wars and conflict are currently underway (Iraq, Afghanistan, Syria, Palestine, the Mediterranean Sea) as well as contexts where the opening up of archives of past wars continues to generate pressing effects (particularly Chile and Argentina). While these various contexts are informed by specific political and regional dynamics, we consider that there is much to be gained from examining them in relation to broader technological and material structures pertaining to the extended materiality of war. Moreover, pulling these various contexts into conversation is also crucial to make legible the "imperial formations"[19] that continue to produce devastating effects on the lives of various populations, as well as transnational alliances between these regions and across times.

The book is divided into four parts, each bringing into view different dimensions of the extended materiality of warfare that we wish to foreground:

A ARCHIVING WAR Spatiotemporal Reconfigurations
B THE AESTHETICS OF DRONE FORMATIONS Counter-Archives, Mediations, and Interventions
C SENSING WAR Technologies, Intimacies, and Bodies
D EVIDENTIARY AESTHETICS Documenting, Witnessing, Redressing

In the following pages we discuss how these different dimensions testify to the changing nature of war and archives, and we offer an overview of how the contributions in each section shed light on the extending materiality of war.

ARCHIVING WAR
Spatiotemporal Reconfigurations

In contemporary warfare, the collecting and archiving of large amounts of data through digital surveillance technologies has led to altered notions of spatiality and temporality. In the nineteenth century, Prussian general and military historian Carl von Clausewitz, informed by the Napoleonic Wars, defined the battle site as "a sector of the total war area which has protected boundaries and so a certain degree of independence."[20] He continued that as being "not just a part of the whole, but a subordinate entity in itself," the "theater of operations" was affected not directly but only indirectly by events happening elsewhere in the war area.[21] According to this conceptualization, the theater of operations refers to the spatio-geographical territory where a war event takes place, and where men who are equally willing to put their lives on the line meet face-to-face. At the same time, however, the concept suggests the existence of a plurality of theaters of operations, which all follow their own rules and only indirectly affect one another. Arguably, Clausewitz's notion reflects above all the wish to project an order of sorts onto the unpredictable and violent condition of war. Nonetheless, the suggested autonomy of the theater of operations on the ground may serve as an important backdrop against which to pinpoint the ways in which contemporary war takes place across a multiplicity of different sites.

As James Der Derian points out in *Virtuous War* (2001), computer simulation, mediatization, global surveillance, and network-based information technologies are deeply entangled with the battle on the ground in contemporary warfare.[22] Indeed, with digital technology permeating all levels of warfare from communications to weapons technologies, the means of *representing* war can almost be collapsed with the means of *waging* war. A case in point is the first Gulf War, often referred to as the video game war. This war is famous for its footage of air raids and so-called precision bombing recorded by cameras aboard US bombers, and its unreal, "virtual" character for global spectators has often been emphasized. By the same token, the Western media's live transmission of footage during the war, supporting the narrative of surgical strikes and the notion that it was a war without bloodshed, has been foregrounded as a success for the Pentagon and US military.[23] Since then, the phenomenon of image war—the shaping of collective imaginaries through visual, often live representations of war events circulated across various media platforms—has established itself as an increasingly important factor to be reckoned with in today's warscape.[24] In other words, mediatized representations of violent events, and the continuous addition of these representations to the gigantic digital (w)archive, have effectively dissolved the autonomy of the material battle site envisaged by Clausewitz.

More recently, the ability of digital technologies to disrupt spatial as well as temporal constraints has reached new levels with the consolidation of drone warfare. Drone warfare renders obsolete Clausewitz's notion of war as entailing a face-to-face battle between two bodies putting their lives on the line. As Grégoire Chamayou observes, it may be the notion of the *manhunt*, rather than war, that applies to the profoundly asymmetrical situation where a drone operator seated in a container in Nevada can follow the annihilation of men, women, and children on the other side of the planet in real time.[25] For populations subjected to this predatory and radically asymmetrical war, this spatiotemporal reconfiguration means that war has become integral to their everyday embodied lives: it is constant and everywhere, drawing no distinctions between the battlefield, the home, and other everyday spaces.

In different ways, the contributions in this section investigate how contemporary warfare breaks with the autonomy of Clausewitz's theater of operations and instead unfolds across multiple, deeply entangled sites, ranging from geographical territories to digital and virtual sites. Moreover, the essays shine a light on transformations in the archival rationale of wars and conflict by examining how different technologies have reconfigured the archive as a structure of war.

In "Archives of Enmity and Martial Epistemology," Kevin McSorley explores the ontologies of enmity that are produced in and through new archival practices characterized by ubiquity and automation. These mark a reconfiguration of spatiotemporal relations that result in "discontinuous and open-ended military violence directed across the globe against networked and individual antagonists." Central here is the anticipatory logic of the predatory war, which entails not only the traditional idea that particular suspect communities might become subject to more targeted surveillance, but also that the mass archiving of the lifeworlds of entire populations might lead to the emergence of new forms of knowledge and targets, surfacing currently unknown unknowns. Paving the way for pattern-of-life analyses that may enable military data analytics and algorithms to "connect the dots" in the behavior of those under surveillance, big data is increasingly deployed not only to monitor the present, but also to predict security risks that may emerge in the future. Thus, in data-driven warfare, models of causality give way to a preemptive logic according to which military action is triggered by potential, not-yet emergent future threats.[26]

In "Event Maps: The Cartographic Archive and Imagined Futures of War," Anders Engberg-Pedersen shows that the historical phenomenon of the war map can indicate how attempts to imagine and thereby control the futures of war have long been key to military tactics. Moving from the astrological chart in Friedrich Schiller's *Wallenstein* (1799) to the topographic map in Leo Tolstoy's *War and Peace* (1869) and thence to the war game in Roberto Bolaño's *The Third Reich* (1989), he outlines how recent developments in computer simulation, and its instantiation in ever more advanced war games used for military purposes, mark a shift toward increased control over the futures of war, and also toward a widening of the military future and its increasing virtuality.

In the final essay in this section, "The Cerrillos Archive Project: Machines, War, and Nonhuman Rights," Cristián Gómez-Moya looks at the archival potential of land through a study of the territories of the University of Chile. The essay focuses on a historical event from 1976, when the military dictatorship moved the Faculty of Architecture from the Cerrillos campus, located in a peri-urban industrial zone, to a central area in the city of Santiago, and handed over the campus territory to the Carabineros (the Chilean national police force). As a result of this intervention, of which there is limited documented evidence, around thirty hectares of the Cerrillos plot were lost. Through the Cerrillos Archive Project, Gómez-Moya reads this loss of land as an "archaeological wound," and approaches the land itself as a document. The Cerrillos Archive Project today seeks to provide an activist counter-archive through the use of drone footage that surveys and recomposes the lost land. In this context, the drone functions as an archival machine that registers the traces in echographic terms, a non-human documentary trace that also activates other forms of human rights. Ultimately, by considering the nonhuman rights of the territory of Cerrillos through drone technology, Gómez-Moya prompts us to think about human rights beyond legal subjects, and to think of archives beyond their recognizable human forms by means of other archival machines.

THE AESTHETICS OF DRONE FORMATIONS
Counter-Archives, Mediations, and Interventions

Within the spatiotemporal reconfigurations charted in the first section, the drone repeatedly emerges as a key vehicle for transformations of the archiving of war. The reorganization of space, time, and lived experience produced by drone warfare is therefore a prime example of the expanded materiality of war that we foreground in *(W)archives*. As Lisa Parks and Caren Kaplan suggest in *Life in the Age of Drone Warfare* (2017), drones are part of extended drone formations, which have wide-ranging material effects: they embody broader cultural imaginaries, drawing upon and generating particular ways of perceiving the world; they are biopolitical machines that have the potential to alter life in the most material ways; they are sensory and perceptual machines embedded within histories of aerial observation and remote sensing, intensifying colonial aerial practices that have evolved over time; and they interact with embodied difference and affect, generating new racializing and gendering processes, and radically redefining the affective experiences and everyday social realities of populations targeted by drone surveillance.[27] Across these different registers, drones produce numerous material effects, across the sky and from the ground up.

Although drones are often referred to as "vision machines" and associated with recent developments in digital technologies, the privileged view from above offered by the drone can be traced back to phenomena such as anchored balloons equipped with telegraph wires, airborne cameras on reconnaissance aircraft, and remote sensing satellites.[28] In *Aerial Aftermaths: Wartime from Above* (2017), Caren Kaplan shows the importance of aerial imagery to modern visual culture and its ability to enforce colonial power, demonstrating both the destructive force and the potential for political connection that come with viewing from above.[29] As scholars and researchers such as Priya Satia and Madiha Tahir have argued,[30] the technological novelty of the drone often obscures these historical continuities—hence Chamayou's description of the drone as a "weapon of an amnesiac postcolonial violence."[31] Yet Kaplan also challenges the notion that the view from above must always entail power and control; she argues that the view from above can also be appropriated by artists and activists to challenge military claims, collect and make visible new data, and draw attention to otherwise obscured experiences on the ground.[32] The contributions in this section examine this extended materiality of drone warfare by homing in on the drone's "techno-aesthetic"[33] dimensions, bringing into view drones' relationships to imperial histories and biopolitical encroachments, their sensorial and perceptual complexity, and their potential to disrupt power through artistic experimentation.

In "Drones as Big Data Archives: Mimesis and Counter-Archiving in Contemporary Art on Military Drones," Kathrin Maurer goes beyond the scopic regime of the drone by attending to drones as "archival machines" implicated in the accumulation and storage of memories, images, experiences, and situations. The chapter turns to theories of mimesis as conceptualized by the Frankfurt School, which she argues can be productive to capture the deterritorializing aspects of drone technology and its archiving modes. Through the notion of mimesis, Maurer foregrounds how artworks that engage with military drones can create counter-archives to the drone "by problematizing its fluid forms of surveillance." The chapter focuses on two films to examine how the aesthetic production of counter-archives takes shape. First, it suggests that Trevor Paglen's *Drone Vision* (2010) performs an aesthetic mimesis of the temporality of drone archiving, aligning itself with the perceptual apparatus of the drone in ways that enable threshold moments of critical engagement. The chapter then turns to how Omer Fast's *5,000 Feet Is the Best* (2011) accentuates the spatial disruptions of drone archives by mimicking them, thus tackling the drone's unstable spatial orders. As a "form of sensory imitation and enactment," mimesis emerges as a way of making visible "the drone's decentralizing and disorienting effects" and thereby foregrounding the vulnerabilities of those targeted by the drone strikes enabled by big data archives.

In "Avian Prophecies and the Techno-Aesthetics of Drone Warfare," visual artist Heba Y. Amin discusses her ongoing project *The General's Stork* in conversation with visual culture scholar Anthony Downey. Accompanied by video stills and installation shots from the project, the conversation discusses the relationship between the techno-aesthetic dimension of drones and broader histories of colonial occupation in the Middle East. *The General's Stork* revolves around a viral media story about a migratory stork to which a tracking device had been attached by Hungarian scientists. The stork was detained and accused of espionage in Egypt in 2013, an episode through which Amin explores the historical conditions of paranoia, and the politics of aerial surveillance from both a bird's-eye view and remote-controlled drones. Embedded in a vertical power hierarchy, both gazes are associated with airborne technologies used to survey, map, and administer Middle Eastern territories and to fix and produce subjects in a political economy of difference and inequality. With this project, Amin speculatively investigates how conquest from the sky and its techno-aesthetics are inherently tied to the Greater Middle East, while also speaking to broader issues pertaining to sovereignty and the right to access and interpret information under growing conditions of digital obscurity.

The relationship between the techno-aesthetics of the drone, biopolitical encroachments, and the potential of artistic experimentation to disrupt such techno-political developments is central to "Watched by Drones: Photographic Surveillance in Art, War, and Protest," a conversation between Svea Braeunert, Sarah Tuck, and Louise Wolthers based on their individual and collaborative curatorial practices on drones. Reflecting on three exhibition projects in the United States, Sweden, Cyprus, and Pakistan, the conversation skillfully navigates numerous questions: the drone as an object to explore the changing ways of defining and describing images in digital culture; the drone's vertical relationships of power and domination; the use of drones as counter-hegemonic tools to challenge and claim power; the history of photography, colonialism, and visual sovereignty; the relationship between local and global histories, and the possibility of forging solidarity across time and space. Throughout the conversation, Braeunert, Tuck, and Wolthers discuss the contributions of various artists to the critical understanding of drone formations, while also charting new directions for scholarly and curatorial engagement with drone warfare and datafication. Crucially, the conversation foregrounds the ethics of curatorial (re)presentation, the curatorial and institutional responsibility of actively producing and shaping the (w)archive, and the need to tackle the power asymmetries of visibility and invisibility that arise with datafication and the wider sensorium that a technology such as the drone brings forth.

SENSING WAR
Technologies, Intimacies, and Bodies

The relation between war and the senses is central to the third section of the book. In *Frames of War*, Butler suggested that any effort to understand how war is waged and experienced must consider the technologies of war and how they work on the field of the senses. For Butler, the question of the senses is fundamental because war functions as an assault on the human senses—for its victims and survivors, but also, in a radically different way, for its global spectators. For this reason, she argues, transforming the senses is crucial to "develop an anti-war politics that focuses on the dispossessed and those rendered precarious."[34] Written a decade ago, these reflections emerged at a tipping point for the war sensorium. At the time, Butler's text was concerned with the perception of wars in Iraq and Afghanistan, how war photography and media reports established the "sensuous parameters of reality itself," how images recruited publics into the wars waged by US empire, and how these images ultimately rendered non-Western lives ungrievable. These reflections were situated within a specific war sensorium, one mostly defined by a field of human vision delimited by photographic cameras and publics solicited by visual and narrative media discourses. Yet as Butler's book was being completed, one month after Barack Obama's election to the US presidency, the "sensuous parameters of reality" were already undergoing decisive transformations that were then perhaps too opaque to discern.[35] This period witnessed a new stage in the "forever war,"[36] in which the front lines more clearly began to expand into spaces of computation and complex human-machinic assemblages, "beyond the thresholds of human perception and their attendant regimes of publicity."[37] Due in particular to the expansion of the US drone program, these new computational spaces have splintered the frames of war into a complex field of sensors and data signals across the electromagnetic spectrum. While these changes have not entirely replaced but have rather transformed earlier regimes of the perception of war, they prompt a reconsideration of the relationship between war and the senses. How does this new war sensorium challenge the ways in which wars are waged, experienced, and felt? How does it solicit different publics, both ethically and politically? As Susan Schuppli contends, if we are to "to intervene politically in the electronic fields of weaponized data," we need to bring about new critical vantage points and new decoding practices."[38]

The contributions in the third section of *(W)archives* engage with the sensory, phenomenological, and embodied aspects of war to think about questions of distance and proximity to war raised by historical and current archival regimes. Throughout this section, the question of "transforming the senses" to bring about more capacious ways of registering and accounting for the experience of war beyond predominant (w)archival regimes emerges as crucial. Common to the various essays is the question of how to develop archival and aesthetic strategies to go against prevailing frames of war, and which in turn may help to surface the underlying and different ways in which we are situated in relation to war. As such, the essays in this section also consider how to account for the situated and partial perspectives of those representing and witnessing conflict.

In the essay "Cruel Intimacies," Daniela Agostinho reflects on the transformations that datafication has brought upon the global war sensorium through the lens of intimacy. The essay contends with the modes of perceptual proximity enabled by datafication, which have led to the emergence of notions such as "distance-intimacy" to refer to the ways in which war is brought up close. In dialogue with Richard Mosse's video installation *Incoming* (2014–2017) and Solmaz Sharif's book of poems *LOOK* (2016), Agostinho thinks through the moral, affective, and material intimacies afforded by the global war sensorium through the term "cruel intimacies." The chapter argues that the proximities enabled by digitization fold global spectators into the (w)archive of violence and conflict through relations of cruel intimacy. These cruel intimacies, she suggests, form the very sensorial-material infrastructure through which global spectators sense, feel, and engage with war. Cruel intimacy thus translates the materialist realization that we are always implicated in—and in relationship with—the suffering of others through everyday engagements with the digital materiality that makes up our networked lives. Finally, the chapter suggests that these cruel intimacies can lay the foundations for conjuring more reparative forms of intimacy in spite of the sensorial solicitations of the global war sensorium. Informed by Tina Campt's notion of hapticity and Wendy Hui Kyong Chun's considerations on touch, Agostinho concludes that the cruel intimacies of the global war sensorium may elicit a sensorial transformation toward "haptic intimacies" that bring about more textured affective grammars and ways to tend to one another.

In "*A Probable Female, a Probable Child*: Civilian Casualties, Remote Monitoring, and Recognition Work in the Air War against ISIS," Sophie Dyer addresses the perceptual and ethical challenges that remote wars pose to the reporting of civilian casualties. Drawing on her experience as a researcher and advocacy officer at Airwars, a nongovernmental organization that monitors civilian harm claims in conflict zones, Dyer draws attention to the growing importance of remote monitoring projects in the context of the West's increasingly remote and air power-dominated military operations, which tend to underreport harms to civilian populations. Drawing on Christina Sharpe's writings, she proposes the term "mis/seeing" to describe the ways in which civilian casualties go unseen and unrecognized by the Coalition in the war against ISIS, and asks whether remote monitoring can become a practice of seeing and properly recognizing the lives that constantly go unaccounted for. Her chapter shows that remote monitoring has been made possible by the growing archive of documentation by civilians, state militaries, and militants alike—who upload content to the Internet in near real time—and how this documentation can be leveraged to demand accountability. At the same time, Dyer examines the ethical challenges raised by such archives, the relationship between sensed and sensing bodies, and how investigators are positioned in relation to the lives for which these archives are meant to account. In particular, she describes how "remote" translates into a position in which one has a "restricted view" that requires one to rely on others who are more proximate to the violence. As a consequence of this "remote" position, Dyer notes that these monitoring projects also risk reinscribing the detached colonial optics that render killable the very lives these projects seek to record and recognize. In response to such ethical challenges, Dyer proposes imagining a civilian casualty-recording project on explicitly feminist and anticolonial terms, and offers notes toward what such a remote monitoring project might look like.

The question of distance and proximity to sites of violence is also taken up by artist and scholar Oraib Toukan in "(Touring)," where she expands her earlier reflections on "cruel images" to think through the cruelty of capturing and touring tragedy and ruins. Moving through different photographic and filmic scenes, from Mohammad Malas's *Quneitra 74* (1974) to Omar Amiralay's *A Plate of Sardines—or the First Time I Heard of Israel* (1997) and Susan Sontag's *Promised Lands* (1974), Toukan's essay reflects on distance not only as a phenomenological question of detachment and degrees of separation from a cruel event, but also—and more crucially—in terms of who has the right to capture that cruel event. Toukan thus asks how one can navigate images in a way that allows one to think of "I" and "Other" as more than visual elements, and rather in terms of the prerogative of who has the right to call herself local when representing cruelty.

The following two essays in this section deal with the question of how to represent cruel events through embodied practices, thus opening up the sensoriality of war through the incorporation of voices, bodies, gestures and textures.

In the visual essay "The Subversive Body," Dutch-Argentinian visual artist Aimée Zito Lema shows installation shots and archival images from a project whose starting point is images of revolutionary and guerrilla movements during the last dictatorship in Argentina, gathered from the Argentinean national archive. The original archive images have been rephotographed to focus primarily on bodily gestures. Close-up and abstracted, the images become traces of physical resistance against political terror. The images are then printed in black and white on large paper that has been shaped and stiffened into a new corpus, the mold for which was the artist's own body. According to the artist, once paper has taken a certain form, the fiber "remembers" this information, resulting in a sculpture that has a "double memory": it recalls a shape as well as a historical event. With "The Subversive Body," Zito Lema investigates bodily memory, the traces that sociopolitical conflicts leave behind, and how to capture those traces beyond documentary inscription. The project thus intimates that the materiality of historical archives might be understood in extended ways to encompass how the human body and different materials register and remember events, thereby gesturing toward more sensuous ways of inscribing, accounting for, and witnessing the experience of war and violence.

Also pursuing the question of how archives can be embodied, in "Archives of the Flesh: Reenacting Memories of Torture" performance artist and scholar Sofie Lebech reflects on her performance piece *This Is for Her* (2017), in which she discusses the relationship between torture and therapy in three parts. In the first part (reproduced in the essay), she reenacts interviews conducted with survivors of torture during Argentina's Dirty War; the second part reenacts the Abu Ghraib photos through bodily gestures and language to reflect on the use of torture in armed conflicts; and the third part discusses the effect of therapy on victims of torture and soldiers coming home from war. The performance links these three seemingly disparate events and geographies in order to discuss Denmark's different engagements with and positions on torture. In linking these events, Lebech reflects in turn on her own situatedness, and on the limits and possibilities of narrating and embodying the archives of others. Informed by Rebecca Schneider's ethics of call and response, Lebech prompts us to consider testimony not as an isolated moment in time but as a "durational act." The essay traces testimony as a figure that navigates between the people she interviewed, the script, the performance, and the audience, "and how in each of these instances a new layer of testimony arises, creating a written, spoken, and embodied archive that exists both then and there and here and now." In seeing testimony as a durational event, Lebech proposes to understand moments of violence as something that we continue to witness and that continues to call for account, gesturing toward the need to reconceive the meanings of witnessing to more capaciously register the effects of violence of war across time.

EVIDENTIARY AESTHETICS
Documenting, Witnessing, Redressing

While relying upon the logics of the archive—collecting, interpreting, and circulating streams of archival data—contemporary war practices also pose major challenges to the notion of the archive as a repository of evidentiary documents and to the formation of "witnessing communities."[39] While the evidentiary and testimonial status of documents and archival material has never been unproblematic, current warfare practices further complicate archives' potential to demand accountability. Historically, the document has been associated with its indexical, evidentiary function. Assumed to point back toward or even provide a link to reality, documents have been characterized by their authenticating, proof-like quality, and by their ability to confirm that events took place.[40] This applies particularly to photographic documents, which, as Charles Peirce famously suggested, have been considered physical traces that index back to reality.[41] However, the "proof of truth" character of the visual document has been decidedly shaken since the latter part of the twentieth century by the emergence of a global visual culture marked by mediatization and digitization. Indeed, within today's connective, digital mediascape, images are produced, distributed, recontextualized, altered, and recirculated at such dizzying speed and to such an extent that we have almost come to expect them to have been digitally manipulated. Alongside insights gained from post-structuralist critiques of representation, these technological innovations—including the spread of cheap DIY technology for producing and distributing visual and audio documents—have put unprecedented pressure on the notion of indexicality associated with the document.[42] In addition, the emergence of the aforementioned operative images, produced by and aimed at machines rather than human perception, have further complicated received notions of the evidentiary character of visual documents. As a result of the use of operative images in automated, remote-led warfare, traditional evidentiary images are increasingly rare, which brings forth new "regimes of unaccountability."[43] Consequently, the concept of evidence has been revisited and critically expanded to include virtual imagery production, which is increasingly utilized as evidence where there is none.[44]

While the evidentiary status of documents and materials seems to have become ever more debated, the relation between the archive and prevailing power structures has been equally emphasized. As Eyal Weizman and Thomas Keenan contend, when considering the documents that do make it into the archive and are granted evidentiary status, it is by no means a question of simply stating "what is objectively there." Instead, the status allotted to documents is heavily dependent on the conditions and political context in which they are embedded. Positioning themselves against prevailing "police forensic practices," Weizman and Keenan have proposed the concept of forensis or counter-forensics. While the former could be said to rest on a notion of the ability of facts and evidence to provide a scientifically approved account of truth, as it were, the latter pays just as much attention to the nontransparent processes and the conditions that determine, for instance, whether something in the courtroom is or is not assigned the status of evidence.[45] As Weizman phrases it: "Forensis [...] introduces both the production of evidence and the querying of the practice of evidence making."[46]

Investigating, probing, and challenging processes of evidence making amounts to challenging the laws of the archive, and in turn, the ways in which history is preserved and handed over to posterity. This point echoes Derrida's *Archive Fever* once again, where he reminds us that the archive is, in fact, not so much of the past as of the future: "The question of the archive is not the question of a concept dealing with the past that might already be at our disposal or not at our disposal [...]. It is a question of the future, the question of the future itself."[47]

The contributions in the last section of *(W)archives* all grapple with the vexed question of evidence and of how to take responsible action for tomorrow by claiming the right to access, build, challenge, reinvent, and interpret the archive. A revised version of a previously published essay, Ariella Azoulay's "The Imperial Condition of Photography in Palestine: Archives, Looting, and the Figure of the Infiltrator" approaches the archive as a place of imperial violence, a site where documents of the past are neutralized and naturalized, thereby making history seem inevitable. She is particularly interested in the performative—and very real—effects of the archive's categories and taxonomies, that is, in how documents can work to violently manufacture material worlds. Refusing to accept the address of imperial archives—specifically the logics and categories according to which the Palestinians' expulsion in 1948 was documented by not only the Israeli state but also the international community—Azoulay sets out to enter the archive with a Palestinian companion. The companion is an elderly Palestinian man whom she encountered in the archive, in a photograph that shows him sitting down and refusing to leave his home, even though the state of Israel commanded him to do so voluntarily. Rather than adopting the categories with which he has been labeled—"infiltrator," "refugee"—as *evidence* of a certain identity or behavior, Azoulay insists on investigating the *conditions* for the fabrication of those categories. Furthermore, the essay relates to the categories and taxonomies of the imperial Israeli archive, as well the ongoing looting of Palestinian archives, not merely as a violation of Palestinian property and rights, but also as a continuous performance of national sovereignty. Performed as an ongoing project of the partition of populations into distinct, differentiated groups, Azoulay contends, sovereignty makes violence between the two groups both the pretext and the effect. In a new addition to the essay, she focuses on the Great March of Return, a series of demonstrations that took place in the Gaza Strip during 2018 and 2019, when thousands of demonstrators demanded that Palestinian refugees be allowed to return to the lands from which they were displaced in 1948. By connecting the march to the figure of the archive, Azoulay's analysis makes clear how the challenging of imperial documents and categories may make the past liquid, as it were, and allow a radically different imagining of the future.

In "Necropolis: Walking through a List of Deaths," choreographer and performer Arkadi Zaides offers insight into the research and working process behind his stage project *Necropolis* (2019–). Acclaimed for his investigations and transformations of archives of violence into what he terms "documentary choreographies," Zaides has dealt consistently with the ways in which political and social contexts affect bodily movements and gestures. In the artistic research project *Necropolis*, he turns to Europe's current so-called refugee crisis (or as he suggests, following Gurminder K. Bhambra, "crisis for refugees"[48]) to explore—together with his team of collaborators—the notion of collective responsibility. In his essay, Zaides accounts for the hybrid methodology developed by the project, which consists partly of a documentary and investigative approach inspired by the expanded practices of forensics, represented by Forensic Architecture mentioned above, and partly of a physical choreographic investigation. The project takes its point of departure in a list (carefully assembled by the organization UNITED for Intercultural Action) of the many thousands who have perished on their way to Europe. Referring to the list as both "a digital archive" and a "mass grave of evidence," *Necropolis* sets out to acknowledge and account for the dead by digitally locating and marking their burial sites, subsequently visiting them in person to pay last respects. As its title indicates, the project at the same time gestures toward a city of the dead, an invisible community or ghostly double that continues to haunt and demand a response from the world of the living.

In "Forensic (Im)probabilities: Entering Schrödinger's Box with Rabih Mroué and Hito Steyerl," Solveig Gade is preoccupied with the notion of evidence as it is formulated in several art theory discourses informed by the concept of forensics. Contesting the often surprisingly positivist take on the concept of evidence, and pointing to the danger in some discourses of reducing documentary works to unambiguous showgrounds for the presentation of equally unambiguous evidence and "truth-telling," Gade turns to Hito Steyerl and Rabih Mroué's lecture performance *Probable Title: Zero Probability*. Engaging with persons that have gone missing in war or conflict and been left unaccounted for by official archives, the lecture performance argues that the missing inhabit "a space of zero probability." This space is able to swallow "all sorts of objects. Whole buildings and even whole landscapes. Lots of people have disappeared into this space, which is just slightly beyond the edges of representation."[49] Entering the work through an approach that could be described as a combination of the forensic and the hauntological, Gade is interested in how the notion of evidence can be read not just as a "proof of truth" that points objectively to reality, but rather as a testament to the political conditions—and in a broader sense, the distribution of the sensible—that determine when something is allotted the status of evidence and when it is not. Furthermore, she argues that unlike supposedly objective facts modeled according to the prevailing distribution of the sensible, uncertainty and improbability may contain a critical potential that can challenge and make us rethink the framings through which we perceive reality.

In the last essay in the book, "*Transitional What?* Perspectives from Syrian Videographers on YouTube Takedowns and the 'Video as Evidence' Ecology," media scholar Dima Saber examines the stakes of the increasing reliance on corporate social media platforms such as YouTube to store and preserve documentation and evidence of human rights violations, particularly from the war in Syria.[50] Such documentation is often removed by these platforms for various reasons pertaining to their content moderation policies, putting at risk important evidence-gathering efforts. In her essay, Saber makes a case for including the Syrian videographers themselves in discussions about the value of their documentation of the uprising and war. Drawing on interviews with fifteen visual content creators based both inside and outside of Syria, she argues that while Western-based legal, intergovernmental policy and human rights stakeholders mourned YouTube's removals of videos of the Syrian war with reference to concepts such as "postwar accountability" and "video as evidence of human rights violations," the videographers themselves (particularly those still based in Syria) did not necessarily identify with those notions. Rather, what was valuable to them was that these materials allowed them to bear witness to the experiences of their people in community-centered, affective, and personal ways. While making clear the limitations of relying on social media platforms to preserve crucial evidence of wars and conflicts, Saber's analysis also highlights that it is vital to take account of the desires and needs of those who produce such content in the first place within ongoing and emerging efforts to create sustainable archives of war. Without their input, she argues, there will be no hope for transitional justice, or for postwar accountability.

Guided by the archive as a conceptual prism, material object, and imaginative practice, *(W)archives* thus seeks to shed light on and help us better understand the increasingly structuring role played by digitization and digital archives in contemporary warfare. Throughout the book, the (w)archive emerges as a term to grasp the extended materiality of contemporary war, wherein immanent digital archiving, as a structuring condition, intersects with images, bodies, senses, infrastructures, environments, imaginaries, memories, textures, emotions, and structures of feeling. By foregrounding this extended materiality, our hope is to capture the material effects of digital archiving, but also to more clearly reposition archives as sites for making political demands, to invent new forms of evidence-making, and to make sensuous the experience of living with war. These are urgent questions which, we argue, call for new epistemic alliances to more capaciously register, account for, and oppose war. If we are to make sense of and respond to the current era of warfare, we need to be able to navigate between different and constantly shifting perspectives, forms of knowledge, and epistemic practices. We are grateful to the authors for trusting us to edit their work and for advancing our understanding of the materialities of war in such generative and enriching ways.

1. Jacques Derrida, *Archive Fever: A Freudian Impression*, trans. Eric Prenowitz (Chicago: University of Chicago Press, 1998), 36.

2. Ibid., 1.

3. Ibid., 77.

4. Michel Foucault, *The Archaeology of Knowledge*, trans. A. M. Sheridan Smith (New York: Vintage, 2007), 4.

5. According to Annie Ring, Foucault's writings present an especially dynamic vision of the archive, stemming from what he saw as "an an-archic energy that pushes out from the lives that [the archive] ostensibly governed." Annie Ring, "The (W)hole in the Archive," *Paragraph* 37, no. 1 (2014): 387-402.

6. For an overview of these various theoretical contributions to a critical understanding of archives in digital times, see Nanna Bonde Thylstrup, Daniela Agostinho, Catherine D'Ignazio, Annie Ring, and Kristin Veel, "Big Data as Uncertain Archives," in *Uncertain Archives: Critical Keywords for Big Data*, ed. Nanna Bonde Thylstrup, Daniela Agostinho, Catherine D'Ignazio, Annie Ring, and Kristin Veel (Cambridge, MA: MIT Press, 2021), 5-8.

7. Foucault, *Archaeology of Knowledge*, 143.

8. Derrida, *Archive Fever*, 19.

9. Thylstrup et al., "Big Data as Uncertain Archives," 5-8.

10. See Anthony Downey, *Dissonant Archives: Contemporary Visual Culture and Contested Narratives in the Middle East* (London: I. B. Tauris, 2015).

11. Basel Abbas and Ruanne Abou-Rahme, "The Archival Multitude," *Journal of Visual Culture* 12, no. 3 (2013): 345-63, https://doi.org/10.1177/1470412913502031.

12. See also Donatella Della Ratta, Kay Dickinson, and Sune Haugbolle, eds., *The Arab Archive: Mediated Memories and Digital Flows* (Amsterdam: Institute of Network Cultures, 2020); and Dima Saber and Paul Long, "'I Will Not Leave, My Freedom Is More Precious than My Blood': From Affect to Precarity: Crowd-Sourced Citizen Archives as Memories of the Syrian War," *Archives and Records*, 38, no. 1 (2017): 80-99.

13. On the politics of such truth-telling gestures, see Daniela Agostinho and Nanna Bonde Thylstrup, "'If Truth Was a Woman: Leaky Infrastructures and the Gendered Politics of Truth-Telling," *Ephemera: Theory and Politics in Organization* 19, no. 4 (2019): 745-75.

14. As Louise Amoore notes, more than algorithmic calculation leading to a militarization of society, or to a commercialization of security, what we are witnessing is algorithmic war as a "continuation of war by other means" in the Foucauldian sense, "where the war-like architectures of self/other, here/there, safe/risky, normal/suspicious are played out in the politics of daily life." Louise Amoore, "Algorithmic War: Everyday Geographies of the War on Terror," *Antipode* 41, no. 1 (2009): 49.

15. Harun Farocki defines "operative images" as "pictures, made neither to entertain nor to inform [...]. Images that do not represent an object, but rather are part of an operation." Harun Farocki, "Phantom Images," *Public*, no. 29 (2004): 17.

16. Judith Butler, *Frames of War: When Is Life Grievable?* (New York: Verso, 2010), xi.

17. Hal Foster, "An Archival Impulse," *October*, no. 110 (2004): 3-22.

18. Ronak K. Kapadia, *Insurgent Aesthetics: Security and the Queer Life of the Forever War* (Durham, NC: Duke University Press, 2019).

19. Ann Laura Stoler, *Duress: Imperial Durabilities in Our Times* (Durham, NC: Duke University Press, 2016).

20. Carl von Clausewitz, *On War*, ed. and trans. Michael Eliot Howard and Peter Paret (Princeton, NJ: Princeton University Press, 1976), 280.

21. Ibid., 280.

22. James Der Derian, *Virtuous War: Mapping the Military-Industrial-Media Entertainment Network* (New York: Routledge, 2009).

23. See Nathan Roger, *Image Warfare in the Age of Terror* (London: Palgrave Macmillan, 2013); Kevin McSorley, ed., *War and the Body: Militarisation, Practice and Experience* (London: Routledge, 2013).

24. See Nicholas Mirzoeff, *Watching Babylon: The War in Iraq and Global Visual Culture* (London: Routledge, 2005); W. J. T. Mitchell, *Cloning Terror: The War of Images, 9/11 to the Present* (Chicago: University of Chicago Press, 2011); Jens Eder and Charlotte Klonk, *Image Operations: Visual Media and Political Conflict* (Manchester: Manchester University Press, 2016); Jan Mieszkowski, *Watching War* (Stanford, CA: Stanford University Press, 2012); Anders Engberg-Pedersen and Kathrin Maurer, eds., *Visualizing War: Emotions, Technologies, Communities* (London: Routledge, 2017); Mette Mortensen, *Journalism and Eyewitness Images: Digital Media, Participation, and Conflict* (London: Routledge, 2014); Lina Khatib, *Image Politics in the Middle East: The Role of the Visual in Political Struggle* (New York: I. B. Tauris, 2012).

25. Grégoire Chamayou, *A Theory of the Drone*, trans. Janet Lloyd (New York: New Press, 2015), 30.

26. See also Brian Massumi, *Ontopower: War, Powers, and the State of Perception* (Durham, NC: Duke University Press, 2015); Louise Amoore, *The Politics of Possibility: Risk and Security Beyond Probability* (Durham, NC: Duke University Press, 2013); Claudia Aradau and Tobias Blanke, "Politics of Prediction: Security and the Time/Space of Governmentality in the Age of Big Data," *European Journal of Social Theory* 20, no. 3 (2017): 373-91; Johan Lau Munkholm, "The Pursuit of Full Spectrum Dominance: The Archives of the NSA," *Surveillance & Society* 18, no. 2 (2020): 244-56.

27. Lisa Parks and Caren Kaplan, *Life in the Age of Drone Warfare* (Durham, NC: Duke University Press, 2017), 9-11. See also Lauren Wilcox, "Embodying Algorithmic War: Gender, Race, and the Post-Human in Drone Warfare," *Security Dialogue* 48, no. 1 (2017): 11-28; and Caroline Holmqvist, "Undoing War: War Ontologies and the Materiality of Drone Warfare," *Millennium: Journal of International Studies* 41, no. 3 (2013): 535-52.

28. Nicholas Mirzoeff, *How to See the World* (New York: Basic Books, 2015), 102-18.

29. Caren Kaplan, *Aerial Aftermaths: Wartime from Above* (Durham, NC: Duke University Press, 2017).

30. Priya Satia, "Drones: A History from the British Middle East," *Humanity: An International Journal of Human Rights, Humanitarianism, and Development* 5, no. 1 (2014): 1-31; Madiha Tahir, "Bombing Pakistan: How Colonial Legacy Sustains American Drones" (paper, Costs of War, Brown University, Providence, RI, 2015).

31. Chamayou, *A Theory of the Drone*, 95.

32. See also Caren Kaplan, "Atmospheric Politics: Protest Drones and the Ambiguity of Airspace," *Digital War*, https://doi.org/10.1057/s42984-020-00005-y; J. D. Schnepf, "Unsettling Aerial Surveillance: Surveillance Studies after Standing Rock," *Surveillance & Society* 17, no. 5 (2019): 747–51.

33. The phrase "techno-aesthetics" is drawn from Anthony Downey's "There's Always Someone Looking at You: Performative Research and the Techno-Aesthetics of Drone Surveillance," in *Heba Y. Amin: The General's Stork*, ed. Anthony Downey (Berlin: Sternberg Press, 2020), 8–30.

34. Butler, *Frames of War*, x.

35. The acknowledgments in the 2010 paperback edition of *Frames of War* end with a tantalizing reference to Obama's election, and with the caveat that "we have yet to see what concrete ameliorations of war may take place under his administration." Butler, *Frames of War*, viii. According to the Bureau of Investigative Journalism, there were ten times more air strikes in the covert war on terror during Obama's presidency than under his predecessor, George W. Bush. Jessica Purkiss and Jack Serle, "Obama's Covert Drone War in Numbers: Ten Times More Strikes Than Bush," *Bureau of Investigative Journalism*, January 17, 2017, https://www.thebureauinvestigates.com/stories/2017-01-17/obamas-covert-drone-war-in-numbers-ten-times-more-strikes-than-bush.

36. Our usage of the term "forever war" here echoes Kapadia's critical appropriation of the term. Rather than reproducing the temporality of the original military term, which described the open-ended war against terror inaugurated by September 11, 2001, Kapadia locates the genealogy of the forever war in the *longue durée* of US colonial expansion and war-making in the Greater Middle East throughout the long twentieth century and into the early twenty-first century. He thus examines not the US "at war" but the US "as war." Kapadia, *Insurgent Aesthetics*, 5–8.

37. Susan Schuppli, "Media as Conflict Zones" (paper, (W)archives workshop, University of Copenhagen, August 21, 2017).

38. Ibid.

39. Michael Richardson and Kerstin Schankweiler, "Affective Witnessing," in *Affective Societies: Key Concepts*, ed. Jan Slaby and Christian von Scheve (New York: Routledge, 2019), 166.

40. Phillip Rosen, *Change Mummified: Cinema, Historicity, Theory* (Minneapolis: University of Minnesota Press, 2001), 234. See also Daniel Schultze, *Authenticity in Contemporary Theatre: Make It Real* (London: Bloomsbury, 2017).

41. Charles Sanders Peirce, *Collected Papers of Charles Sanders Peirce*, vol. IV, book II (Cambridge: Cambridge University Press, 1933), 447.

42. Solveig Gade, "The Promise of the Index in Contemporary Documentary Performance," *Nordic Journal of Aesthetics*, nos. 55–56 (2018): 41–64.

43. See Kris Paulsen, "Rogue Pixels: Indexicality and Algorithmic Camouflage," *Signs and Society* 6, no. 2 (2018): 412–34; and Lila Lee-Morrison, "The Forensic Architecture Project: Virtual Imagery as Evidence in the Contemporary Context of the War on Terror" (paper, Virtual Zones of Peace and Conflict, University of Copenhagen, Centre for Resolution of International Conflicts, January 12–13, 2015).

44. Lee-Morrison, "The Forensic Architecture Project."

45. Eyal Weizman, "Introduction: Forensis," in *Forensis: The Architecture of Public Truth*, ed. Forensic Architecture (Berlin: Sternberg Press, 2014), 12.

46. Ibid.

47. Derrida, *Archive Fever*, 36.

48. Gurminder K. Bhambra, "The Current Crisis of Europe: Refugees, Colonialism, and the Limits of Cosmopolitanism," *European Law Journal* 23, no. 5 (2017): 399.

49. Rabih Mroué and Hito Steyerl, "Probable Title: Zero Probability" (unpublished script, 2012).

50. See Jeff Deutch and Hadi Habal, "The Syrian Archive: A Methodological Case Study of Open-Source Investigation of State Crime Using Video Evidence from Social Media Platforms." *State Crime Journal* 7, no. 1 (2018): 46-76.

A ARCHIVING WAR
Spatiotemporal Reconfigurations

ARCHIVES OF ENMITY AND MARTIAL EPISTEMOLOGY

Kevin McSorley

How might we think the linkages between war and the archive? At a foundational level, war is itself an act of political contestation *and* inscription, a continuous and injurious process of archiving that is written upon the myriad bodies of the victims it generates and the lifeworlds it transforms. As Elaine Scarry notes, it is bodily injury that is ultimately crucial to war's political mattering, that provides the radical material force to suture and substantiate the political "crisis of substantiation" that war entails.[1] War unmakes and remakes worlds, then, its outcomes recorded in an archive of broken bodies and destroyed lives, a transubstantiation of political ideals into flesh.

At another level, war-fighting is also underpinned by myriad processes of intelligence-gathering, surveillance, and reconnaissance, and other techniques of operational data collection about the nature of "enemy" forces, formations, and activities. The planning of military violence fundamentally depends upon the compilation, organization, and interrogation of such information to generate actionable reports in the form of kill lists, enemy orders of battle, target mappings, and matrices. It is through such archival procedures that particular bodies, infrastructures, and environments ultimately become identified as targets for the subsequent injury and destruction that underwrites political mattering. However, as Jacques Derrida notes, the process of "archivization produces as much as it records,"[2] and the question of *how* particular understandings of the structure of enmity get inscribed and produced in these archival regimes and manipulations is the focus of this chapter.

As one historical example, consider the United States Air Force's (USAF) establishment post-World War II of a Directorate of Targets, which was responsible for compiling what eventually came to be known as the Bombing Encyclopedia of the World (BEW).[3] This was an archive constructed at a global scale containing records of thousands of military installations, industrial plants, and other elements of vital infrastructural systems—electricity, petroleum, transportation, water, steel, etc.—the destruction of which would cut across [...] the enemy's ability to defend himself."[4] Although initially focused upon the Soviet Bloc, the project rapidly expanded throughout the 1950s to cover Western Europe, the Far East, and beyond. By 1959, seventy-eight thousand potential bombing targets had been produced, rendering large parts of the world through a particular military grid of intelligibility.

While images from aerial reconnaissance became crucial as the project developed, the initial key source of data for the BEW in its early years was human intelligence obtained via Project Wringer.[5] This was a vast program of mass debriefing and interrogation of over three hundred thousand human subjects, mostly German and Japanese ex-servicemen, returning from postwar detention and forced labor in the Soviet Union. Elliott Child details how millions of oral accounts and memory sketches of installations and plants were systematically obtained from these "human sources" and fed back to USAF target compilers in Washington, DC, where, guided by rationalized and productivist principles of industrial managerialism, the accounts were "stripped of subjectivity" and bureaucratically transformed, disarticulated, and recombined to form abstract and codified targeting records.[6]

Importantly for the purposes of the current discussion, the material form in which individual records were initially stored was punched cards that could be read by early Univac computers built specifically for the Department of Defense. Subsequently, the records were encoded in a standardized format, the Consolidated Target Intelligence File, on magnetic tapes that allowed more rapid automatic machine processing.[7] Each record in the archive had multiple data fields, detailing the geolocation, industrial outputs and capabilities, and various other aspects of the site. As these records were not organized by a single, rigid system of classification, they could be queried on machine runs that would generate targeting reports according to various strategic criteria such as all the sites within a specific area that might contribute to particular production cycles, like that of fighter planes, for example.[8]

This, then, was an open-ended archiving of the vital infrastructures and productive capacities of modern military-industrial economies and societies, where the specific information architecture facilitated the flexible generation of myriad targeting reports detailing multiple material flows, interdependencies, and critical vulnerabilities. The archive thus encoded a particular martial epistemology and enabled the production of new knowledge about various ways in which the military capabilities of enemy societies might be constituted and could be vulnerable to attack.[9] It marked an important moment in twentieth-century war-fighting in which a particular type of database storage and querying system emerged as a key technocultural form for the flexible planning of military violence, as well as offering an early instantiation of a totalizing ambition to disclose the entire world's existent and emergent structures of enmity.[10]

It is the construction of such *archives of enmity* through the organization of "military information regimes," defined by Alfred McCoy as "sophisticated systems for collecting, codifying and operationalizing voluminous amounts of data about whole societies,"[11] and in particular the development of new computational and database technologies, that is the focus of attention here. What distinct understandings of enmity, what "ontology of the enemy,"[12] gets inscribed and produced through such archival developments? While war is undoubtedly a crucible of technological innovation,[13] it is beyond the scope of this essay to provide a comprehensive genealogy of the ways in which changes in war-fighting and transformed understandings of enmity have coevolved with historical transformations in computational and data-processing technologies.[14] Rather, I will predominantly focus upon exploring the advent of specific forms of data-driven warfare that are associated particularly with recent developments in ubiquitous sensing and immanent archiving, evolutions in "post-relational" database architectures and analytics, and certain doctrinal and operational shifts away from conventional large-scale warfare against nation-state adversaries and regular formations, and toward forms of discontinuous and open-ended military violence across the globe against networked and individual antagonists.[15]

The contemporary moment is one marked by increasingly ubiquitous, networked, and automated forms of "data" production, with ever more interactions and practices of quotidian life—communication, consumption, finance, travel, leisure, social networking, online identity curation, interfacing with the "Internet of Things," simply moving while carrying a cell phone—generating immanent data trails that are recorded as a matter of course across permanently updating and reconfigurable archives that stretch the very definition of the word.[16] Much of embodied existence is thus now productive of "data exhaust" or "ontic exhaust,"[17] with being-archived increasingly an ontological condition of contemporary living, producing an oceanic cacophony of data.[18]

It is worth noting here that many of the technologies, protocols, and logics that are central to this datafication of everyday life have been significantly shaped by defense funding and military aspirations. For example, the genealogy of Internet protocols such as TCP/IP is fundamentally entangled with military desires for resilient networking,[19] and the development of location-based services and targeting is fundamentally dependent upon GPS technology originally designed for the navigation of weapons systems.[20] Martial desires have thus long been intertwined with the wider parameters of everyday technocultural becoming, enframing human life in complex recursive processes of technogenesis,[21] with "civilianized" technologies becoming central to the way that the contemporary (post)human subject has increasingly become constituted as an informational entity or node, as a signal transmitter in military terms.

These and related developments have been variously theorized in terms of "surveillance capitalism,"[22] "data colonialism,"[23] the "sensor society,"[24] and the rise of "big data."[25] The emergence of big data is said to be changing the overall ways in which sense-making might occur, ushering in a paradigm shift in how knowledge of the world may be generated, and with it transformations in the ways in which life may be governed through such data.[26] Rob Kitchin argues that "big data analytics enable an entirely new epistemological approach for making sense of the world; rather than testing a theory by analyzing relevant data, new data analytics seek to gain insights "born from the data.'"[27] For Chris Andersen, the data deluge is ushering in an "end of theory," whereby pattern recognition and correlation outstrip the understandings offered by models of causality, intentionality, or ideology: "Out with every theory of human behavior, from linguistics to sociology. Forget taxonomy, ontology and psychology. Who knows why people do what they do? The point is they do it, and we can track and measure it with unprecedented fidelity. With enough data, the numbers speak for themselves."[28]

Further, unlike "modernist" processes of knowledge production, immanent data collection that happens as a by-product of daily life is more speculative and occurs without necessarily anticipating the uses to which it may be put, without a clear question or purpose in mind.[29] Mark Andrejevic and Mark Burdon thus note that "function creep is not ancillary to the data collection process but is built into it, the function *is* the creep,"[30] and as such commercial and military information regimes often overlap and inform one another in deeply symbiotic relationships. Indeed, recent histories have detailed longstanding dual-use hybridity and the continuing inseparability of military interests from the shaping of the structures of innovation, regulatory frameworks, practices, and values of the commercial data-tech giants of Silicon Valley.[31]

This epistemological approach is transforming numerous domains of social life, but particularly the realm of security broadly conceived, and notably in a context in which it was argued that the 9/11 attacks could have been predicted if only the US security agencies had somehow been able to "connect the dots" in already existent data,[32] to see the patterns of emergent enmity prior to the event, rather than in post hoc reconstruction. Haunted by this question of "how did we miss it?" the US security state has increasingly been concerned with how to unlock the potential that was felt to exist in the broad dataverse, to recombine or manipulate or reterritorialize it in ways that might be specifically revelatory for security and military concerns. With data seen as a potential reservoir of previously untapped insights, the possibility of preemptively tracing the latent "threatprint,"[33] the emergent signature of insecurity or enmity, within and across various data archives has assumed new salience.

The idea that new knowledge production might occur through big data analytics, operating at speeds and scales exceeding human perception and cognition,[34] has thus increasingly become a significant new *doxa* of the security professions,[35] with intelligence agencies and analytic labor being restructured for an age of "digital warfare."[36] There has been massive investment in an amalgam of practices including interoperable data exchange and database interconnectivity, new forms of social network analysis, risk profiling and predictive analytics, machine learning and artificial intelligence, advanced data visualization, and so on. Such practices are transforming intelligence work, policing, homeland security, counterterrorist practice, and counterinsurgency warfare.[37]

With the rise of automated and ubiquitous forms of mass data collection across entire populations, one key epistemological principle of the big data paradigm is that the very heterogeneity of the mass is reconceptualized not as an obfuscatory haystack, but as an asset whose very complexity can reveal new patterns and connections.[38] The economy of knowledge, then, is to *archive it all*,[39] in order that heterogeneous plural normalities and the anomalous, the haystack and the needle, might emerge together.[40] Indeed, the bigger the data, the more self-correcting it is understood to be. The logic here, then, is not simply the traditional disciplinary idea that particular suspect communities might become subject to more targeted surveillance, but that the mass archiving of the lifeworlds of entire populations might lead to the emergence of new forms of knowledge and targets, might surface currently unknown unknowns: "The population-level portrait allows particular targets to emerge, and once they do, their activities can be situated in the context of an ever-expanding network of behaviors and the patterns these generate."[41]

While patterns of suspicious activity may be sought in individual and discrete archives of, for example, travel data, financial transactions, or communicative metadata, in addition, databases and archives, unmoored from their commercial purposes, are also fused together via new combinatorics to generate a multidimensional higher-level feature space that offers new possibilities for inquiry and intervention.[42] Vast computational power and new-generation database designs and query languages mean that the rapid, dynamic, and generative interrogation of massive open-ended, semi-structured, and scalable data sets is now possible. With the definition of a few rules or boundary conditions, algorithms may rapidly search such a problem space for data patterns and anomalies. A one-way airfare between particular locations, a pattern of chatter on social media, a GPS trace along a particular route, or a large transaction between particular accounts may all be meaningless and absolutely inauspicious in isolation, part of the curves of many everyday normalities.[43] But if associatively traced and linked across a higher-level feature space, then the network mapped and the traces conjoined may be calculated and recognized as the potential surfacing of threat or enmity. As Louise Amoore and Marieke de Goede note, "the deviant other, then, is identified not so much through her individual aberration from a norm, but through an assembly of transactions or associations seen as signifying suspicious activity."[44]

The threatprint of the enemy-to-come is thus now understood in terms of this complex ontology of *association* across a multi-dimensional feature space, the relations between elements more significant than the individual elements per se. The inductive and iterative generation of new security derivatives assembled from the myriad relationships between heterogeneous sources of data widens the analytic field and creates new potentialities for investigation and possible intervention, surfacing patterns for the attention of the analyst.[45] For Matteo Pasquinelli, this "introduction of the topological perspective to large datasets is the birth of a new symbolic form that is comparable to the birth of modern perspective using techniques of optical projection from astronomy."[46] Furthermore, enmity is increasingly understood in terms of the *anomalous*,[47] whereby "an anomaly can be detected only against the ground of a pattern regularity."[48] And recursive algorithms may continuously find, learn, and apply new rules from data contingencies and variations, generating new derivatives of derivatives, while patterns that are not anomalous are continuously folded back into the calculation of normalities. In this way, algorithms and thresholds may constantly modulate, change, and evolve. In cases of deep machine learning, the ultimate rationale for the emergence of outcomes may thus become increasingly opaque and inscrutable even to the analysts deploying it.

Drawing partly upon such principles, the twenty-first century battlespaces of the "everywhere war"[49] have become laboratories for experimentation in the archival and analytic underpinnings of military violence. The US wars in Iraq and Afghanistan in particular involved the transformation and accelerated tempo of special forces-led operational intelligence cycles, the society-wide "reality-mining" of myriad data sources for programs of "computational counterinsurgency,"[50] and an analytic preoccupation with disclosing networked forms and patterns of enmity within the wider population rather than understanding social and political concerns at the local level.[51] Furthermore, beyond these specific wars of occupation, rolling programs of punctuated military violence, particularly in the form of targeted drone strikes, have also been carried out by the United States Joint Special Operations Command and the Central Intelligence Agency (CIA) under the sign of counterterrorism across many other territories including Pakistan's Federally Administered Tribal Areas (FATA), Yemen, and Somalia, as will be discussed below.

While the drone strike is the signature motif of this form of "predatory war,"[52] it is important to initially emphasize that the drone itself is merely one element in a whole archival apparatus of sensors, databases, and algorithms, and that "cut off from its back end, from its satellite links and its data processors, its intelligence analysts and its controller, the drone is as useless as an eyeball disconnected from the brain."[53] Predatory war exemplifies both the individuation of warfare and the dissolution of the spatiotemporal and normative constraints of the conventional battlefield.[54] As Derek Gregory and Grégoire Chamayou note,[55] the locus of violence for drone strikes is defined by the presence of the individualized enemy, with "the target contracted to the individual human body even as the field of military violence expands to encompass the globe."[56]

One aspect of predatory war that deserves particular attention here is the procedure for the disclosure, the anticipatory surfacing, of particular targets—so-called signature strikes—who may never be known or identified, but who emerge on the basis of activity rather than identity from a "vast and continually evolving database, known as the disposition matrix."[57] This archive does not just amass information on certain individuals, but rather records comprehensive data across a whole population, across the entire "life of the populace described as pre-insurgent,"[58] with blanket surveillance and targeted killing going hand in hand. As Ian Shaw notes, "in order to individualize, the security state must first totalize."[59]

The disposition matrix draws on multiple sensors and sources in the generation of its open-ended kill lists, principally the many billions of elements of communicative metadata that the United States National Security Agency (NSA) routinely harvests daily, alongside further signals intelligence collected from drones acting as virtual base towers. Many US military drones capture all the available wireless data traffic in the areas through which they fly,[60] and the felt value of communicative metadata in particular is such that NSA General Counsel Stewart Baker has argued that "it absolutely tells you everything about somebody's life [...]. If you have enough metadata, you don't really need content."[61] This data is supplemented by human intelligence from agents and informants, and visual surveillance imagery from drone feeds.[62]

From the combinatoric manipulation of all these various anonymous and "dividualized" traces of communication, geolocation, and activity, an archive of overall "patterns of life" in a digitally enclosed battlespace can be derived (indicating bodily movements and rhythms in space and time, gatherings of bodies, networks of speech and chatter, durational intensities of social connectivity, etc.). The interrogation of this multidimensional data topography is then conducted via algorithmic inquiry, including forms of social network analysis, time series analysis, and rhythmanalysis, with the hermeneutic goal of identifying anomalous patterns of suspicion linked to particular networked nodes and "bodies out of place."[63] The process by which "an archive of lives [...] will constitute a death warrant"[64] is thus one where anonymous and anomalous "data bodies" are fundamentally derived from digital traces of *activity*, as opposed to forms of individual *identity* anchored in, for example, biometric data. Via "cross-sensor cueing,"[65] such emergent targets may also become subject to further granular and more intense visual surveillance, including full-motion video feeds that may be watched by drone personnel or become subject to further machinic vision and interrogation,[66] and which ultimately inform the triggering of strikes.

As Astrid Nordin and Dan Oberg note, one of the dangers of such a process of producing targets is that it is theoretically endless: "There will always be more targets than it is possible to destroy."[67] The logic of big data is ultimately one of continuous recommendation on the basis of noting similarities between patterns. Indeed, Paul Pillar, former director of the CIA's counterterrorism center, has stated that "we are looking at something that is potentially infinite."[68] For Jameel Jaffer, relatedly, the institutional danger is that, once established, "the legal and bureaucratic infrastructure required to sustain this practice [...] will demand a [further] targeted-killing campaign."[69] Further, the likelihood of identifying false positives is heightened by such an archival reliance on metadata, where the meaning of communication or the qualitative context of association is abstracted.[70]

Moreover, the total archiving of an entire population inevitably introduces wider transformations of the social for all those living under drones, ruptures that are regularly elided in narratives of precision targeting. As Neal Curtis notes, "the implicit aspects of the social that the drone apparatus targets are that a person speaks and acts, moves and comes together with others [...]. Drones make this very being-with explicit and problematic, if not dangerous and lethal."[71] Indeed, testimonies of the lives of those wider populations in territories such as FATA reveal widespread experiences and feelings of danger, exposure, paranoia, incomprehension, and helplessness.[72] Many mundane social interactions are felt to be newly precarious lest they attract drones, with a consequent and profound undermining of all routines of everyday living, a stable interaction order, and any sense of ontological security and trust in the world.[73]

As Scarry notes, such a radical inversion and contraction of everything that is traditionally experienced as safe and benign, the unmaking of the victim's world, describes the very phenomenology and methodology of torture. However, in predatory war, this profound reversal and negation is scaled up from the site of the individual torture room to the assay and enclosure of the entire population and social lifeworld. As myriad everyday sayings and doings, moving and being-with others become targeted by the drone apparatus, the entire social environment is both unmade and weaponized, "the appropriation of the world into the torturer's arsenal of weapons."[74] For those already highly vulnerable populations who are subject to the intense necropolitical assay of predatory war, the phenomenology of their embodied experiences is thus not just of targeted killing, nor even of more widespread death, injury, grief, and destruction, although it is all of those. Rather, it is the very unmaking of their world, a profoundly asymmetric unmaking that increasingly approaches the underlying structure of mass torture, whereby an entire population may be "kept in a state of radical embodiment by its awareness that it is at any moment deeply woundable."[75]

FUTURE DEVELOPMENTS

In this essay, I have pointed to the production and naturalization of various ontologies of enmity through archival procedures underpinned by historical transformations in military information regimes and associated shifts in computational power and database architectures. Given that war is a constantly shape-shifting, but enduringly injurious, transhistorical, and transcultural social institution, this is clearly a very partial genealogy of the archive as a technology of epistemic and military violence,[76] one that invites further complication. By way of conclusion, I wish to highlight just a few of the issues that are provoked by immanent digital archiving and the associated rise of forms of predatory war.

Firstly, and quite apart from the crucial ethico-political issues and violences that accompany such developments, it is important to note that many historical precursors and ambitious experiments in forms of total information awareness, granular targeting, and datafied warfare have been characterized by significant overreach, blowback, and failure to disrupt adaptive enemy capacity in the ways envisaged. For example, during the Vietnam War the establishment of the "electronic battlefield" to try to stop the north-south flow of enemy combatants and trucks along a key jungle supply route, the so-called Ho Chi Minh Trail in southeastern Laos, ended up being a costly fiasco.[77] Programs of reality-mining and computational counterinsurgency such as Nexus 7 in Afghanistan were unproven at best in their abilities to predict insurgent behavior.[78]

Indeed, as Chamayou notes, the prosecution of the entire global war on terror has only exacerbated the incidence of terrorism worldwide, with the underlying premise of the existence of reliable individualized signatures of enmity yet to be found to hold up.[79] History thus suggests that caution is advisable when assessing the martial significance of any such developments, beyond noting the recurring attraction to militaries of technical systems and abstractions that promise to "project power without projecting vulnerability."[80] This hubristic compulsion also underpins the digital archive fever of contemporary martial power.[81]

That said, the promise of immanent archiving and big data analytics has clearly been inspiring renewed devotional and even magical thinking in military circles in recent years, with the notion of the algorithm in particular taking on its own performative force, becoming "an evocative shorthand for the power and potential of objective calculative systems that can think more accurately than humans."[82] "Algorithmic warfare" is a sign under which increasing quantities of resources, research, and development are being mobilized worldwide,[83] with the big data paradigm only strengthened by its hermetically sealed understanding of error and failure as that which gets enfolded back into the iterative refinement of its discriminatory powers.[84] As Katharine Kindervarter notes, visions of total access, infinite searchability, and digital omniscience have thus decisively entered the contemporary martial imagination.[85] The future trajectories of brutal developments such as predatory war thus remain troublingly unclear. While, as noted, previous martial experiments in total information awareness have often ultimately offered only ephemeral advantages and illusions of control, current archival assemblages in the laboratories of the imperial peripheries may nonetheless be harbingers of a much wider "great war of enclosure,"[86] one that increasingly turns its attention back toward the homeland, to "domestic societies conceived as battlespaces *in potentia*,"[87] and to producing the enemy within.

Finally, it remains crucial to study not only how such datafied targeting occurs, as well as its archival infrastructure and algorithmic rendering of particular patterns of life and enmity, but also to explore how the knowledge of being permanently subject to this regime of intense necropolitical assay is understood and experienced by those who actually live with its torturous uncertainties, with the very unmaking of their social world. There are clearly numerous significant ethico-political issues that accompany the rise of predatory war—its lack of algorithmic transparency and the militarized culture of secrecy, its logic of endless expansion, its redistribution of the sovereign decision across recursive loops of automation, its adaptive driving of its actual adversaries further into civilian "hypercamouflage,"[88] even its cybernetic reconfigurations of its own operators' subjectivities. However, perhaps the most acute, particularly for those currently living under the drone apparatus, is its potential for apophenia, for "seeing patterns where none actually exist, simply because massive quantities of data can offer connections that radiate in all directions."[89] While from one point of view this may seem like a technical issue—the procedural collateral of radically opening up a search space—for those who are currently subject to predatory war, it is a matter of life and death.

1. Elaine Scarry, *The Body in Pain: The Making and Unmaking of the World* (Oxford: Oxford University Press, 1985).

2. Jacques Derrida, *Archive Fever: A Freudian Impression*, trans. Eric Prenowitz (Chicago: University of Chicago Press, 1995), 17.

3. Stephen Collier and Andrew Lakoff, "The Bombing Encyclopedia of the World," *Limn*, no. 6. (2016), http://limn.it/the-bombing-encyclopedia-of-the-world/; Derek Gregory, "Bombing Encyclopedia of the World," August 3, 2012, https://geographicalimaginations.com/2012/08/03/bombing-encyclopedia-of-the-world/.

4. James Lowe cited in Collier and Lakoff, "The Bombing Encyclopedia of the World."

5. Elliott Child, "Through the Wringer: Mass Interrogation and United States Air Force Targeting Intelligence in the Early Cold War," *Political Geography*, no. 75 (2019), https://doi.org/10.1016/j.polgeo.2019.102052.

6. Ibid.

7. Gregory, "Bombing Encyclopedia of the World."

8. Ibid.

9. Collier and Lakoff, "The Bombing Encyclopedia of the World."

10. Collier and Lakoff argue that this Cold War analysis of enemy societies was also turned inward in the second half of the twentieth century, leading to a new reflexive self-understanding and governance of domestic urban and infrastructural planning according to principles of "vital systems security." The enemy city targeted thus became the homeland city dispersed and suburbanized in preventive anticipation of attack. Stephen Collier and Andrew Lakoff, "Vital Systems Security: Reflexive Biopolitics and the Government of Emergency," *Theory Culture and Society* 32, no. 2 (2015): 19-51.

11. Alfred McCoy, "Imperial Illusions: Information Infrastructure and the Future of US Global Power," in *Endless Empire: Spain's Retreat, Europe's Eclipse, America's Decline*, ed. Alfred McCoy, Josep Fradera, and Stephen Jacobson (Madison: University of Wisconsin Press, 2012), 361-62. McCoy proposes an overarching schema of three main "military information regimes"—manual, computerized, and robotic—that have characterized US conventional and counterinsurgency/pacification war-fighting over the last century, all designed to reduce complex societies to "serviceable data": "Despite an enormous expansion into a global system during World War II, Washington's data management remained, until the 1950s, largely manual with typewritten files, numeric codification, and limited mechanical assistance for transmission and tabulation. From the 1960s onward, however, a computerized information infrastructure emerged during the Vietnam War with automated data processing and electronic communications. After a decade of combat in Iraq and Afghanistan, the Pentagon was, by 2010, at the edge of a robotic information regime that will fuse aerospace, cyberwarfare, and biometrics into a worldwide surveillance and strike network of unprecedented power" (362).

12. In an analysis of Norbert Weiner's development of cybernetic defense systems, Peter Galison argues that the way the enemy figure was understood and inscribed within such human/machine assemblages differed from the racialized figure of the enemy "other" that existed in public discourses. Peter Galison, "The Ontology of the Enemy: Norbert Wiener and the Cybernetic Vision," *Critical Inquiry* 21, no. 1 (1994): 228-66.

13. While cautioning against simplistic narratives that stress either the overwhelming determining force of the exigencies of war-fighting upon technical change, or the uniquely transformative effects of particular technologies upon the conditions of war, Antoine Bousquet nonetheless notes that "armed conflict is undoubtedly a particularly potent accelerant for technological evolution, concentrating minds and resources and subject to an intense dynamic of action-reaction between belligerents that singularly spurs innovation." Antoine Bousquet, "A Revolution in Military Affairs? Changing Technologies and Changing Practices of Warfare," in *Technology and World Politics: An Introduction*, ed. Daniel McCarthy (Abingdon: Routledge, 2018), 173.

14. For studies that might contribute to such an undertaking, see Josef Ansorge, *Identify and Sort: How Digital Power Changed World Politics* (Oxford: Oxford University Press, 2016); Oliver Belcher, "The Afterlives of Counterinsurgency: Postcolonialism, Military Social Science, and Afghanistan 2006-2012" (PhD diss., University of British Columbia, 2013); Oliver Belcher, "Sensing, Territory, Population: Computation, Embodied Sensors, and Hamlet Control in the Vietnam War," *Security Dialogue* 50, no. 5 (2019): 416-36; Antoine Bousquet, "Cyberneticizing the American War Machine: Science and Computers in the Cold War," *Cold War History* 8, no. 1 (2008): 77-102; Paul Edwards, *The Closed World: Computers and the Politics of Discourse in Cold War America* (Cambridge, MA: MIT Press, 1996); James Gibson, *The Perfect War: Technowar in Vietnam* (New York: Avalon, 2000); Katherine Hayles, *How We Became Posthuman* (Chicago: University of Chicago Press, 1999); McCoy, "Imperial Illusions"; Ian Shaw, *Predator Empire: Drone Warfare and Full Spectrum Dominance* (Minneapolis: University of Minnesota Press, 2016).

15. Frédéric Gros, *States of Violence: An Essay on the End of War* (Chicago: University of Chicago Press, 2010); Derek Gregory, "The Everywhere War," *Geographical Journal* 177, no. 3 (2011): 238-50; Glenn Voelz, "The Individualization of American Warfare," *Parameters* 45, no. 1 (2015): 99-111.

16. Holger Potzsch, "Archives and Identity in the Context of Social Media and Algorithmic Analytics: Towards an Understanding of iArchive and Predictive Retention," *New Media & Society* 20, no. 9 (2018): 3304-22.

17. Mark Jarzombek, *Digital Stockholm Syndrome in the Post-Ontological Age* (Minneapolis: University of Minnesota Press, 2016), 2.

18. Ed Finn, *What Algorithms Want: Imagination in the Age of Computing* (Cambridge, MA: MIT Press, 2017).

19. Janet Abbate, *Inventing the Internet* (Cambridge, MA: MIT Press, 1999).

20. Caren Kaplan, "Precision Targets: GPS and the Militarization of Everyday Life," *Canadian Journal of Communication* 38, no. 3 (2013): 397-420.

21. Hayles, *How We Became Posthuman.*

22. Shoshana Zuboff, *The Age of Surveillance Capitalism* (London: Profile Books, 2019).

23. Nick Couldry and Ulises Mejias, "Data Colonialism: Rethinking Big Data's Relation to the Contemporary Subject," *Television & New Media* 20, no. 4 (2019): 336-49. Couldry and Mejias emphasize how colonial and capitalist logics of extraction, accumulation, and commodification, rather than, for example, securitization, underpin contemporary "data" production. They argue that increasingly, the very texture of social life itself is being reconfigured as a potential resource for expropriation,

whereby "digital platforms [...] produce a new type of 'social' for capital: that is, the social in a form that can be continuously tracked, captured, sorted and counted for value as 'data'" (341).

24. Mark Andrejevic and Mark Burdon, "Defining the Sensor Society," *Television & New Media* 16, no. 1 (2015): 19-36.

25. David Lyon, "Surveillance, Snowden, and Big Data: Capacities, Consequences, Critique," *Big Data & Society* 1, no. 2 (2014): 1-13; Rob Kitchin, "Big Data, New Epistemologies and Paradigm Shifts," *Big Data & Society* 1, no. 1 (2014): 1-12.

26. David Chandler, "A World without Causation: Big Data and the Coming of Age of Posthumanism," *Millennium* 43, no. 3 (2015): 833-51.

27. Kitchin, "Big Data, New Epistemologies and Paradigm Shifts," 2.

28. Chris Andersen, "The End of Theory: The Data Deluge Makes the Scientific Method Obsolete," *Wired*, no. 16 (2008), http://archive.wired.com/science/discoveries/magazine/16-07/pb_theory.

29. Chandler, "A World without Causation."

30. Andrejevic and Burdon, "Defining the Sensor Society," 32.

31. John Foster and Robert McChesney, "Surveillance Capitalism: Monopoly-Finance Capital, the Military-Industrial Complex, and the Digital Age," *Monthly Review* 66, no. 3 (2014), https://doi.org/10.14452/MR-066-03-2014-07_1; Yasha Levine, *Surveillance Valley: The Secret Military History of the Internet* (London: Icon Books, 2019); Margaret O'Mara, *The Code: Silicon Valley and the Remaking of America* (London: Penguin, 2019). Levine's analysis of the "military-digital complex" thus argues that "the Internet was hardwired to be a surveillance tool from the start. No matter what we use the network for today [...] it always had a dual-use nature rooted in intelligence gathering and war" (2). Foster and McChesney conclude their analysis of the history and political economy of surveillance capitalism by arguing that "the digital revolution must be demilitarized and subjected to democratic values and governance, with all that entails."

32. United States Joint Inquiry, "Report of the Joint Inquiry into the Terrorist Attacks of September 11, 2001," Washington DC: House Permanent Select Committee on Intelligence and the Senate Select Committee on Intelligence, 2003.

33. Alexandra Hall and Jonathan Mendel, "Threatprints, Threads and Triggers: Imaginaries of Risk in the 'War on Terror,'" *Journal of Cultural Economy* 5, no. 1 (2012): 9-27.

34. Louise Amoore, "Cloud Geographies: Computing, Data, Sovereignty," *Progress in Human Geography* 42, no. 1 (2016): 4-24.

35. Claudia Aradau, "The Signature of Security: Big Data, Anticipation, Surveillance," *Radical Philosophy*, 191 (May-June 2015): 21-28.

36. David Rohde, "Digitizing the CIA: John Brennan's Attempt to Lead America's Spies into the Age of Cyberwar," *Reuters*, November 2, 2016, https://www.reuters.com/investigates/special-report/usa-cia-brennan/.

37. See inter alia Louise Amoore, "Algorithmic War: Everyday Geographies of the War on Terror," *Antipode* 41, no. 1 (2009): 49-69; Louise Amoore, *The Politics of Possibility: Risk and Security Beyond Probability* (Durham, NC: Duke University Press, 2013); Eli Berman, Joseph Felter, and Jacob Shapiro, *Small Wars, Big*

Data: The Information Revolution in Modern Conflict (Princeton, NJ: Princeton University Press, 2018); Roberto Gonzales, "Seeing into Hearts and Minds: 'Big Data,' Algorithms, and Computational Counterinsurgency," *Anthropology Today* 31, no. 4 (2015): 13-18.

38. Aradau, "The Signature of Security"; Charlotte Heath-Kelly, "Algorithmic Autoimmunity in the NHS: Radicalisation and the Clinic," *Security Dialogue* 48, no. 1 (2017): 29-45.

39. As encapsulated in DARPA's "Total Information Awareness" program (see, e.g., Lyon, "Surveillance, Snowden, and Big Data") and the National Security Agency's (NSA) characterization of its own data collection posture as "Sniff it all, know it all, collect it all, process it all, exploit it all." Jon Queally, "NSA Global Spy Stations Revealed: 'Sniff It All, Collect It All, Know It All, Process It All, Exploit It All,'" *Common Dreams*, March 7, 2015.

40. Aradau, "The Signature of Security."

41. Andrejevic and Burdon, "Defining the Sensor Society," 23.

42. Amoore, *The Politics of Possibility*.

43. Louise Amoore, "Data Derivatives: On the Emergence of a Security Risk Calculus for Our Times," *Theory, Culture and Society* 28, no. 6 (2011): 24-43.

44. Louise Amoore and Marieke de Goede, "Transactions after 9/11: The Banal Face of the Preemptive Strike," *Transactions of the Institute of British Geographers* 33, no. 2 (2008): 178.

45. Amoore, "Data Derivatives." Amoore notes that derivatives are a speculative mode of data derived from, but also necessarily different than and hence partially indifferent to, the individual values or singularities of the underlying phenomena or data fields.

46. Matteo Pasquinelli, "Arcana Mathematica Imperii: The Evolution of Western Computational Norms," in *Former West: Art and the Contemporary after 1989*, ed. Maria Hlavajova and Simon Sheikh (Cambridge, MA: MIT Press, 2017), 290.

47. Claudia Aradau and Tobias Blanke, "Governing Others: Anomaly and the Algorithmic Subject of Security," *European Journal of International Security*, no. 1 (February 2018): 1-21.

48. Matteo Pasquinelli, "Anomaly Detection: The Mathematization of the Abnormal in the Metadata Society," 2015, http://matteopasquinelli.com/anomaly-detection/.

49. Gregory, "The Everywhere War."

50. Belcher's analysis of computational counterinsurgency details how the US occupation accumulated massive amounts of disparate data on Afghan society through traditional means such as informants and police reports, significant activities reports from patrols, biometric technologies deployed at checkpoints, cell phone data, and even metrics supposedly indicating local "confidence and security" such as commodity prices in markets. Military projects such as Nexus 7 then subjected this disparate data to "dynamic network analysis" in order to produce models, predictions, and visualizations thought to reveal the structural patterns, rhythms, and movements of insurgency through the Afghan population, with the results used to orient the deployment of further military resources. As Belcher notes, the fundamental working assumption of this program was an underlying vision of the "networked enemy," an ontology of enmity that was further naturalized

in these programs of computational counterinsurgency. Belcher, "The Afterlives of Counterinsurgency." See also Gonzales, "Seeing into Hearts and Minds"; Sharon Weinberger, *The Imagineers of War: The Untold Story of Darpa, the Pentagon Agency That Changed the World* (New York: Alfred A. Knopf, 2017).

51. Belcher, "The Afterlives of Counterinsurgency"; Grégoire Chamayou, "Oceanic Enemy: A Brief Philosophical History of the NSA," *Radical Philosophy*, 191 (May-June 2015): 2-12; Matthew Ford, "Finding the Target, Fixing the Method: Methodological Tensions in Insurgent Identification," *Studies in Conflict and Terrorism* 35, no. 2 (2012): 113-34.

52. Kevin McSorley, "Predatory War, Drones and Torture: Remapping the Body in Pain," *Body and Society* 25, no. 3 (2019): 75-99.

53. Mark Bowden, "The Killing Machines: How to Think about Drones," *Atlantic*, August 14, 2013, http://www.theatlantic.com/magazine/archive/2013/09/the-killing-machineshow-to-think-about-drones/309434/.

54. Antoine Bousquet, *The Eye of War: Military Perception from the Telescope to the Drone* (Minneapolis: University of Minnesota Press, 2019); Voelz, "The Individualization of American Warfare"; Kyle Grayson, "Six Theses on Targeted Killing," *Politics* 32, no. 2 (2012): 120-28; Gros, *States of Violence*.

55. Derek Gregory, "Lines of Descent," in *From Above: War, Violence and Verticality*, ed. Peter Adey, Mark Whitehead, and Alison Williams (Oxford: Oxford University Press, 2013), 41-70; Grégoire Chamayou, *A Theory of the Drone*, trans. Janet Lloyd (New York: New Press, 2015).

56. Derek Gregory, "Drone Geographies," *Radical Philosophy*, no. 183 (2014): 14.

57. Greg Miller, "Plan for Hunting Terrorists Signals US Intends to Keep Adding Names to Kill Lists," *Washington Post*, October 23, 2012.

58. Neal Curtis, "The Explication of the Social: Algorithms, Drones and (Counter-)terror," *Journal of Sociology* 52, no. 3 (2016): 528.

59. Ian Shaw, "The Urbanization of Drone Warfare," *Geographica Helvetica*, no. 71 (2016): 25.

60. Andrejevic and Burdon, "Defining the Sensor Society."

61. Stewart Baker cited in David Cole, "We Kill People Based on Metadata," *New York Review of Books*, May 10, 2014, https://www.nybooks.com/daily/2014/05/10/we-kill-people-based-metadata/. Indeed, General Michael Hayden, former director of the NSA and the CIA, has similarly attested that "we kill people based on metadata," cited in ibid.

62. Derek Gregory, "The Territory of the Screen," *Mediatropes* 6, no. 2 (2016): 126-47; Jutta Weber, "Keep Adding: On Kill Lists, Drone Warfare and the Politics of Databases," *Environment and Planning D: Society and Space* 34, no. 1 (2016): 107-25.

63. Lauren Wilcox, "Drone Warfare and the Making of Bodies out of Place," *Critical Studies on Security* 3, no. 1 (2015): 127-31.

64. Chamayou, *A Theory of the Drone*, 49.

65. Pratap Chatterjee and Christian Stork, "Drone, Inc.: Marketing the Illusion of Precision Killing," *Corpwatch*, 2017, http://www.corpwatch.org/droneinc.

66. United States Department of Defense, "Project Maven to Deploy Computer Algorithms to Wars," 2017, https://www.defense.gov/News/Article/Article/1254719/project-maven-to-deploy-computer-algorithms-to-war-zone-by-years-end/.

67. Astrid Nordin and Dan Oberg, "Targeting the Ontology of War: From Clausewitz to Baudrillard," *Millennium* 43, no. 2 (2015): 401.

68. Paul Pillar cited in Miller, "Plan for Hunting Terrorists."

69. Jameel Jaffer, *The Drone Memos* (New York: New Press, 2016), 7.

70. For example, the prominent Al Jazeera journalist Ahmad Muaffaq Zaidan was identified as a member of Al Qaeda by the NSA SKYNET program on the basis of communicative metadata generated in the course of his investigative work on the group (for further examples, see Chamayou, *A Theory of the Drone*, 49-51).

71. Curtis, "The Explication of the Social," 531.

72. James Cavallaro, Stephan Sonnenberg, and Sarah Knuckey, *Living under Drones: Death, Injury and Trauma to Civilians from US Drone Practices in Pakistan* (Stanford, CA: International Human Rights and Conflict Resolution Clinic, Stanford Law School, 2012), https://law.stanford.edu/projects/living-under-drones/.

73. McSorley, "Predatory War, Drones and Torture."

74. Scarry, *The Body in Pain*, 45.

75. Ibid., 80. As Metin Başoğlu relatedly notes, "the overlap between features of drone warfare and torture is so striking that it deserves attention from both moral and legal perspectives [...]. Inflicting severe and prolonged mental suffering on people essentially trapped in an 'inescapable shock' situation is no less morally abhorrent than torture and, at least from a behavioural science perspective, may well amount to mass torture." Metin Başoğlu, "Drone Strikes or Mass Torture? A Learning Theory Analysis," November 11, 2012, https://metinbasoglu.wordpress.com/2012/11/25/drone-warfare-or-mass-torture-a-learning-theory-analysis/.

76. Gayatri Spivak uses the term "epistemic violence" when discussing the silencing and othering of marginalized groups and the privileging of colonial epistemic practices over local forms of knowledge. Gayatri Spivak, "Can the Subaltern Speak?," in *Marxism and the Interpretation of Culture*, ed. Cary Nelson and Lawrence Grossberg (Champaign: University of Illinois Press, 1988), 271-313. In an analysis of the computerized Hamlet Evaluation System deployed by the United States in the Vietnam War, Belcher argues that "acts of translating the rich texture of hamlet and village life into an objectified information format constituted a unique form of 'epistemic violence,' rooted not so much in the narrative subjection of the 'Other,' but in the pure abstraction of life into a digitally stored data trace." Belcher, "Sensing, Territory, Population," 420.

77. Gibson, *The Perfect War*; Bernard Nalty, *The War against Trucks: Aerial Interdiction in Southern Laos 1968-1972* (Washington, DC: US Air Force History and Museums Program, 2005).

78. Belcher, "The Afterlives of Counterinsurgency"; Gonzales, "Seeing into Hearts and Minds"; Weinberger, *The Imagineers of War*.

79. Chamayou, "Oceanic Enemy."

80. Lieutenant General David Deptula, United States Air Force, cited in Chamayou, *A Theory of the Drone*, 12.

81. Relatedly, the broad US doctrine of low personnel, high-tech networked warfare characterized as the Revolution in Military Affairs (RMA) failed to survive the initial realities on the ground in the US occupations of the early twenty-first century. However, as Jeremy Black notes, whatever objective assessment one might make of its military successes or failings, its very existence was revelatory of a wider set of Western cultural and political assumptions: "The RMA acts as a nexus for a range of developments and beliefs, including an unwillingness to accept conscription, a very low threshold for casualties, an assertion of Western superiority, and the ideology of machinism." Jeremy Black, *New Century War: Past, Present, Future* (London: Continuum, 2003), 97.

82. David Beer, "The Social Power of Algorithms," *Information, Communication & Society* 20, no. 1 (2017): 11.

83. United States Department of Defense, "Project Maven to Deploy Computer Algorithms to Wars"; Hague Center for Strategic Studies, "Artificial Intelligence and the Future of Defense," 2017, https://hcss.nl/report/artificial-intelligence-and-future-defense.

84. Aradau, "The Signature of Security."

85. Katharine Kindervarter, "The Emergence of Lethal Surveillance," *Security Dialogue* 47, no. 3 (2016): 223-38.

86. Shaw, *Predator Empire*.

87. Bousquet, *The Eye of War*, 193.

88. Reza Negarestani, "The Militarization of Peace: Absence of Terror or Terror of Absence?" in *Collapse* I, ed. Robin Mackay (Oxford: Urbanomic, 2007), 53-92.

89. danah boyd and Kate Crawford, "Critical Questions for Big Data," *Information, Communication & Society* 15, no. 5 (2012): 668.

EVENT MAPS
The Cartographic Archive and Imagined Futures of War

Anders Engberg-Pedersen

Warfare has long been a driving force in the development of cartography.[1] It is easy to understand why: orientational knowledge is indispensable in times of war, when the specific topographic lay of the land, the details of the terrain, and the possible routes through it can be decisive for the outcome of the conflict. In his *History of the Peloponnesian War*, Thucydides wrote that the sudden death of a native guide could have as a consequence the destruction of almost an entire Athenian army.[2] A reliable topographic map has therefore historically been an indispensable tool for the military commander. An apocryphal but often quoted statement by Napoleon summarizes it well: "A detailed map is a weapon of war."[3] As such, military maps have been surrounded by secrecy, and sharing maps with competitor nations has been considered an act of treason.[4] On the other hand, national cartographic centers have often published incorrect maps of their own territory with intentionally misplaced cities and nonexistent rivers so as to confuse the enemy.[5]

All these efforts have left us a large, diverse, and, given the material, often fragile archive of spatial representations. Deployed here as a broad notion of the totality of extant historical military maps, this general Archive is of course accessible and organized in numerous concrete archives such as Le service historique de l'armée de terre in Vincennes, the Kartenabteilung in the Staatsbibliothek zu Berlin, or Det Kongelige Bibliotek and Forsvarets Bibliotek in Copenhagen. Disconnected from their historical context, the maps in such collections at first sight appear as what they of course also are: detailed topographical representations of space. Yet, for all the importance of topography within military cartography, war maps also reveal an important linkage of spatial representations and temporal projections. As an instrument of tactics and strategy, the orientational knowledge of space serves as the basis for attempts to orient oneself in time. From the ancient astrological divination of celestial constellations and star charts, via the gradual development of an accurate topographic military cartography in the eighteenth century, to the birth of the modern war-game and its transformation in contemporary virtual simulations, cartography has formed the site where possible worlds, scenarios, and hypothetical events are imagined, projected, and tested. Above all else, the war map is a symbolic tool for the management of future events.[6]

In this respect, war maps give rise to a precarious epistemology. They produce knowledge, not of the actual world, but of possible worlds whose very existence is in the balance. They operate with conjectures and probabilities, and serve as tools to govern the type of event that Aristotle termed "potentialities."[7] Via Boethius's Latin translation *contingens*, they have become known as "future contingents" and designate events that are neither impossible nor necessary.[8] Evidently, like all plans for the future, the projections of military strategy are highly uncertain, but they are based on a specific and carefully calculated transformation of spatial order into events, and this translation is authorized in different ways depending on the historical period and the type or genre of map that is used.

We might therefore regard war maps as *event maps*—that is, maps that in various ways serve the complex translation of space into time and virtual scenarios into actual deeds. How does that happen? Under what conditions, to what extent, and with what validity do war maps convert symbolic spatial arrangements into actions and events?[9]

This essay sketches out a brief history of the imagined futures of war. On the one hand, I will sample from the Archive of military cartography three examples of its main genres: the astrological chart, the topographic map, and the war game. At the same time, in a parallel track, I will examine three artistic reappropriations of this cartographic Archive, namely Friedrich Schiller's *Wallenstein* (1799), Leo Tolstoy's *War and Peace* (1869), and Roberto Bolaño's *The Third Reich* (1989). These texts, among many others, have served as a kind of laboratory in which the intentions and assumptions of military cartography are put to the test. From this perspective, literary history comes to function as a running commentary on the precariousness of the link between war cartography and the imagined futures of war.

I. THE CELESTIAL EVENT MAP

Let us begin with a celebrated debate about the power of astrological maps. In 1625 Johannes Kepler responded to a request he had received from Albrecht von Wallenstein, Duke of Friedland, and soon to be Generalissimus of the Holy Roman Empire. Wallenstein had asked Kepler to update the horoscope he had made for him some years earlier in 1608, since his life seemed out of sync with the original horoscope. Some of the predicted life events had occurred too early, and some too late. In particular, he wanted to know how long he would continue in military service, and whether he would be blessed with luck in all his military endeavors.[10] He probably had not expected the response he then received from Kepler, who began to lecture him on the limits of the science of astrology: the stars did indeed influence events in the sublunary realm, but, he said, it was mere superstition to believe that it was possible "to predict particular matters and *futura contingentia* from the skies."[11] Nevertheless, Kepler updated the horoscope and predicted a series of general events until the winter of 1634, in which, as he wrote, "horrible disorder" threatened.[12]

By turning to the stars for guidance in earthly affairs, Wallenstein was following a long tradition in politics and war. Since its emergence in ancient Mesopotamia, the science of astrology had informed the decisions of rulers and generals seeking the most propitious moment of action for their political and military endeavors. The basic assumption was that celestial constellations carried a potent force; in other words, that spatial arrangements in the sky translated into terrestrial events. As Ptolemy put it in *Tetrabiblos*, the standard reference for all things astrological for over a thousand years: "The cause of both universal and of particular events is the motion of the planets, sun, and moon; and the prognostic art is the scientific observation of precisely the change in the *subject* natures which corresponds to parallel movements of the heavenly bodies through the surrounding heavens."[13]

The science of astrology was therefore infused with a spatial metaphysics: the celestial configuration in itself carried what Ptolemy called an "effective power."[14] In other words, star events were made possible because astrologers projected a spatial field infused with metaphysical assumptions onto the planets and their movements. For the astrologer looking up at the skies, the heavens constituted not only a mobile spatial arrangement but a field of possible events.[15]

That double reference point transformed the heavens themselves into a vast *event map*. Royal astrologers therefore read and interpreted the heavens as war maps that offered glimpses into the future of a given military conflict.

So much for the heavens, but what about actual maps, as we would say today? The most important astrological map was the horoscope. In this representation the metaphysical spatial projection was particularly evident, as can be seen in the horoscope Kepler made for Wallenstein in 1608. → Fig. 1

Wallenstein's horoscope is divided into twelve contiguous triangles, each representing the houses of the zodiac, and the horoscope shows the exact position of the sun, the moon, and the planets within this spatial order at the time of Wallenstein's birth. Kepler observed the various positions and alignments of the planets at that time and proceeded to predict a number of events in Wallenstein's life. He concluded that the horoscope "was not a bad nativity, but contained exceptionally important signs."[16]

But Kepler's subsequent wry response to Wallenstein marks a fundamental limitation in the epistemology of the astrological nativity map. Kepler writes: "I state this solely for the purpose of removing the illusion entertained by the subject of the nativity that all the *Particularia* can be predicted from the heavens. This much is true, that from the heavens follow heavenly *Particularia*, but not terrestrial ones [...] rather, all terrestrial *Eventus* take their form and shape from terrestrial causes, since every particular has its particular cause."[17] According to Kepler, the celestial pattern of Wallenstein's horoscope can only be regarded as an indicator of general trends, but astrology is unable to predict particular events. Too many terrestrial factors muddle the picture. As an event map, the horoscope does not contain a detailed topography of events, only general tendencies and probabilities. So, while the

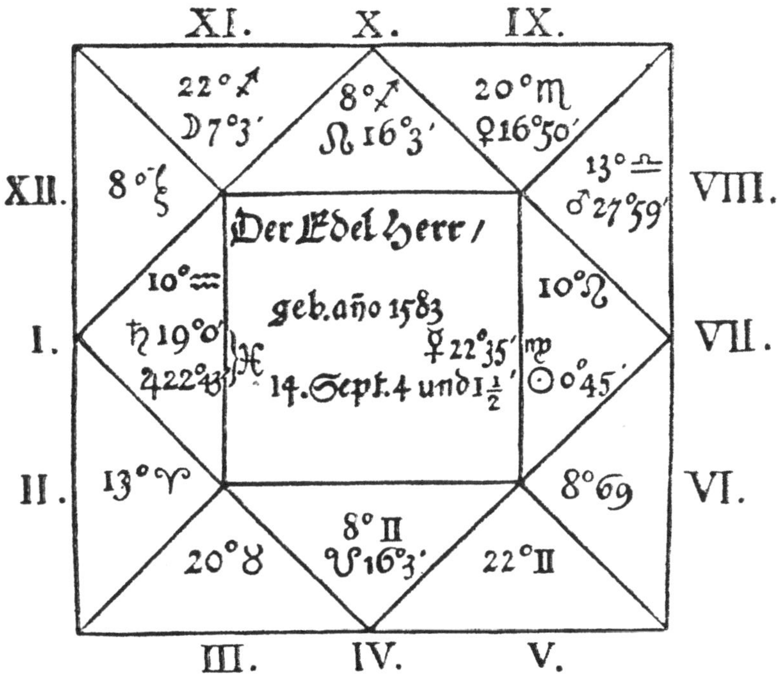

Fig. 1 The original horoscope Kepler made for Albrecht von Wallenstein in 1608

metaphysics of the astrological system remains intact, Kepler goes out of his way to emphasize that his map *cannot* provide the information Wallenstein demands of it.

What do we see in this debate? Well, we encounter the clash of opposing conceptions of the epistemology of astrological maps. From Wallenstein's perspective, the horoscope is an epistemically highly robust representation that accurately maps spatial constellations onto future contingents at all levels, if only for the trained beholder. From Kepler's perspective, the horoscope is a representation that accurately maps the positions of the stars onto supra-individual future events, but it generates no reliable knowledge at the level of the individual and the particular, only random fictions. That Kepler nevertheless agrees to update the horoscope and offers a series of often fairly particular predictions is a good example of what Dan Edelstein has called the

"Super-Enlightenment"—the curious blend of the hermetic and the occult with what we today recognize as well-reasoned science. With its amalgamation of astronomical observation and astrological metaphysics, the horoscope precisely maps the "epistemological no-man's land" in which many scientists operated at the time.[18]

Schiller's Poetic Stars

About 175 years later, another man would enter this debate: in fictionalized form, the celestial event map plays a central role in Schiller's war play *Wallenstein*, composed in the 1790s. There is a key scene that reveals how the drama engages with astrology. We encounter Wallenstein surrounded by maps, globes, and quadrants, facing a large blackboard, and inspecting a *speculum astrologicum*—a diagram of the planets' current positions. According to the diagram, three planets have entered into a significant conjunction: Jupiter, Mars, and Venus. In Wallenstein's interpretation, their alignment is the outcome of celestial warfare. Jupiter and Venus act as military commanders who have outmaneuvered the cause of the conflict, Mars, and have forced him into submission.

Thrilled by the favorable constellation visible on the blackboard, Wallenstein is, in his own interpretation, looking at a diagram of his military future. Indeed, the astrological belief of Wallenstein is such that he has transformed his palace into a vast map of the heavens, painting the zodiac signs on the walls and surrounding himself with pictures of the planets.[19] Immersed in this enormous star chart, he has become oblivious of its alleged referent—what Kepler called the "terrestrial causes." So when one of Wallenstein's allies is captured and his military plans are revealed, this unforeseen event challenges the entire metaphysical order of his belief system. The favorable constellation on his star chart did not translate into favorable military events on the ground.

In an attempt to save the science of astrology, however, Wallenstein then reconceptualizes the celestial event map. No longer a representation of the immediate future as it is about to unfold, the stars now represent what *ought* to unfold according to the natural course of things:

> The stars don't lie, that however
> took place against the course of the stars and against destiny.
> The art is honest, but this false heart
> brings lie and deceit into the truthful heavens.
> Divination is based only on truth,
> Where nature exceeds its bounds, all science errs.[20]

The event map of the heavens is transformed from an *ontological* map into a *normative* map: from events that *will* be, to events that *should have* been. And in the end Wallenstein's celestial map loses all its metaphysical underpinnings. Paying no heed to the warnings of his astrologer Seni, Wallenstein eventually abandons astrology as a guide in military affairs. Deprived of their signifying power, the heavens have ceased to be a map and now constitute only an infinite, meaningless territory. Where Kepler lectured the historical Wallenstein on the limits of astrological predictions, Schiller's fictional Wallenstein seemingly dismisses their power entirely.

Readers and Astrologers

Seemingly. For even though *Wallenstein* dismisses military astrology and its metaphysical underpinnings, Schiller at the same time endows the stars with a poetic function as literary plot devices. He does so in at least two ways. At a fundamental level, the dramatic action is organized by the malfunction of the astrological map as a transformer of spatial constellations into actions and events. Throughout the play, the heavens are filled with potentially significant movements, but *Wallenstein* as a play is pervaded by an almost complete terrestrial eventlessness—nothing happens. The stars and star charts and diagrams generate a wealth of hypothetical scenarios, but Wallenstein is paralyzed by all the options in front of him, and none of them are ever actualized.[21] Schiller transforms conventional dramatic progression into a prolonged debate about the meta-choice of choosing whether to choose or not to choose. And this peculiarly undramatic structure of the drama is a direct effect of the celestial map—of the failure to choose among its multiple latent possibilities. In other words, Wallenstein gets lost among all the virtual futures the map generates.

At a different level, however, Schiller addresses the *hermeneutics* of the map. Schiller does indeed recapitulate the demise of the heavens as an astrological and military signifying system, but he also refunctionalizes the stars and grants them a positive hermeneutic significance within the symbolic economy of literature. For just when Wallenstein's own belief in the stars begins to waver, they appear to carry an actual predictive force. At the end of the play Schiller intervenes in the natural celestial order and rearranges the stars. Although this is astronomically impossible, Schiller's literary stars morph into a threatening celestial pattern a mere three days after their favorable alignment. His astrologer is quick to issue a warning:

> The signs are in a horrible position, close, close
> Are the nets of doom. […]
> Come, read it yourself in the constellation of the planets,
> That calamity threatens you from false friends.[22]

Wallenstein dismisses the warning entirely, but the readers and spectators, with their superior knowledge of the plot against Wallenstein, are invited to offer an interpretation of future events that confirms the astrological signs. Astrological authority is transferred from Wallenstein and Seni to the readers, whose superior hermeneutics establishes the tragic irony of the play: just when the stars cease to signify to their main disciple, their astrological power is confirmed. At this level, astrology is not dismissed out of hand. Rather, Schiller transforms astrological maps into a literary device in order to capitalize on their suggestive predictive powers. What is useless for military strategy turns out to be quite useful for managing literary expectations.

II. TOPOGRAPHIES OF WAR

Just as Schiller was writing, however, a different cartographic genre became particularly important. From the metaphysics of the astrological map we move to the immanent workspace of the topographic military map. By 1800 the large-scale warfare of the Revolutionary and Napoleonic Wars had replaced the smaller cabinet wars that had dominated the eighteenth century. As Carl von Clausewitz wrote, the French had unshackled "the horrible element of war from its old diplomatic and financial fetters: it now marched forth in its raw violence."[23] The scale and extensiveness of the new wars meant that accurate topographic military maps became absolutely necessary for military operations. To manage their troops in the vast theater of war, commanders and officers became deeply reliant on the topographic knowledge that a detailed map could offer. As a result, the period around 1800 witnessed an explosion in the production, dissemination, and use of military cartography.[24]

The effects of this media event were varied and profound. The Swiss military theorist Antoine-Henri Jomini developed a cartographically inflected theory of war, and he even went so far as to claim that "strategy is the art of waging war upon the map."[25] In
Fig. 2 ← Prussia, the leading topographer Johann Georg Lehmann sought to improve cartographic literacy among military topographers and planners, because, as he wrote, "if even the best maps become dangerous objects in the hands of the strategist who does not know how to read and use them, how much more the bad ones that can lead even the most skilled officer astray if he does not know how to check them."[26] Meanwhile his fellow Prussian officer, Georg Heinrich von Berenhorst, claimed that the officers should *themselves* be mediatized. In the absence of maps, they should be able to project triangles and other geometrical figures directly onto the terrain in order to transform it into a legible and manageable mental map. The inside of an officer's skull must, as he put it, be "wallpapered with maps."[27]

As the ideas of these military thinkers indicate, the topographic military map was a tool that encompassed both spatial and temporal orientation. Commanders and officers needed detailed knowledge of the terrain, but their two-dimensional planes also served as the workspace on which various contingent futures were projected, simulated, and compared. This function is perhaps most clearly evidenced by the reports of some of the people who witnessed Napoleon's work habits at first hand. Napoleon's personal secretary, Agathon Jean François Fain, described the process thus: "D'Albe was called whenever the Emperor wanted to read the dispatches on the map; with red and black pins d'Albe marked the sites occupied by our troops; he then highlighted the

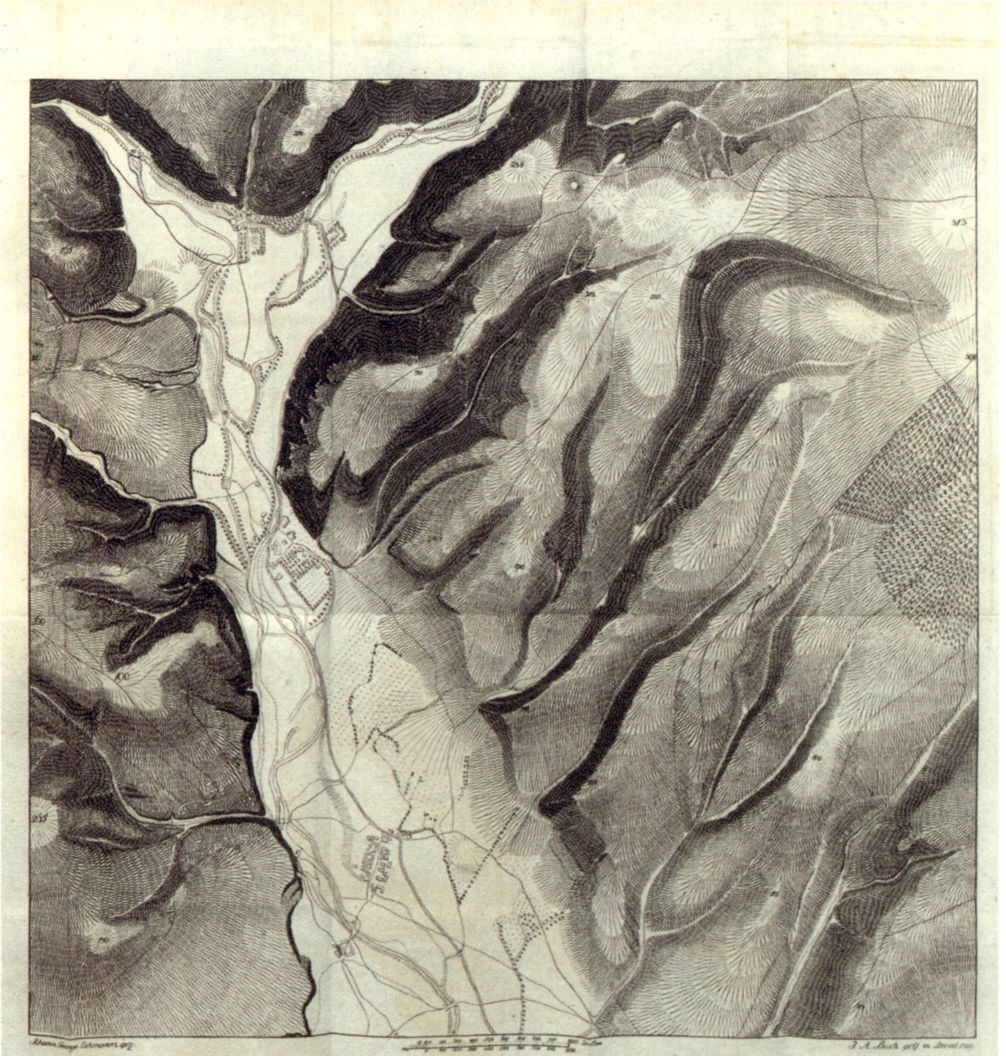

Fig. 2 A topographic map by Johann Georg Lehmann from 1799, displaying hachures to mark the differentiations between various degrees of incline

signs of the most important rivers, mountains, and borders with nuanced colors; finally he prepared the calculations of distance; underlined the scale and opened the compass next to the map. Once the dispatches had been applied to the map in this manner, the Emperor would begin to study it."[28] In this setup, the map serves as the pivot of an information-processing system. First, reports are procured from the actual world, which Bacler d'Albe, Napoleon's chief cartographer, proceeds to visualize with symbols on the map. Then Napoleon reaches a decision and dictates it to his secretary, who eventually transmits it back to the actual world. In this information-processing system, the two-dimensional plane of the map, along with the pins and the compass, functions as an experimental workspace in which various hypothetical scenarios can be tested. The military map, the instruments of inscription, and the pins together constitute a tool that can generate a plurality of worlds and a plurality of battles—all hypothetical, to be sure, but worlds and battles whose hypothetical management had immediate effects.

Compared with the star chart, the topographic military map constitutes a very different kind of event map. In the transition from celestial constellations to topographic maps of the terrain as the central cartographic tool for managing war, the mode of engagement with the maps shifts from *hermeneutics* to *manipulation*, from teasing out the future by way of astrological interpretation, to the invention of the best possible future by way of practical operations on a piece of paper.[29] The colored pencils, the pins, the compass are part of an operational praxis that seeks to realize the latent tactical and strategic knowledge that lies hidden within the map. Louis Marin has suggested that the printed, completed map constitutes a matrix of all possible movements.[30] Using it as a workspace for the projection of hypothetical military scenarios, however, the commanders sought to weigh the best possible movements against one another and choose the optimal virtual world with the greatest chance of being actualized in real events. According to the regulatory ideal of military cartography, the future is a map effect generated by the strategist.

Map Illusions

But was this regulatory ideal valid? To what extent might contingent futures invented on a map actually be realized out in the field? For a number of nineteenth-century war novels, that was precisely the question. With different emphases, authors such as Balzac, Stendhal, and Tolstoy articulated a critique of the assumptions of the military event map. Tolstoy is the most explicit. In several scenes throughout *War and Peace*, maps are at the center of attention. Maps are more than mere literary props that illustrate the pervasive use of cartography during the Napoleonic Wars; Tolstoy interrogates the military map as an object of knowledge.[31] He asks us to consider how information is ordered on maps, what semiotic models they rely on, what governing power they possess, and how virtual scenarios are transformed into actual events. At one point during a Russian war council, the Prussian General Phull has had enough of the vocal critique of his dispositions: "'Where's the difficulty? Nonsense—it's child's play!' He went over to the map and began poking at it with a desiccated finger, jabbering away as he demonstrated that the effectiveness of the Drissa camp was immune to all contingencies, every development had been foreseen, and if the enemy did try a pincer movement, then the enemy would inevitably be destroyed."[32] The map spread out on the table is the emblem of Phull's theory of warfare. Phull excludes a consideration of time, of probability, of the opponent's moves. Such exclusions are highlighted when another general dismisses the objection that his disposition is useless because it assumes knowledge of the enemy's situation and such knowledge is highly doubtful. "A certainty," the general retorts; his elaborate battle plan will be as effectual on the terrain as it is on the map.[33] In Tolstoy's satire on military cartography, the map guarantees the actualization of virtual scenarios. But this is only because the map has lost all connection to the territory. Accordingly, Tolstoy claims that not one but two Battles of Borodino took place—the one that was planned, and the one that actually occurred: "On paper, every one of these columns arrived in position exactly on time and destroyed the enemy. As always in such dispositions everything had been superbly thought through, but as with all dispositions not a single column arrived anywhere on time."[34]

The split between the map and the territory reveals just how radical Tolstoy's claim really is. In war, symbols lose all referential power. The glue that connects signifiers to their signifieds is dissolved in the haze of chaotic events. As Tolstoy's own narrative depictions suggest, war is a stochastic phenomenon that comprises, as he writes, "[a] hundred million contingent factors" in which his characters continually get lost. As such, warfare can be neither managed nor comprehended. All cartographic attempts to govern contingent futures with scenarios and projections are doomed from the very beginning. In Tolstoy's view, Phull's desiccated finger tapping on the map during the war council touches a fantastic object: static, a-chronous, manageable, comprehensible, the map illustrates everything war is not. Confined to the sphere of virtual events, the military event map is a grand illusion.

III. PLAYING AT WAR

But might contingency be trained? Might the individual faced with numerous contingent futures somehow be taught to bring them under control, instead of getting lost in them as did Schiller's Wallenstein? The third major genre in the cartography of war was developed as a response to these questions. Along with the advancement of military cartography, the period around 1800 also witnessed the development of an elaborate tool designed to provide tactical war experience by proxy—*das Kriegsspiel*, or the modern war game.[35] Against the backdrop of large-scale Napoleonic warfare, the game underwent two important changes. Earlier games had been only slightly more elaborate versions of chess. Now, however, to the two-dimensional board inventors added the illusion of a third dimension in the form terrain differentiations. Johann Hellwig's game from 1803, *The War Game—an Attempt to Illustrate the Truth of Various Rules of the Art of War*
Fig. 3 ← *in an Entertaining Game*, includes a board of 1,617 squares with two different obstacles represented by the colors green and red.[36] To increase verisimilitude, other officers and inventors suggested playing directly on one of the topographic maps that were made and used for actual warfare.[37]

The second major change was the simulation of chance. In 1806 Johann Ferdinand Opiz brought a minor revolution to the war game.

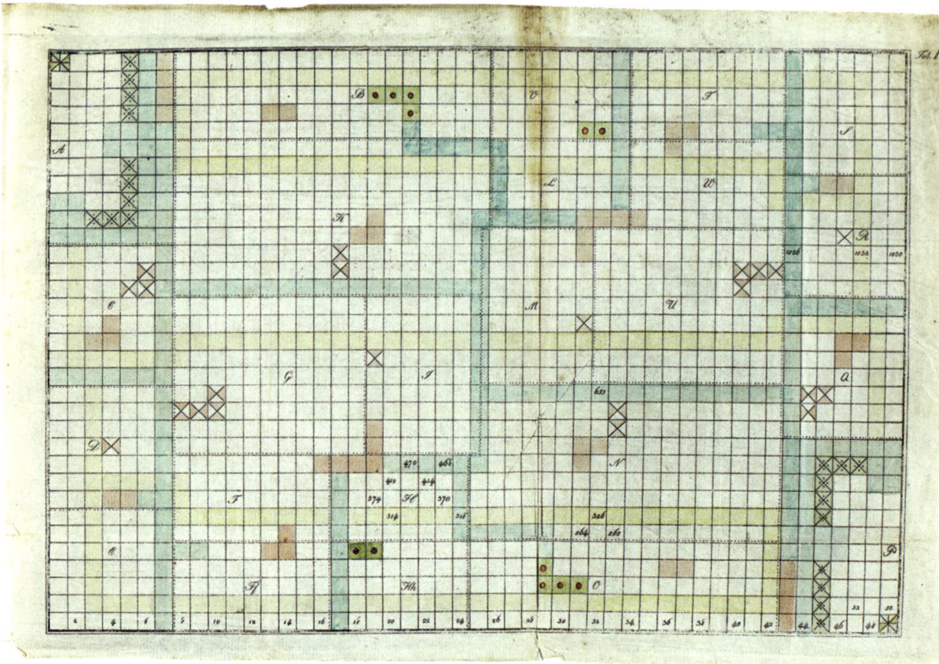

Fig. 3 The board for Hellwig's war game features a space of 1,617 squares. The colors indicate different terrain types that complicate movement.

The Opiz War Game included dice as a key component. Chance was thereby installed as the basic operative logic of the war game. As Clausewitz would later advocate in his treatise, *On War* (1832), commanders had to contend not just with the inscrutable will of the enemy, but also with "friction"—the numerous unforeseen chance events that beset any concerted action in war. With Opiz's invention, these unforeseen events were given a material correlate in the form of the dice.

As indicated by the various subtitles, the purpose of war games was and is to offer military training by proxy, to teach soldiers the basic rules of tactics and strategy in circumstances pervaded by contingency, and to do so in the comfort and safety of their homes or in the military academy. Karl Venturini, another inventor, wrote in 1797 that war games were the best tools with which "to teach young soldiers the often difficult doctrines of the art of war *as if* through experience."[38] While today computer simulation has become the preferred military training technology, board games still play a pedagogical role in training in tactics and strategy. As Philip Sabin writes in his book *Simulated War* (2012): "The most important function of wargames is to convey a vicarious understanding of some of the strategic and tactical dynamics associated with real military operations. Besides learning about the force, space and time relationships in the specific battle or campaign being simulated, players soon acquire an intuitive feel for more generic interactive dynamics associated with warfare as a whole."[39]

Compared with the two other cartographic genres, horoscopes and topographic maps, the war game constitutes a new kind of event map. Blending entertainment with serious purpose, war games create purely potential events separated from the immediate context that would allow them to be realized. Unlike the horoscope, whose power is supported by a metaphysical belief, and unlike the commander's military map, which forms a part of a concrete political and military situation, the war game is not tethered to an immediate reality. Instead it allows for an almost infinite set of situations and variations designed to teach the general logic of military operations in the form of a varied set of patterns. While hypothetical scenarios mushroom, the probability that they will ever be actualized—their chances of ontological success, so to speak—are greatly diminished. In the particular genre of historical war games that simulate famous wars and battles of the past, the inability of the game to have an impact on military events is obvious from the beginning. The simulation of historical events might change our understanding of them, but never the events themselves. Yet, as in the genre of counterfactual historiography, they lure us with their nimbus of virtual alternate versions of the past.[40] As an event map, the war game in its different forms functions as a generator of a multiplicity of military fictions with, even in the best of cases, only a general and very slim chance of realization.

The Third Reich

How might a literary work interact with this third genre of military mapping and its very tenuous link to actual events? Roberto Bolaño's *El Tercer Reich* (*The Third Reich*)[41] is named after a famous war game developed by John Prados in 1974: *The Rise and Decline of the Third Reich*, known to gamers simply as *The Third Reich*. Bolaño not only takes this specific game as the gravitational center of the plot, but he also models his text on a war game. Narrated by the protagonist himself, the novel follows the increasingly nervous and unreliable German war-gaming champion Udo Berger during a vacation with his girlfriend Ingeborg in Spain. Udo sets up *The Third Reich* in his hotel room and spends most of his time trying to come up with a new "strategic variant" that will guarantee a German victory. → Fig. 4

The world outside his hotel room, however, slowly begins to take on the properties of the game. Not only do games of all sorts appear—local and international soccer games, card games, TV shows featuring simulations of accidents (that is, various forms of sublimated warfare that all seem on the verge of breaking out of their sphere of virtuality)—but the world itself appears to be a series of variations on Udo's life. The vacation is a repetition of his childhood vacations; Udo and Ingeborg befriend another couple of about the same age, who also hail from Germany; the women are "almost the same size"; the man, Charly, mistakes their town for the next one up the coast, which, coincidentally, also has a hotel with the same name as the one they are staying in; and so on. Just as the playing board and the pieces in *The Third Reich* are, as the narrator puts it, "like a stage set where thousands of beginnings and endings eternally unfold, a kaleidoscopic theater," so the actual world appears to be "something unreal"—a proliferation of alternate versions of Udo, his game, and the Third Reich.[42] An avatar of the past, Udo himself appears to be living in a game, a ludic multiverse whose variations dissolve any sense of a solid, singular reality.

On the other hand, the events in the game gradually begin to leave the realm of fiction and break through the border between the virtual and the real. A game of entertainment, *The Third Reich* is not designed to have immediate consequences. The board ought to produce only virtual events. Increasingly, however, the

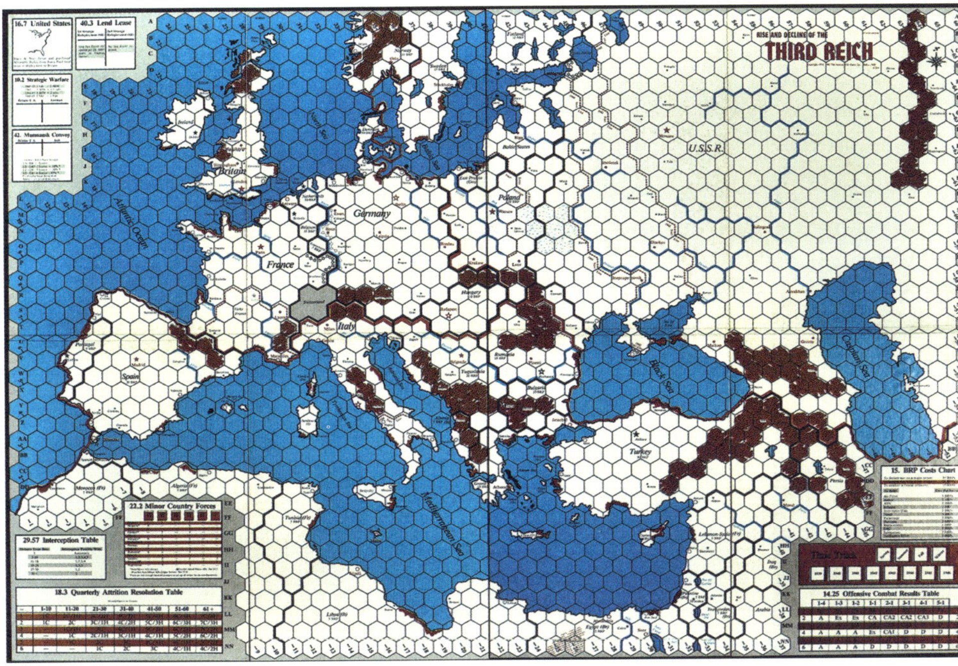

Fig. 4 The board of John Prados's war game *The Rise and Decline of the Third Reich*, 3rd ed., 1974

events in the actual world seem to be directly influenced by the action on the map. When Udo's local opponent, a man charred beyond recognition who goes by the name of El Quemado, or the Burn Victim, slowly gains the upper hand over the German champion, the stakes seem to have risen to a new level where Udo's life is in the balance. People in town now believe that Udo is not just a commander of virtual Nazis on the board, but an actual Nazi, and the game a "trial of the war criminals."[43] Against the protestations of the increasingly unstrung Udo, who insists that *a game is just a game*, *The Third Reich* serves as a catalyst that transforms fiction into reality and the past into the present. It forms the basis not merely of a replay or a reenactment, but of a veritable repetition of World War II in miniature. Unlike conventional war games that produce only a nimbus of hypothetical worlds, Bolaño's literary war game becomes indistinguishable from actual war.

Blending actuality and games, realism and the fantastical, the past and the present, Bolaño fuses what the narrator tries to keep apart as "categorically opposed things."[44] The result is a novel made up of a haze of fictions, its events hovering in an undecidable ontological realm between the virtual and the real. Out of the entertaining or pedagogical virtual events of the traditional war game, Bolaño fashions a war delirium in which all distinctions collapse. Fictional war and actual war are merely variations of one another.

What is the point of these blends, we might ask? If we consider the literary war game as an event map, its curious temporality alerts us to the underlying purpose. Like Schiller's astrological event map in *Wallenstein*, *The Third Reich* serves the poetic function of generating and managing reader expectations. Everything gravitates toward a literary future in which a fatal event will bring the game to a conclusion. But at the same time Bolaño turns the event map around, so to speak. The game repeats a historical war, not a war to come. Udo's strategic variant turns out to be a perverse form of *Vergangenheitsbewältigung*. The variant is a "past contingent" with which he tries to rectify not the Nazis' actions, but their mistakes. In his own words: "It's as if we want to know exactly how everything was done in order to change what was done wrong."[45] Not performing an act of retribution in a "game of atonement" as a compatriot sees it, Udo plays to lead the Nazis to victory.[46] Ostensibly pointing the readers' expectations toward a calamitous future, the map instead becomes a tool for dealing with the problematic events of the German past. The military mindset, Udo's latent belligerence, the insanity of the fanatical war delirium that made generals ponder their maps to conceive the best possible world of destruction, all have been forgotten and repressed by "an amnesiac Europe," but now it all becomes manifest on the hexes of the board.[47] By means of a game, the novel makes explicit that war is anything but that. The entertaining virtual "events" produced by gamers with maps and dice are sublimations that repress their serious purpose as instruments of death and charred flesh.

In the end, all reader expectations are thwarted. Udo loses the game, but only to return to Germany and withdraw from all gaming activities. The curiously anticlimactic nonevent of the game, however, precisely marks the central event of the game-novel: the end of the obsession with war. As a response to the traditional war game, *The Third Reich* inverts its rationale. Instead of teaching us to handle the potential events of future wars, it conjures from the past their horrific reality to make us desist from military activities altogether, be they actual or invented.

THE FUTURES OF WAR

In 1570 Abraham Ortelius famously wrote that geography is the "eye of history."[48] When we survey the main genres within the cartography of war, we might want to reorient his gaze. Within the military sphere, the map serves as a strategic tool that offers a glimpse of the plural futures of war. Ortelius's statement is nevertheless relevant, for the futures of war have a history. While star charts and horoscopes, military topographic maps, and war games exist side by side as distinct cartographic genres, their genealogy marks three significant moments in the development of the military future. From the metaphysical grounding of astrological predictions in the movement of the celestial orbs, the future of the topographic map becomes an immanent product of strategic planning. Now grounded in the skill and creative genius of the commander rather than in a cosmological belief system, the future loses some of its givennness and emerges as an artifact that can, at least partially, be made. And with the emergence of war games and their recent instantiations in computer simulations, the future takes the form of a repetition, but a repetition of something that has never happened, of an imagined future that has already been played through multiple times. Accordingly, the primary mode of engagement with military maps shifts from hermeneutics, to manipulation, to play. These shifts in cartographic habitus would suggest a growing control over the futures of war, but they are accompanied by a widening of the military future and its increasing virtuality, as possible scenarios burgeon and the nexus between map and event becomes ever more hypothetical.

In some of the main literary works that examine this nexus, the very notion of a "cartography of war" even appears to be a contradiction in terms. For authors such as Stendhal and Tolstoy, conventional cartographic virtues such as control, visibility, and power, which should ground temporal projections and ensure the tractability of contingent futures, are deemed impotent in the context of war. In these texts, it seems that war is not simply a complex object that is difficult to govern, but one that evades the government of maps entirely. Texts and maps are linked not as supplemental media that enmesh literary history with the cartographic Archive, but as opposing media in perpetual conflict. Yet all the authors examined here at the same time co-opt military cartography, adapting and retooling it into productive poetic devices that structure the literary representation of war and the way we are instructed to read their texts. Whether the war map malfunctions as in Schiller, whether it serves as a foil for the narration of war as in Tolstoy, or whether it is turned around and its purpose inverted as in Bolaño, the military event map has shaped the ways in which literature has represented and imagined the events of war—just as these literary works have given us pause to reflect on what it even means to map the imagined futures of war.

1. This essay is a revised version of my article "Cartographies of War: Star Charts, Topographic Maps, War Games," which appeared in the volume *Literature and Cartography: Theories, Histories, Genres*, ed. Anders Engberg-Pedersen (Cambridge, MA: MIT Press, 2017), 411-41.

2. Thucydides, *History of the Peloponnesian War*, vol. 2, bk. 3, , trans. C. F. Smith (Cambridge, MA: Harvard University Press, 2005), 173-75.

3. Unless otherwise indicated, all translations are my own. See Martin Rickenbacher, "Französische Kartierungen von Schweizer Gebieten zwischen 1760 und 1815," *Cartographica Helvetica*, no. 41 (2010): 12. While the use of military maps reached new heights during the Napoleonic Wars, Napoleon's statement does not only apply to the period around 1800; as John Hale writes of the Renaissance, "Maps and conquest seemed to go together." John Hale, "Warfare and Cartography, ca. 1450 to ca. 1640," in *The History of Cartography*, vol. 3, bk. 1, *Cartography in the European Renaissance*, ed. David Woodward (Chicago: University of Chicago Press, 2007), 719.

4. See for example Ute Schneider, *Die Macht der Karten: Eine Geschichte der Kartographie vom Mittelalter bis heute* (Darmstadt: Primus, 2006), 116. For numerous examples during the Napoleonic Wars, see Henri Marie Auguste Berthaut, *Les Ingénieurs géographes militaires 1624-1831* (Paris: Impr. du Service géographique, 1902). In our time the geographical knowledge now provided by satellites is also surrounded by secrecy. For years the US military followed a policy of "selective availability" after they launched GPS, considering it a "dual-use technology" that allowed only limited accuracy for civilians (they scrambled the signals), and retaining its actual pinpoint capabilities for military purposes. See Laura Kurgan, *Close Up at a Distance: Mapping, Technology, and Politics* (New York: Zone Books, 2013), 40.

5. See Mark Monmonier, *How to Lie with Maps* (Chicago: University of Chicago Press, 1996), 115-17; Christian Jacob, *The Sovereign Map: Theoretical Approaches in Cartography Throughout History*, trans. Tom Conley, ed. Edward H. Dahl (Chicago: University of Chicago Press, 2006), 274.

6. See Anders Engberg-Pedersen, *Empire of Chance: The Napoleonic Wars and the Disorder of Things* (Cambridge, MA: Harvard University Press, 2015), 146-83.

7. Aristotle, *The Basic Works of Aristotle*, ed. Richard McKeon (New York: Modern Library, 2001), 47.

8. Boethius, *Commentarii in librum Aristotelis Peri hermeneias*, vol. 1 (Lipsiae: In aedibus B. G. Teubneri, 1877-1880), 21.

9. As Benjamin Bühler and Stefan Willer note, all knowledge of the future relies on media, on language, models, and simulations. Examining the specificities of the formal makeup of event maps and their development over time is therefore necessary if we are to account for the changing nature of map events. See "Einleitung," in *Futurologien: Ordnungen des Zukunftswissens*, ed. Benjamin Bühler and Stefan Willer (Paderborn: Wilhelm Fink, 2016), 9.

10. Johannes Kepler, *Die Astrologie des Johannes Kepler: Eine Auswahl aus seinen Schriften*, ed. H. A. Strauss and S. Strauss-Kloebe (Fellbach: Adolf Bonz, 1981), 244-45.

11. Ibid., 233.

12. Ibid., 256.

13. Ptolemy, *Tetrabiblos*, ed. and trans. F. E. Robbins (Cambridge, MA: Harvard University Press, 1940), 221.

14. Ibid., 225.

15. The basis that ensured the validity of the correspondence between the superlunary and sublunary realms was a cosmological world picture in which the universe was considered a single entity with all elements connected, from the celestial spheres to human beings, animals, and the botanical and mineral realms. For the classic explication of the "cosmic order" in the Elizabethan period, see E. M. W. Tillyard, *The Elizabethan World Picture* (New York: Vintage Books, 1959).

16. Kepler, *Die Astrologie*, 225.

17. Ibid., 238-39. In the original German the quotation reads: "Dies melde ich allein zu dem End, auf daß ich dem Geborenen den Wahn nehme, als ob so ganz die *Particularia* aus dem Himmel vorzusagen seien. Einmal ist dies wahr, daß aus dem Himmel zwar wohl himmlische *Particularia* folgen, nicht aber irdische, [...] sondern alle irdischen *Eventus* nehmen ihre Form und Gestalt aus irdischen Ursachen, allda ein jedes Particular seine Particular-Ursach hat."

18. See Dan Edelstein, "Introduction to the Super-Enlightenment," in *The Super-Enlightenment: Daring to Know Too Much*, ed. Dan Edelstein (Oxford: Voltaire Foundation, 2010), 33. See also David Bates's essay "Super-Epistemology" in the same volume. The persistence in Kepler's thought of astrological themes such as the *harmonia mundi*, the analogy of macro- and microcosmos, can be seen even in his mathematical calculations. See Hania Siebenpfeiffer, "Astrologie," in *Futurologien*, 385.

19. Schiller, *Wallenstein* (Frankfurt am Main: Deutscher Klassiker Verlag, 2005), 175, 155. In 1623, the historical Wallenstein commissioned Italian artists to decorate the twenty-one-meter-long Astrological Corridor in his palace with frescoes that depicted the seven known planets personified as ancient gods, along with the signs of the zodiac. See Alena Hadravová and Petr Hadrava, "Science in Contact with Art: Astronomical Symbolics of the Wallenstein Palace in Prague," in *Acta historiae rerum naturalium necnon technicarum*, vol. 8, *Science in Contact at the Beginning of Scientific Revolution*, ed. Jitka Zamrzlová (Prague: National Technical Museum, 2004), 181-84.

20. Schiller, *Wallenstein*, 213. "Die Sterne lügen nicht, das aber ist / Geschehen wider Sternenlauf und Schicksal. / Die Kunst ist redlich, doch dies falsche Herz / Bringt Lug und Trug in den wahrhaft'gen Himmel. / Nur auf der Wahrheit ruht die Wahrsagung, / Wo die Natur aus ihren Grenzen wanket, da irret alle Wissenschaft."

21. See also Joseph Vogl's analysis of the proliferation of virtual scenarios in *Über das Zaudern* (Zurich: Diaphanes, 2008).

22. Schiller, *Wallenstein*, 282. "Die Zeichen stehen grausenhaft, nah, nahe / Umgeben dich die Netze des Verderbens. [....] / Komm, lies es selbst in den Planetenstand, / Dass Unglück dir von falschen Freunden droht."

23. Carl von Clausewitz, "Über das Leben und den Charakter von Scharnhorst 1817," in *Verstreute kleine Schriften*, ed. Werner Hahlweg (Osnabrück: Biblio, 1979), 228.

24. A comprehensive account of Napoleonic war-mapping is still to be written. I offer what is merely an initial sketch in *Empire of Chance*. See also Berthaut, *Les Ingénieurs*; Max Eckart, *Die Kartenwissenschaft*, vol. 1 (Berlin: Walter de Gruyter, 1921).

25. Antoine-Henri Jomini, *Précis de l'art de la guerre ou nouveau tableau analytique des principales combinaisons de la stratégie, de la grande tactique et de la politique militaire*, vol. 1 (Paris, 1855; repr., Osnabrück: Biblio, 1973), 155. See also *Tableau analytique des principales combinaisons de la guerre* (St. Petersburg: Bellizard et Cie, Libraires de la Cour, 1830), 50.

26. Johann Georg Lehmann, *Die Lehre der Situation-Zeichnung oder Anweisung zum richtigen Erkennen und genauen Abbilden der Erd-Oberfläche in topographischen Charten und Situations-Planen*, vol. 1 (Dresden, 1816), 46. For a similar advocacy of a proper cartographic "critique," see also Ernst Heinrich Michaelis, *Einige durch die Fortsetzung der Bohnenberger-Ammonschen Karte von Schwaben veranlasste Bemerkungen über die topographische Kunst* (Bern, 1825), 130-31.

27. Georg Heinrich von Behrenhorst, *Betrachtungen über die Kriegskunst, über ihre Fortschritte, ihre Widersprüche und ihre Zuverlässigkeit*, vol. 2 (1797-1799; repr., Osnabrück: Biblio, 1978), 345.

28. Agathon Jean François Fain, *Mémoires du Baron Fain* (Paris: Arléa, 2001), 29.

29. Discussing the early use of military maps in Holland, Wolfgang Schäffner labels such simultaneously practical and tactical engagement with maps "operational topography." Wolfgang Schäffner, "Operationale Topographie: Repräsentationsräume in den Niederlanden um 1600," in *Räume des Wissens: Repräsentation, Codierung, Spur*, ed. Hans-Jörg Rheinberger, Michael Hagner, and Bettina Wahrig-Schmidt (Berlin: Akademie, 1997), 63-90.

30. Louis Marin, "Les voies de la carte," in *Cartes et figures de la terre* (Paris: Centre Georges Pompidou/CCI, 1980), 50.

31. For a more comprehensive account of the role of maps in *War and Peace* see Anders Engberg-Pedersen, "Critique of Cartographic Reason: Tolstoj on the Media of War," *Russian Literature* 77, no. 3 (2015): 307-36; Engberg-Pedersen, *Empire of Chance*, ch. 6.

32. Tolstoy, *Polnoe sobranie sochinenii*, vol. 11, ed. V. G. Chertkov (Moscow: Gosudarstvennoie Izdatelstvo, 1928), 50.

33. Tolstoy, *Polnoe sobranie sochinenii*, vol. 9, 322.

34. Tolstoy, *Polnoe sobranie sochinenii*, vol. 12, 74.

35. See, above all, Philipp von Hilgers, *Kriegsspiele: Eine Geschichte der Ausnahmezustände und Unberechenbarkeiten* (Munich: Wilhelm Fink, 2008); Claus Pias, *Computer Spiel Welten* (Munich: Sequenzia, 2002). See also Peter P. Perla, *The Art of Wargaming* (Annapolis, MD: United States Naval Institute, 1990); Hajo Holborn, "The Prusso-German School: Moltke and the Rise of the General Staff," in *Makers of Modern Strategy: From Machiavelli to the Nuclear Age*, ed. Peter Paret (Oxford: Oxford University Press, 1986), 281-95.

36. For an in-depth analysis of the earlier version of Hellwig's game from 1780, see Pias, *Computer Spiel Welten*, 204-13.

37. See for example Karl Venturini, *Beschreibung und Regeln eines neuen Krieges-Spiels, zum Nutzen und Vergnügen, besonders aber zum Gebrauch in Militair-Schulen* (Schleswig: J. G. Röhss, 1797), xvi; Ludwig Freidrich Erck, *Anleitung zum zweckmäßigen Studium der Kriegswissenschaft: Von einem norddeutschen Officiere* (Leipzig: Hahn, 1828), 35, 49, 57-58.

38. Venturini, *Beschreibung und Regeln*, xvi.

39. Philip Sabin, *Simulating War: Studying Conflict through Simulation Games* (London: Continuum, 2014), 31. Indeed, Christian Jacob suggests that the map is "the role-playing game par excellence." Jacob, *The Sovereign Map*, 328.

40. See for example Niall Ferguson, *Virtual History: Alternatives and Counterfactuals* (New York: Basic Books, 1999).

41. The novel was written in 1989, but it was only published posthumously in 2010. The English translation followed in 2011.

42. Roberto Bolaño, *The Third Reich*, trans. Natasha Wimmer (Basingstoke: Picador, 2012), 49, 108, 200, 41.

43. Ibid., 250.

44. Ibid.

45. Ibid., 206.

46. Ibid., 234.

47. Ibid., 83.

48. Abraham Ortelius, "Benevolis lectoribus," in *Theatrum orbis terrarum* (Antverpiae: Apud Aegid. Coppenium Diesth, 1570), n.p.

THE CERRILLOS ARCHIVE PROJECT
Machines, War, and Nonhuman Rights

Cristián Gómez-Moya

In what follows, I will present a problem of the archive from a territorial perspective on human rights.[1] This means addressing archival practices as forms of political agency in specific or situated spaces. I will speak about a form of agency that seeks to intervene in the memory of a university space, a space where a process of deterritorialization has rendered identifiable the effects of state violence during Chile's civil-military dictatorship (1973–1990): first, the illegitimate occupation of a plot of land originally designated for higher education (1976); second, the transformation of that plot into a place for the formation of apparatuses of police repression, which still continues at the time of writing (2019).

The problem is as follows. The University of Chile's loss of real estate during the 1970s and 1980s is fundamentally related to the matter of human rights during wartime; furthermore, it is also connected to the dispute over nonhuman rights to territory. Fig. 1 ← In the case of the university's Cerrillos campus,[2] which opened in 1957 in a peri-urban industrial zone far from the civic center, the territory was intervened in through an operation that involved General Augusto Pinochet himself. Along with Pinochet, it also involved members of the senior leadership of the University of Chile: the Delegate Rector, General Agustín Toro Dávila,[3] and the Dean of the Faculty of Architecture, architect Gastón Etcheverry Orthous—both of whom were appointed by executive mandate during the dictatorship.

The key aspects of this historical event are defined by an intervention that began in 1976, when the military dictatorship decided to move the University of Chile's Faculty of Architecture to a central zone in the city of Santiago.[4] Although the decision appeared to

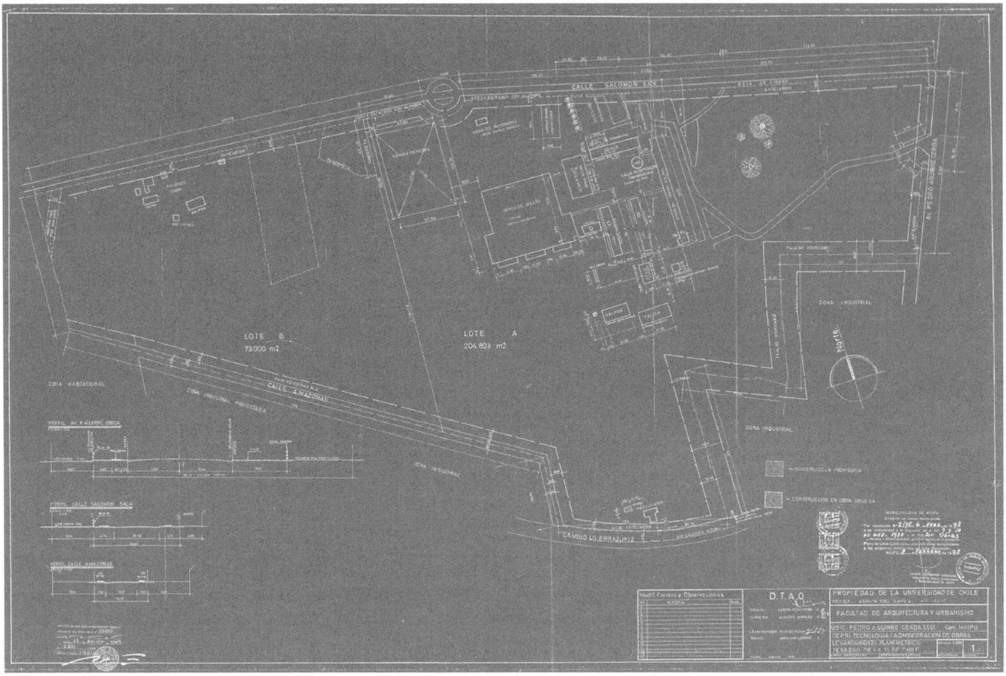

Fig. 1 Planimetric survey of Cerrillos campus, 1957

be in line with the need to be close to an urban pole, thereby strengthening cultural life in an area of historic conservation, it also enabled a glimpse into the dictatorship's opaque maneuvering in relation to the state transfer of real estate. It is worth mentioning that this operation, as documentary records show, was enacted through a series of modifications to fiscal property agreements that progressively altered the territorial rights in question.

More than forty years later, we can see that around thirty hectares of the Cerrillos plot, which had been donated to the educational institution in 1957, were lost as a result of the 1976 intervention. The Faculty of Architecture currently owns only two hectares, which it has been able to hold onto despite the fraudulent operations—for which, incidentally, there is still a lack of evidence to prove the actual financial transfers. To this we might add another precedent, perhaps the most controversial: the handing over of this land to the Carabineros (Chilean National Police Force) in the midst of the dictatorship—the moment when, we might say, the university gave up its symbolic and material heritage.

It is difficult to determine the size of the loss of patrimonial heritage that the University of Chile suffered as a result of the dictatorship. We might say that this deterritorialization is a genuine legacy of what is bitterly known as the "shock doctrine"[5] promoted by the state terrorism of the period. It ultimately mutilated the country's civil, economic, and cultural life, as well as the extensive cultural heritage of the whole Chilean state. The military regime's self-endowed institutionality led to the loss of various lands at the metropolitan level, which also had an impact on regions outside of the capital. The various regional faculties were disconnected from the University of Chile and turned into autonomous unities without central resources. Their fiscal territories were expropriated, and the development of the notion of private university education was initiated.[6] In brief, Pinochet's coup d'état in 1973, along with the complicity of the business and political system of the day, brutally and definitively transformed the university space, giving rise to neoliberalism and a subsidiary state that ultimately consolidated itself through constitutional laws that favored a culture of private goods over and above public interest.[7]

If public interest is the matter of concern, the University of Chile—a historical site for the cultivation of knowledge and the sustainability of public university education—appears as a locus of prime interest. This discussion in favor of public interest, however, also encompasses territories that manifest that interest's social complexity—which we must assume consists of a heterotopic narrative plot with multiple and uneven layers—since it is ultimately on and through these territories that public power is exercised, be they physical or virtual spaces.

As regards the object of analysis, I will examine the matter of the political archive with the aim of producing a contemporary reading of the historical land of Cerrillos. Through the case of this territory, I will raise the following discussion; first, I will argue that there exist nonhuman rights associated with the natural vestiges of that lost space, and that these constitute a problem concerning the relationship between archive, humanity, and territory; second, I will present a heuristic strategy for addressing this problem. This strategy concerns a perspective of political agency that requires us to examine the notion of the "archival machine" doubly: as an archival practice that examines the document under the custodial care of state law and as a practice of territorial activism by means of a scopic apparatus whose register introduces a form of humanism through a nonhuman object. Thus, throughout this text, I will review the parabola between archive and territory, the arc of which makes visible a core aspect of the violence associated with the loss of real estate and human rights—a violence in whose depths rests a form of war marked by deterritorialization and nonhuman rights.

NONHUMAN RIGHTS

If we were to consider the University of Chile's loss of land as a result of juridical mechanisms engendered by the dictatorship, it would suffice to take the state to court to retrieve the lost hectares. This would mean a trial in which the state (in this case, the public university) confronted the state (the tax authority as public administration). However, if we adopt another perspective, the problem is not limited to restoring rights over the territory—in terms of land use—but extends to safeguarding the rights of the territory as an objecthood in itself.[8] This, which might sound somewhat eccentric, consists in exploring other forms of historical understanding: on the one hand, understanding that territory is a complex entity where subjects, objects, and representations cross paths; on the other, understanding that territory is also an abstract entity with regard to the agency of social subjection. As such, with the aim of understanding an expanded notion of *topos*, it is fitting to examine Félix Guattari's suggestion: "A territory can be relative to both a lived space and a perceived system within which a person feels like 'a thing.' The territory is synonymous with appropriation, with subjectification enclosed on itself [...]. It is a set of representations that leads, pragmatically, to a series of behaviors and investments, in social, cultural, aesthetic and cognitive times and spaces."[9] Thus, given that things fulfill an apparent ontological condition, the relationship between subject and thing cannot pass by unperceived.

Now, if we read the territory of Cerrillos as an archival form of nonhuman rights, it becomes plausible—and perhaps at the same time trivial—to recognize the origins of "the human" in another order of things, which may be documents or objects, but also paths, trees, demarcations, grounds, etc. Evidently, this comprehensive notion of the nonhuman thing will lead to a kind of neo-animism[10]—even more so if we consider things to be facts foreign to politicized life. Nevertheless, we are referring to things that operate as public things, and consequently as possible political agencies. Therefore, we must recognize that, inasmuch as territory has been transformed into a simple space of occupation and exchange, it is into these very things that the human has strayed. The territory's value has become diluted between that which violently rules its condition as transferable and that which transforms its ecosystem into a place with an exchange value. Thus, if we think of the nonhuman rights of the territory of Cerrillos, then we must also think of an ethics beyond that of an economy of the human—a *topos* that declares the normative history of that which is and is not patrimonial heritage.

I therefore believe that the possibility of constructing a territorial archive also operates through an aesthetic agency that is capable of generating or activating other comprehensive forms of human rights. This implies, moreover, an unusual detour for these very archives. We may say that this practice of documenting does not necessarily target the custodial value of the documentary sources, funds, and collections[11]; rather, it directs itself toward declassifying the origin of classification, understood as the surface of inscription where the only trace of the human is in the writing itself as a document of law. It is for this reason that an archival strategy can also be deployed through a declassification of archives obtained from a public institution. Indeed, we should pause over the political meaning that declassification acquires in this context. I contend that this consists less in what is revealed from the secret of the archive, and more in a problem associated with classification as an instituting norm. More precisely, I understand the declassification of archives as a destructive operation on that which has been instituted as the norm. Promoting a discursive politics against this norm's classificatory form, this operation organizes and generates tensions in the ordering of facts itself.[12]

If we consider the operations of declassification related to matters of human rights that were carried out during the dictatorship, we can observe that the main operations were produced through a politics of images. This means that the declassifications transformed analogue objects, recorded within the realm of military and dictatorial secrets, into virtual objects that were diverted toward new ways of organizing and constructing visual and collective memory.[13] Of course, many cases of declassification aim to reveal secret state crimes in countries where regimes of terror have been installed; in so doing, they present the truth and consequences of those crimes and their violent practices, as well as access to information as a human right. But in these cases, we can do more than conceive of declassification as simply a humanist revelation with a humanitarian end, since we must also contemplate the nonhumanist action entailed by the declassification itself: an action that creates another conception of the subjective world that lives within the document.

A declassification of archives, more than the mere revelation of documents, constitutes a critical technological practice carried out by nonhuman objects. This practice, posited in the "forensic turn" that authors such as Thomas Keenan and Eyal Weizman have promoted in recent discussions of human rights archives,[14] entails recognizing the coexistence of testimony and evidence. Thus, documentary objects, although they may well carry the traces and residues of the human, must also be understood as nonhuman things related to existence. This means that the document must not bring us only to a single judgment on the inhuman as a violent and abusive practice of state terrorism; rather, it must also allow us to question the history of the human itself by means of its own forms of preservation—which are based, paradoxically, on the technology of the document.

Let us pause over this: state terror is not solely defined by the exercise of force that the document clearly evidences. There are innumerable cases where evidence is transformed into a discursive form that depends on the impetus of the speaker and the scene evoked. As Weizman and his team have demonstrated on diverse occasions, the conception of evidence in terms of documents and forensic tests also requires activation: "Evidence requires someone to present, defend and mobilize it."[15] Indeed, evidence's sole place is within the dispute over the building of the inapprehensible space of truth: that space where documents are required to be visible, legible to others, and thus able to build a common politics on the basis of their apparent veracity. Despite the fact that this focus brings with it all of the problems associated with the politics of representation that post-structuralism inaugurated, it also rests fundamentally on an anachronistic inference related to the pressure that "evidence" exercises once it has been presented and mobilized. As this is the most fragile and arguable point of the "forensic turn," given that it appears to abandon the critique of the document as a positivist technology of domination, what is relevant here is understanding that the document's evidence functions as an interval between the human and the nonhuman; that is, it is an intermediary space where the certainty of being human is conditioned by the cold object, which in turn determines all the ideas that one might have about humanity and its future.

Let us not forget that in these practices of documentation one appeals to the archive, but also, and above all, one aims to produce and create new documentary "evidence"—in relation to both what can be seen and what constructs the space of the right to see.[16] At stake, incidentally, in this way of activating and expanding the notion of archive, is a critique of the aesthetic order, or an aesthetic agency over the archive itself. This means widening the sensorium effect of all human action associated with the perception of human documents, and, at the same time, moving forward with the political conviction of turning such documents and images into active forms.[17] In this I ultimately seek to move beyond the blind faith in the historical and cognitive document as the only way of measuring human statute according to the law.

WAR MACHINES/ARCHIVAL MACHINES

If machines, in Marx's sense, are "knowledge's objective force," then they produce value within a collective frame of knowledges. It is pertinent to examine the distinction that Marx makes between tool and machine in the chapter of *Capital* entitled "Machinery and Modern Industry":

> Again, some people try to explain the difference between a tool and a machine by saying that in the case of the tool, man is the motive

> power, whereas the power behind the machine is a natural force independent of man, as for instance an animal, water, wind and so on. According to this, a plough drawn by oxen, which is common to the most diverse epochs of production, would be a machine, while Claussen's circular loom, which weaves 96,000 picks a minute, though it is set in motion by the hand of one single worker, would be a mere tool. Indeed, this same loom, though a tool when worked by hand, would be a machine if worked by steam.[18]

The distinction is relevant insofar as Marx identifies the machine with a strength that surpasses that of humans; that is, he invokes a nonhuman energy to define a machine that nevertheless reverberates in the ongoing life of "the human." Following this line of thought, some thinkers have expanded the logic of machines and taken it onto an even more functional plane. It is consequently worth highlighting what Gilles Deleuze and Guattari have presented in relation to the notion of the "abstract machine." We must note the meaning acquired by territorialization and deterritorialization as itself a machine whose operations necessarily transform the original machine:[19]

> There is no abstract machine or machines in the sense of a Platonic Idea, transcendent, universal, eternal. Abstract machines operate within concrete assemblages: They are defined by the fourth aspect of assemblages, in other words, the cutting edges of decoding and deterritorialization. They draw these cutting edges. Therefore they make the territorial assemblage open onto something else, assemblages of another type, the molecular, the cosmic; they constitute becomings. Thus they are always singular and immanent. [...] They surpass any kind of mechanics. They are opposed to the abstract in the ordinary sense. Abstract machines consist of unformed matters and nonformal functions. Every abstract machine is a consolidated aggregate of matters-functions (phylum and diagram).[20]

So, in the way we have been thinking thus far, a critical understanding of the archive would be closer to the machine-like perspective that Deleuze and Guattari invoke: the machine's becoming-agent. Many other authors have subsequently begun to problematize Deleuze and Guattari's work, particularly in relation to the need to address human rights from machine-like forms of action—which is, in part, what Michael Hardt and Antonio Negri, following Baruch Spinoza and then Gilbert Simondon, have identified as the "ontological plane" to which humans and machines belong. Nonetheless, these authors have also stated that the problem is located more on the political than the ontological plane.[21]

In an undeniably sophisticated and not unmetaphorical way, these abstract machines have the capacity to transform into greater functionality—even within the order behind the system of every machine. We are referring to the very notion of war that, in this case, appears to be subsumed under the binary that leads one to think of democracy as its opposite. Nevertheless, all of this strays far from what Deleuze and Guattari imagined as the "war machine" that generates modal agencies of conflict and resistance. It would consequently be worth asking whether different kinds of war might exist, as the authors suggest: "Writing and music can be war machines."[22]

In light of the discussion above, we can argue that the machine is an aesthetic agency, while the concept of war is here defined in terms of tactical circumstances. The latter actually correspond more to the grammatical, scopic, and technological use of documents than to the conception of war in terms of a belligerent arms race. Hence, by pushing further the analogy between the concepts, we can introduce the idea of "archival machines."

THE CERRILLOS ARCHIVE PROJECT

The Cerrillos Archive Project is the product of a team of individuals who have set themselves the task of problematizing the idea of the machine in relation to the territorial archive.[23] Through collaborative and critical laboratory work based on the search for facts and documents, the team has discovered the lack of an archive on the former Cerrillos campus. Although this has severe implications for the documentary understanding of the history of the university, the team has also seen the need to create an archive from a machine-like perspective: that is, to pick up the archival norm that already exists surrounding the territory of Cerrillos, and to submit the order of these documents to a discursive apparatus with political intent.

Underlying this political intent is the examination of a few techno-political processes that we can briefly comment on: first, the exploration of the real-estate public archive, whose technology reflects traditional thinking based on jurisdiction and state-administered writing; second, the production of a videoscopic dispositive whose aerial technology has captured the trace of an over-monitored zone controlled by the state's police apparatuses.

Behind these technologies lie notions regarding visual technologies of the territory, as well as political questions about how to activate archives of nonhuman rights. What identificatory markers need to be present in these actions so that they will constitute archival practices? More importantly, what kind of humanist narrative do these archival forms constitute in the domain of nonhuman technologies?

Real-Estate Technology

Beyond the violent political experiences documented in the records and publications of the post-dictatorship period, it is key to begin with the reason for the activation of the Cerrillos Archive Project. Although its technical infrastructure and classification protocols do not yet exist, the archive's mere creation turns it into a political agency that is greater than its own material conditions. This means that behind the desire for an archive, there lies a discursive and historic micropolitics of the discussion of the human and the nonhuman.

Typically, architecture archives consist of records of plans and objects, designed within the paradigmatic frame of projects for livable spaces. Recognizing that this focus is pertinent for the presentation of the formal and technical aspects of a disciplinary field, I have here sought instead to present evidence that is less suggestive of the architectonic object as a visual counterpoint to the archival problem. This basically means reviewing the juridical archaeology that lies beneath the right to territorial space, the layers of which reveal the genealogy of complex bureaucratic operations that were carried out in a spurious and fraudulent manner during the dictatorship in Chile.

In light of these precedents, the configuration of the Cerrillos Archive Project has implied thinking through at least two fundamental characteristics that produce political agency: time and territory. Time, which is defined by the loss of the documentary history associated with the Faculty of Architecture in Cerrillos between 1957 and 1976, carries that suspended dimension that all violent interventions leave behind on the advent of a new epoch: what Walter Benjamin called the crack of progress, which means leaving history suspended, and consequently letting the ruin appear as what it has left behind.[24] Thus, one would have to begin by reconstructing the documentary bases of the personal records of students, professors, and public servants, as within them there forms a parabola between individual and collective memory in relation to historical time.[25] At the same time, through archival mechanisms as surfaces of historical inscription, an object-related territorial memory also forms.[26]

In fact, a few former students and professors have saved papers, plans, and photographs in their personal files, in some cases handing over their records to university libraries and archives, and in others maintaining simple and vague memories of a turbulent period. The scarce records that have been found through work carried out in laboratories, workshops, or experimental institutions might constitute a potential archive. Nevertheless, here the documentary findings are less important than the agential capacity that mobilizes thought, stirring it to consider the historical discourse that justified this suspension of time—as if it consisted in a strange normalcy. This, in other words, is nothing other than the condition of exceptionality that prevailed in those days. The state of exception was, precisely, a continuum whose normalcy ultimately annulled all need for an archive. As we know already, this entails the closing down of history: if historical time has been annulled, there is no need for a record of it.

On another point of note, the territory in this case acquires a transversal importance and archival condition that is perhaps more relevant than ever. The territory refers not only to the measurable perimeter in terms of hectares and surfaces, but also to its material features, as expressed by the nature of the place, the infrastructure, and its artificial objects. The donation consisted not only of the thirty hectares, but also of the transfer of use of the buildings, which were architectonically thought out both for technical and intellectual development and sought to provide a space for the leisurely and inert idle time implied in every educational activity. The area consisted of trees and bushes in the middle of floral gardens designed at human scale, areas for eating and recreation, athletic infrastructure, classrooms, workshops, and hallways connecting technological manufacturing sheds—all of these crossed by paths, roads, and an irrigation canal. The natural space conjugated with the useful living space provided by the designed artifact.

Thus, in light of the archive, one of our tasks has been to explore the architectural archaeology of two of the main occupied buildings, designed by architects Simón Perelman and Ventura Galván respectively. Perelman's building was destined to be the School of Architecture, while Galván's developed progressively to provide workshops for textile, graphic, and industrial arts, within the School of Design. From the documentation of the infrastructure, only a few plans and photographic views have remained classified. These are held in the Archivo Central Andrés, which belongs to the University of Chile itself.

Beyond the donation of the designed space and its described artifacts, we still need to ponder the state's intervention into the destiny of the University of Chile's patrimonial heritage. Thus, the first documents that we needed to bring to light were those concerning the event of the deterritorialization itself, that is, the military traces of the land transfer. → Fig. 2

A visit to the Registry of Lands, Mines, and Industrial Properties of the city of Santiago de Chile[27] allowed us to begin to reconstruct the spurious genealogy around this state bureaucracy. It is worth emphasizing at least three markers concerning the rights over the university's estates, which have remained in an obscure juridical dimension. A series of documents serve as evidence of strange transfer mechanisms maintained by means of diverse juridical forms, including: (1) bailment (1976), (2) exchange (1989), and (3) sale and purchase (1981).

We can observe these types of transfer on Folio 12146 No. 14413, → Fig. 3
which corresponds to the Property Register for the year 1980. These → Fig. 4
records demonstrate a long genealogy of imprecise documentation of the extension of the lots and the hectares involved, as well as of the nature of the transfer. Although we can note that the case calls for profound juridical study—which would probably lead to

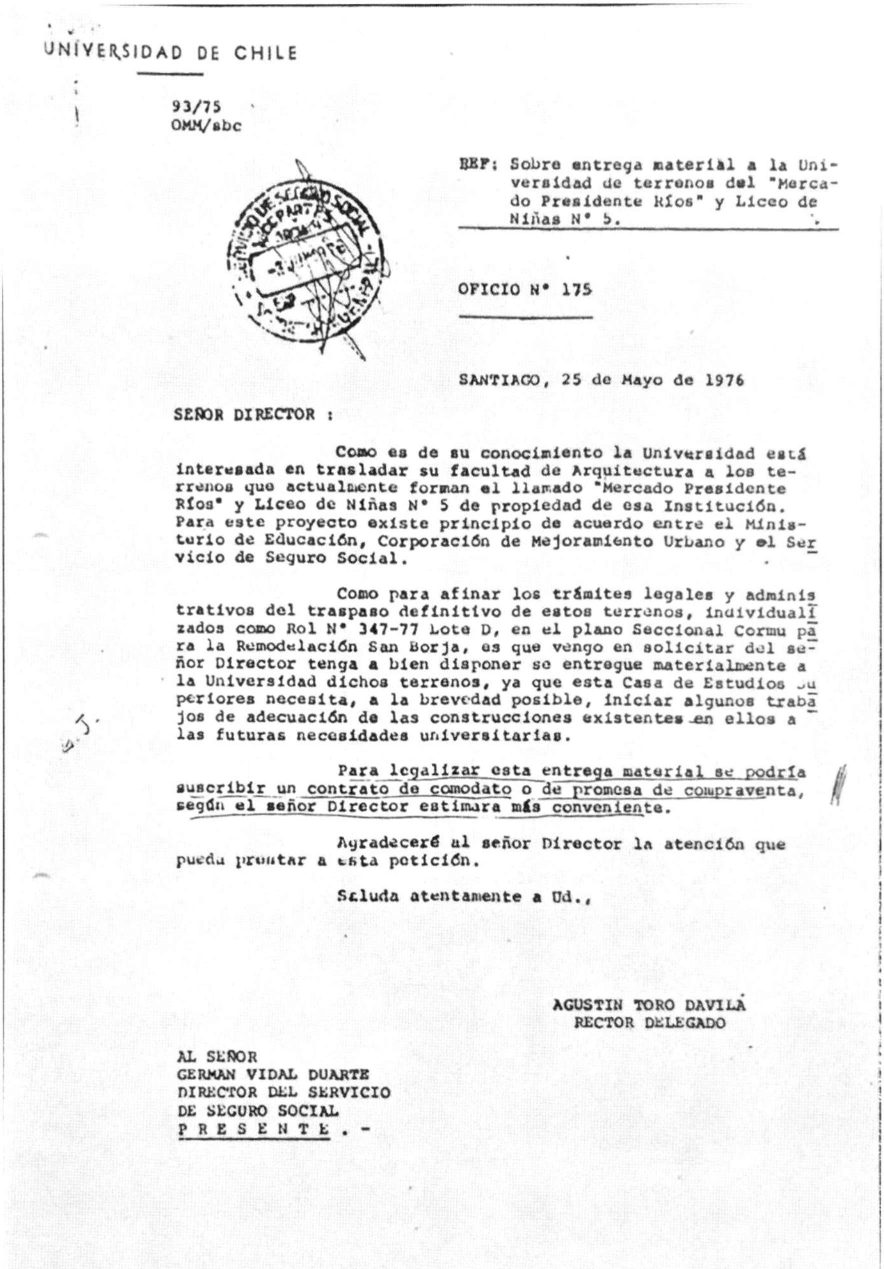

UNIVERSIDAD DE CHILE

93/75
OMM/sbc

REF: Sobre entrega material a la Universidad de terrenos del "Mercado Presidente Ríos" y Liceo de Niñas N° 5.

OFICIO N° 175

SANTIAGO, 25 de Mayo de 1976

SEÑOR DIRECTOR :

Como es de su conocimiento la Universidad está interesada en trasladar su facultad de Arquitectura a los terrenos que actualmente forman el llamado "Mercado Presidente Ríos" y Liceo de Niñas N° 5 de propiedad de esa Institución. Para este proyecto existe principio de acuerdo entre el Ministerio de Educación, Corporación de Mejoramiento Urbano y el Servicio de Seguro Social.

Como para afinar los trámites legales y administrativos del traspaso definitivo de estos terrenos, individualizados como Rol N° 347-77 Lote D, en el plano Seccional Cormu para la Remodelación San Borja, es que vengo en solicitar del señor Director tenga a bien disponer se entregue materialmente a la Universidad dichos terrenos, ya que esta Casa de Estudios Superiores necesita, a la brevedad posible, iniciar algunos trabajos de adecuación de las construcciones existentes en ellos a las futuras necesidades universitarias.

Para legalizar esta entrega material se podría suscribir un contrato de comodato o de promesa de compraventa, según el señor Director estimara más conveniente.

Agradeceré al señor Director la atención que pueda prestar a esta petición.

Saluda atentamente a Ud.,

AGUSTIN TORO DAVILA
RECTOR DELEGADO

AL SEÑOR
GERMAN VIDAL DUARTE
DIRECTOR DEL SERVICIO
DE SEGURO SOCIAL
P R E S E N T E .-

Fig. 2 Official letter 175, transfer document, “On the Material Delivery of Land to the University of Chile,” 1976

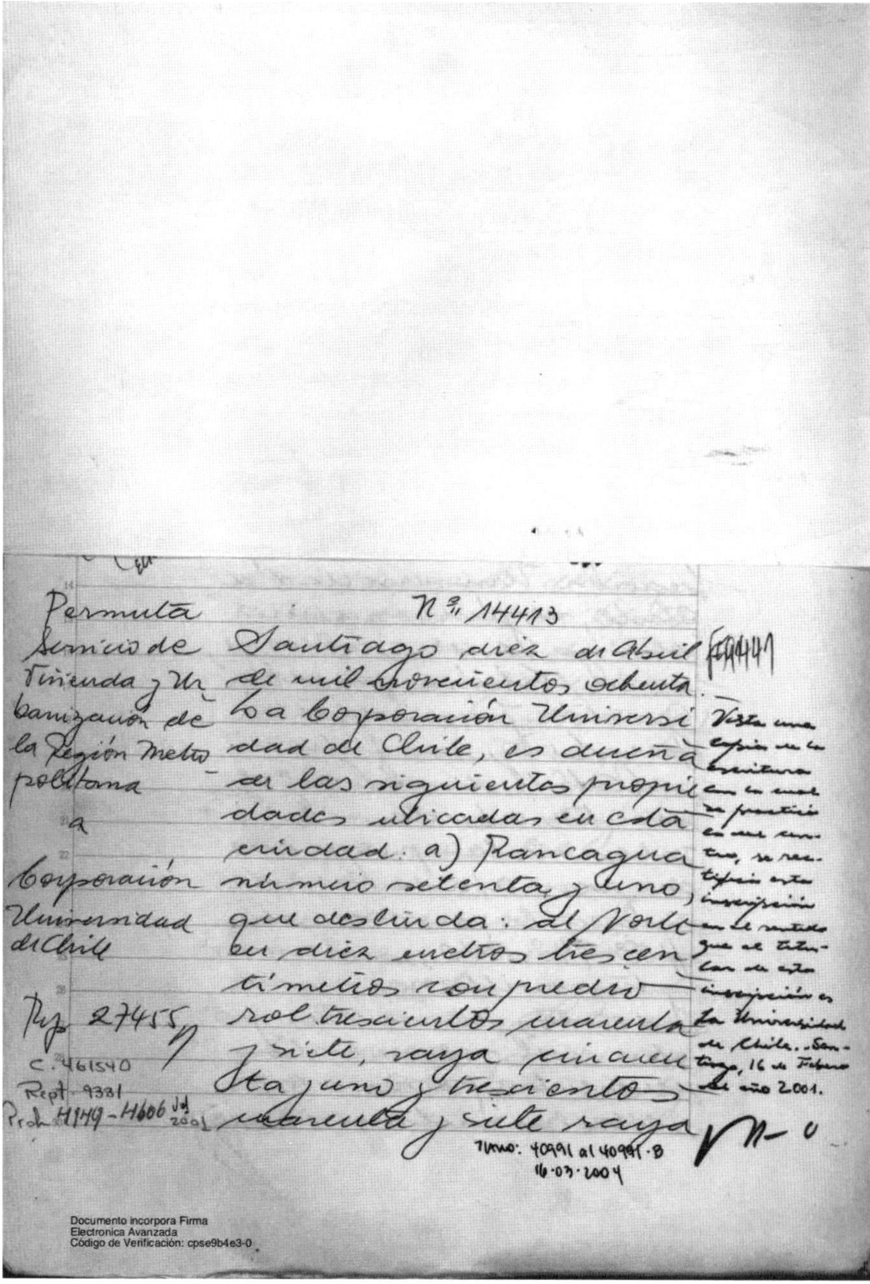

Permuta
Servicio de Vivienda y Urbanización de la Región Metropolitana
a
Corporación Universidad de Chile

Nº 14413

Santiago diez de Abril de mil novecientos ochenta. La Corporación Universidad de Chile, es dueña de las siguientes propiedades ubicadas en esta ciudad: a) Rancagua número setenta y uno, que deslinda: al Norte en diez metros tres centímetros con predio rol trescientos cuarenta y siete, raya cincuenta y uno y trescientos cuarenta y siete raya

Rep. 27455
C. 461540
Rept 9381
Proh 4149-4606 Vol 2001

Vista una copia de la escritura en la cual se practicó la presente inscripción, se rectifica esta inscripción en el sentido que el titular de esta inscripción es la Universidad de Chile.- Santiago, 16 de Febrero del año 2001.

Turno: 40991 al 40991-B 16-03-2004

Documento incorpora Firma Electronica Avanzada
Código de Verificación: cpse9b4e3-0

Fig. 3 Records on folio 12146, no. 14413, "Exchange Deed of the Land of Cerrillos," 1980

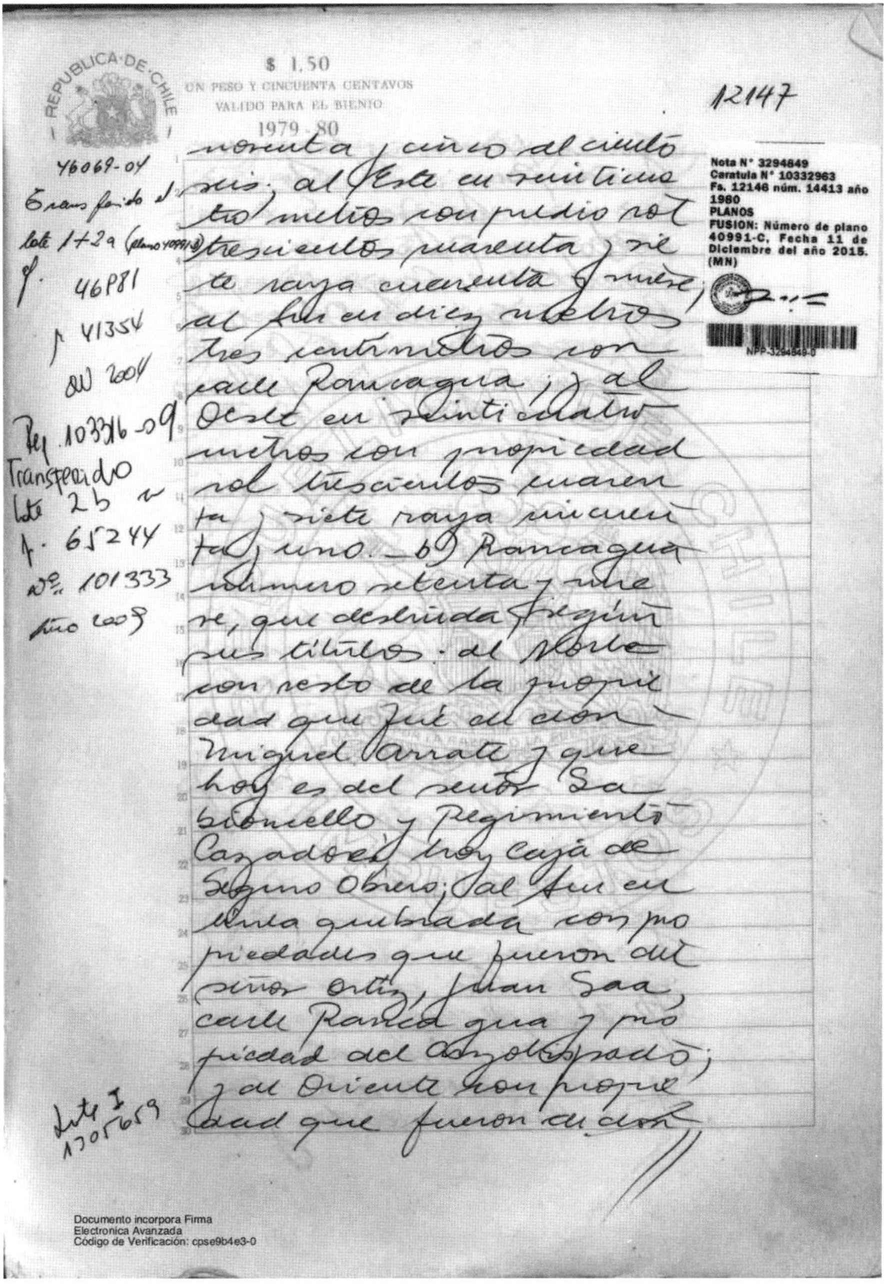
$ 1,50
UN PESO Y CINCUENTA CENTAVOS
VALIDO PARA EL BIENIO
1979-80

12147

Nota N° 3294849
Caratula N° 10332963
Fs. 12146 núm. 14413 año 1980
PLANOS
FUSION: Número de plano 40991-C, Fecha 11 de Diciembre del año 2015.
(MN)
NPP-3294849-0

noventa y cinco al ciento seis; al Este en veinticuatro metros con predio rol trescientos cuarenta y siete raya cuarenta y nueve; al Sur en diez metros tres centímetros con calle Rancagua; y al Oeste en veinticuatro metros con propiedad rol trescientos cuarenta y siete raya cincuenta y uno.- b) Rancagua número setenta y nueve, que deslinda según sus títulos: al Norte con resto de la propiedad que fue de don Miguel Arratte y que hoy es del señor Sabionello y Regimiento Cazadores, hoy Caja de Seguro Obrero; al Sur en una quebrada con propiedades que fueron del señor Ortiz, Juan Saa, calle Rancagua y propiedad del Arzobispado; y al Oriente con propiedad que fueron de don

Documento incorpora Firma Electronica Avanzada
Código de Verificación: cpse9b4e3-0

Fig. 4 Records on folio 12146, no. 14413, "Exchange Deed of the Land of Cerrillos," 1980

a more meticulous examination of the abuses committed by the dictatorship during the supposed "state of war" that began in 1973[28]—what is relevant here is the military intervention against the educational principle bestowed on the University of Chile by the benefactor Don Salomón Sack Mott.

The University Council Act, published in the Annals of 1957, puts it eloquently. Upon examining its content, we are able to discern that, given that the donation had to strictly fulfill the benefactor's mandate, there was a lack of ethical adherence to his will: "d) Within a term of two years from the date of the donation deed, the University of Chile must begin to satisfy the educational aims of the Foundation; and e) This donated property cannot be alienated nor destined to any other ends than the aforementioned."[29] This principle was violated by the irruption of the dictatorship into territories that had been designated exclusively for education with the aim of providing the country with technicians and university professionals. Furthermore, the situation appears even more controversial given that the Carabineros Training Academy[30] and Special Police Operations Group[31] were installed in its place; the latter, approved by the Organic Constitutional Law of the Carabineros of the State of Chile, is to this day the main militarized police force in the country.

→ Fig. 5
→ Fig. 6

If the former Cerrillos campus offers a documentary trace of the problematic of war, it is essentially this trace that entails the discursive conditions behind these juridical, authoritarian, and yet rudimentary documents. The confusing norms of the bureaucracy of the time left uncovered a form of territorial war—perhaps a less ominous one in terms of the loss of human life, but sufficiently damaging to patrimonial heritage records, and to the politics of nonhuman rights.

Scopic Dispositive

Although it is evident that all technology constitutes a technical apparatus, whether artificial, foreign, or beyond the ontological dimension of the human being, it is pertinent to point out that its condition as a material apparatus does not exclude it from having a humanistic becoming. In that sense, it is important to problematize the reasons that led us to use a scopic dispositive,[32] and the implications of a vertical gaze for activating an archive-in-progress

- 9 -

XII.- A propuesta de la Facultad de Ciencias Físicas y Matemáticas y después de oir las explicaciones del Decano señor Mori, se acordó crear en la Carrera de Ingeniería Civil Electricista el Seminario de Electrotecnia, destinado a fomentar entre los alumnos de 4°, 5° y 6° años el espíritu de investigación en los temas que abarca el estudio de esta carrera, y determinar que el cargo de Profesor Encargado de dicho Seminario tendrá carácter universitario, con una equivalencia de 8 horas semanales de clases. El tiempo que dedicarán a estas tareas los alumnos será una parte del contemplado para ejercicios en los planes de estudio vigentes.-

XIII.- Refiriéndose a la donación que hace a la Universidad la Fundación Salomón Sack Mott y de la cual impusiera al Consejo en la sesión anterior, el señor Rector dió lectura a la siguiente carta firmada por el donante :

" Nos es muy grato poner en conocimiento del señor Rector, y por su digno intermedio del Honorable Consejo, que esta Fundación acordó en su última sesión donar a esa Universidad la totalidad de terrenos y edificios de su propiedad ubicados en esta ciudad, en el lugar denominado "Fundo Los Cerrillos".

Para cumplir el objetivo de la referida donación se acordó asímismo condicionarla a los siguientes puntos : a) La Universidad de Chile deberá mantener permanentemente y a perpetuidad en los establecimientos que funcionen el nombre de Donación "Fundación Salomón Sack Mott"; b) Los actuales edificios y los que se construyan en el futuro se destinarán al cumplimiento de los fines educacionales y de investigación de la Fundación, manteniéndose el nombre de la misma; c) Se creará una Junta de Administración de la donación; d) Dentro del plazo de dos años contados desde la fecha de la escritura de donación, la Universidad de Chile deberá empezar a cumplir los fines educacionales de la Fundación; y e) No podrá enajenarse el inmueble donado ni destinarlo a otros fines que los ya señalados.

En instrumento separado nos permitimos someter a vuestra consideración el proyecto aprobado por esta Fundación para la Junta de Administración de la Donación y copia del acta de la sesión en que se aprobó la Donación.

Además tenemos el agrado de comunicar al señor Rector y al Honorable Consejo que existe el deseo de introducir reformas en los Estatutos de nuestra Fundación, en forma tal que esa Universidad llegue a tener la tuición docente de la misma.

Fig. 5 Council of the University of Chile. Donation deed, Salomón Sack Foundation, 1957.

- 10 -

Este Consejo tiene la certeza que el propósito del Fundador se verá cumplido bajo la prestigiosa dirección de esa Universidad, y que la presente Donación no sólo significará un aporte material a la educación pública chilena, sino que será también aliciente para quienes la dirigen y ejemplo para otros hombres y entidades.

Con los mejores deseos para esa Universidad, el señor Rector y Honorable Consejo, se despiden S.S.S.-(Fdo.) Salomón Sack M., Presidente Ejecutivo.- "

Informó el señor Rector que la donación comprendía en total, 30 hectáreas de terreno con 211,90 metros frente a la Av. Pedro Aguirre Cerda y 6.700 m2. de edificación, lo que significa un valor aproximado de quinientos millones de pesos.

La donación será administrada por una Junta de 5 miembros : 3 que representarán a la Universidad -el Rector y los señores Héctor Mardones y Carlos Mori G., Decanos de las Facultades de Arquitectura y de Ciencias Físicas y Matemáticas, respectivamente - y dos que representarán a la "Fundación Salomón Sack Mott" - su Presidente don Salomón Sack Mott y don Luis Parentini Castro.-

Destacó el señor Rector que se trataba de una de las donaciones más valiosas hechas hasta ahora a la Universidad y posiblemente en todo Chile, en vida del donante. Ella permitirá a la Corporación desarrollar e incrementar sus programas coincidentes con los de la Fundación. Se instalarán por ahora en los inmuebles donados la Escuela de Construcciones Civiles y la Escuela de Artes Aplicadas y se estudiará en el futuro la ubicación en ellos de otros servicios y establecimientos que se relacionen con la finalidad de la Fundación, cual es la de intensificar la enseñanza industrial en el país, en todos sus aspectos.

Recordó, además, que en la sesión última el Consejo acordó aceptar esta donación, acuerdo que pidió se ratificara a fin de hacer pública la noticia en tres actos diferentes : recibimiento a don Salomón Sack por el Consejo, al término de la sesión y conferencia de prensa; acto oficial de firma de los documentos correspondientes ante S.E. el Presidente de la República y señor Ministro de Educación, en fecha próxima, y visita oficial a los terrenos y edificios donados en compañía de las autoridades respectivas.

Los señores Decanos y Consejeros apoyaron las proposiciones del señor Rector y algunos de ellos agregaron otras informaciones relacionadas con la personalidad del donante, las características de los terrenos e inmuebles destinados por él a la Universidad y los objetivos de la Fundación Salomón Sack, después

Fig. 6 Council of the University of Chile. Donation deed, Salomón Sack Foundation, 1957

such as the Cerrillos Archive Project. As Alberto Toscano and Jeff Kinkle note when they call aerial cartographic dispositive into question, a *politics of verticality* is also a politics of the globality that ultimately mitigates the necessary geopolitical disorientation.[33]

First, let us note the prosthetic dimension of a gaze that opens up archival rights, as it concerns the right to enter the gaze of the other with technological dispositive—which themselves are always biopolitical means of entering another entity.[34] As various authors have commented, technologies of the gaze, such as drone machines, not only monitor, like panopticons; they also exercise a differed gaze over a given space. Having been televisually spanned, this space enables access into the other's gaze, thereby interfering in their own subjectivity.

"Where is the field of battle?" Grégoire Chamayou asks himself every time a drone is used as a machine of war.[35] In effect, the field, as a material target that provokes deterritorialization, is diluted in the viewing enabled by this technology of distanced registering. Nonetheless, since the matter concerns a weapon loaded with a missile, this technology affects the field in a profoundly destructive way. In the case of the drone video as archival machine, the aim is not to let a missile fall, but to allow the gaze to fall on the territory. Thus, the question is worth asking, but in different terms: what kind of field is being disputed from the heights? This battlefield is evidently mediated by a technological artifact that flies over the area, carrying information in such a way that the dispute over the territory seems to occur in a different space and time, that is, once the image constitutes an archive and this archive is put to use.

Now, this archival machine is never fully a nonhuman object, as it also assembles anatomical structures between the operator and the object of the gaze. These objects, incidentally, are not just databases, institutional protocols, or codes of technological vigilance, but also subjects of violence. In this sense, there would not be a drone gaze without an embodied subject on which the gaze falls[36]—hence the existence of zones of bodily violence. Following Judith Butler, we would say that there exist diverse material instruments of violence that acquire their own agency: "Of course, persons use technological instruments, but instruments surely also use persons (position them, endow them with perspective, establish the trajectory of their action); they frame and form anyone who enters into the visual or audible field, and, accordingly, those who do not."[37] In effect, the drone gaze is a violent machine that enters the dwelling of the other, and in so doing generates a record of the event. The gaze planes over a territory that was once a source of public education, and the trace that its register leaves is not just a trace of what was observed, but also of the fact itself, the fact of interfering in the aerial space of monitored military space. Although ultimately this operation → Fig. 7 may well be circumstantial and unable to produce a change in → Fig. 8 the lands expropriated by the state, I believe it also allows us to → Fig. 9 advance toward a critical ecology of technologies of the gaze.

This is what we might identify, perhaps in a more precise way, with an "echography"—that is, with the care of the place, the *oikos*, which is at the same time the home, the heritage, and with the *grafia*, which is writing as a technology of political critique.[38] When we speak about technological action, then, we are referring to an echo-graphy—a concern over heritage that is expressed through a gaze on its materiality: a kind of writing that sustains a form of humanism that, paradoxically, is also a form of the nonhuman documentary trace. It is important, in this line of thought, to return to Timothy Morton's reflections on the relationship between humanism and geology.[39] It concerns a strange curl, the author says, where a completely dark thread of progress appears: a place among places that at the same time is also a *space*. From there, then, we think of the *oikos*, and along with it the *grafia*, which operates as both image and sound. It is not too much to say that an echo-graphy positions itself in the space that borders writing, but it does so in a way that necessarily generates a situation of crisis (*krisis*) in the very ecosystem where writing is learned.

The drone dispositive orbits in the invisibility of the sky, flying unauthorized over the perimeter of the former Cerrillos campus. → Fig. 10 In a grazing turn, the drone video shows us an area that once → Fig. 11 belonged to the University of Chile and whose current condition is → Fig. 12 marked by drought, bulletproof roofs, and signs of military exercises, among other features. Today occupied by the Carabineros and their militarized wing, the Special Police Operations Group, this *space* has been transformed precisely into the trace of a dark ecological progress. Thus, in putting to work the technological

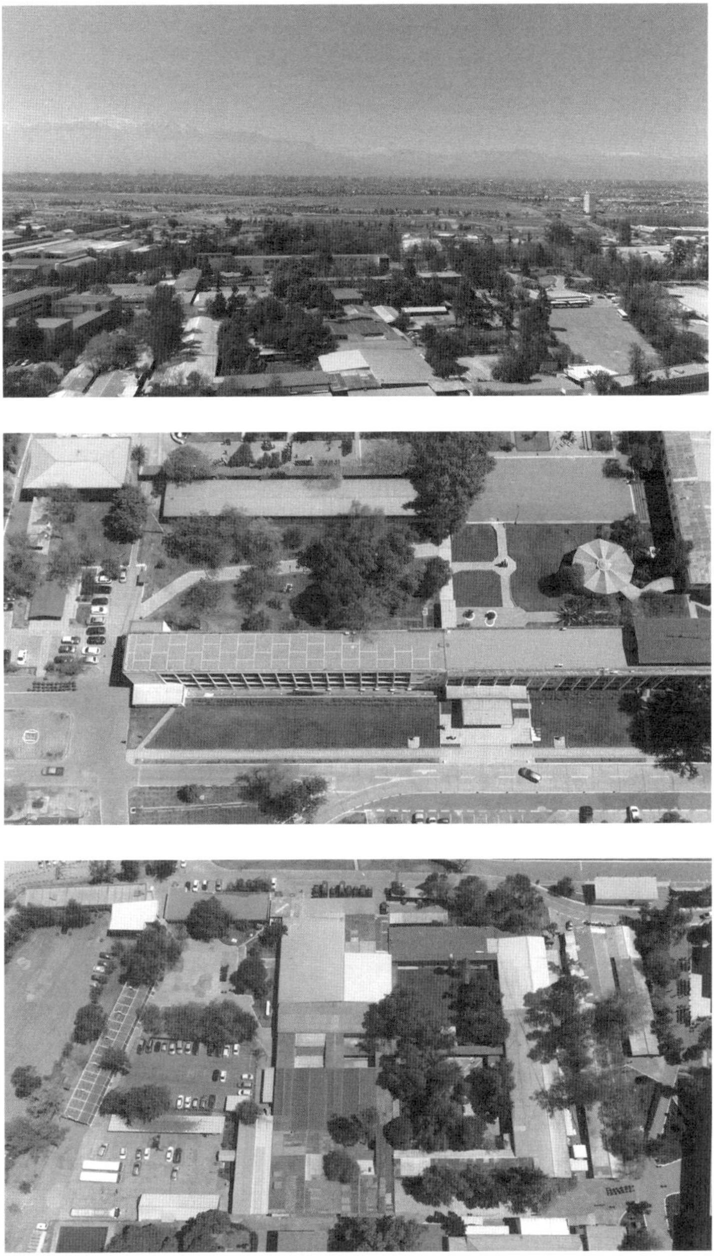

Figs. 7, 8, 9 Aerial views of area in former Cerrillos campus. Currently property of Carabineros Training Academy and Special Police Operations. Digital images taken with drone technology, 2019.

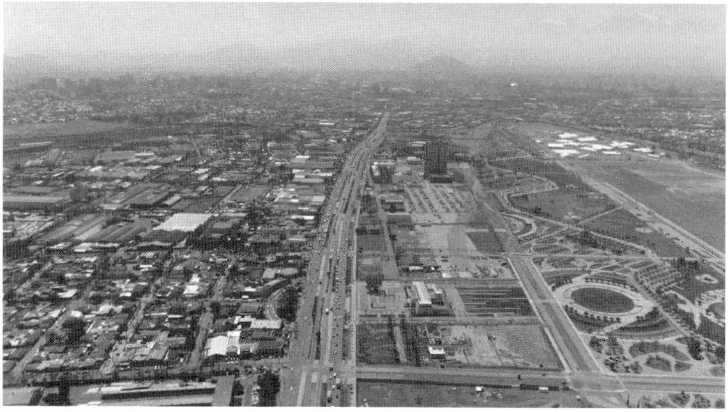

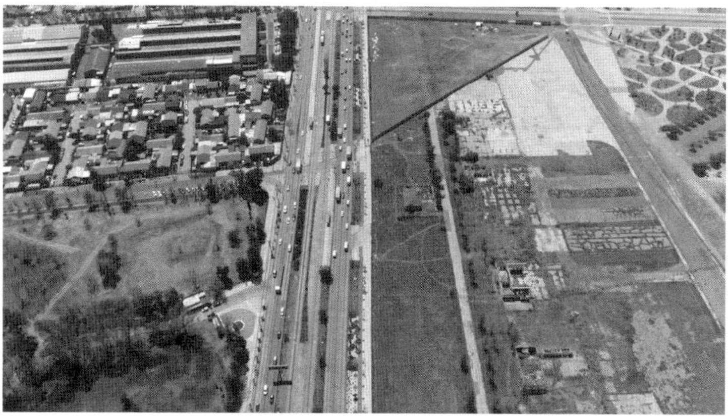

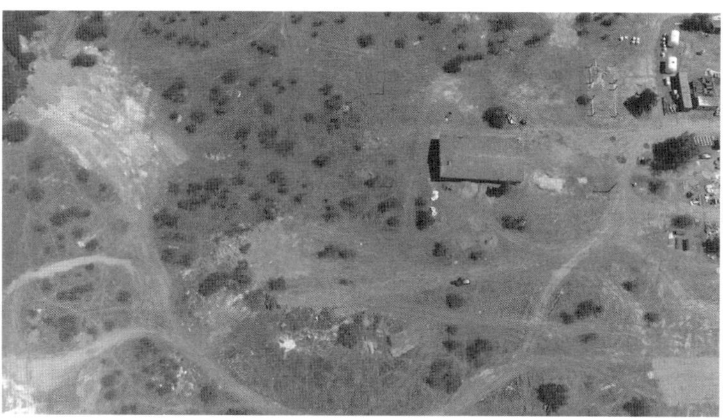

Figs. 10, 11, 12 Aerial views of area in Cerrillos. Digital images taken with drone technology, 2019.

dispositive of the gaze, an echo-graphy over the territory is also activated. Turned today into a zone for security training, the land has remained suspended between heritage buildings, systems of landscaping, and paths destined for walks for leisure and thought. Through audiovisual means, this dispositive becomes a system of written register whose data points describe decaying and degraded panoramic views, which in turn attest to violent forms of deterritorialization.

We must understand this archival machine, therefore, as a political agency that sets in motion an ecology common to all: a common space that undoubtedly corresponds with the domain of human rights. In view of this, however, we must keep in mind that we are considering human rights that have been lost in time: they do not stand in front of us. For this reason, it is useful to speak of nonhuman rights within documents. We might express it as follows: the drone's record is a nonhuman document that stirs ecological thought about the question of the human itself. Nevertheless, for this reason, it is fitting to ask: what kinds of human rights does the drone video produce? At this stage, we cannot say that there are rights assigned to these documentary forms. It would be fitting, however, to suggest that such nonhuman forms allow us to remember and rethink all kinds of rights. We can even suggest that the drone video is a nonhuman strategy for entering the domain of the other, whose alterity conditions all comprehensive and uniform forms of human rights.

Second, let us highlight the observation of bodily practices developed in the heritage buildings of Cerrillos, which could have not been revealed without the scopic dispositive. This vertical gaze allows us to note the military exercises carried out in the area: assault training, exercises with explosives, war simulations, etc. It is also worth highlighting how disciplined bodies move on the streets of the former Cerrillos campus. We can recognize forms of walking there that are both uniform and standardized. All of these practices attest to a disciplinary regime that exerts Fig. 13 ← itself not only on bodies, as is evidently the case, but also on the Fig. 14 ← educational space that is altered around its movements.

As Guattari argued in 1989—in what was perhaps a prelude to the global discussion of the environment—the ecological crisis is the result of the imperialism of a global market that has not

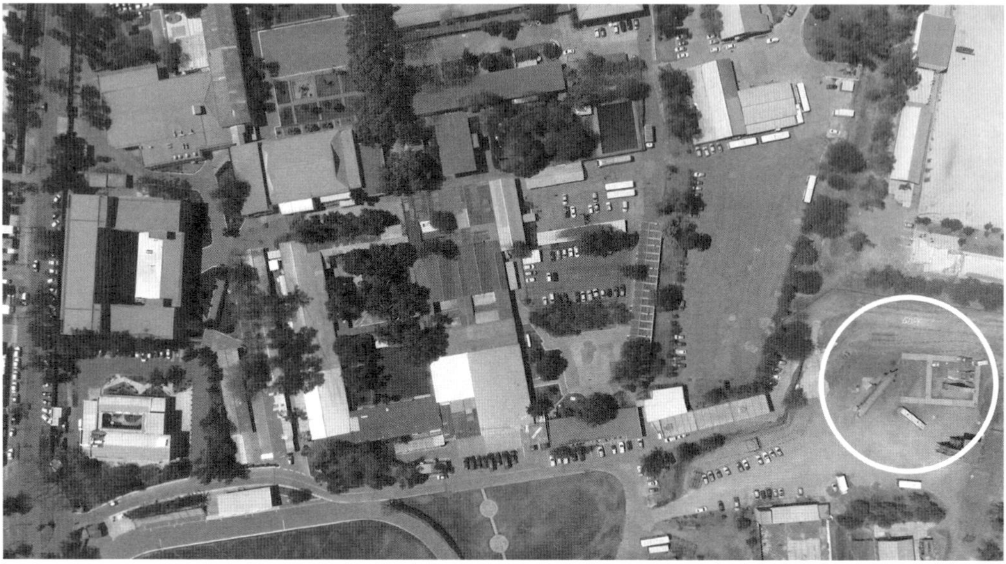

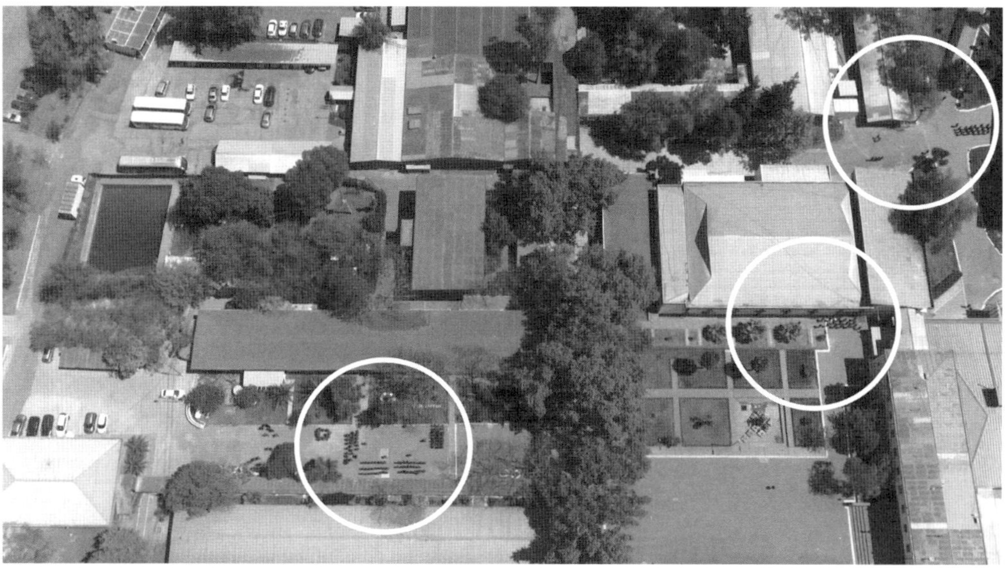

Figs. 13, 14 Aerial views of area in former Cerrillos campus. Targets on police and military activity of Special Police Operations. Digital images taken with drone technology, 2019.

just eliminated all the different layers of value and standardized it around goods, but has also subjected social relations to the domination of police and military machines.[40] It is due to this that the archival machine constructs itself in antagonism to regimes of social subjection, leaving in plain sight not only the loss of a territory, but also the predominance of police practices that, in the domains of value and public goods, have become naturalized.

In the area of Cerrillos today, we can observe artificial objects once designed for a humanistic education coexisting with disciplined bodies training—however ironically—under the watchtower of humanist thinking. This mode of thinking is that of national security and police force, of calculated power, of the training required for the war to come.[41] Understood as a nonhuman object, the drone video allows us to make note of the rights behind every gaze—even a forbidden gaze in a militarized zone. But the most relevant thing that emerges when we activate a dispositive of this kind is the possibility of hinting at the rights of technological gazes, which are crucial for the declassification and resignification of the human rights that must prevail over the use of such things, over their meaning, over their patrimony.

It is relevant to add, furthermore, that a thinking of the nonhuman seeks to reorient the order of sad humanist history consecrated, for example, in Martin Heidegger's ontological writings composed at the end of World War II. In his 1946 "Letter on Humanism," the German philosopher took great pains to reclaim a sense of humanism through language: that *clearing* in the woods where being meets language, that is, the language of being. The traditional encounter with humanism has consisted in this scene. Further, we must signal that these are the key features of the onto-anthropology of Heideggerian humanism that Peter Sloterdijk observed in turn, showing how the philosopher of *Being and Time* (1927) managed to free himself from the taint that he acquired after the collapse of Nazism. This encounter with language would have consisted precisely in Heidegger's reconciliation with humanism and a history of humankind through an epistolary community, that is, through writing as a strong emblem of humanism.

Contrarily, a thinking of the nonhuman has the task of critically addressing writing as a history of humankind, since the humanism behind it is being's ontic encounter—the same being that has led us to preserve the "Letter on Humanism" as a valid and enduring reconciliatory response to the war that this same humanist belief in modernity produced. Thus, it is important to highlight the fact that archivists did not escape this belief either: "Can the archival basement also come into the clearing? Everything suggests that archivists have become the successors of humanists."[42]

This reflection is not of minor importance, especially when we expect archives to preserve the history of humankind. But it is not necessarily a matter of preserving that history; rather, it is about creating machines that allow us to disassemble and declassify history through other technologies. It is not about preserving, but about transforming the history of objective and humanist writings on war.

Following Donna Haraway's notion that every divergent idea of the human must move toward one dissociated from the human-made binary of humans and nature, we can posit that the history of humanism based on that masculine epistolary community has its vanishing point in machine-like tactics. This is one of the essential ingredients of the *cyborg*, according to the scientist Haraway—whose epitome would be "communication systems, texts, and self-acting, ergonomically designed apparatuses."[43] This machine aims at the functioning of monstrous designs that, seeking to escape reductive conditions of gender, coloniality, and sexuality, explore other capacities of the textual and visual dispositive; that is, they open up the question of the textual-visual as an apparatus of humanist continuity in order to locate themselves in the hybrid logic between machine and organism, between social reality and fiction.

Haraway warns us that the partial gaze is a form of subversion of totalizing vision. Hence, all machine-like apparatuses allow us to catch a glimpse of the world as what cannot but be an intentional, organized, and political construction: "There is no unmediated photograph or passive camera obscura in scientific accounts of bodies and machines; there are only highly specific visual possibilities, each with a wonderfully detailed, active, partial way of organizing worlds."[44] What is appealing in this view is the fact that the ability to read humanism through the scopic becomes strangely paradoxical at the very moment when the author suggests that we continue to do so: "Vision requires instruments of vision; an optics is a politics of positioning."[45] Perhaps it sounds redundant to speak about politics and positioning when all optics require a position, a place from which one looks (reflects). Nonetheless, here the premise rests less on the one who observes and more on the technological instruments used to carry out that observation, such that every instrument of vision, as a prosthetic monitored at a distance, has the capacity to provide a place from which to look at/reflect the world.

To sum up, a territorial gaze occupying a nonhuman dispositive is indeed a partial gaze on things. It is a nonobjective and at the same time impure gaze at the truth within the sciences of humankind—not objective, and not pure, in its response to all univocal talk on the machine-like, the human, or their rights.

CODA

Far from positing itself as a custodial archive, the Cerrillos Archive Project has found ways to articulate a critical technology by means of documents and records. These documents constitute sources to activate an archive, but more than that, they come forward as evidence from which the right to recompose these territories can be exercised, given that these territories also possess rights—common rights.

I have attempted to indicate that the deterritorialization that affected the former Cerrillos campus did not simply represent a loss of hectares, or the state's abuse of power over heritage property. In the depths of its operation, a profound archaeological wound has remained—in the discursive sense that governs a conception of humanity centered on the origin (*archē*) of its archive. It is not possible to understand the effect that Cerrillos had without recognizing the dictatorship's system of deterritorialization in strategic places like this one: in this particular locale, a solid industrial belt had been established for a working class that was burgeoning with a new pedagogical thinking founded on public education.

As we know already, the deterioration of the University of Chile's estate was not a result of its territorial loss. I insist, rather, that it was generated by the trace of the police humanism that cemented a large part of the state's bureaucracy. Perhaps one of the aspects that best reveals the archaeological wound, along with the tearing up of origins, is the advent of that same wound within contemporary humanism. I am referring to historical events where an ideology that favors the human in opposition to land has prevailed: “humans versus nature” appears to meet at these points with the original premises of force, control, and domination.

Finally, keeping in sight that a territory, like an object, requires dispositives of recording, action, and representation, it would be naive to think that we are dealing with the experience of human inhabitance. At the same time, however, we also cannot deny that we are dealing with the experience of inhabitance in the document. Land transforms itself into document every time control, jurisdiction, and the right to see are exercised over it. The documents extracted from the Cerrillos archive are indeed territorial forms, or forms that attest to the process of deterritorialization that we have described. In virtue of these transformative processes in relation to the archive, it appears viable, then, to think of human rights as beyond legal subjects: to think instead of the subjection behind all archival forms of the human, as well as its declassifications by means of other archival machines.

Translated from Spanish by Vanessa Gubbins

1. This essay was written in the context of the research project "Archival Machines: The 'Archival Turn,' Communities, and Declassification in Contemporary Visuality (2010-18)," ANID, FONDECYT Initiation Research 2018, N° 11181193, led by the author.

2. The Faculty of Architecture began on this campus, which later also became home to the School of Applied Arts (later the School of Design) and various specialized institutes, including the Institute of Experimental Edification; the Institute of Experimental Stability; the Institute of the History of Architecture; the Institute of Housing, Urbanism, and Planning; and the Department of Construction.

3. General Toro served as Delegate Rector between May 24, 1976, and December 1, 1980. "Período de rectores delegados durante la intervención militar," Universidad de Chile, http://www.uchile.cl/portal/presentacion/historia/rectores-de-la-u-de-chile/4720/periodo-de-rectores-delegados-1973-1990.

4. The space that was taken over comprised a part of the Juan Antonio Ríos Market and a part of the No. 5 School for Girls. It is worth mentioning that between 1893 and 1933, the Barracks of Cavalry Regiment No. 2 had operated in that very space. "Cazadores," in "Historia," Facultad de Arquitectura y Urbanismo, Universidad de Chile, http://www.fau.uchile.cl/facultad/presentacion/63270/historia.

5. This form of state engineering has been described as the shock doctrine (understood by various authors as a form of shock therapy) because it introduces violence under the guise of efficiency. It impacts on at least two spheres: human rights and economic development. Applied with strategic violence, the doctrine produces sustained confusion, but it does so on the pretext that it is a desired and inevitable process. The shock doctrine was implemented in Chile in the middle of the 1970s, when the country served as a neoliberal economic laboratory for the Chicago School of Economics. Led by the economist Milton Friedman, the model was intended to be implemented throughout Latin America. Consequently, it has often been understood as a prelude to globalization. See Naomi Klein, *The Shock Doctrine: The Rise of Disaster Capitalism* (Toronto: Knopf, 2007).

6. Until 1973, the University of Chile had nine regional locations, whose role was to guarantee access to university education in provinces that were marked not just by differing geographical climates, ecosystems, and cultures, but also by highly specific forms of economic development. The latter was a result of the complex infrastructure and technologies used to exploit natural resources, and of labor relations that were contingent on the difficulties of trade union and social politics. At this stage, the public state university fulfilled a fundamental role in the ecosystem of knowledge, granting egalitarian rights to education, guaranteeing the development of scientific investigation and artistic creation, and constructing a collective consciousness of the whole country's environmental context. "Una mirada a la historia," Universidad de Chile, https://www.uchile.cl/portal/presentacion/historia/resena-historica/4727/una-mirada-a-la-historia.

7. The key contemporary symptoms of the social unrest that broke out in Chile on October 18, 2019, can be recognized in these features. On this date there began a wide debate about the incongruous relationship between the subsidiary and solidary state. This led to more than three months of profound social mobilization that aimed to change the Constitution of 1980, which had been validated during the dictatorship.

8. This discussion, which is still only beginning, will be determined by what some authors have called a critique of the nonhuman within the ample field of post-humanist theory. This critique centers on debates around the relationship between writing and anthropodicy, see Peter Sloterdijk, *Regeln für den Menschenpark* (Frankfurt am Main: Suhrkamp Verlag, 1999); humanity, science, and nature, see Donna Haraway, *Simians, Cyborgs, and Women: The Reinvention of Nature* (New York: Routledge, 1991); gender and capitalism, see Judith Butler, *Gender Trouble: Feminism and the Subversion of Identity* (New York: Routledge, 1990), and Rosi Braidotti, *The Posthuman* (Cambridge: Polity Press, 2013); and ecologies and natures, see Timothy Morton, *Ecology without Nature: Rethinking Environmental Aesthetics* (Cambridge, MA: Harvard University Press, 2009).

9. Félix Guattari and Suely Rolnik, *Micropolítica: Cartografías del deseo* (Buenos Aires: Tinta Limón, 2016), 323. It is interesting to review the terminology that Rolnik extracts from her correspondence with Guattari in relation to the triple domination of territory: "Territoriality, deterritorialization, reterritorialization: the notion of territory is here understood in a very tall sense, one that overflows the way it is used in ethology and ethnology. A territory can be relative to a lived space as well as to a perceived system where a subject feels 'at home.' Territory is synonymous with appropriation, with subjectification enclosed on itself. Territory can be deterritorialized, that is, it can open up and undertake lines of flight and even fall apart and be destroyed. Deterritorialization would consist in an attempt to recompose a territory entrenched in a process of reterritorialization." Ibid., 372, translated by Vanessa Gubbins. In the Spanish version, the word "thing" (*cosa*) is replaced with the word "home" (*casa*).

10. The discussion of animism has become relevant to cultural practices, as well as to the constitutional rights of persons and the environment. Beyond the complexity that a reclaiming of the animist position implies, it is important to remember its appearances in political reformulations of Constitutions: recall, for example, Ecuador's Constitution, where "the rights of nature" were recognized in 2008, or the constitution of New Zealand, which grants rights to national resources that belong to native communities. A relevant text is Paulo Tavares, "Nonhuman Rights," in *Forensis: The Architecture of Public Truth*, ed. Forensic Architecture (Berlin: Sternberg Press, 2014), 564-65. In the domain of decolonial aesthetics and material expressions of the artificial and the natural, it is useful to review the catalogue of the exhibition "Animism," which took place at Haus der Kulturen der Welt, in Berlin in 2012. See Irene Albers and Anselm Franke, eds., *Animismus: Revisionen der Moderne* (Zurich: diaphanes, 2015).

11. Terry Cook's archival turn of 1980, which questioned the idea that custodial preservation is the only practical form of archive work, is well known. The author took on the task of going beyond an inert archive to argue for the "post-custodial" as a way to activate all the forms of a document. See Terry Cook, "Electronic Records, Paper Minds: The Revolution in Information Management and Archives in the Post-Custodial and Post-Modernist Era," *Archives and Manuscripts* 22, no. 2 (1994): 300-28.

12. As Jacques Rancière argues, the possibility of exercising a disidentification or declassification depends on this; in other words, it is a kind of resistance to the classificatory force that arises from forms of breaking with the visible (and invisible). Jacques Rancière, *Aux bords du politique* (Paris: Osiris, 1990); Jacques Rancière,

"The Use of Distinctions," in *Dissensus: On Politics and Aesthetics*, trans. Steven Corcoran (New York: Continuum, 2010), 205-18.

13. See Cristián Gómez-Moya, ed., *Human Rights/Copy Rights: Visual Archives in the Age of Declassification* (Santiago de Chile: VID/Universidad de Chile, 2013).

14. See Thomas Keenan and Eyal Weizman, *Mengele's Skull: The Advent of a Forensic Aesthetics* (Berlin: Sternberg Press, 2012).

15. Forensic Architecture, *Forensic Architecture: Hacia una estética investigativa* (Barcelona: Museu d'Art Contemporani de Barcelona, 2017), 14; translated by Vanessa Gubbins.

16. A discussion along these theoretical lines takes place in the seminal text *Droit de regard* (Paris: Les Éditions de Minuit, 1985) by Jacques Derrida, whose positions were in part collected later in interviews with Bernard Stiegler in *Échographies de la télévision: Entretiens filmés* (Paris: Galilée, 1996). A partial revision appears in Nicholas Mirzoeff, *The Right to Look: A Counterhistory of Visuality* (Durham, NC: Duke University Press, 2011), and in my own book, Cristián Gómez-Moya, *Derechos de mirada: Artes y desclasificación* (Santiago de Chile: Palinodia, 2012).

17. See the pertinent Deleuzian discussion of "social machines" in André M. Tello, *Anarchivismo: Tecnologías políticas del archivo* (Buenos Aires: La Cebra, 2018).

18. Karl Marx, *Capital*, trans. Ben Fowkes (London: Penguin, 1976), 493.

19. "Every abstract machine is linked to other abstract machines, not only because they are inseparably political, economic, scientific, artistic, ecological, cosmic-perceptive, affective, thinking, physical, and semiotic—but because their various types are as intertwined as their operations are convergent. Mechanosphere." Gilles Deleuze and Félix Guattari, *A Thousand Plateaus: Capitalism and Schizophrenia*, trans. Brian Massumi (Minneapolis: University of Minnesota Press, 1987), 514.

20. Ibid., 510-11.

21. Michael Hardt and Antonio Negri, "We, Machinic Subjects," in *Assembly* (Oxford: Oxford University Press, 2017), 107-24.

22. Deleuze and Guattari, *A Thousand Plateaus*, 513.

23. The Cerrillos Archive Project team, led by the author, includes the researchers Daniel Opazo, Luciana Pastor, Diego Vallejos, Pablo Marchant, Bernardita Ebensperger, Camila Vicencio, Diego Salinas, Sofía Murray, and Carolina S. Elissetche, primarily architects, designers, lawyers, and historians who work at the University of Chile. Their work, whose goal was to create an archival machine, took place between the 2018 and 2019 as part of the project FONDECYT 11181193.

24. Walter Benjamin, *Über den Begriff der Geschichte* (Frankfurt: Institut für Sozialforschung, 1942).

25. Maurice Halbwachs's account of collective memory, presented in *La mémoire collective* (Paris: Presses Universitaires de France, 1950), is well known. From it one can extract a plausible explanation that allows us to assume that all memory is always collective, and thus that all of history is common. Nonetheless, we can also reflect on the kind of memory left behind by narratives—by aesthetics—that function as memory traces. See Nelly Richard, ed., *Políticas y estéticas de la memoria* (Santiago de Chile: Editorial Cuarto Propio, 2000).

26. Michel Foucault, *L'archéologie du savoir* (Paris: Éditions Gallimard, 1969), 58.

27. The Registry of Lands, Mines, and Industrial Properties in Santiago de Chile (Conservador de Bienes Raíces de Santiago) is a public institution dedicated to the collection and registration of public and private properties. It is operated by "ministers of faith in charge of the real-estate records, whose principal objective is maintaining the history of immovable property and granting complete publicity to the levies that may affect real estate." "Conservador de Bienes Raíces de Santiago," Chile Atiende, https://www.chileatiende.gob.cl/instituciones/zc002; translated by Vanessa Gubbins.

28. Let us remember the famous words of the authoritarian group linked to Pinochet's military junta, who took power after the coup of September 11, 1973: "The Marxist resistance is not over yet, extremists still remain. I must declare that Chile in this moment is in a state of internal war." Quoted in Verónica Valdivia, "'¡Estamos en guerra, señores!' El régimen militar de Pinochet y el 'pueblo,' 1973-80." *Historia* 43, no. 1 (2010): 163-201, http://dx.doi.org/10.4067/S0717-71942010000100005; translated by Vanessa Gubbins.

29. "Fundación Salomón Sack Mott," Universidad de Chile, Actas del Consejo Universitario, sesión 2ª ordinaria, 9 de enero de 1957, 9; translated by Vanessa Gubbins.

30. The Alguacil Mayor Juan Gómez de Almagro Carabineros Training Academy (Escuela de Formación de Carabineros) is an establishment for technical police education that in turn makes up the Personal de Nombramiento Institucional (PNI) of the Carabineros of Chile, the personnel in charge of appointing officials. "The student Carabineros, after a year of training, graduate with the degree of Carabinero and become a part of the 'Escalafón' PNI, a rank of military subofficials within the Carabineros of Chile. Later, throughout their police career, they are promoted to higher ranks according to their capacities and experience." Escuela de Formación de Carabineros, Carabineros de Chile, https://www.esfocar.cl; translated by Vanessa Gubbins.

31. The Special Police Operations Group (Grupo de Operaciones Policiales Especiales, GOPE) is a grouping of commandos from the Carabineros of Chile who develop and execute high-risk police operations throughout the whole country. The following can be read on their website as a description of their operations: "Bomb deactivation, rescue of people and corpses from places of difficult access, search and entry of property, among other tasks. The GOPE constitutes a uniformed elite team of military police, as stipulated by the Constitutional Organic Law of the Carabineros of Chile. It is the only military team that faces real-life conflict in the present day, carried out in the context of the battle against crime." Carabineros de Chile, http://www.carabineros.cl; translated by Vanessa Gubbins.

32. My use of the term "dispositive" (*dispositif* in the original French version, and *apparatus* in English translations) is indebted to its long epistemic genealogy in relation to forms and networks of power. It comprises the strategic meaning of laws, institutions, things, objects, or technologies; that is, anything that produces a network of historical power relations and controls discourse. See Michel Foucault, *Dits et écrits (1954-1988)*, vol. III (Paris: Éditions Gallimard, 1977); and Giorgio Agamben, *Che cos'è un dispositivo?* (Roma: Nottetempo, 2006). My specific use of the term "scopic dispositive" alludes to Deleuze's notion of a machine that makes see or makes speak, conceived in relation to a dispositive's

lines of assemblage (visibility, articulation, strength, and subjectivation). See Gilles Deleuze, "Qu'est-ce qu'un dispositif?" in François Ewald, ed., *Michel Foucault philosophe* (Paris: Seuil, 1989).

33. Alberto Toscano and Jeff Kinkle examine a kind of geovisuality to defend an argument that Frederic Jameson in turn would describe as a geopolitical aesthetic. At the same time, they also review an essay by Eyal Weizman ("The Politics of Verticality," *OpenDemocracy*, April 23, 2002, https://www.opendemocracy.net/en/article_801jsp/) that analyses the new and sophisticated geopolitics that control airspace through the dispositives of optical urbanism. Alberto Toscano and Jeff Kinkle, *Cartographies of the Absolute* (London: Zero, 2015). See also Fredric Jameson, *The Geopolitical Aesthetic: Cinema and Space in the World System* (Bloomington: Indiana University Press, 1995).

34. This is the thesis that Derrida and Stiegler discuss in *Échographies de la télévision.*

35. Chamayou's text, like many others that follow this line of thought, has established a discussion of the drone as a bellicose apparatus of distanced precision, as well as of the new colonial conditions of the geopolitical gaze—although this aspect is not fully developed in his text. Grégoire Chamayou, *Drone Theory* (London: Penguin, 2015). See also Hugh Gusterson, *Drone: Remote Control Warfare* (Cambridge, MA: MIT Press, 2016); Jamie Allinson, "The Necropolitics of Drones," *International Political Sociology* 9, no. 2 (June 2015): 113-27, https://doi.org/10.1111/ips.12086.

36. As Lauren Wilcox has argued, "Drone warfare must instead be theorized for the multiple modes of corporealizing posthuman subjects and the zones of violence they occupy." Lauren Wilcox, "Embodying Algorithmic War: Gender, Race, and the Posthuman in Drone Warfare," *Security Dialogue* 48, no. 1 (2017): 25.

37. Judith Butler, *Frames of War: When Is Life Grievable?* (New York: Verso, 2009), xii.

38. The work that the Chilean writer Nelly Richard has developed over the course of several decades deserves close attention in relation to understanding critique as a problem of the political, that is, as an intermediary place that has been left out of specialized academic knowledge production and studies of the social sphere—but also as a place that expresses the theoretical, intellectual, and aesthetic as practices of the "political-poetic" text. See Alejandra Castillo and Miguel Valderrama, *Nelly Richard, Crítica y política* (Santiago de Chile: Palinodia, 2013). See also Willy Thayer's *Technologies of Critique*, trans. John Kraniauskas (New York: Fordham University Press, 2020), where he presents relevant work on machines and critique, but importantly does so on condition that the word "critique" is situated in relation to the "performative position of crisis." According to the author, crisis appears, then, as a "form" of life, as a "form" of critique.

39. See Timothy Morton, *Dark Ecology: For a Logic of Future Coexistence* (New York: Columbia University Press, 2016).

40. Félix Guattari, *Les trois écologies* (Paris: Galilée, 1989).

41. In this regard, it is important to remember the unfortunate statement by the current President of Chile, Sebastian Piñera, in an address to the nation after the social unrest of October 18, 2019: "We are at war against a powerful enemy." "Piñera: 'Estamos en guerra contra un enemigo poderoso,'" CNN Chile, https://www.cnnchile.com/pais/pinera-estamos-en-guerra-contra-un-enemigo-poderoso_20191021/; translated by Vanessa Gubbins. The consequences of

this statement led to the declaration of a state of exception, and to the repressive measures that the Carabineros and Special Forces took during massive protests in Chile between October and December 2019. Amnesty International and Human Rights Watch produced a report on the attacks on citizens during these protests. They condemned the actions of the Carabineros and their various police apparatuses, demonstrating systematic violations of human rights. The Carabineros were responsible for the blinding, torture, and death of various people during that period. According to the figures, there were more than 220 eye injuries caused by the use of lead pellets, and more than 442 accusations of sexual abuse, torture, attempted homicide, homicide, etc. These reports are proof of the pedagogical connection that the Carabineros Training Academy maintains with the syndrome of war. "Chile: Llamado urgente a una reforma policial tras las protestas," Human Rights Watch, https://www.hrw.org/es/news/2019/11/26/chile-llamado-urgente-una-reforma-policial-tras-las-protestas.

42. Peter Sloterdijk, "Rules for the Human Zoo: A Response to the 'Letter on Humanism.'" trans. Mary Varney Rorty, *Environment and Planning D: Society and Space* 27 (2009): 12-28.

43. Donna Haraway, "A Manifesto for Cyborgs: Science, Technology, and Socialist Feminism in the 1980s," *Socialist Review*, no. 80 (1985): 65.

44. Donna Haraway, "Situated Knowledges: The Science Question in Feminism and the Privilege of Partial Perspective," *Feminist Studies* 14, no. 3 (1988): 583.

45. Ibid., 586.

B THE AESTHETICS OF DRONE FORMATIONS

Counter-Archives, Mediations, and Interventions

DRONES AS BIG DATA ARCHIVES
Mimesis and Counter-Archiving in Contemporary Art on Military Drones

Kathrin Maurer

"Getting into the Ground Control Station was surreal. I can remember every moment like my very being was recording the event. It's probably one of the few memories I have that I'm not sure I ever want to keep. The sun was pale, the wind blowing like it was straight out of hell with enough sand to get into uncomfortable places. It was hot for a January afternoon. The inside of the Ground Control Station was cold, arctic even, and the only lights inside were from the multitude of computer monitors on the other side of the trailer."[1] Brandon Bryant, who has spoken publicly about his traumatic experiences as a sensor operator during 2006 and 2011, wrote these words in a letter to Lisa Parks, the coeditor of the anthology *Life in the Age of Drone Warfare* (2017). Bryant's observations point to the fact that military drones are not just another technology of warfare, but are also directly implicated in the accumulation and storage of memories. They produce archives of images, experiences, and situations of war; they make (w)archives. Memories of drone attacks can get stuck in the minds of sensor operators as well as in those of their targeted victims (as far as the latter survive).[2] But drones also do more than create individual memories: drone technology itself has an archiving function. Drones register, collect, compile, and store information about war. In fact, they create archives of big data streams, which are in turn selected, ordered, and interpreted by algorithms and data analysts. Bryant's observations already highlight the specifics of this kind of archiving: the disruption of time and space.[3] His words describe the lasting presence of his experiences: the drone attacks conducted seem unable to become part of the past ("every moment like my very being was recording the event").[4] In terms of space too, Bryant refers to the disruptive power of drone archives: being in the container transposed him into a hell-like state of emergency ("getting into the Ground Control Station was surreal").[5] Drone archiving and its relentless recording disrupts organic, ordinarily embodied, and linear experiences of time and space on the level of individual recollection, as well as on the level of how this technology organizes and structures data collection.

The goal of this chapter is to explore these specific modes through which military drone technology archives war, as well as to discuss how drone archiving is problematized in contemporary art on drone warfare. The realm of aesthetics provides a privileged channel for observing the disruptive power of drone archiving by experimenting with, recycling, and even mimicking the archival dimensions of drone warfare. Aesthetics can thus be understood on two levels in this context. Firstly, aesthetics is understood in respect to contemporary art that engages with drone warfare. This chapter investigates examples of art that deal with drone technology as a political subject, and it analyzes the ways in which these artworks negotiate drone archiving. Secondly, the chapter also links aesthetics to a theoretical category, namely mimesis. In this context, theories of mimesis from the Frankfurt School, such as those by Theodor W. Adorno and Walter Benjamin, serve as trajectories.

Often, drone criticism makes use of the notion of the "scopic regime" to express the hierarchical, violent, and asymmetrical power regime of drone surveillance. The term refers to the drone's visual framing, its ocular operations of capture, its optical perspective on the target, and its powerful, violent, "hunting" gaze; the term is also important to Grégoire Chamayou's *A Theory of the Drone* (2013).[6] My analysis aims to go beyond the concept of the scopic regime by making use of the term "mimesis." Although this term might seem outdated in light of current theoretical approaches to contemporary art on drone warfare, I nevertheless suggest that it can help us to grasp the critical power of contemporary art on drone warfare. Not only can mimesis sense the sensorial aspects of power, but it can also provide a trajectory for performing the decentered and deterritorializing aspects of drone technology and their archiving modes—aspects that are often difficult to articulate within a scopic critique. By employing this term as a critical analytical tool, I hope to provide some insights into how artworks can create counter-archives to the drone by problematizing its fluid forms of surveillance, its spatial and temporal disruption, and its decentralized and dispersed modes of executing power. Before getting into the analysis of mimesis and contemporary art, a discussion is in order of how we can understand military drone technology as archives, since this will help us to grasp how some examples of contemporary art can be seen as counter-archives to the drone.

MILITARY DRONES AS BIG DATA ARCHIVES

During the nineteenth century, archives played a dominant role in defining and delimiting what constituted knowledge, and through their systematic collection and accumulation of historical documents they contributed to the scholarization of the past. In what Michel Foucault called the "age of history," the storage of temporal records was key to historians understanding the human subject and its historicity.[7] In this context, archives are often described as sites of pleasure where the archivist can immerse themselves in the data, within an enclosed space filled with documents and other records of the past. Leopold von Ranke, for example, saw the archive as a house of knowledge where the beauty and rationalization of the past were entwined.[8] Ranke's conception of the archive as pleasure was heavily gendered, since he also described the archive through the image of the virgin, thus premising it on a male gaze as well as a powerful position of privilege.[9] In addition to gendered power, during academic historicism archives were often conducive to the creation of "authentic" historical narratives that privileged powerful individuals (monarchs, war heroes, generals), systems, and institutions.

This scholarization of historical archives also played a role in the rise of national war museums and their ways of archiving the data of war. The Bundeswehr Military History Museum in Dresden, founded in 1897 as the Militärhistorisches Museum, a military archive and weapons display for Prussia, is a case in point. At first, its collections were clearly ordered according to historicist categories: they focused on grand narratives and events, and on prominent political figures. (W)archiving in this museum meant collecting evidence that constructed the history of war, and the archival material acquired testimonial status. The work of evidence collection was certainly connected to the exercise of power and the strategic planning of war. Only recently, in 2011, was the museum reconceptualized and architecturally restructured, with some parts of the exhibition taking a clearly anti-historicist turn in representing war.[10]

In the digital age, when the archivist can be supplanted by an algorithm and the walls of the archive (previously a physical house of knowledge) have dissolved, how do war archives work? How does the technology of drone's big data streaming shape archives and redefine their role and function? A discussion of the military drone technologies referred to as "Gorgon Stare" and "Argus-IS" may provide some answers to these questions.[11] I am well aware that these are only two of many existing drone surveillance technologies, but they have been chosen because they exemplify three crucial features of official military drone archives: their fluid forms of surveillance, their disruption of spatial and temporal paradigms, and their execution of a decentralized form of violence.

Scholars of the humanities know gorgons well as a species of monster in Greek mythology, comprised of three sisters—Medusa, Stheno, and Euryale. Of those, Medusa is specifically famous for turning anyone who looks at her into stone. That a powerful surveillance technology goes by the name Gorgon Stare is no accident. Gorgon Stare is a wide-area surveillance technology able to capture motion imagery of a whole city, which in turn can be analyzed by humans and artificial intelligence.[12] This technology incorporates a spherical array of nine cameras attached to an aerial drone armed with Hellfire missiles. Together with the surveillance technology Argus-IS (named for the many-eyed giant Argus Panoptes), which contains over a hundred cellphone-like cameras, Gorgon Stare can quilt together a mega-stream of images into a large-scale mosaic and feed them into ground stations' big data networks. In fact, a drone operator is never quite alone; they are always connected to different ground stations that interpret the visual data. For example, Creech Air Force Base in Nevada, where drone pilots sit glued to their computer screens in an office-like container, is linked to the Combined Air and Space Operations Center (also called the IMAX) in Qatar, which houses visual data analysts, military commanders, and advisors.

Gorgon Stare's real-time, full-motion, and high-definition video feeds, and its connection to a "theater" of war, can certainly be seen as a big data war archive. Surveillance images from multiple cameras on the move are fed onto one large data screen. Images of daily life (family gatherings, markets, schoolchildren on the streets), as well as images of attacks and terrorist activities, are merged together into one big data mass. These data masses are often no longer sorted and systematized by human subjects, but pre-sorted and selected by a variety of algorithms. In this context, big data drone archives disrupt fixed configurations of space, since these data streams do not distinguish locations but propose alternate concepts of "terrain." As the philosopher Zygmunt Bauman pointed out, the drone's field of surveillance (and mode of archiving data) is rather different from the panopticon's. While the panopticon requires a single viewer from whose perspective data is captured and analyzed, drone surveillance requires neither spatial partitions nor fixed architectural demarcations. This multiscopic aspect of this form of surveillance becomes quite clear when one looks at the spherical distribution of the Gorgon Stare and Argus-IS cameras: no longer organized via a centralized verticality (i.e., the panopticon's watchtower), theirs is rather a multifaceted gaze that can change its configuration constantly. Drones constitute what Bauman calls a "liquid technology," not perpendicularly ordered, but a-central and flexible.[13]

In this context, drone archives disrupt, invert, and destabilize traditional concepts of space and time. When a sensor operator enters a container in Nevada, they also enter a different geography and "are" in Pakistan or Afghanistan (for example). This experience is what Bryant called "surreal." Space is no longer experienced according to known conventions (such as a fixed conception of territory), but rather as distorted and beyond the real. Drones and their big data streams are not bound to a place. Surveilling the world in a fluid mode that transgresses spatial boundaries, they are constantly on the move. Certainly, the drone archive then also becomes a storage place that disrupts conventional notions of spatial order. The physical spaces of drone data storage centers often remain obscure to the public. Like premodern elitist archives, drone archives are often only accessible to a select few. In addition, digitalization also makes this data independent of its physical location, and the "data cloud" can (if one has the relevant privileges) be accessed from any place where there is an Internet connection.

Besides this spatial disruption, drone surveillance archives also disrupt linear concepts of temporality. While archives are usually associated with the temporal modus of the past, drones' big data streams change this temporal pattern. Drone data surveillance archives no longer exclusively collect data from historical events in order to reconstruct and interpret what has already happened; the archive is now oriented toward the future.[14] Drone archives collect masses of data about what could happen, and especially about security risks that might emerge at a later point in time. Although the images originate in the past, they nevertheless acquire a sense of futurity. Indeed, Jacques Derrida made this aspect of futurity a feature of all archives (including the traditional historical ones): "The question of the archive is not, I repeat, a question of the past [...] but rather a question of the future, the very question of the future, question of a response, of a promise and of a responsibility for tomorrow."[15] Derrida highlights that archives are often determined by the idea of storing documents to make changes for future generations. The archive thus becomes a type of remedy and antidote to future crises of history, society, and humankind.

This archival futurity becomes evident when one considers the Stasi archives of former East Germany. These archives, which documented the daily activities of suspected citizens, did not report on actual crimes, but rather on their future potentiality. However, the difference between the Stasi archives (or any other nondigital political surveillance [w]archive) and big data archives lies not only in the sheer mass of information, but also in the fact that drone data archives follow much more of a pre-crime ideology whereby criminal activities are estimated before they have even happened. While the Stasi collected specific information that might signal the potential for political crime—and which they considered evidence—drones collect *all* data. Theoretically, every binary digit can index a future threat. Thus, the digital drone archive works much more with the temporal concept of preemption. Collecting big data is a preemption of a threat of immediate aggression; thus collecting becomes an action based on hypothetical knowledge targeted toward a potential security issue in the future.[16]

Lastly, it is important to understand that big data drone archives must be seen as an assemblage of risk assessment that involves many agents, functions, and technologies. The Stasi archives were still administered by subjects, and the information was collected and interpreted by individual agents. In drone archiving, however, automated surveillance technology plays a central role. Algorithms perform calculation, data processing, and automated reasoning tasks.[17] Drones can even conduct automated processes of selective vision. However, it is important to note that the (human) eyes of the drone pilot—who observes potential target areas through an extended sensorium—remain. Algorithms are coded by humans, and as I have demonstrated with my discussion of Gorgon Stare and Argus-IS, big data surveillance technologies are connected to a whole array of human subjects and agents. However, the difference from the analogue war archive is that the digital one comprises a whole assemblage of human-machine interactions. Derek Gregory has stated in his research on remote warfare that "the kill-chain can be thought of as a dispersed and distributed apparatus, a congeries of actors, objects, practices, discourses and affects."[18] This form of assemblage creates dispersed knowledge, which in turn decentralizes decision-making about executing violence.

CONTEMPORARY ARTWORKS ON DRONE WARFARE, MIMESIS, AND COUNTER-ARCHIVING

Despite the relative obscurity and invisibility with which drones operate, this late modern war technology is quite present in public media as well as in scholarly discourses. Indeed, Caren Kaplan has coined the term "drone-o-rama" to characterize the current hype and interest in drone technology.[19] In addition to their prominence in public media and diverse scholarly disciplines, drones have also reached the art scene. There is a whole array of artists that use the drone as a medium (a tool, but also a representation) to problematize the military drone's execution of power and violence. The exhibition catalogue *To See Without Being Seen: Contemporary Art and Drone Warfare* (2016) offers an insightful overview and critical discussions of the media and political diversity of contemporary art on drone warfare.[20] In particular, the three thematic sections of the exhibition—"Bringing the War Home," "Tracking and Targeting," and "Countersurveillance"—show the diversity of these artworks, which engage with machinic vision, uncertainty, and the execution of violence and power by drone technology. Svea Braeunert discusses key artists in this context: web-based art by James Bridle and Josh Begley, photography by Tomas van Houtryve and Trevor Paglen, Björn Schülke's spider-shaped sculpture *Spider Drone* (2011–2015) Hito Steyerl's installations about countersurveillance, and films by Harun Farocki on simulation and war, to name but a few examples. Although all of these artists and their works are very different in medium, shape, message, and context (and hence it is difficult to establish a generic term for drone art), one could perhaps formulate one common thread: they all engage with the drone as a political subject, and thereby aim to criticize the logic and execution of military drone strikes. However, one should handle this assumption with care. As my discussions of some exemplary artworks will show, the critical power of drone art ought to be thoroughly reflected on. There are examples of artworks that engage with the power regime of military remote technology but end up reinforcing narratives of remote warfare by racializing and "othering" the victims of drone wars. An example is the discussion around the collectively-made art installation *#NotABugSplat* (2014), a gigantic photograph of a Pakistani child on the ground in a drone target zone. That said, however, I also do not believe that every form of liberalizing idea in art is always already doomed; that is why my analysis will foreground the critical and constructive potential of certain artworks, while remaining aware of their possible pitfalls.

Although contemporary artworks that engage with drone technology are highly diverse, this chapter will focus on some examples that in my view do share one specific feature: they are artworks that attempt to perform a type of counter-archive to the official drone archives produced by military technologies. With the term "counter-archive," I refer to the idea that an aesthetic artwork performs gestures of storing, gathering, and collecting—archiving—that go against the official parameters of big data archiving, and in doing so problematize the temporal and spatial forms of disruption, as well as the decentralization of violence and surveillance, in official big data military drone archives. In this context, I have chosen Trevor Paglen's film *Drone Vision* (2010) and Omer Fast's film *5,000 Feet Is the Best* (2011) as exemplary cases. Although these works are almost canonical classics of art that engage with military drones, they are particularly productive in respect to the discussion of how artworks can construct a counter-archive that problematizes the power of the official drone archive.

The key question for my analysis of these artworks is to find out how they become, precisely, counter-archives. How are they able to voice a critique and perform a counter-gesture in relation to official drone archiving and its rhetoric of power and exclusion? Art historian Thomas Stubblefield has raised the compelling question of whether drone art (and its criticism) can be characterized as a form of "scopic criticism" based primarily on oppositional and binary thinking.[21] In this context, the concept of a scopic regime expresses the hierarchical, violent, and asymmetrical power regime of drone surveillance. Stubblefield shows that drones—military drones in particular—process information in decentered and a-linear modes. Art on drone warfare, according to Stubblefield, can reiterate this fluid networking, which in turn escapes narratives of criticism based on concepts such as hierarchy, authority, and repression. Such categories are based on duality and binary oppositions, which do not take into the account the drone's amorphous and decentered mechanisms: "In articulating hierarchies of repressions along binary oppositions, such critiques enact a kind of rhetorical drone hunting, which may not only miss the target, so to speak, but also obscures its dual character."[22]

While Stubblefield consequently tries to approach drone art beyond binary discourse by applying network theory as a theoretical toolbox, I suggest making use of the category of mimesis. Mimesis as an aesthetic category, as I hope to show, can be productive in describing the potential modes of counter-archiving, since this term can develop not only an experiential dimension but also a critical trajectory, and even forms of resistance. The popular idea of mimesis is that it signifies a form of imitation. Etymologically stemming from *mimos* (an actor onstage), mimesis represents (but can also creatively reproduce) processes of real life. For the philosophers of the Frankfurt School, mimesis gained the status of an epistemological category that could provide an alternative, privileged form of knowledge (*Erkenntnis*). According to Adorno, art is the house of mimesis ("Kunst ist die Zuflucht des Mimetischen"), and hence art can activate a non-instrumental form of knowledge by engaging with the "other" and the "incommensurable."[23]

In ways similar to Adorno, in Benjamin's essays "Doctrine of the Similar" and "On Mimetic Faculty," mimesis also embodies a concept of creative reflection in the arts that differs from traditional theories of imitation. Mimesis is more than just a gage of the levels of reality-processing in artistic productions; rather, it is an active form of behavior and way of experiencing. Mimesis describes the ability to produce and perceive similarities at a prerational level of experience. This term, for Benjamin, unfolds a critical energy, since mimesis can show alternative modes of perception, experience, and knowledge that go beyond (or precede) oppressive forms of instrumental reason. This mimetic faculty, according to Benjamin, was diminished by the rise of rationality, and survives primarily in the realms of language. However, this is not just in relation to natural language but can also refer to the language of poetry, dance, and even cosmology.[24] Mimesis, for Benjamin, is a human faculty of aesthetic symbolization, understood not as sheer representation but also as form of prerational world-making. This aspect also closely interlinks mimesis with the realm of memory and archiving. In particular, for Benjamin, these realms are essential for his work, and they determine his philosophy of history, his writings on modernity, and his insights into modern art. Via mimesis, not only can the human subject create stores of remembrance, but memory can also activate mimetic residues from childhood.[25]

For Benjamin as well as Adorno, this prerational configuration of mimesis opens up the potential for a form of political critique. Via mimesis, the subject and art alike can counteract the logic of instrumental reason, objectivization, and commodification. It is important to note that mimesis must also always be considered a dialectical process, which follows from Benjamin's conception of criticism. The mimetic approach cannot be thought without rational reflection, but rather it embodies one aspect of critique that in turn has to be understood in a sociopolitical context. That is, art criticism should not just describe mimetic processes; it should also dialectically reflect on the processes of instrumental reason in modern society. In this light, the mimetic in art can become a type of ironic mimicry that effectuates an act of political sabotage.

In sum, for Benjamin and Adorno, mimesis not only occurs as a human capacity (rooted in anthropological history) but can also be carried by different forms of culture techniques (*Kulturtechniken*), such as language, theater, music, and dance. Although Benjamin was fascinated by film and photography, and also attributed residues of auratic experience to these media, the primary realm for mimesis is language. How does this category of mimesis then work in conjunction with contemporary art that engages with digitalization, remote technologies, algorithms, and big data? Can art on drone technology even have or activate mimesis? The big data archives of drones do not seem to work with a form of experiential mimesis. Gorgon Stare and Argus-IS seem to be closed systems that no longer need the world; they invented the world a long time ago. As much as language seems to assert mimetic potentials, algorithms seem to exist without mimesis. No longer imitation but simulation, the construction of virtual, potential, and future worlds is at stake. In the next parts of this essay, my goal is twofold: my discussions of the artworks will show that (1) mimesis is in fact present as an aesthetic strategy for representing drone technology, and (2) these artworks, precisely through their mimesis of drone technology, can engage critically with the ways in which official drone archives function and instrumentalize data.

THE TEMPORAL DIMENSION OF THE DRONE ARCHIVE: TREVOR PAGLEN'S FILM *DRONE VISION*

The artist Trevor Paglen is well known for his photographs and films about mass surveillance, data mining, and military security technology. For example, his collection and exhibition of the official and semiofficial military patches worn by US soldiers demonstrate secret visual codes and clusters of signification within military discourse. He also engaged with the topic of military drone operations by making several photographs called *Untitled (Reaper Drones)* in 2010. These images show colorful impressions of open sky where one can only barely make out the almost invisible traces of the Reaper drone. Of particular interest for this analysis is Paglen's film *Drone Vision* (2010), since it raises critical issues about big data archiving, and it also employs mimesis as both an

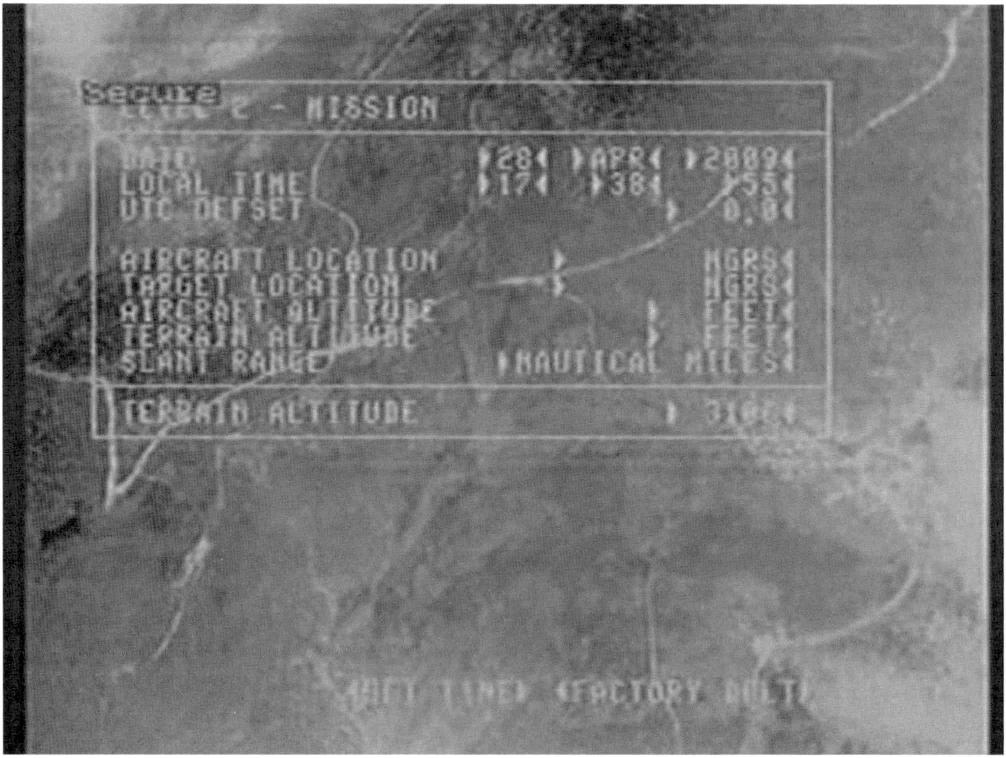

Fig. 1 Trevor Paglen, *Drone Vision* (video still), 2010. Archival pigment prints, 40×50 cm.

aesthetic strategy and a critical term. Paglen's video exploits a security glitch in the transfer of images from drones to a US-based pilot via unencrypted satellite uplinks. The source material for this video was intercepted by an amateur satellite hacker from an open channel on a commercial communication satellite over the Western hemisphere. Already this use of "raw" and "archival" material provides a trajectory for using mimesis as an aesthetic strategy, since the actual artwork (Paglen's film) suggests an (illusionary) identity with the very material it represents. Paglen's film performs an aesthetic mimesis of the temporal dimension of drone archiving. The five-minute film mostly shows aerial images from the perspective of the drone, which hovers in the sky, filming mountains, roads, trucks, houses, and clouds.

Fig. 1 ← Paglen's film begins with aerial views shot by drone. In the margin of the images, all the technical data (date, location, aircraft, altitude, and mission) can be seen. At first, the images are panoramic, giving views of the sky; at times one sees parts of the aircraft; then the gaze shifts downward to the ground. The latter represents the more familiar view one associates with drone vision. The film then shows how the drone circles around one specific point, then zooms into the landscape (mountains, a road with a tractor, trees, and cars). These surveillance pictures do not connect smoothly. The images are sometimes disrupted, scattered, black, and the drone goes back and forth. The image quality is rather grainy and often hindered by fog or clouds.

Time is a central theme in this short video. Toward the end, the camera stops showing aerial footage and instead focuses on an analogue wall clock inside of a living room. The clock face displays 2:30, its small emblem in the center reminiscent of a military patch from a drone mission. The analogue clock introduces a sense of a different but parallel time universe in addition to the digital information about time in the air scan picture. This convergence of analogue and digital time disrupts linear and chronological models of archiving. The artistic insertion of the analogue clock highlights and points to a simultaneity of temporal layers. As mentioned in my discussion of Gorgon Stare and Argus-IS, the many parallel eyes of the drone register data simultaneity in their own specific time channel.

This disruption is enhanced by aerial images of the landscape: mountain surfaces, roads, cars, and trucks. The images do not convey a sense of the past as something that should be archived to evidence a historical event. Rather, the landscape images convey a sense of futurity. Nothing has happened there yet, but the images record and anticipate a potential risk, and turn the surveilled area into a threat. The tractor could be steered by a terrorist; the mountains could be hiding places for insurgents. The aerial view of the landscape transmits fear, risk, and danger. Thus, the recorded images do not neatly fit the traditional concept of the archive, which is supposed to document events that have already happened. Rather, Paglen's drone film shows that big data drone archives record events under the auspices of futurity and hypotheticality. This temporal alignment to futurity imitates the futurity of drone archives.

In what ways, then, does Paglen's installation reflect critically on military drone archives? Paglen's film certainly does not clearly portray the drone's scopic regime, in which the drone and its operators observe and obstruct the enemy. Rather, his art installation performs a type of mimesis of the temporal modes of drone big data archiving and surveillance: it imitates and performs the disruptions in time, and in doing so it highlights the aspect of futurity. The art installation temporarily adopts the same rhythms as the drone; the eye of the viewer merges with the "eye" of the drone. The critical potential of Paglen's film lies precisely in this moment of mimesis. When the viewer's eyes merge with the drone's—seeing as the drone sees—the viewer experiences the disruption of time in an almost bodily, affective fashion. No discursive markers explain the way in which drones archive, but the work makes the viewer feel and sense it. As noted above, the work shows not only aerial views; at some moments, the drone seems to be looking under the wings of the airplane, spinning around itself. Indeed, one has the feeling that the drone is not a machine made by humans, but a curious human eye that looks around. This subtle ironic twist hints at the idea that drones are often less precise than is assumed, and that they can become disoriented—that they might have a life of their own. Thus, in a pre-discursive mimetic fashion, it also shows that drones' modes of archiving disrupt our conventional conceptions of data collection by attaining an autonomous mode of vision, unsettling models of linear time, and creating evidence for something that has not happened yet.

On the one hand, this mimetic alignment between Paglen's *Drone Vision* and the perceptual apparatus of the drone could be seen as a problematic taking of sides, and even as a reiteration of the posthuman fantasy that technology is gaining a life of its own. Certainly, the artwork invites such observations. On the other hand, following Benjamin's thoughts regarding mimesis (and the more general assumption that art can invite contradictory and paradoxical views), one can also read this aesthetic mimetic activity as a critical reflection. For Benjamin, mimesis is never understood as a permanent return to the nonreflective and prerational. Rather, the mimetic is always already thought in a dialectical dynamic, as entwined in a sudden moment that clashes with rationality. Winfried Menninghaus has termed these "threshold moments" (*Schwellenmomente*): instants in which the mimetic is disturbed, and by means of this interruption can be reflected on and analyzed.[26] Paglen's *Drone Vision* seems to indulge in drone technology, but at the same time, the processes of mimesis do not create a continuum. *Drone Vision* distorts these processes of mimesis through the visual static, the analogue clock, the abrupt cuts, and also the manner in which the drone itself almost seems to look around. These are the threshold moments from which the artwork can open up a critical trajectory. The sensory energy in the film sheds light on the fact that official drone archives and their algorithms still have a sensory and experiential sphere, that they bear a trace of a human agent, and that they are connected to the external world. This does suggest the idea that drones are not just some kind of automated technology beyond human control; they are created by us, and we are therefore responsible for them.

THE SPATIAL DIMENSION OF THE DRONE ARCHIVE: OMER FAST'S *5,000 FEET IS THE BEST*

Omer Fast has also engaged with the idea that drones are not only killing machines, but also producers of memory and data. Fast's film specifically tackles the drone's spatial aspects in conjunction with the construction of archives, and mimesis again plays a role as an aesthetic strategy and critical category. Fast's thirty-minute cinematic work *5,000 Feet Is the Best* (2011) stems from a series of conversations the artist conducted with a former US Air Force Predator drone operator working in Las Vegas as a casino security guard; the former pilot reflected on his daily duties as a security guard and the psychological effects of his drone missions in Pakistan and Afghanistan. The film narrates three episodes about a man who loves trains, a con-artist couple operating in Las Vegas, and a family being attacked in a drone strike while taking a drive through Nevada. The frame for these diverse and in many ways disjunctive episodes is the former drone pilot's therapy sessions in a Las Vegas hotel. The film repeats the dialogues in the hotel room, and the piercing beeping sound in the former pilot's head connects the different episodes and the layers of remembrance of his personal experiences during drone operations. The film weaves together scenes from original footage of interviews with actual drone pilots and their fictional restaging. The real former drone pilot is only seen as a blurred image, and his role is mainly performed by a professional actor. Fast's film does not follow the rules of fact-based documentary. By means of imaginative elements, strong light-and-shadow effects, and the inversion of locations, Fast constantly estranges and distorts the boundaries between fiction and fact.

The film's last episode depicts a drone strike on a family on a road in the Nevada desert landscape. The father drives, while the children in the back and the mother in the front seat have fallen asleep. Aerial images from a drone above are woven into the episode. When the car is stopped by a roadside patrol, a bomb is thrown at the car, and the vehicle explodes. The explosion is seen from above; the aerial view of the family, in color, is entwined with a black-and-white air scan picture of the kind that appears on drone sensor operators' monitors. The drone strike, which has taken place on US soil, has seemingly erased this family. In the Western public's imagination, drone strikes do not occur in the United States or Western Europe. They take place in faraway places associated with terror and endless war.

The location of the drone strike on US territory calls up the spatial paradigm of the drone: deterritorialization. Not only does the act of killing trespass spatial boundaries (by staging a drone strike in the United States), but the film also demonstrates the drone's archiving, and the spatial disruptions that come with that. The way the film records images, taking pictures and filming from above, signals Fast's interest in the drone as a deterritorialized locus of data storage. This big data archive can be everywhere and nowhere at the same time. It is everywhere in that data pools can be streamed across continents; the film portrays and even exaggerates the drone archive's "everywhereness" by an inversion of place (as the United States becomes a target for drone attacks). However, drone data is also nowhere, since these drone archives, with their images and statistics about potential targets, remain hidden, top secret, and invisible to the public. The drone archive's obscurity is clearly evident in Fast's film. The mother and children have no idea what is going on, and the father, clueless, has no idea that they are being watched from above.

As in Paglen's drone film, the drone strike is neither explained nor commented on. Rather, Fast's film at times also takes the drone's perspective and mimetically imitates the spatial paradigms of its archiving activity. The film shows (but does not explain) the drone's deterritorializing effects (its trespassing, encroaching, and intruding on space). For example, the film shows aerial views of Nevada settlements, and of Las Vegas. The drone's archives of these US landscapes and its view from the sky suggest the ground as a potential target. The film mimetically follows the ways in which drones hover, surveil, and film landscapes. However, and similar to Paglen's film, Fast's work then also disturbs and brings the mimetic continuum to a halt: the viewer understands that these are US landscapes that are being filmed, and that the family targeted via a drone strike is American. After being bombed, the family gets out of the car unhurt, they continue their journey on foot, and remain unbelievably invulnerable. These surreal twists and absurd elements open up a critical energy within the mimetic process. This image of the family as revenants powerfully shows us the killing logic of the drone and its asymmetrical vulnerability. While this moment comes across as surreal, the film in fact precisely points to the drone's logic of killing: the US family remains unhurt, which speaks to the fact that the United States is protected from drone strikes.

In addition to the aspect of spatial configuration, Fast's film also sheds light on another dimension of the drone archive, namely the archiver. The drone archiver and his or her associated technologies no longer conserve and collect data to reconstruct the past. Rather, the archiver uses data to kill. Of course, analogue war archives have also always been strategic, and military analysts of analogue wars have been part of the military chain of command. However, never before in warfare has the connection between killing and data interpretation been so close. The image a sensor operator sees on-screen is no longer simply a part of an operation. Rather, the image becomes operative in itself: it is the operation and the weapon, as Harun Farocki has shown and formulated in his writing, and in his films on cyberwarfare such as *Serious Games* (2009–2010) and *Eye/Machine* (2000–2003).

The role of the archivist as killer has also been discussed in research on the trauma experienced by sensor operators during drone missions. Scholars have emphasized the intimacy of drone war, and its inversion of distance. Drone operators are often imagined as disengaged “armchair” soldiers who kill at the press of a button, as if playing a computer game. However, drone pilots are far from being remote, detached, and cool.[27] In fact, they are only eighteen inches away from the screen that shows the scene of violence: the killing takes place right in front of their eyes. Drone technology’s dramatic compression of space forces drone pilots into a paradoxical co-presence. At once close to the killing and distant from it, drone pilots experience a new form of intimacy that mirrors neither a cold killer’s attitude nor a detached PlayStation mentality.[28] This intimacy can result in post-traumatic stress disorder (PTSD), with studies showing that drone pilots experience anxiety, stress, hyperarousal, and flashbacks.[29]

This aspect of intimacy and PTSD is a controversial issue in research on military drones. Chamayou has argued that the psychic damage to drone pilots is exaggerated, and that it takes attention away from the victims.[30] Cara Dagget has discussed how the recognition of drone pilots as wounded soldiers is conducive to a process of reinstalling masculinity through woundability.[31] While aware of these discourses, I nevertheless find the aspect of trauma in Fast’s film rather crucial: the film does not show any form of empathy for the drone operators, but rather portrays the psychopathology of the drone—that is, the psychological damage, the disorientations, the uncertainties of drone operations, and the processes of alienation entwined with technology. Fast’s film does not explain this discursively, but rather attempts to capture this psychopathology via processes of mimetic imitation.

The former drone pilot depicted in Fast’s work suffers from severe PTSD. The sequences in the hotel show his shadowy, disturbed face. His eyes are constantly searching, his gaze conveys restlessness, and his whole body communicates emotional collapse. The hunter seems to have become the hunted, haunted by nightmares and images of automated killings. The film does not take the former drone pilot’s side; any moment of potential empathy with him is undermined by alienation effects, repetitions, and hermeneutic gaps. There is, for example, a constant shift between fiction and the factual narrative. Not only does the therapist repeat the same questions over and over, but the actor playing the former drone pilot even reproaches him for not being real. In addition, the "real" former drone pilot in the documentary is substituted by an actor, and when he is interviewed his face is unrecognizable. The film "senses" itself into the drone's spatial dis-order and its archiving functions, and thereby unravels the emotional ramifications of the technology. It does so by imitating the drone's spatial deterritorialization, inverting geographical and national boundaries between home and foreign, enemy and friend, and known and unknown, as well as showing the affective (traumatic) effects of these spatial orders for the subject, in this case the former drone pilot. By means of such mimetic gestures toward the spatial logic of the official drone archive as well as the role of the archiver as a killer, the film constructs a type of counter-archive. However, this counter-archive does not establish clear binary oppositions between good and evil, victim and perpetrator; rather, it shows the disorientating and decentralized forms of power at stake in drone war.

Perhaps a short excursion into James Bridle's work will further illuminate my point. In his *Drone Shadow* series, Bridle films himself drawing monumental outlines of the MQ-1 Predator drone on street corners or parking lots. The making of the diagram on the ground and the aerial filming are all part of the artwork. One can find his *Drone Shadows* in many places, including London, Istanbul, and Ljubljana. Like Fast, Bridle works with the idea of spatial deterritorialization and bringing the war home. As in the marking of a crime scene, the aerial views of these diagrams seem to enact a profound displacement. Bridle has also made available to his audiences a manual on how to make a drone diagram, thus mimicking in his own process the proliferative nature of drone-based data collection (or production), in which data can be reiterated endlessly.

In its production, technology, and mode of dissemination, then, Bridle's drone artwork both imitates and reflects on the power of military drones. The video about the production of a *Drone Shadow* in Dublin shows the drone's diverse body parts being put together by its assemblers. While making the drone, the builders do not have a total view from above. Rather, they only see its parts, limbs, and individual pieces. The drone's fragmentation and its builders' scattered movements symbolize the drone's dispersed collective power. This dispersion of the drone's power is inherent in the fact that any drone operation requires the disparate but simultaneous participation of more than a hundred people. Bridle's *Drone Shadow* mimetically imitates this diffusion of power, since the film shows the builders moving back and forth, and the fast-forward effect illustrates and even exaggerates the processes of automatization. The people involved in building the drone, according to Bridle's manual, move according to the idea of completeness, but the artwork never really shows the drone as a whole. Its totality remains hallucinatory, and the individual movements are fragments of a virtual future. The drone remains a grid, a shadow, and a transitory image.

In similar ways, Fast's film intensifies and even accentuates the spatial disruptions of drone archives by mimetically imitating them. As drone archives dissolve spatial as well as temporal boundaries, the film also displays the gaps, ruptures, and logical disjunctions inherent to the archive. Moreover, the film emphasizes the disordering effects on the archiver's psyche, and his new role as an "image soldier." This critique of the archive is not enunciated by means of a discursive narrative about drones and their regimes of power. Rather, the film sabotages the drone by executing a type of mimesis of it, and by reenacting its modes of re-collection.

My analysis has aimed to demonstrate that military drones can be understood as archives that transmit, collect, and accumulate images, information, and statistics on a big data scale. These drone archives no longer adhere to the long-standing analogue matrix of data collection. Rather, official drone archives deploy a-linear modes of temporality and unstable spatial orders. My analysis has tried to show how contemporary artists react to these new modes of drone archiving and surveillance by creating visions of aesthetic counter-archives. In this the notion of mimesis has been crucial, since this form of sensory imitation and enactment is key to constructing these counter-archives. The aesthetic drone archives make visible the drone's mode of sensing, storing, and collecting, and in doing so provide insights into the ways that drones execute power. As shown in my discussion of Paglen's film, drones work under the auspices of preemption and securitization, whereby they can create, construct, and select targets on the basis of their sensing practices and image analyses. In a way, Fast's film performs the drones' archiving function by itself becoming an archive that stores disjunctive traumatic memories and evidence of the psychological toll taken on those engaged in drone warfare.

This aesthetic counter-archive is not constructed on the basis of binary oppositions. These aesthetic works offer no guidance for discerning between enemy and friend, good and bad, machine and human, peace and war, just and unjust, or victim and perpetrator. Rather, these works replay the decentering effects of drones and their archiving activity. Their artistic drone memory inserts itself into the dynamics of drone archiving, and, through this somewhat "perverse" mimesis of the drone's mode of remembering, makes visible the drone's decentralizing and disorienting effects. Drone technology's decentering effects in terms of time and space should not just be understood as a different way of storing data. These new forms of archiving execute political power precisely by diffusing necessary differentiations between the machine and the subject, war and peace, civilian and soldier. Contemporary art that engages with military drones can critique this by imitating these processes of diffusion, making them visible, and in doing so also reflecting the vulnerabilities of those targeted by drone strikes imposed by big data archives.

1. Brandon Bryant, "Letters from a Sensor Operator," in *Life in the Age of Drone Warfare*, ed. Lisa Parks and Caren Kaplan (Durham, NC: Duke University Press, 2017), 315.

2. Concerning survivors of drone attacks, the report "Living under Drones" provides crucial insight into the traumatic recollections of people living in drone-surveilled zones. James Cavallaro, Stephan Sonnenberg, and Sarah Knuckey, "Living under Drones: Death, Injury and Trauma to Civilians from US Drone Practices in Pakistan" (Stanford, CA: International Human Rights and Conflict Resolution Clinic, Stanford Law School, 2012), https://law.stanford.edu/projects/living-under-drones/.

3. It is important to note that one has to handle these pilot testimonies with great care. Often these personalized (eyewitness) accounts are fetishized by media and researchers, which in turn may reinforce the narratives of remote warfare that the testimonies seek to reverse. See Michelle Bentley, "Fetishized Data: Counterterrorism, Drone Warfare, and Pilot Testimony," *Critical Studies on Terrorism* 11, no. 1 (2018): 88-110.

4. Bryant, "Letters from a Sensor Operator," 319.

5. Ibid.

6. Grégoire Chamayou, *A Theory of the Drone*, trans. Janet Lloyd (New York: New Press, 2015).

7. Michel Foucault, *The Order of Things: An Archaeology of the Human Sciences*, trans. Alan Sheridan (London: Routledge, 2002 [1966]), 235-40.

8. Ranke's pleasure at being in the archive is described in Anthony Grafton's *The Footnote: A Curious History* (Cambridge, MA: Harvard University Press, 1997), 36.

9. Terry Cook, "The Archive(s) Is a Foreign Country: Historians, Archivists, and the Changing Archival Landscape," *Canadian Historical Review* 90, no. 3 (2009): 497-534.

10. Gorch Pieken and Matthias Rogg, *Militärhistorisches Museum der Bundeswehr* (Dresden: Sandstein-Verlag, 2012).

11. The following passages are based on my work on scopic regimes and drones in Kathrin Maurer, "Visual Power: The Scopic Regime of Military Drones," *War, Media, Conflict* 10, no. 2 (2017): 141-51. I have used some of the same material in this chapter, but I have modified it to focus on drones as archives rather than as scopic regimes.

12. My knowledge about this system stems from Derek Gregory's work on drones. Derek Gregory, "The Everywhere War," *Geographical Journal* 177, no. 3 (2011): 238-50; Derek Gregory, "From a View to a Kill: Drones and Late Modern War," *Theory, Culture & Society* 28, nos. 7-8 (2014): 188-215.

13. Zygmunt Bauman and David Lyon, *Liquid Surveillance: A Conversation* (Cambridge: Polity Press, 2012), 67.

14. Mark Hansen, *Feed-Forward: On the Future of Twenty-First Century Media* (Chicago: University of Chicago Press), 2015.

15. Jacques Derrida, "Archive Fever: A Freudian Impression," trans. Eric Prenowitz *Diacritics* 25, no. 2 (1995): 36.

16. See also the discussion of risk and uncertain futures in contemporary warfare in Louise Amoore, *The Politics of Possibility: Risk and Security Beyond Probability* (Durham, NC: Duke University Press, 2013).

17. For a discussion of algorithms and cultural agency, and of how drone warfare thereby reproduces gendered and racialized bodies, see Lauren Wilcox, "Embodying Algorithmic War: Gender, Race, and the Posthuman in Drone Warfare," *Security Dialogue* 48, no. 1 (2017): 11-28.

18. Gregory, "From a View to a Kill," 196.

19. Caren Kaplan, "'Drone-O-Rama': Troubling the Temporal and Spatial Logics of Distance Warfare," in *Living in the Age of Drone Warfare*, 161-57. Kaplan's research is central to my approach to drones as archives, since she also discusses temporal and spatial disruptions within drone warfare.

20. Svea Braeunert, "To See Without Being Seen: Contemporary Art on Drone Warfare," in *To See Without Being Seen: Contemporary Art on Drone Warfare*, ed. Svea Braeunert and Meredith Malone (Chicago: University of Chicago Press, 2016), 11-12. For a discussion of this exhibition see also the conversation between Svea Braeunert, Sarah Tuck, and Louise Wolthers in this volume.

21. Thomas Stubblefield, "In Pursuit of Other Networks," in *Living in the Age of Drone Warfare*, 195-219.

22. Ibid., 196.

23. Theodor W. Adorno, "Ästhetische Theorie," in *Gesammelte Schriften*, vol. 7 (Frankfurt am Main: Suhrkamp Verlag, 1970), 86.

24. See also Michael Taussig, who analyzes mimesis as an anthropological category in the context of ethnography. Michsel Taussig, *Mimesis and Alterity: A Particular History of the Senses* (New York: Routledge, 1993).

25. See also the child as "role model" for mimesis in Kathrin Maurer, "Mimesis aus Poesis: Anmerkungen zu Walter Benjamins Berliner Kindheit um Neunzehnhundert," *Text und Kontext*, no. 30 (2008): 150-66.

26. Winfried Menninghaus, *Walter Benjamins Theorie der Sprachmagie* (Frankfurt am Main: Suhrkamp Verlag, 1980).

27. Gregory, "The Everywhere War."

28. Ibid.

29. Wayne Chappelle et al., "Symptoms of Psychological Distress and Post-Traumatic Stress Disorder in the United States Air Force Drone Operators," *Military Medicine*, no. 179 (2014): 63-70.

30. Chamayou, *A Theory of the Drone*.

31. Cara Dagget, "Drone Disorientations," *International Feminist Journal of Politics* 17, no. 3 (2015): 361-79.

AVIAN PROPHECIES AND THE TECHNO-AESTHETICS OF DRONE WARFARE

Heba Y. Amin and Anthony Downey

I first became aware of Heba Y. Amin's project *The General's Stork* in 2016, when I met her in Berlin and she outlined the research that she had been undertaking as part of the project.[1] The facts were simple enough, but the implications, as we will see below, were far from straightforward. In 2013, Egyptian authorities detained a migratory stork that was accused of espionage. Reportedly captured by a fisherman who viewed the bird with suspicion after noticing an electronic device attached to it, the unfortunate stork was handed over to the local police station in Qena, a city situated on the east bank of the Nile in Upper Egypt. Upon further investigation, it transpired that the "camera device" was in fact a functioning tracking instrument, attached by Hungarian scientists who were researching avian migratory habits. While the entire incident may at first appear risible, the event pointed to a nationwide level of mistrust in Egypt of both the skies and what they hold. In a broader geo-political and regional context, as *The General's Stork* amply demonstrates, the episode also directly relates to the politics of aerial surveillance from both a bird's-eye view and, in an age of digitally defined warfare, remote-controlled drones. Against the backdrop of biblical prophecies, uncrewed aerial vehicles, and colonial narratives, *The General's Stork* speculatively investigates how conquest from the sky—through land surveying, mapping, bombing, and advanced drone technologies—has transformed Western power into the spectacle of high-tech weaponry.

Focusing on how military techniques were developed in the specific context of Middle Eastern geographies, the project, as Amin observes throughout the following conversation, decisively delineates the contemporary condition of paranoia that led to a migrating bird being accused of spying. Drone surveillance, in these contexts, not only produces a psychopathological relationship to airspace based on anxiety, fear, and trepidation, but also consigns and delivers the Middle East to new forms of visibility and visualization to combat such fears. Conflict, in this logic, is viewed as a regionwide phenomenon capable of emerging from anywhere and everywhere at once, while territorial control is contingent on the technological means of visualization rather than occupation.

The apparent ubiquity of hostility was, of course, a mainstay of colonial discourse, but its technological manifestation through the means of a digital eye exposes a set of circumstances whereby the techno-aesthetics of visualization—the (operational) means of envisioning and the synchronized manifestation (appearance) of the image—is irredeemably imbricated within a seemingly unending replay of future conflict and threat. To this end, and while this project takes the region as a starting point for its development, these are emphatically global concerns that encompass not only the development of advanced surveillance methods, but the compartmentalization of life—and indeed death—under the conditions of algorithmically defined systems of control.

—Anthony Downey

Anthony Downey Can you talk about the origins of this project—I understand there was a bird involved?

Heba Y. Amin I was struck by an incident in Egypt in late 2013: a viral media story about a bird that was captured and accused of espionage. The story suited the absurdity of that moment in the Egyptian narrative when the Muslim Brotherhood was overthrown by the army, and everyone had their say about it, particularly in Western media. The bird—which was subsequently given the name Menes—was a migratory stork with a scientific tracking device attached to him by a wildlife consortium in Europe. The device raised suspicion when it was spotted by a fisherman in southern Egypt, who captured the bird and handed him over to the police authority in Qena. He was taken to a police station and held in a jail cell.[2] Shortly after the tracking device was authorized and the bird was released, he did not get far before being hunted by local → Fig. 1

children in Aswan and eaten; they had, in effect, consumed their own paranoia. Like everyone else, I was fascinated by the absurdity of the whole thing and the vivid image it conjured, but I also knew that paranoia did not emerge from a void, and I was compelled to investigate the origin of that.

AD Let's discuss the origins of that paranoia. In late 2013, when the bird was found, Egypt had already seen the overthrow of Hosni Mubarak following the 2011 revolution, and Mohamed Morsi, briefly the fifth president of Egypt, had been likewise ousted in July 2013, to be replaced by Abdel Fattah el-Sisi. So the situation was fluid, to say the least. How did this impact people and their general outlook at the time?

HYA Let's say the Egyptian people had been living in paranoia for a long time. In fact, this period following the 2011 revolution was the first time they could express it openly. But leading up to, and especially after, the ousting of Mohamed Morsi, there was plenty of mistrust to go around. However, that we could perhaps link that paranoia to decades of living under oppression from various political factions—both foreign and local—was of particular interest to me. I explain that paranoia through architectures of warfare and the remnants of violence that are embedded in the landscapes in question.

AD Can you talk more specifically about the bird in question and the research you undertook at the time? I understand you spoke to a number of the people involved in its rescue.

HYA I spoke to several people involved with the rescue of the bird. The researchers in Hungary realized something was wrong when their tracking device was no longer recording movement. Tracking storks helps inform researchers about the dangers storks face along their migration routes, and, according to their data, the bird was stuck somewhere in southern Egypt. They proceeded to contact Nature Conservation Egypt, a local NGO, to see what had happened. Because the migratory bird defies political boundaries, it became an interesting allegorical tool for addressing contemporary politics, particularly in relation to the failure of the nation-state as a means

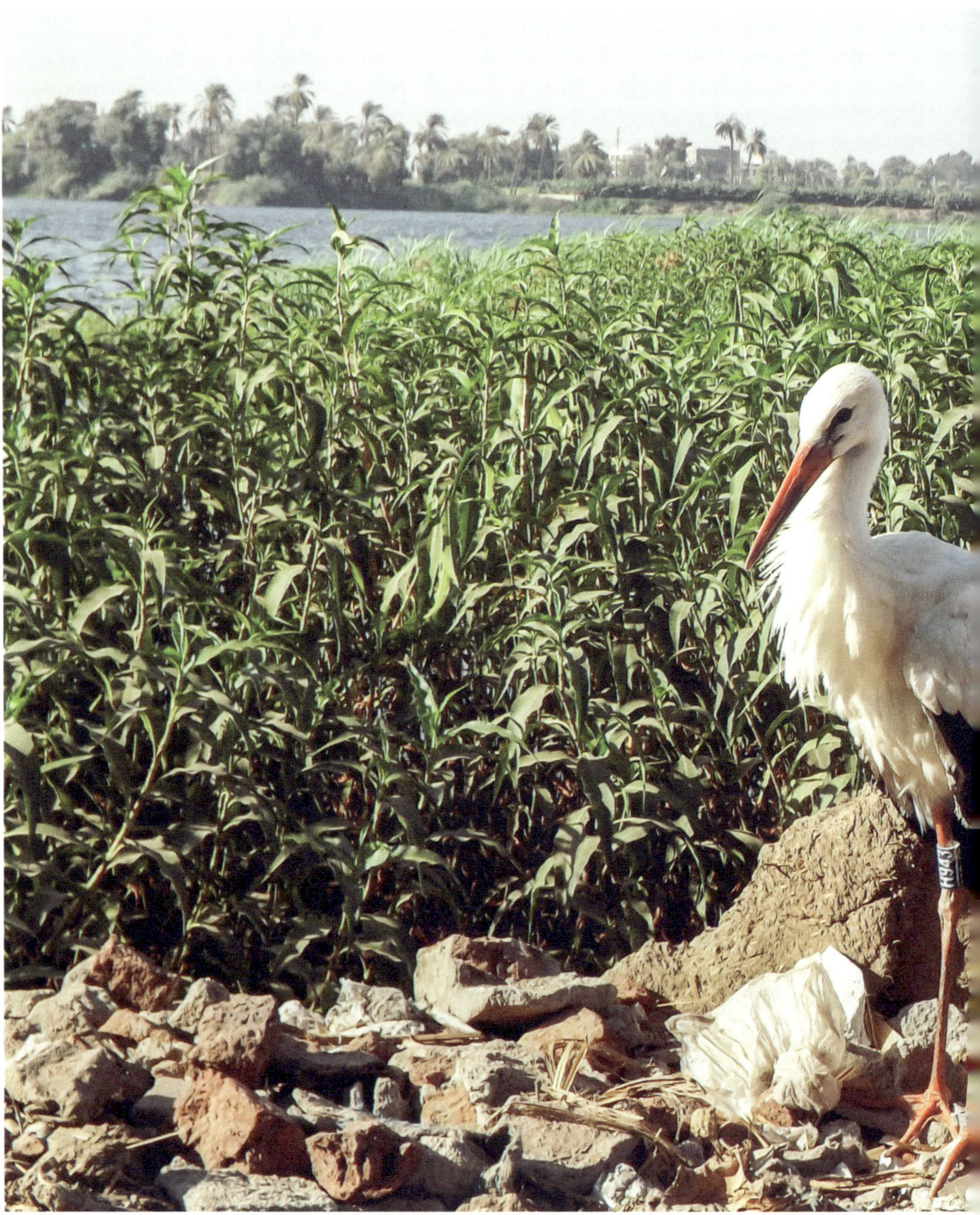

Fig. 1 Menes captured and accused of espionage

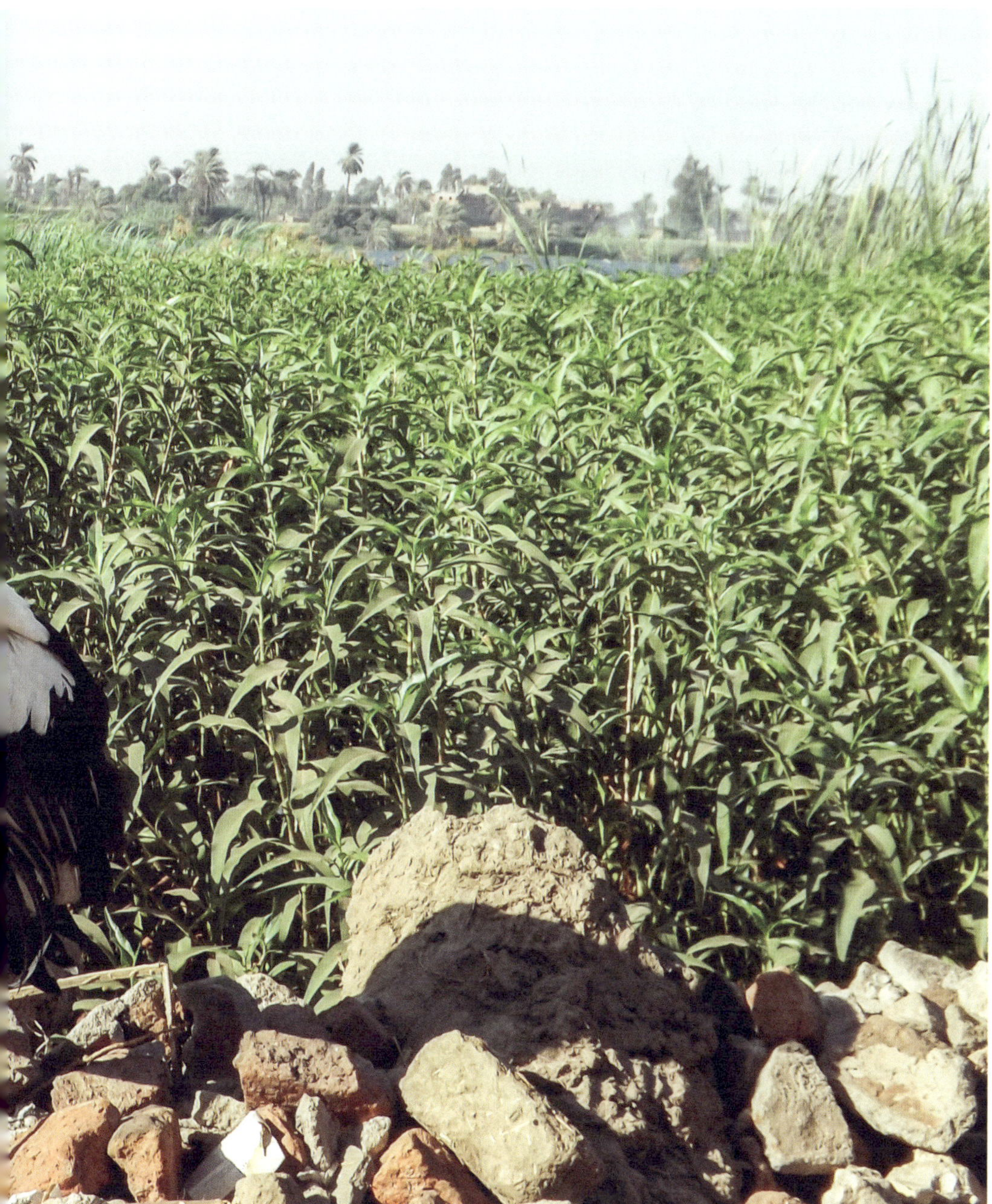

of containment. It allowed me to critique the history of territorial configuration and occupation in the region.

While the bird in question is seemingly innocent, the view from the sky in these particular landscapes represents something much more nefarious—a fisherman from Qena questioning an electronic device on a bird is not so far-fetched when you consider the centuries of colonial occupation, foreign military interventions, archaeological excavation, and extraction of cultural heritage. Among the many narratives I explored, I was particularly struck by a secret US military airbase located just outside of Qena. It was here that Operation Eagle Claw was launched, an attempted rescue mission for the US diplomatic crisis in the late 1970s in Iran, when fifty-two diplomats and citizens were held hostage for 444 days. The operation ultimately failed and brought to the foreground the ways in which imperial power dynamics operate. It is also often cited as the reason Jimmy Carter lost his reelection campaign. I have read somewhere that they were recently using that same airbase to launch drones into Yemen, but I am not certain of that yet.

AD The region has a history of avian prophecy that also references this narrative of colonialism, warfare, and violence—I am thinking here of Lord Allenby and his use of airplanes drop leaflets over the city of Jerusalem in 1917. Can you talk a little about this and how your research developed in relation to that and the work as a whole?

HYA Lord Allenby was the commander of the Egyptian Expeditionary Force in Cairo in 1917, and was given orders by Prime Minister David Lloyd George to capture Jerusalem from the Ottoman Turks. He was persuaded to launch an attack based on a biblical prophecy found in Isaiah 31:5, which states: "As birds flying, so will the Lord of hosts defend Jerusalem; defending also he will deliver it; and passing over he will preserve it." On the basis on this prophecy, Allenby believed it was his duty to send as many planes as possible to fly over Jerusalem, demanding the Turks surrender the city. This put Palestine under British mandate—courtesy of the so-called Balfour Declaration—which set the foundation for the modern-day state of Israel. Allenby's "protective" birds were no more than a mechanism to justify colonial theft. He uses religious prophecy, a strategy that continues to be used one hundred years later, to advocate for the erasure of a people by dehumanizing them or simply pretending they don't exist.

I came across the story of Lord Allenby and his bird prophecy through a peculiar portrait of him in his garden in Cairo with his pet stork in 1917. He had an interest in birds, it seems, and I was struck by the relationship between Allenby and this bizarre-looking bird—in their postures and attitudes, there is a similar disposition. It reminded me of the Berber belief that storks are actually transformed humans. I was also thrilled that the bird was of the stork variety, and I found the connection to Menes, the spy bird located in Qena, an exciting bridge in the story. My research became about connecting the dots and finding ways to narrate the transformation of the geography of the region in the last hundred years through the narrative of birds, a strategy that draws from Farid ud-Din Attar's parable "The Conference of the Birds," which is about the quest to attain enlightenment, told through birds with human qualities.

AD In the years leading up to Allenby's arrival in Jerusalem, other aerial-bound devices were being invented to take photographs, including, in 1908, a form of "pigeon photography" pioneered by Julius Gustav Neubronner, a German apothecary, inventor, and amateur photographer and filmmaker. You make some interesting connections in the project to aerial-bound photography and warfare, not least in the way that the concepts behind Neubronner's ideas are today considered to be forerunners of mechanized drones, or "uncrewed aerial vehicles," and the armed reconnaissance drones that emerged in the 1980s.

HYA Neubronner's pigeons were a fascinating find for me: the German inventor strapped small cameras with timing mechanisms to the birds for aerial photography. This was very quickly adopted by German military intelligence, who reportedly trained pigeons leading up to World War II. Now we have Festo, a research laboratory in Germany investing in what they call "bionic thinking," or robotics that mimic nature. They have developed the SmartBird, a drone that is engineered to mimic the flight of a seagull.[3] Of course, Festo claim they are not engineering these robots for warfare purposes, but these kinds of technological development are almost always used by the military. Where are they being used, and against whom? These are the more pertinent questions here. In 2011, a downed drone bird almost identical to the SmartBird crashed in Chaman, a township bordering Afghanistan. Can you imagine how fearful you would be if you lived in a place like Chaman or Waziristan, which have both seen the heaviest bombardment from drone strikes? Now they can't even tell the difference between a beautiful bird and a killing machine!

AD It seems that Allenby's protective birds, the biblical augury of refuge, have metamorphosed here into the specter of imminent, if not arbitrary, drone-ordained death from above. I want to talk further here about your research into drone technology. When drones are launched from the ground in regions across the Middle East, Afghanistan, and Pakistan, the information from them is typically relayed via satellites to air force bases, where drone operators make decisions—such as whether to fire a Hellfire II anti-armor missile from a Predator drone—that are based on theoretical information received, as opposed to eyes on the ground, so to speak. This has had a huge impact on the psychopathology of airspace across the region. Can you talk about this further?

HYA Whereas the British military went to considerable lengths to understand the Arab mindset, so as to ultimately control the territories in the Middle East through aerial surveillance in the early twentieth century, US army strategists—with the most comprehensive and aggressive drone program in the world today—design fake Arab towns to practice drone warfare through gaming.[4] Surveillance over entire populations has gone beyond anthropometric policing and into biometric data control. This means that the structuring of space is pursued in accordance with the archiving of the global movement of bodies. Drone warfare particularly looks to spatiotemporal mapping, or the analysis of an individual's movements in correlation to space and time. Drones look for so-called outlier data, or anyone who veers from their daily routines and could be deemed a potential target. If someone is being surveilled, a spatiotemporal map can relay the patterns of their life; if they do something that deviates from this pattern, they could be flagged through algorithmic processing. The White House "kill list" criteria are unknown and based on blind trust.

Perhaps even more alarming is that people are now being labeled as potential threats before they have even considered doing anything. In April 2017, over four hundred Palestinians were detained on the basis of an algorithmic determination of the possible danger they posed to Israel. Furthermore, US military rhetoric systematically portrays warfare through aesthetics that not only glorify the destruction of Middle Eastern cities but also reduce the civilian casualties to faceless, abstract figures. The aftermath of 9/11 brought us the postmodern war and Operation Shock and Awe, where scenes of violence and destruction from the aerial bombardment of Iraq in 2001 were broadcast on television and narrated through aesthetic constructs. Sixteen years later, in 2017, the US Shayrat missile strikes in Syria were described as "beautiful pictures" by MSNBC's Brian Williams. The victims of war see their spaces and landscapes simultaneously through experience and through the aesthetics of the machine. Their multilayered perception of landscape becomes like an out-of-body experience where witnessing one's own death is an imminent possibility.

AD Some of this information has of course entered the public domain, thanks to a number of fearless individuals.

HYA Yes, it has, and after Chelsea Manning's disclosure of nearly 750,000 classified documents—including the Baghdad air strike video Collateral Murder, which was released on April 5, 2010—we have clear documentation of the murder of civilians. Our exposure to the casualties of warfare has since become embedded in our contemporary consciousness. Indeed, Manning's release of that particular video greatly transformed our public discourse and collective imaginaries in regard to military conduct and our role in it. The leaks were an attempt to address the accountability of the system, in this case the US government, which not only withholds truths from the public and controls the dissemination of images, but also gets away with war crimes. The leaks did something that military images and the media never do: they humanized victims.

AD I did a lot of reading about this as we were preparing our book on this project, and I was struck by a quote from Martin C. Libicki where he observes how, within this ascendant paradigm of perceptibility and exposure, the very fact of "visibility equals death."[5] But something else needs to be added to this—as you note—and that involves the fact that it is not the corporeal eye (the fleshy, embedded eye) that does the looking under conditions of war and surveillance; rather, it is "operational images," to use the term Harun Farocki deployed—images that are made by machines for machines have now become the autonomous systems of interpretation and empirical deduction that power drones.[6] Uncrewed drones, already implicated in bypassing human operators, could also be vastly improved by algorithmic means—or so we are told—so that human error would be eradicated. It now seems that algorithms control death–delivering missiles—thus further uncoupling any moral obligation from the act of killing.[7] Can you talk a little bit about this, inasmuch as it addresses your concerns around the ethics and techno-aesthetics of visualizing not just people but the region more broadly through the technologies of warfare?

> HYA Techno-aesthetics are inherently tied to the Greater Middle East, as military technologies were developed against the backdrop of Middle Eastern geographies throughout the last century or so. The Royal Geographical Society convened in 1920 to discuss British military strategies and opportunities brought forth by aerial technologies for land expansion, particularly in Europe's new territories on the African continent.[8] They were surveying landscapes not only for visualizing the colonies but also for administrative control and imperial cataloging that was predominantly preoccupied with colonial expansion, particularly in Africa. Paul Virilio writes of "the deadly harmony that always establishes itself between the functions of eye and weapon" when missiles and bombs are fitted with cameras and suddenly "open their eyes."[9] However, the danger of talking about drones or artificial intelligence as having autonomy is that, as you state, we uncouple moral obligation from the act of killing. Algorithms are written by humans within a specific context that is ultimately imbued with racism. There is always accountability to be had. Someone is always ethically and morally responsible.

AD There are echoes of the orientalist or colonial gaze here, don't you think? A gaze that fixes and produces it subjects in a political economy of difference and inequality—except, in this instance, the process is increasingly automated through the operation of algorithmically defined forms of surveillance. I was thinking here again of how "operational images" and drone surveillance would appear to have ushered in their own techno-aesthetic realm for producing the realities of the Middle East—in both subjective and objective terms—based on rampant suspicion and intrinsic fear, not to mention the augury of imminent retaliation. Would you agree with this reading?

HYA The aerial view completely changed the shape and sovereignty of territories. These images do not merely serve as an extension of vision, but rather speak to the moral and social landscapes reflected in the desire and fulfillment of the nation-state. The exoticization of violence through a colonial gaze is embedded in the aerial image, which simultaneously proposes notions of construction and destruction. Seeing the world from above introduced a new imagination of territory that played into the hands of colonial ideology by establishing a vertical power hierarchy. Ultimately, aerial power allowed empires to police territories from above by applying social control over entire populations.

AD There are further dimensions to the research that went into this work. I am thinking here also of *As Birds Flying* (2016), your short allegorical film, and how it responds to similar issues through the use of found drone footage (including aerial views of savannas and wetlands, and settlements in Galilea). Can you talk a little about this film, given that there are many crossovers with this current project?

Fig. 2 ←
Fig. 3 ←

HYA *As Birds Flying* is a short allegorical film pieced together with found drone footage filmed along the flight path of storks migrating through Israel and the occupied territories toward the Egyptian border. The aerial views are accompanied with a cinematic soundtrack of reconstructed audio from Adel Imam's iconic film *Birds of Darkness* (dir. Sharif Arafah, 1995), which addresses political corruption and religious extremism through parliamentary candidates on opposing sides of the political spectrum. My film speaks to the corruption and violence of the nation-state. The voice is presented as though from the perspective of the spy bird, who contemplates ideas such as political sectarianism, democracy, censorship, and surveillance. It was in the process of making this film that I began to connect the various narratives in the project on aerial perspectives and the landscapes of conflict.

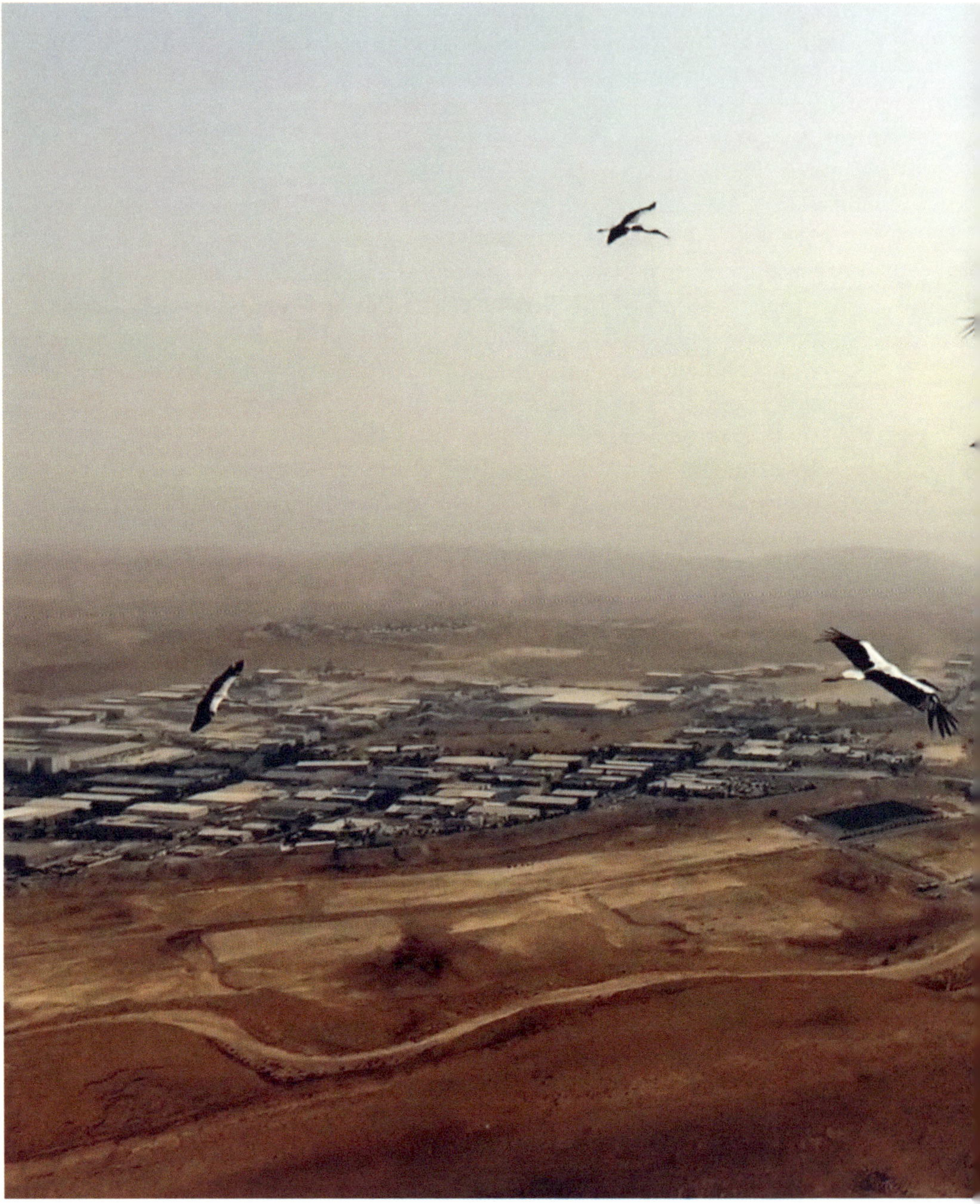

Fig. 2 Still from Heba Y. Amin, *As Birds Flying*, 2016. HD video, 7'11''.

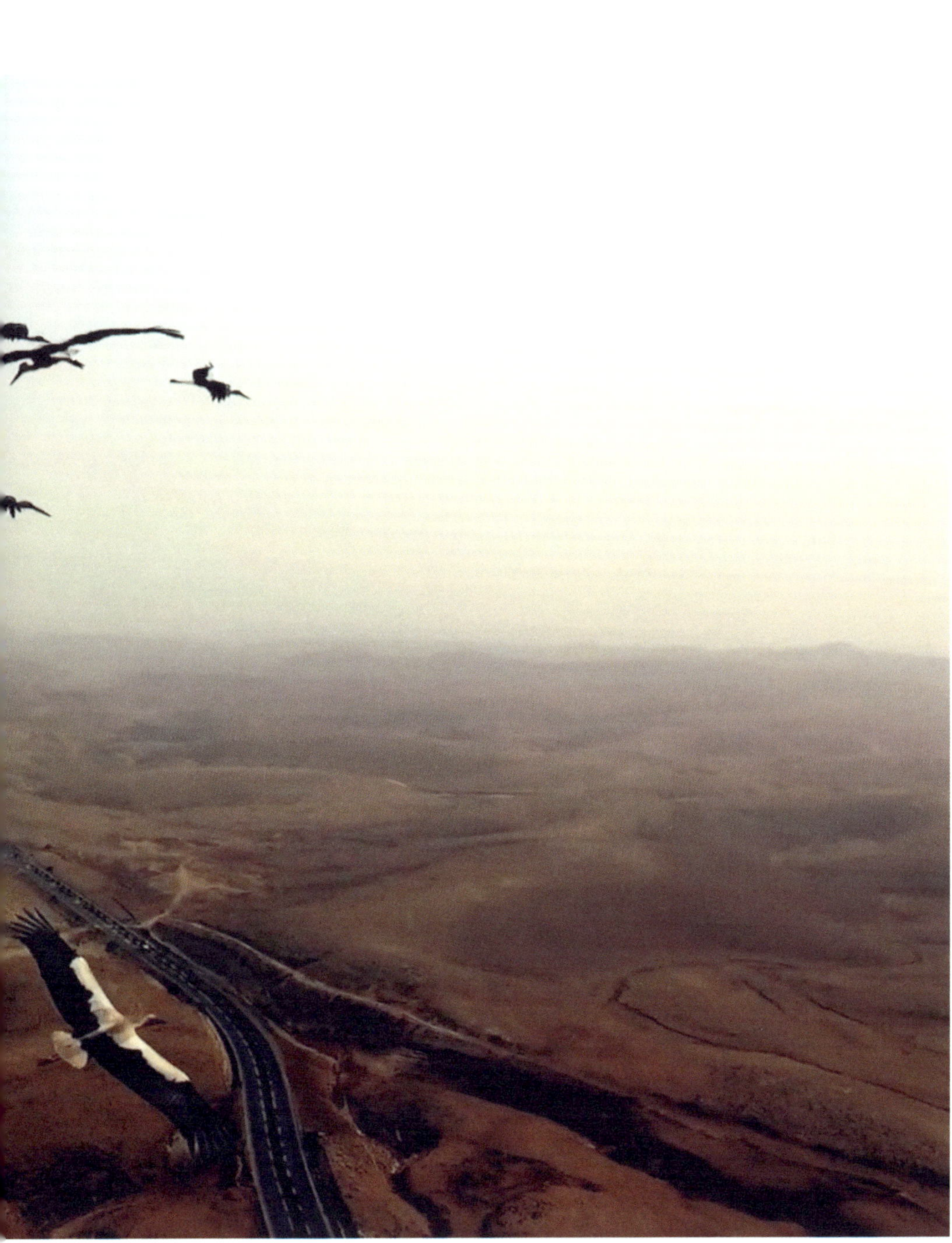

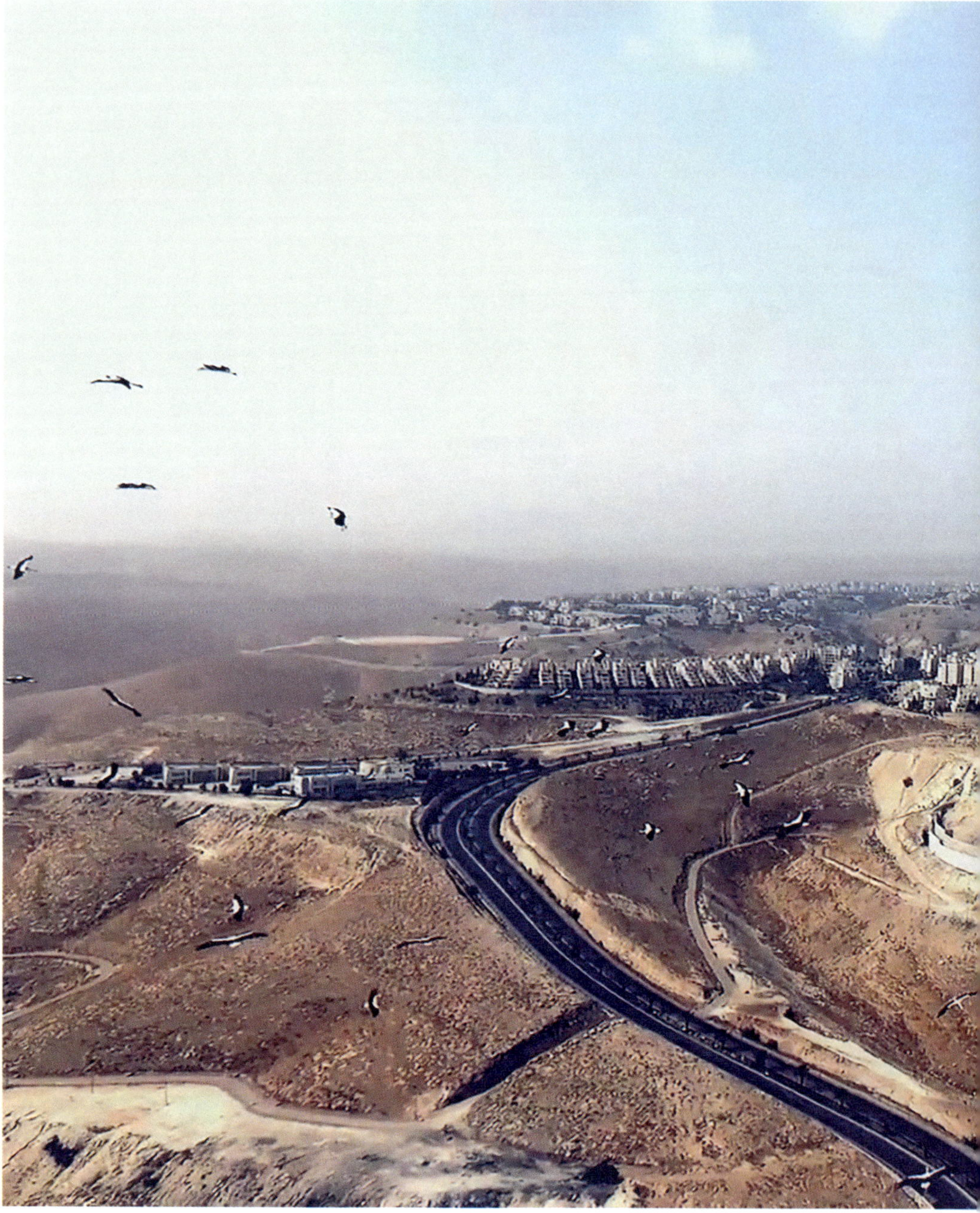

Fig. 3 Still from Heba Y. Amin, *As Birds Flying*, 2016. HD video, 7'11''.

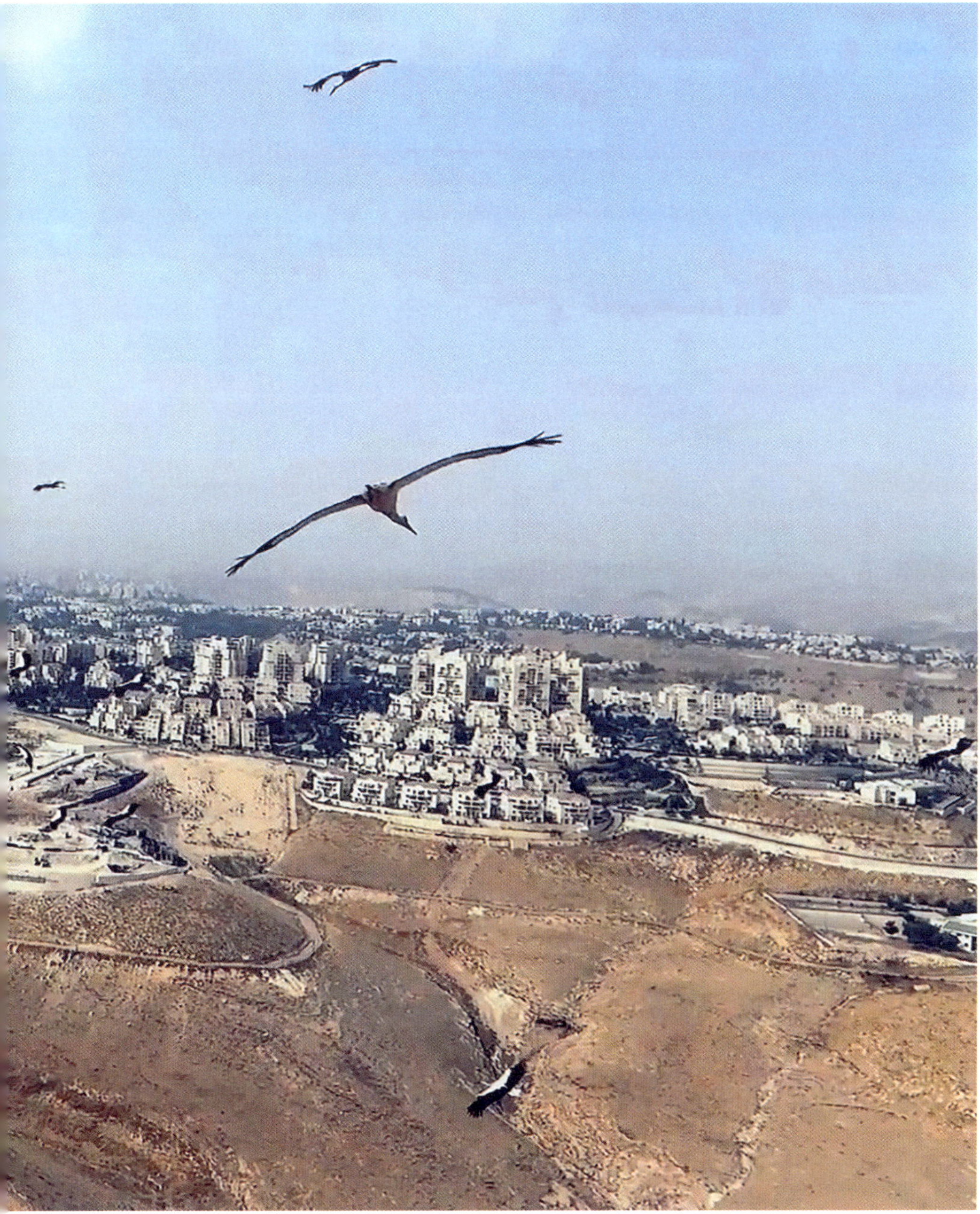

AD I want to zoom out to get a bigger picture here, given that these issues—specifically the anxieties surrounding surveillance, data mining, the state-sponsored use of algorithms to develop machine learning, and the broader role of augmented reality in the development of artificial intelligence—are not specific to the Middle East but have a distinct global context. To what extent do you think the concerns raised in *The General's Stork* relate to broader global issues?

HYA We are dealing with the problem of obscurity, as governments and corporations limit our access to information. This enables opaque methods of strategic decision-making that can be used against us. Ultimately, as a public, we must fully understand space through the canons of technology to avoid perpetuating and legitimizing those systems that control—and this is indeed a global rather than regional concern. The sovereignty of the aerial viewpoint is highly debatable, particularly in the digital age, when suspicion of representation is commonplace in post-representational photography. Rather than questioning whether or not the truth of a photograph is self-evident, we should contemplate our complicity in assuming it to be true in the first place. The new cult of the machine was born out of the doctrine of air power and colonial discourse. The aerial perspective became the symbol of modernity, as it transformed urban reality into an abstract representation of the sociotechnical imaginary.[10] These issues are most definitely global, because the very foundation of our right to survival is at stake.

AD This brings me to a conversation you had with the filmmaker Laura Poitras as part of the development of our book *The General's Stork*. There were two distinct elements that emerged in this discussion: one has to do with the expanded, digitally defined era of state surveillance, but the other has to do with practice and how (and where) you present projects such as yours. I was specifically thinking of how Poitras articulated her own involvement in cultural institutions as a methodology of sorts, inasmuch as she observed how art institutions do not always feel comfortable talking about classified information, but when she puts her projects into such spaces, the project can become both culture and news at the same time. Does this have a bearing upon your practice?

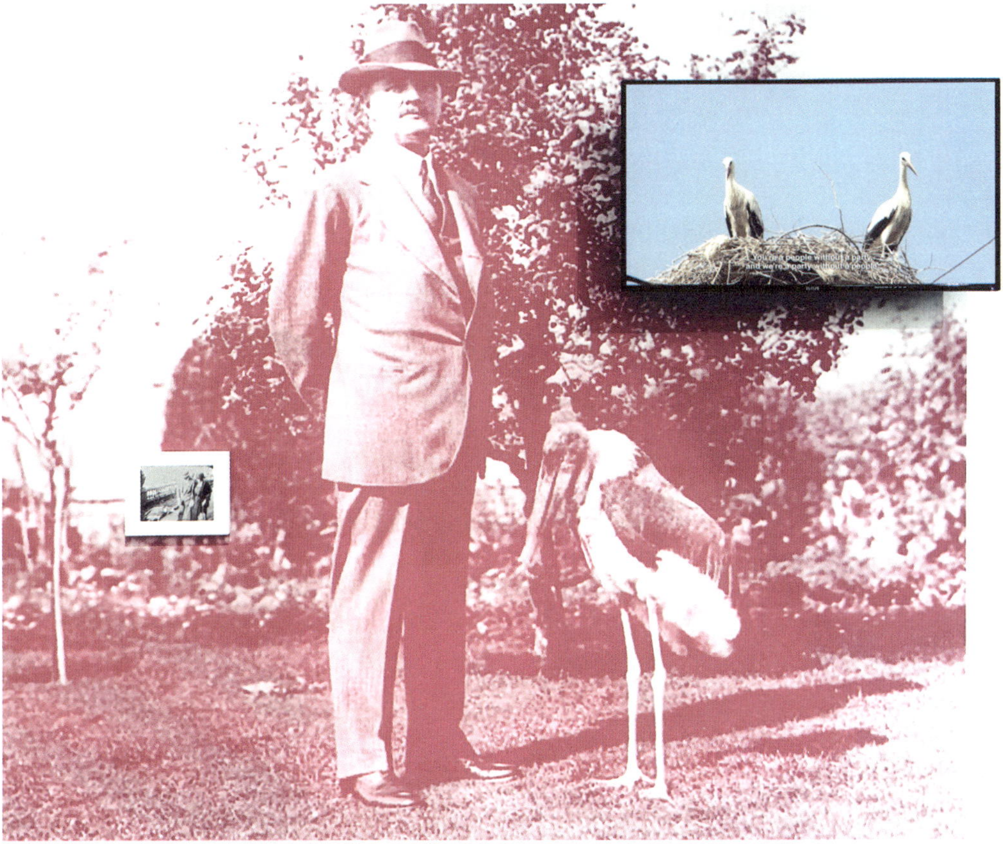

Fig. 4 Heba Y. Amin, *The General's Stork*, 2018. Mixed media installation.

HYA The work that I make is meant to critique systems of power. I am interested in instigating difficult conversations in an attempt to change discourse, or at the very least invite critical perspectives. For that reason, I am constantly thinking of different strategies and questioning the impact of the work that I make, especially at this time, when the situation seems so urgent. On this point, Laura Poitras is an artist I deeply admire and look to as a role model, as I am quite interested in her approach of not only using media as a tool of dissemination beyond the exhibition space, but also using art as a form of investigative journalism. What should we be asking of art at this particular moment in time? That is the question I want to
Fig. 4 ← explore in works such as *The General's Stork*. Can art, moreover,

be instrumentalized to address forms of social reengineering? What strategies can we as practitioners in the art world use to curb a complete disintegration of civil liberties? It seems to me that it is important to find other spaces in which art can live and address these issues head-on.

1. This conversation continued to develop and subsequently culminated in the publication of *Heba Y. Amin: The General's Stork*, ed. Anthony Downey (Berlin: Sternberg Press, 2020).

2. For fuller details, see Conal Urquhart, "Arrested 'Spy' Stork Killed and Eaten after Release in Egypt," *The Guardian*, September 7, 2013, https://www.theguardian.com/world/2013/sep/07/arrested-spy-stork-killed-eaten-egypt.

3. The use of albatrosses fitted with lightweight radar detection devices to identify illegal fishing ships in remote locations has been recently noted too. See Eleanor Ainge Roy, "'Intelligent Drones': Albatross Fitted with Radar Detectors to Spot Illegal Fishing," *The Guardian*, January 31, 2020, https://www.theguardian.com/world/2020/jan/31/intelligent-drones albatross-fitted-with-radar-detectors-to-spot-illegal-fishing.

4. Grégoire Chamayou has observed that "when American army strategists imagine what drones will be like in twenty-five years, they begin by getting an infographist to create a composite image of a typical Arab town, complete with mosque, other buildings, and palm trees." Grégoire Chamayou, *A Theory of the Drone*, trans. Janet Lloyd (New York: New Press, 2015), 56.

5. See Martin C. Libicki, quoted in Antoine Bousquet, *The Eye of War: Military Perception from the Telescope to the Drone* (Minneapolis: University of Minnesota Press, 2018), 3.

6. Farocki used the phrase "operational images" to describe images made by machines for machines, the full implications of which he explored throughout his three-part film *Eye/Machine I, II, III* (2000-2003). These machine-oriented images are not produced in relation to representing either subjects or objects; rather, they are part of an operation. For Trevor Paglen, writing of this phenomenon, Farocki "was one of the first to notice that image-making machines and algorithms were poised to inaugurate a new visual regime. Instead of simply representing things in the world, the machines and their images were starting to 'do' things in the world. In fields from marketing to warfare, human eyes were becoming anachronistic." Trevor Paglen, "Operational Images," *e-flux Journal*, no. 59 (November 2014), http://worker01.e-flux.com/pdf/article_8990555.pdf.

7. Debates about whether drone-based targeted killing programs are indicative of an incipient moral indifference to death caused by armed conflict are widespread within military, ethical, and legal fields. See Michael J. Boyle, "The Legal and Ethical Implications of Drone Warfare," *International Journal of Human Rights* 19, no. 2 (2015): 105-26; Anders Henriksen and Jens Ringsmose, "Drone Warfare and Morality in Riskless War," *Global Affairs* 1, no. 3 (2015): 285-91; Bradley Jay Strawser, "Moral Predators: The Duty to Employ Uninhabited Aerial Vehicles," *Journal of Military Ethics* 9, no. 4 (2010): 342-68.

8. Peter Adey, *Aerial Life* (Malden, MA: Wiley-Blackwell, 2010), 1.

9. Paul Virilio, *War and Cinema: The Logistics of Perception*, trans. Patrick Camiller (New York: Verso, 2009), 83.

10. Sheila Jasanoff describes at length the meaning of the term sociotechnical imaginaries as "collectively imagined forms of social life and social order reflected in the design and fulfillment of nation-specific and/or technological projects." Sheila Jasanoff and Sang-Hyun Kim, *Dreamscapes of Modernity: Sociotechnical Imaginaries and the Fabrication of Power* (Chicago: University of Chicago Press, 2015), 20.

WATCHED BY DRONES
Photographic Surveillance in Art, War, and Protest
A conversation between Svea Braeunert, Sarah Tuck, and Louise Wolthers

The following conversation draws on three research projects that have all been presented as exhibitions and publications: "To See Without Being Seen: Contemporary Art and Drone Warfare" (2016), "WATCHED! Surveillance, Art, and Photography" (2016–2017), and "Drone Vision: Warfare, Surveillance, Protest" (2018–2019).[1] While each project was independently initiated and driven by different research questions, they all share a curatorial engagement with artistic responses to the contemporary surveillance complex, and we, as curators and critics taking part in the following conversation, have been inspired by and collaborated with several of the same artists, projects, and thinkers. Thinking through the theme of (w)archives, we discuss the imperatives and archives informing our projects, as well as the archival dimensions of big data, and the impact of the digital on concepts, logics, and logistics of the archive. Furthermore, based on our different curatorial perspectives, we consider the political effects of viewing the world from above, and we discuss the restriction of space and movement as it plays out against the backdrop of a supposedly unrestricted form of warfare.

Louise Wolthers Let's begin by outlining our different approaches in the three projects. While "WATCHED!" was a fairly broad investigation of everyday surveillance as visualized through photographic and lens-based art under subcategories such as scanning, screening, and tagging, "To See Without Being Seen" and "Drone Vision" focused more explicitly on drones and the view from above. What were your initial research questions and approaches to the drone explored by artists? And following this, what—and how—can we learn from artistic engagement with drone visions in terms of contemporary warfare?

Svea Braeunert I was working on a book on drone warfare and contemporary art when Meredith Malone from the Mildred Lane Kemper Art Museum at Washington University in St. Louis approached me about co-curating a show on the topic. Developing the outline for the project was very intriguing, as it allowed us to combine her expertise in curating and art history with my interest in media and visual cultures.[2] The resulting exhibition was divided into three sections: "Bringing the War Home," "Tracking and Targeting," and "Countersurveillance." It essentially took the drone as an object to explore the changing ways of defining and describing images in digital culture, and how these relate to political practices and conflicts.

When we conceived "To See Without Being Seen," I was very much focused on the use of drones in war, and on works that explicitly reference that connection, such as Tomas van Houtryve's *Blue Sky Days* (2013–2014) or James Bridle's *Dronestagram* (2012–), which, following critics such as Grégoire Chamayou and Byung-Chul Han, led me to emphasize the drone's vertical relationship of power and domination.[3] It was only through Sarah's curatorial approach that I started to pay more attention to projects that use drones as counter-hegemonic tools for reversing the gaze and making visible. As a result, I am currently interested in rethinking the relationship between above and below in more complex ways, taking into account a broader range of works such as Hiwa K's *A View from Above* (2017), Basma Alsharif's *Ouroboros* (2017), or Hito Steyerl's writings. → Fig. 1

LW I agree that both contemporary drone practices and technologies—in warfare, counterculture, and art alike—apply and enable a below-above dynamics in much more nuanced ways than, say, the aerial reconnaissance camera or CCTV. As surveillance scholar Kevin Haggerty suggests, what we have seen in the last decades is an "undermining [of] the neat distinction between watchers and watched through a proliferation of criss-crossing, overlapping and intersecting scrutiny."[4] A useful concept, also coined and applied by Haggerty together with Richard Ericsson, could be the assemblage model.[5] What approaches and understandings of below-above dynamics would you specifically point to in the work of Hiwa K, Basma Alsharif, and Hito Steyerl?

SB There are mainly two aspects I want to stress, and they both have to do with broadening the archive of what is considered "drone art."[6] It was around 2011 that artists and curators started to pick up on the theme of drone warfare, and a number of exhibitions, including Meredith Malone's and my "To See Without Being Seen," were very topical.[7] Now that we have reached a point where awareness of military drone usage has grown alongside the civilian application of drones, and drones have become so much of a topic that Caren Kaplan speaks of a "drone-o-rama,"[8] I believe it is time to complicate things and also take into account works, pensive images (*Denkbilder*), and concepts that are not as directly linked to the topic of drone warfare but nevertheless speak to it—be it on a formal, historical, or perceptual level. I am thinking, for instance, of tilted images such as the famous duck-rabbit, which allows you to see either a duck or a rabbit but never both at the same time, although both figures are always there. Is this a constellation/perceptual phenomenon that might allow me to think through the tension of the seen and the unseen in drone warfare? Is the instance when one shifts from one to the other (and when either both or neither are visible) indicative of the viewing conditions of the drone? Can above and below be conceived as relational when we look at them in this instantaneous moment of shifting? I am not sure yet where this will lead me, but it is something that I am currently thinking about. That is the first point. It concerns integrating non-drone materials in order to think about the drone.

The second point has to do with the uneven representation that comes from the asymmetrical power relations in this war and its viewing conditions, which extend to the realm of art. The majority of works that are shown are by artists based in Europe and North America, and in one way or another they either address the fact that this is a war also waged at home, or they seek to evoke empathy in Western viewers. This once again makes invisible the experience of people who live under the constant threat of drones. I am interested in positions that not only attempt to counter the imbalance in representation but also seek to shift the overall dynamic and trouble binary distinctions between the seen and the unseen, the vertical and the horizontal. In her essay "A Sea of Data," Hito Steyerl takes an image from an Israeli drone that was intercepted by the United Kingdom's Government Communications Headquarters and leaked as part of the Snowden files via *The Intercept*, and she

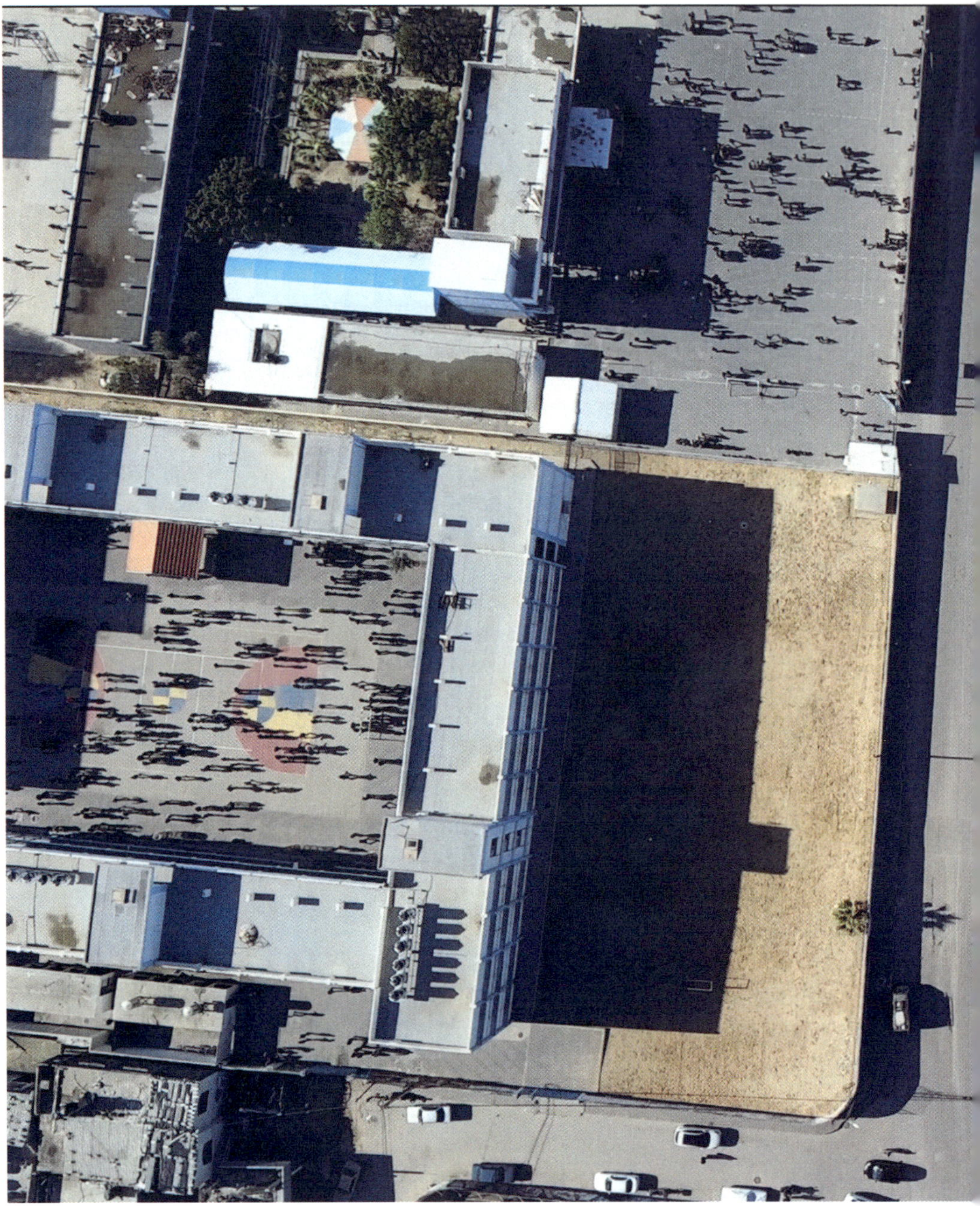

Fig. 1 Still from Basma Alsharif's film *Ouroboros*, 2017

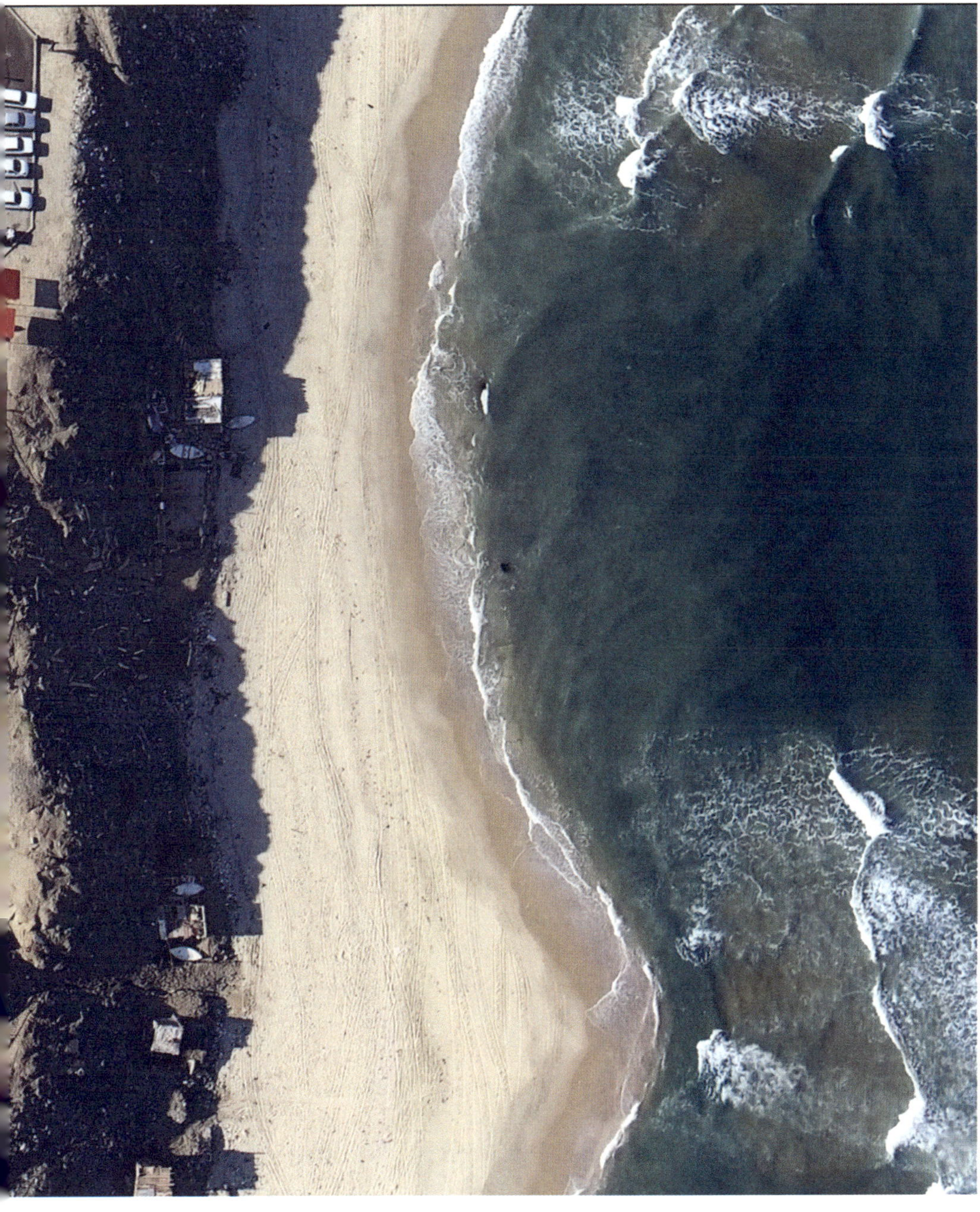

circumscribes that image through apophenia, so that in the end she sees in it the distorted view of Amani al-Nasasra, a woman who was blinded by a drone attack in Gaza in 2012.[9] By doing so, Steyerl takes the experience of blindness to mark the blind spots of drone warfare and turn a document of power into the powerful account of a witness. Similarly, Hiwa K's video *A View from Above* raises the question of what you can know from the ground and what you can know when you look at the world from above. He tells the story of an asylum seeker who, in order to qualify for asylum, memorizes details about a city that correspond to a map of that place. He is granted asylum, although the schematic and ordered view from above has very little to do with what you actually experience when you encounter a city in all of its lived and material density. Last but not least, Basma Alsharif's film *Ouroboros* begins with a strikingly beautiful vertical shot from a drone, showing the passage from the ocean to the shore and land in Gaza. The film continues with poetic episodes that translate the question of violence from the air to the ground and back, thereby setting up a cyclical structure that speaks to the relational thrust of the work. As Justine Smith wrote: "This is a film about Palestine but also about the bonds of trauma and violence that connect seemingly disparate histories."[10] I think it is these kinds of connections, but also more importantly the shifts and translations, that I am interested in in all of these works, along with the testing of skewed perspectives and ways of looking awry that deviate from the artificial order of linear perspective.

Sarah Tuck With "Drone Vision: Warfare, Surveillance, Protest," → Fig. 2 I wanted to understand if civilian use of drone technologies could be thought of as countersurveillance, to think through how drones influence the dynamics of protest on the ground. In short, to see how the politics of visibility connects to the politics of verticality, and in this braiding of the visible and the vertical to understand its meaning for public assembly in the street and, not least, the possibilities of solidarity across time and place enabled by seeing at a distance in real time. Nevertheless, I was concerned that an emphasis on this potentiality of civilian drone use could too readily obscure the lethal role of drones, so for the research project "Drone Vision," a collaborative initiative of Valand Academy, Gothenburg University, and the Hasselblad

Foundation, the three areas explored were warfare, surveillance, and protest. My initial hesitation to produce an exhibition in Sweden that would somehow "speak of" each of the themes led me to work in partnership with the National College of Arts in Lahore, Pakistan, and with Nicosia Municipal Arts Center (NiMAC) in Cyprus, in order that the realpolitik of drone use, civilian and military alike, could be addressed across three simultaneous exhibitions.

SB Can you tell us a little bit more about the collaborations with curators in Lahore and Cyprus, and the idea behind having the exhibition dispersed in three different locations? Does the multiplication of sites, in your opinion, speak to the multiplication of zones of conflict today? Were there discernible differences between the commissioned works in each place, and in the ways audiences reacted and interacted?

ST The three exhibitions were connected by a shared inquiry. Each exhibition hosted edited views from above the cities of Gothenburg, Nicosia, and Lahore by Cypriot artist Vicky Pericleous, and an audio station—designed by Markus Miessen and students of HDK, Academy of Design and Crafts, Gothenburg University, and assembled locally—where audiences could listen to roundtable conversations of an international cohort of artists, geographers, technologists, photographers, and war and defense researchers discussing the ethics and politics of drone technologies.

I did not want to assume the role of curator in Lahore and Nicosia, since I have limited knowledge of the artistic, cultural, social, economic, and political histories that shape those cities. The selection of partners in Pakistan and Cyprus was to understand how proximity to and distance from war affect understandings of the drone, where geographical distance is upended but the intimacy of grief and trauma remains local. How then could an exhibition "stage" this complex extension of geographies of place, and in so doing be alert to the experience of living beneath the threat of a drone strike, of fleeing war, and the trauma that is compounded by the journeys undertaken and the lack of hospitality and refuge provided? And finally, how might the military use of drone technologies be subverted

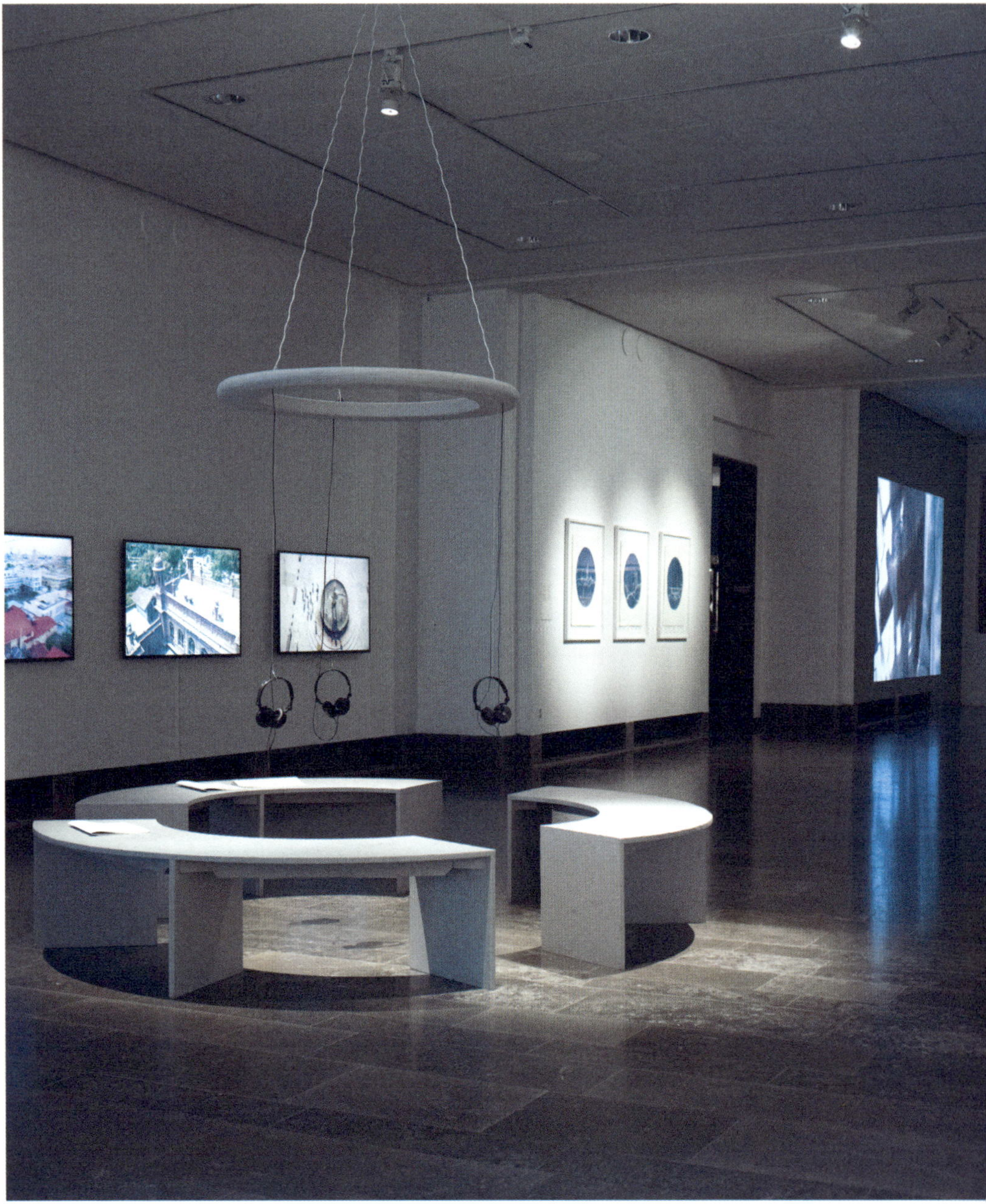

Fig. 2 Exhibition view from "Drone Vision: Warfare, Surveillance, Protest," Hasselblad Center, Gothenburg, May 19–September 19, 2018

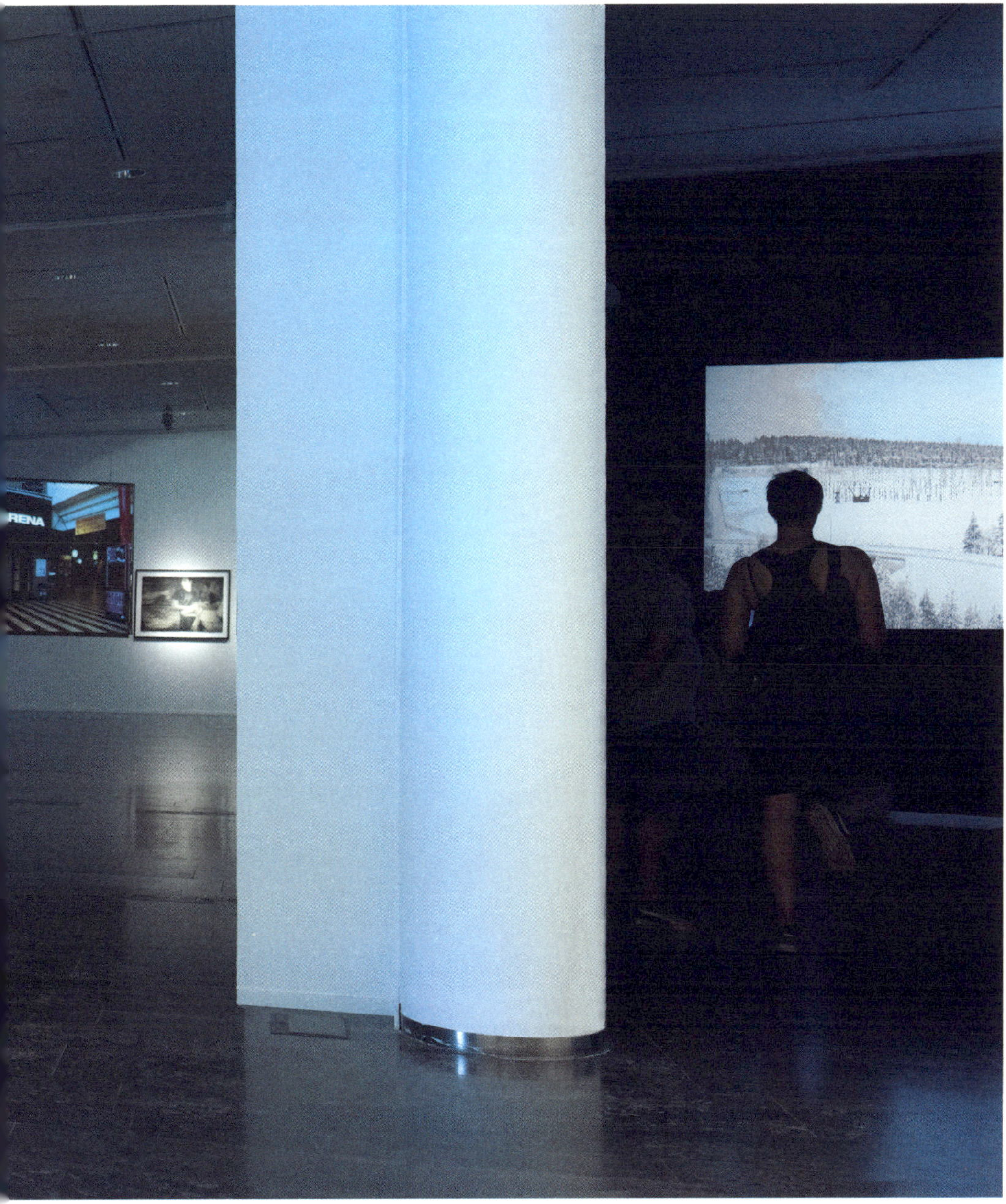
RENA

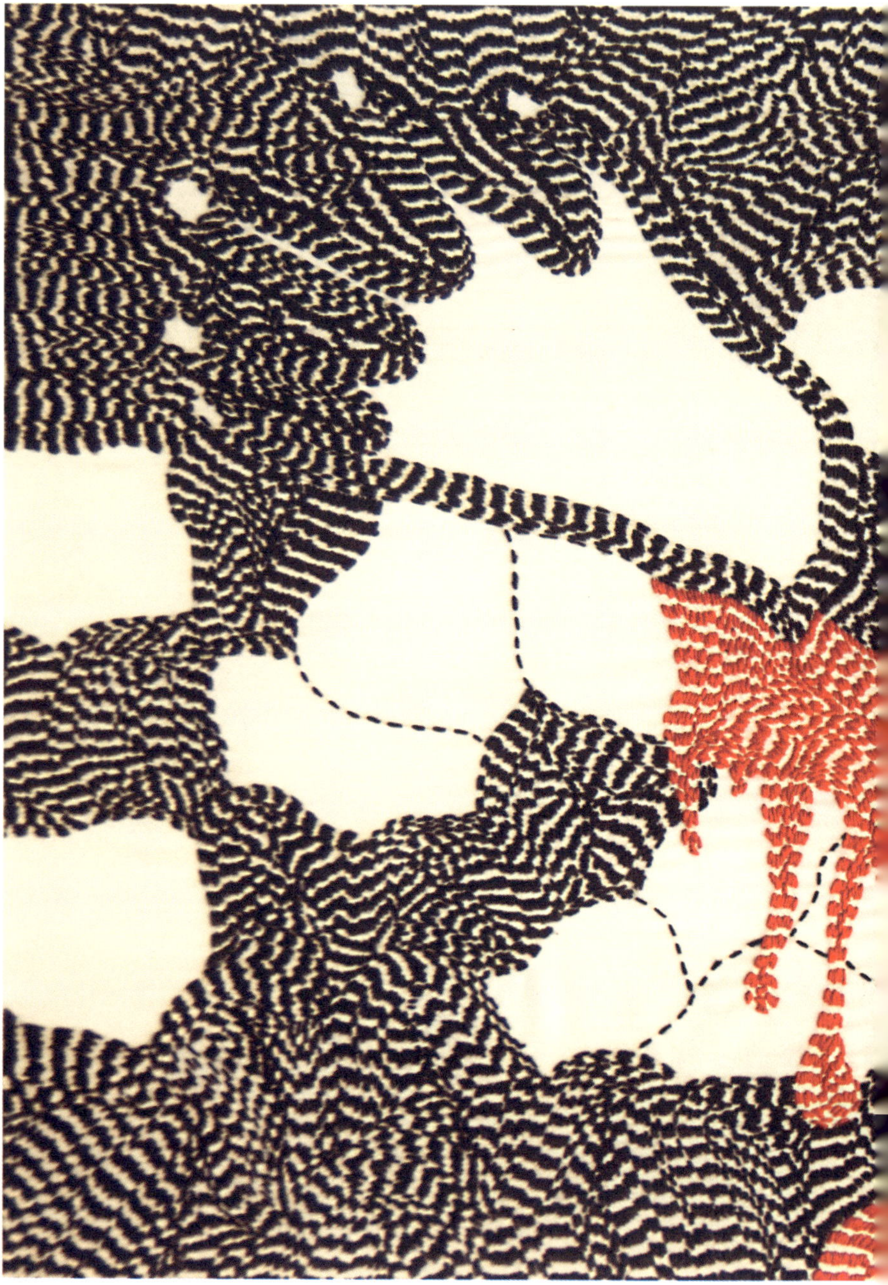

Fig. 3 Wajahat Saeed, *This Vicious Cycle*, 2017. Hand embroidery on fabric, 29.46×47.24 cm.

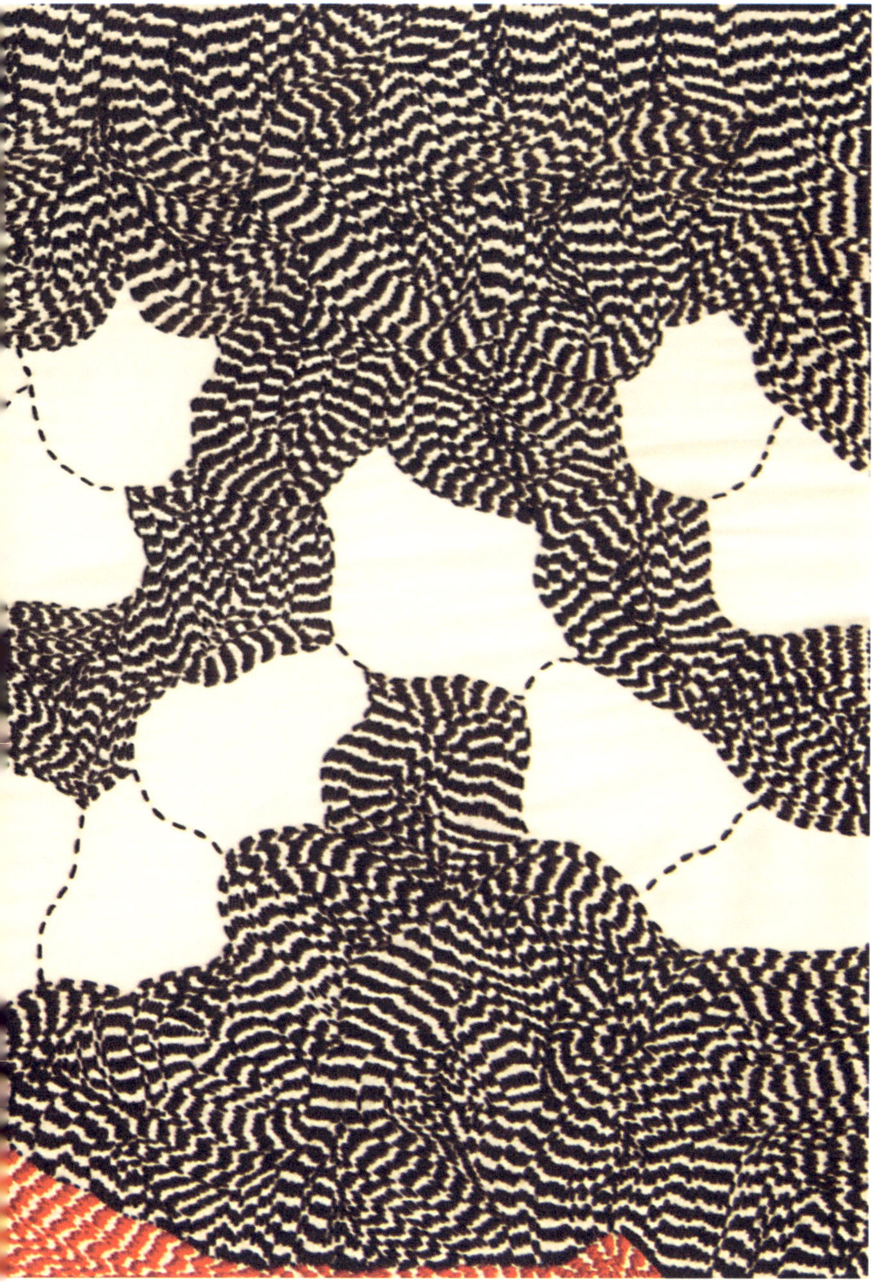

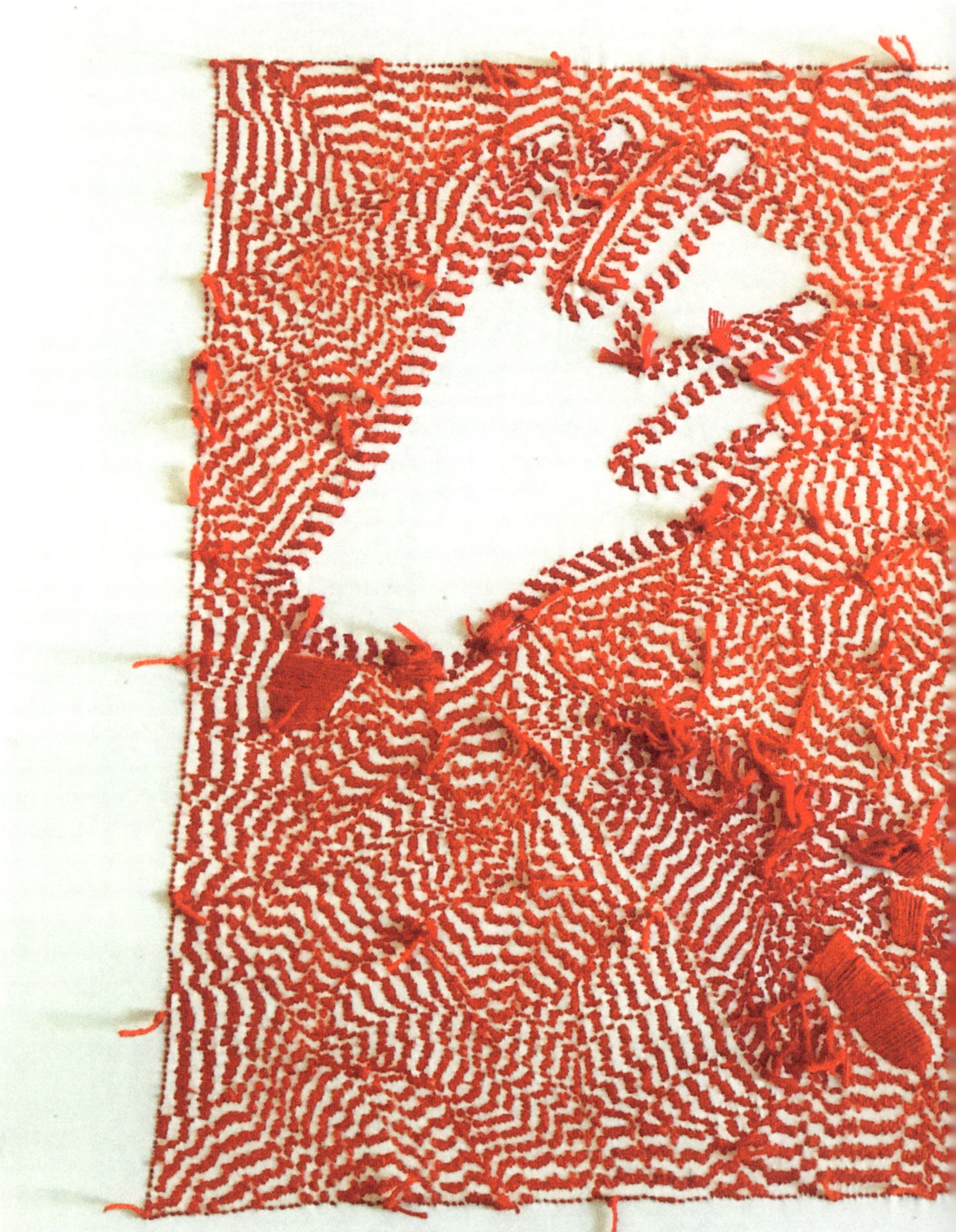

Fig. 4 Wajahat Saeed, *Yet Again! It Happened*, 2017 (work in progress). Hand embroidery on fabric, 29.46×47.24 cm.

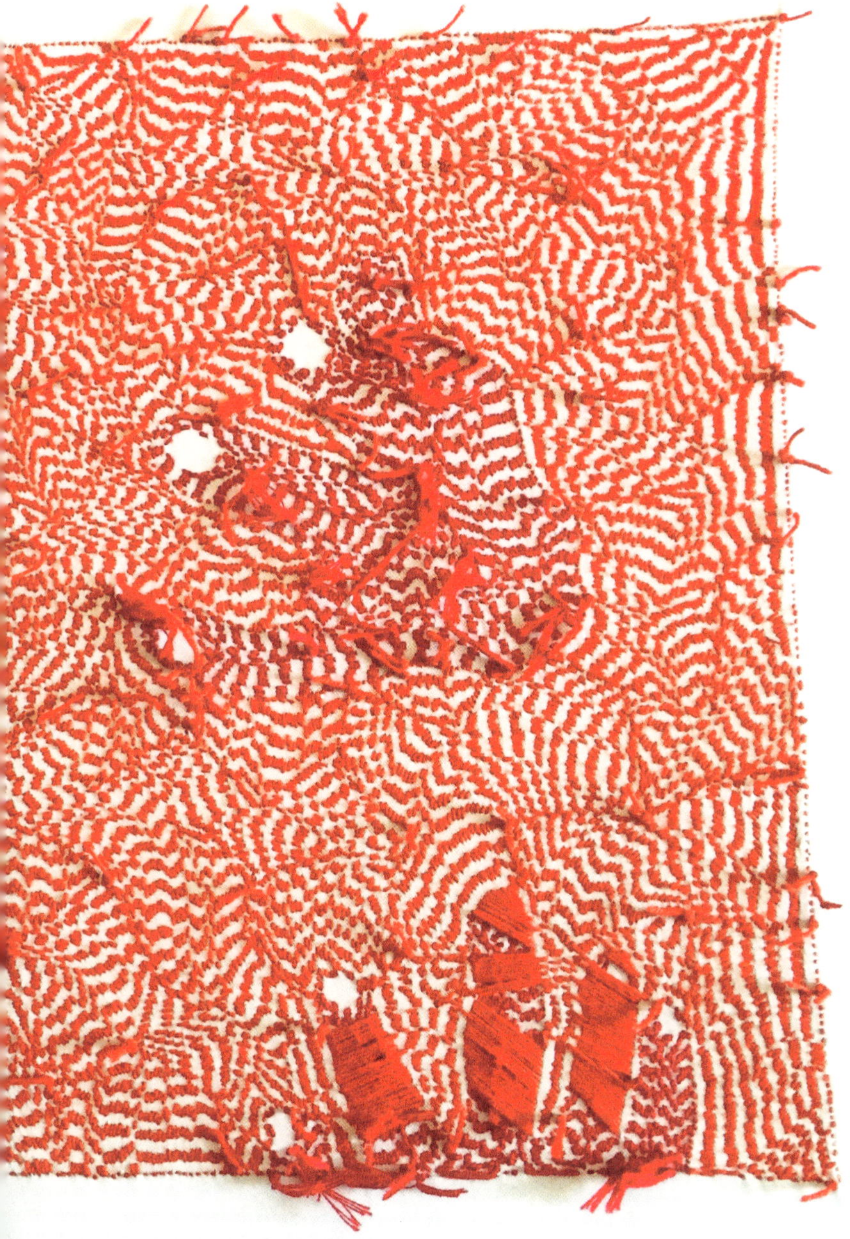

through a civilian use whereby seeing at a distance in real time becomes a possibility for connection and solidarity? This is of course not intended to gloss over destructive uses of drones by civilians, or to suggest that a differentiation and distinction between military and civilian drones can be so easily secured, but is instead to indicate how a civilian use of drones has the potential to reconfigure asymmetries of power. The triptych of exhibitions was therefore a way to think critically about the "elastic geography" that drone technologies enable, without displacing the specific effects of this technology. In Lahore, the exhibition was curated by Imran Qureshi and showed the work of three artists: Salman Khan, Wajahat Saeed, and Sajid Khan, all of whom come from the Federally Administered Tribal Areas (FATA) of northern Pakistan. Each of the artists had experienced US-led drone strikes, and all of them "fit the description" of "military-aged males." Watched from the Creech Air Force Base in Nevada by the US military, the three artists are "seen" as legitimate targets, and it is this experience that shaped the work presented at the National College of Arts in Lahore. The artists Salman Khan and Sajid Khan used miniature painting → Fig. 3
techniques to present the fear of the sky and the trauma of the → Fig. 4
aftermath of a drone strike, and artist Wajahat Saeed produced → Fig. 5
thread paintings where, as the artist described, each stitch → Fig. 6
was an act of resistance against drone attacks and a process of grieving for those killed.

For the exhibition at NiMAC, in association with the Pierides Foundation in Nicosia, curator Yiannis Toumazis selected the three artists: Efi Savvides and Stelios Kallinikou from Cyprus, and Ran Slavin from Israel. The three proposals effectively responded to the thematic axes of the project—warfare, surveillance, and protest. Ran Slavin's work dealt with warfare, Stelios Kallinikou examined surveillance, and Efi Savvides tackled protest. Each work responded to a specific geopolitical circumstance. Ran Slavin documented a disused Israel Defense Forces training site, revealing a facsimile of a Palestinian village, the ruins of an aircraft, and a desert landscape. Stelios Kallinikou chose not to work with drone photography, instead holding the camera to track the histories of militarized surveillance, from fortresses of the Middle Ages to the present-day Haarp (High Frequency

Active Auroral Research Project) found at British sovereign bases in the areas of Akrotiri and Troodos. Efi Savvides worked with the Hassan family, a Kurdish family from Syria, documenting their struggle for citizenship in Cyprus through a video work and the presentation of their correspondence with the authorities, revealing both the administrative violence of the categorization of the family as "stateless" and the lived reality for the family of the state's violence.

With the exhibition at the Hasselblad Center in Gothenburg, the three artists Mhairi Sutherland, Behjat Omer Abdulla, and Ignacio Acosta explored the impacts of drone technologies on the militarization of the everyday and as a tool of protest and countersurveillance. Mhairi Sutherland explored the extension of Saab in the uninterrupted airspace of the Swedish city of Linköping to the city's Saab Arena for ice hockey, with its looped promotional videos for Saab's military hardware. Artist Behjat Omer Abdulla produced a first-person testimony on the aftermath of an aerial bombardment in Daraa in Syria. The radically mobile and machinic gaze of the drone through the corridors and grounds of Sweden's largest asylum center, and the first-person narration, details the interconnection between being subjected to aerial bombing and being policed biopolitically. For Ignacio
Fig. 7 ←
Acosta, the vertical dimension of drone technologies provides a visual method to map the threat to the cultural, social, and economic life of the Saami people by Beowulf Mining, who are seeking a twenty-five-year exploitation concession to establish a mine in Kallak in the county of Norrbotten. The vertical dimension—from the drone view above, to the proposed extractive violence of a mine on Saami land—links the contestation of the subterranean with land surface.

The exhibition in Lahore, with its emphasis on the lived experience of drone strikes, put into circulation the profound emotional consequences of killing at a distance for those targeted. In September 2018, all the artists and curators who had been part of the three exhibitions were invited to Gothenburg for a two-day public conversation. The intention was to share critical approaches as curators and artists, to generate discussion, and, not least, for the commissioned artists to meet one another. The artists Salman Khan, Sajid Khan, and Wajahat Saeed were all

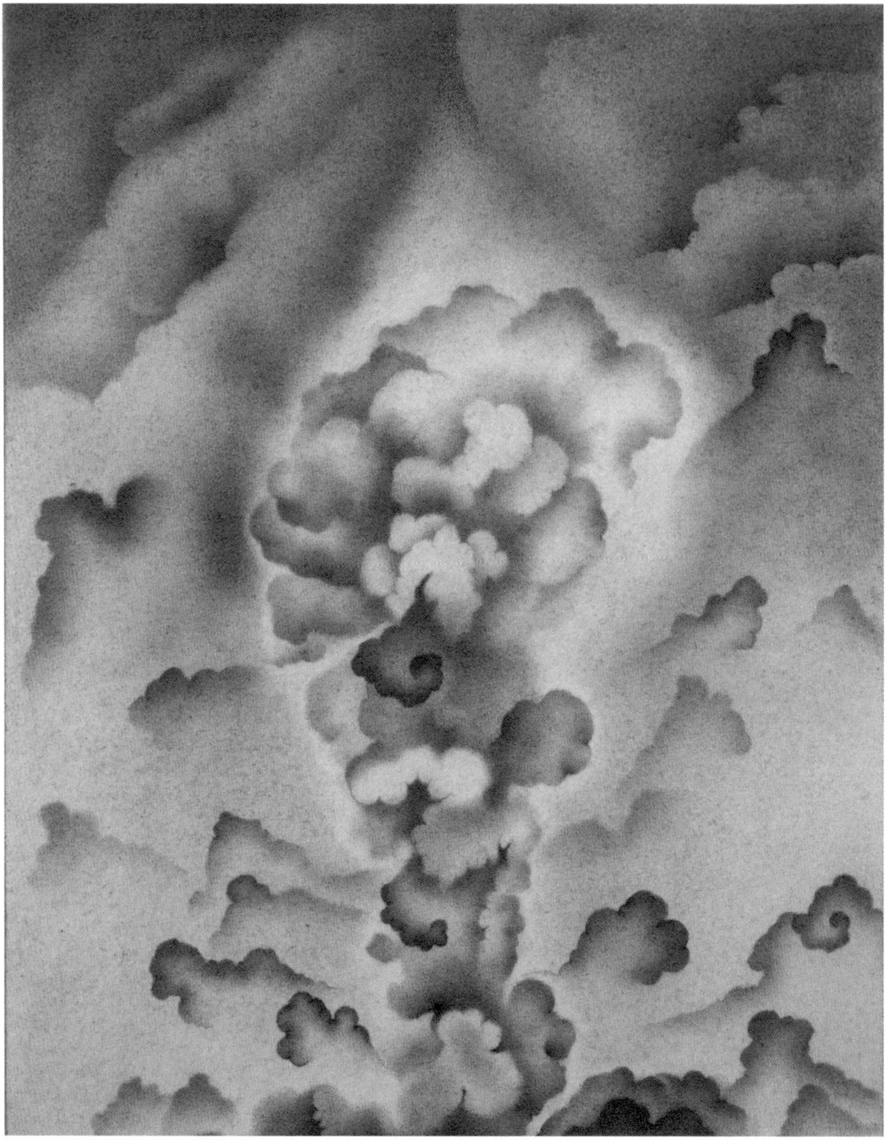

Fig. 5 Sajid Khan, *Untitled II*, 2017. Graphite on paper, 15×11.25 cm.

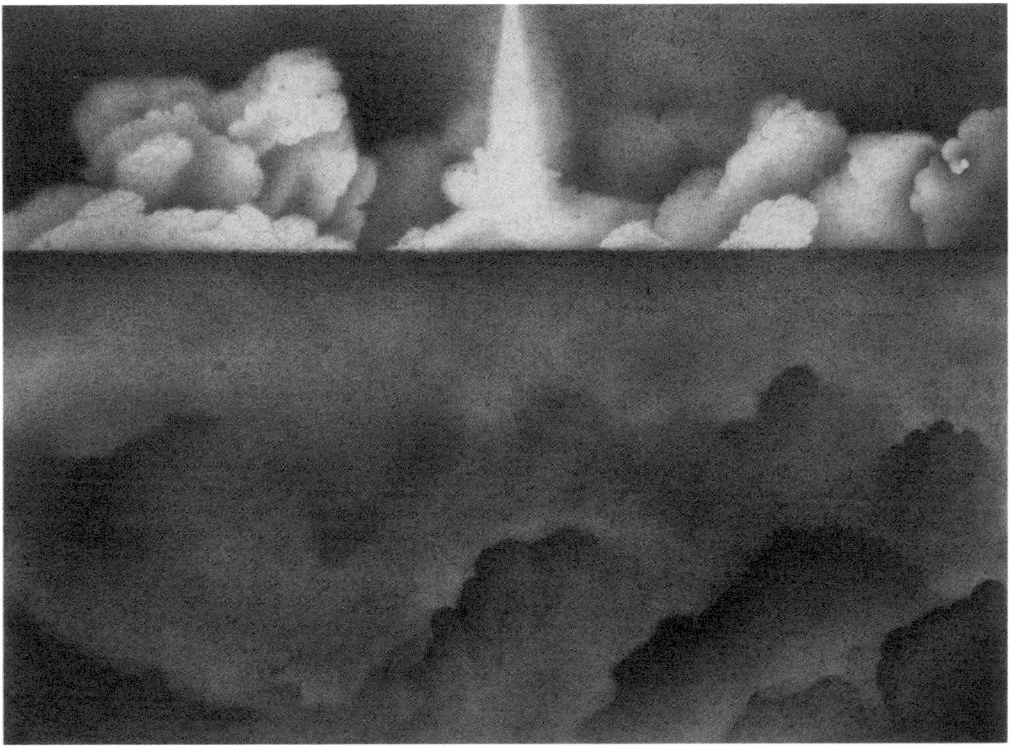

Fig. 6 Sajid Khan, *Untitled III*, 2017. Graphite, color pencil on paper, 11.25×15 cm.

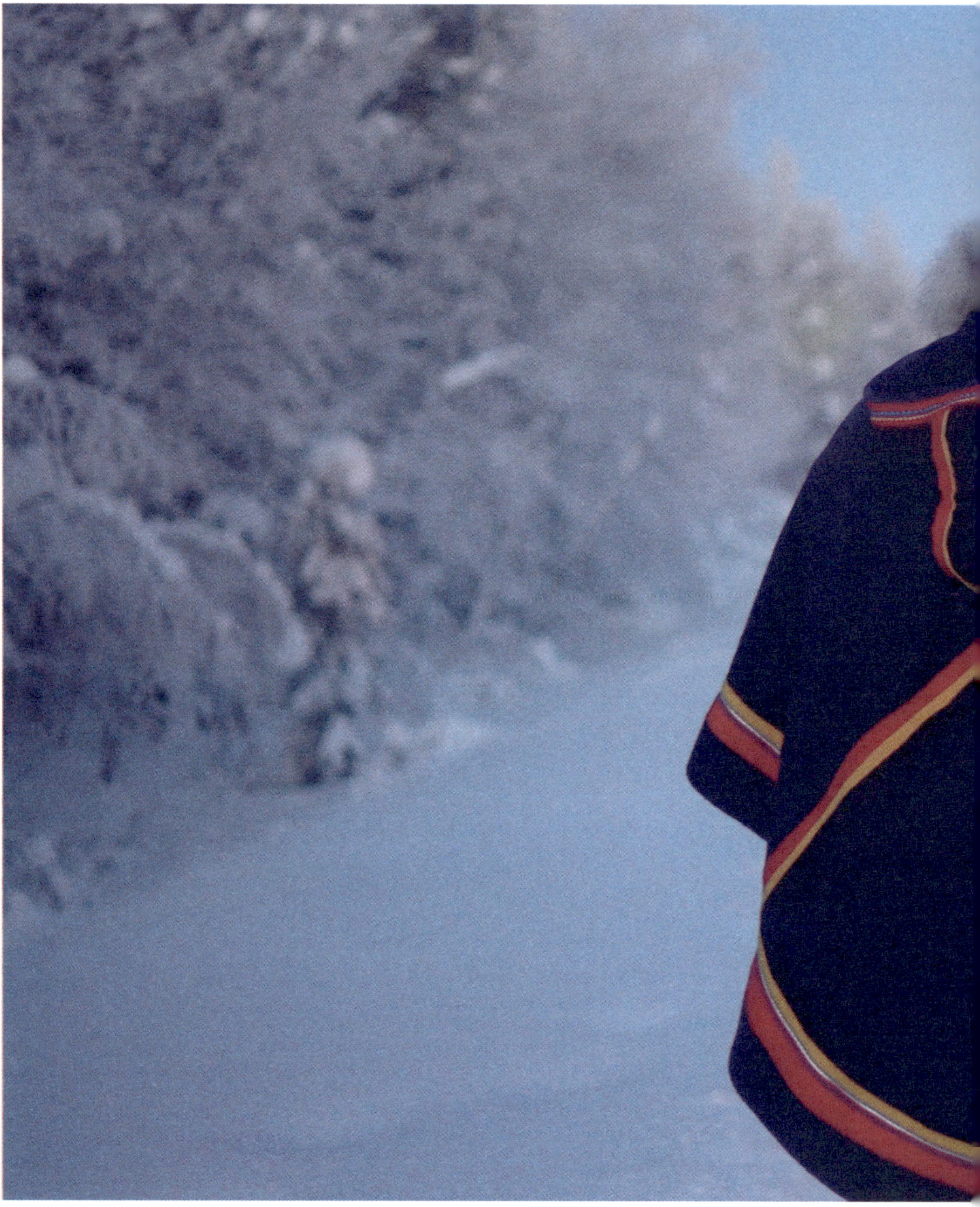

Fig. 7 Still from Ignacio Acosta, *Litte ja Goabddá* [Drones and Drums], 2018

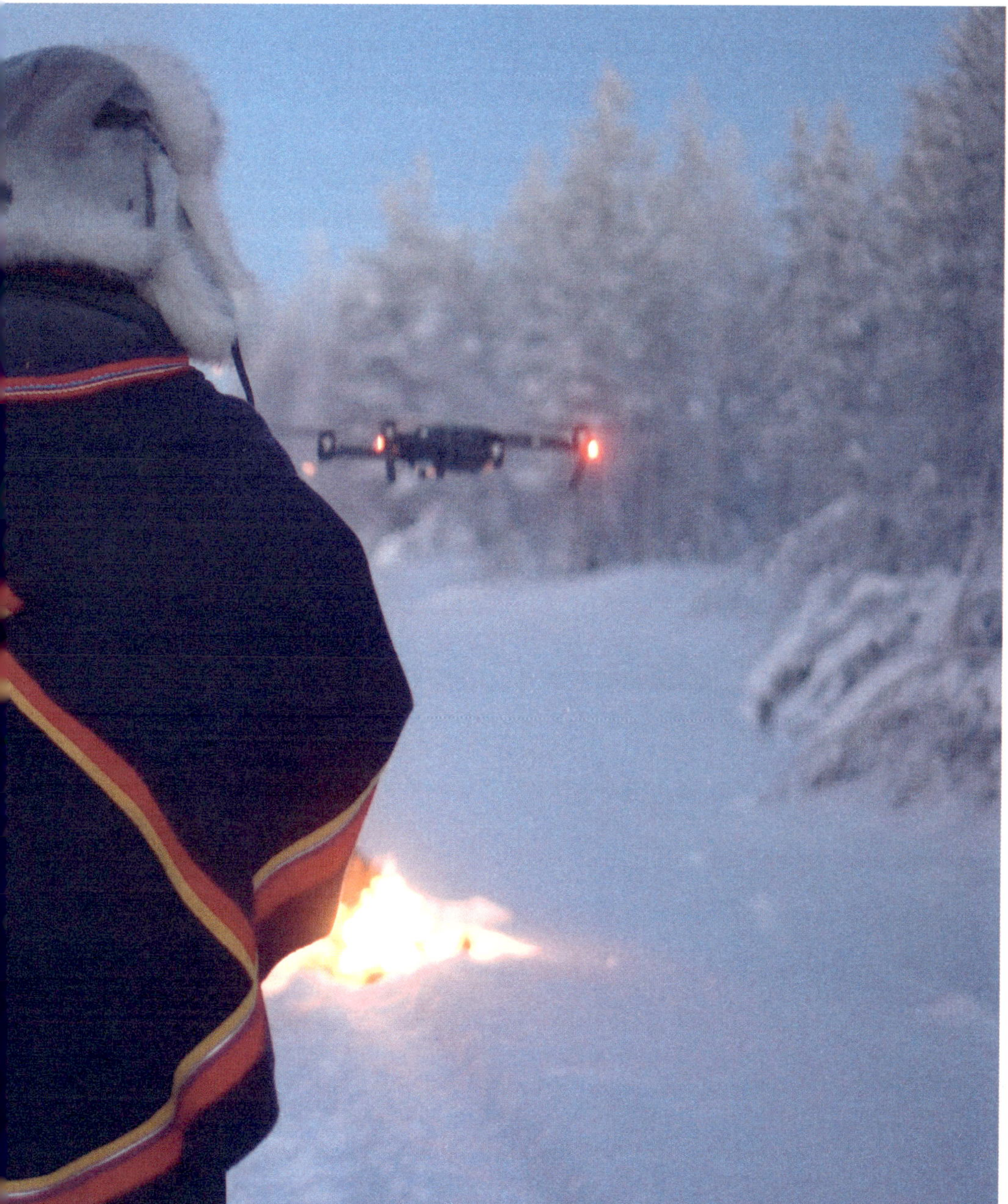

denied visas. A denial that explicitly demonstrated the barriers, boundaries, and bureaucratic opacity of who is allowed to travel and who is not.

SB Looking at our three projects, they clearly share a political agenda of addressing urgent questions of the contemporary moment through art. Yet they do so—maybe to different degrees—against the backdrop of histories. I am thinking in particular of the history of photography, colonialism, and visual sovereignty. In what ways would you say your respective approaches were informed by the archives of art history, visual culture, and the emergence of new media?

LW "WATCHED!" was certainly informed by a double approach. On the one hand, the history of photography as a medium of scientific and social identification, registration, mapping, recording, exposure, etc., including of course the rich history of artists and photographers applying the medium across the whole spectrum, from voyeurism to countersurveillance. Being situated at the Hasselblad Foundation, conducting critical research on the view from above, I also felt the need to emphasize that a predecessor of the acclaimed Hasselblad cameras used in Nasa's Apollo missions was in fact a military reconnaissance camera, the HK7, which only emphasizes how territorial overviews are militarily motivated. One of the artists included in the book, Susanne Kriemann, used a Hasselblad aerial camera from 1942 in her work *One Time One Million (Migratory Birds/Romantic Capitalism)* (2009), to construct a supervisory and visionary view from a bird's-eye perspective on the "Million Program," in which millions of homes were built in the suburbs of Stockholm, Sweden, between 1964 and 1974. Initially seen as progressive, the high-rise concrete blocks later became symbols of segregation and ghetto formation, with a majority of residents marginalized with limited economic resources and immigrant backgrounds. Kriemann's use of "migratory birds" in her title refers not only to the book *Flyttfagelstrak* (The Flight of Migratory Birds), which Victor Hasselblad wrote in 1935,[11] but also to migration as a sociopolitical phenomenon.

On the other hand, the research project and many of the included artworks reflected current developments in surveillance technologies and practices, through, for instance, automated imagery and everyday use of

digital media for tracking and networking. Some artists, such as Hasan Elahi and Alberto Frigo, apply mobile sousveillance and self-tracking technologies to an extreme degree. Elahi's long-term project *Tracking Transience* (2002-) was conceived as a smoke screen response to authorities surveilling him due to unjust racial profiling, and it consists of an overwhelming amount of image and coordination data tracing the (alleged) location of the constantly traveling artist. Frigo follows
Fig. 8 ← the tradition of artists and activists constructing and using wearable cameras, in a project beginning in 2004 and ending in 2040, where he—among several other means of self-documentation—has committed to photograph everything he touches with his right hand. Others, such as Heather Dewey-Hagborg and Zach Blas, engage critically with questions of biometrics, facial recognition technology, and bio-surveillance. Based on the traces of genetic material that strangers unwittingly leave behind in public places, Dewey-Hagborg sculpts portraits by applying analyses and developing technologies of forensic DNA phenotyping—a technology embedded in structural racial bias. Blas's *Facial Weaponization Suite* (2011-2014) consists of community-produced masks that protect against biometric facial recognition. The automated view from above—for instance, through satellites—is being addressed by artists such as James Bridle and Mishka Henner. In his essay for the book, Bridle reminds us that "when discussing [satellite and other data-gathering processes], we often fall back onto the language of photography to describe it, speaking in terms of pictures and images, and to anthropocentric concepts of the eye and vision in order to understand it. But this language is both reductive and deleterious."[12] Instead, elements such as extreme resolution, absence of certain light frequencies, and a planetary timescale force us to rethink how satellites "see."

SB I am glad that you're bringing up the issue of language, or rather, the issue of finding an appropriate terminology for what it is we are dealing with in the digital present. In the case of drones, there is a surprising amount of anthropomorphic vocabulary. It is probably most notorious in the phrasing "the drone sees." Have you found any fitting or intriguing alternatives while doing your research on surveillance and art? What role do artworks play in finding this new vocabulary? Do they mainly point to the deficit in the metaphors that are being implied, or do they actively seek out new ones?

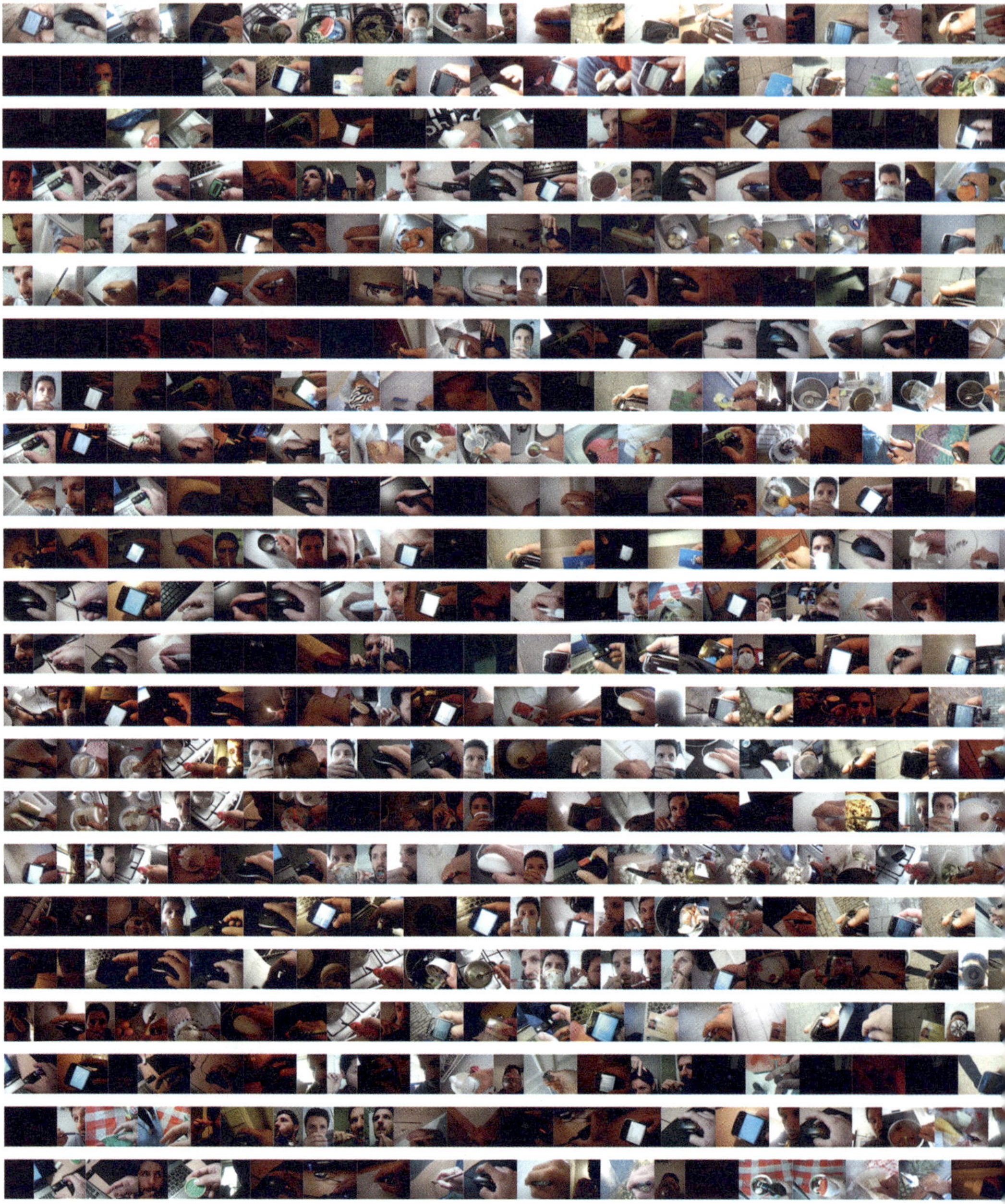

Fig. 8 Alberto Frigo, detail of *Images of the Artefacts Used by the Main Hand* (2004-), from the project *2004-2040*. Month panel 117 (90×30 cm).

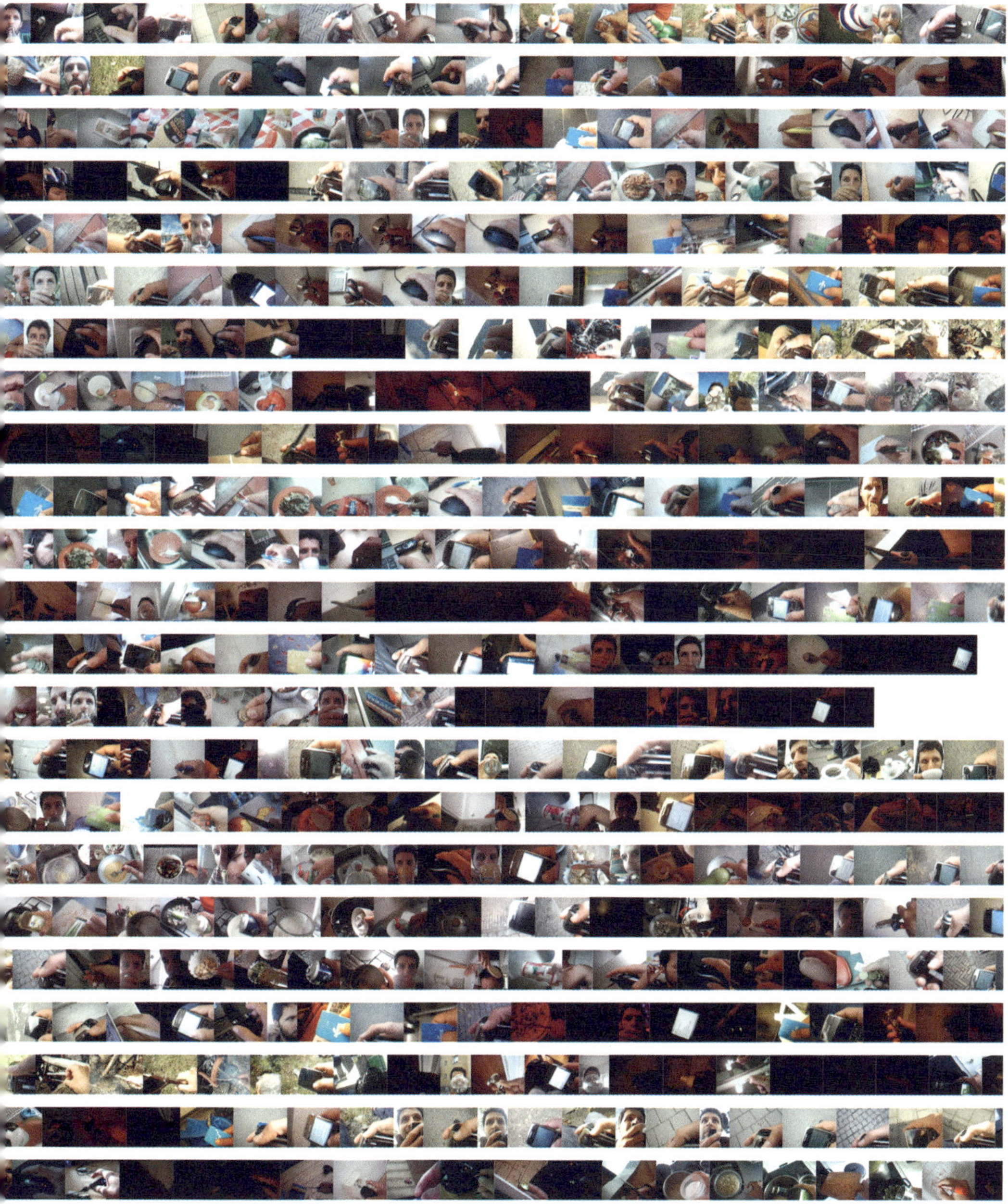

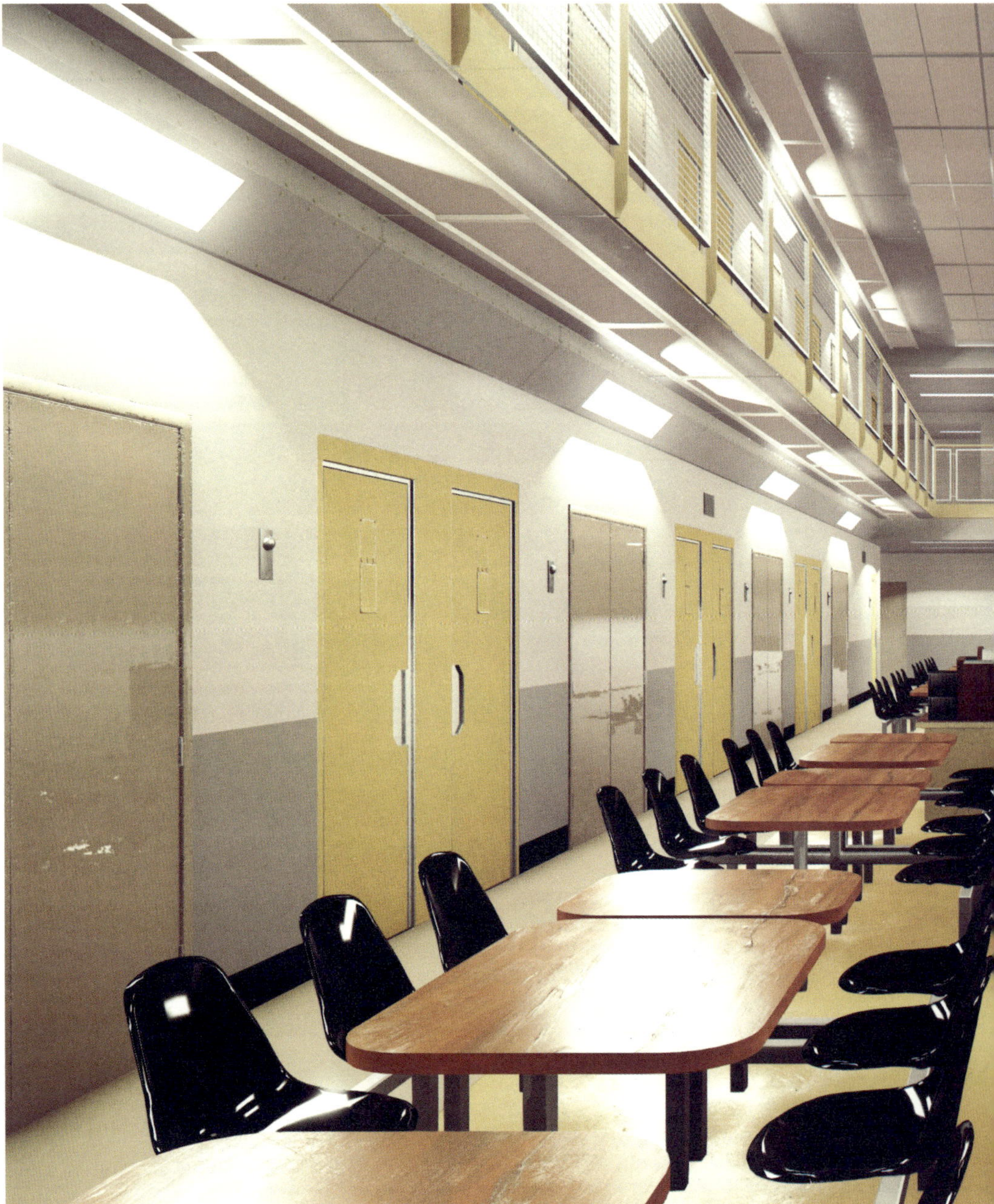

Fig. 9 Still from James Bridle, *Seamless Transitions*, 2015. Animation by Picture Plane.

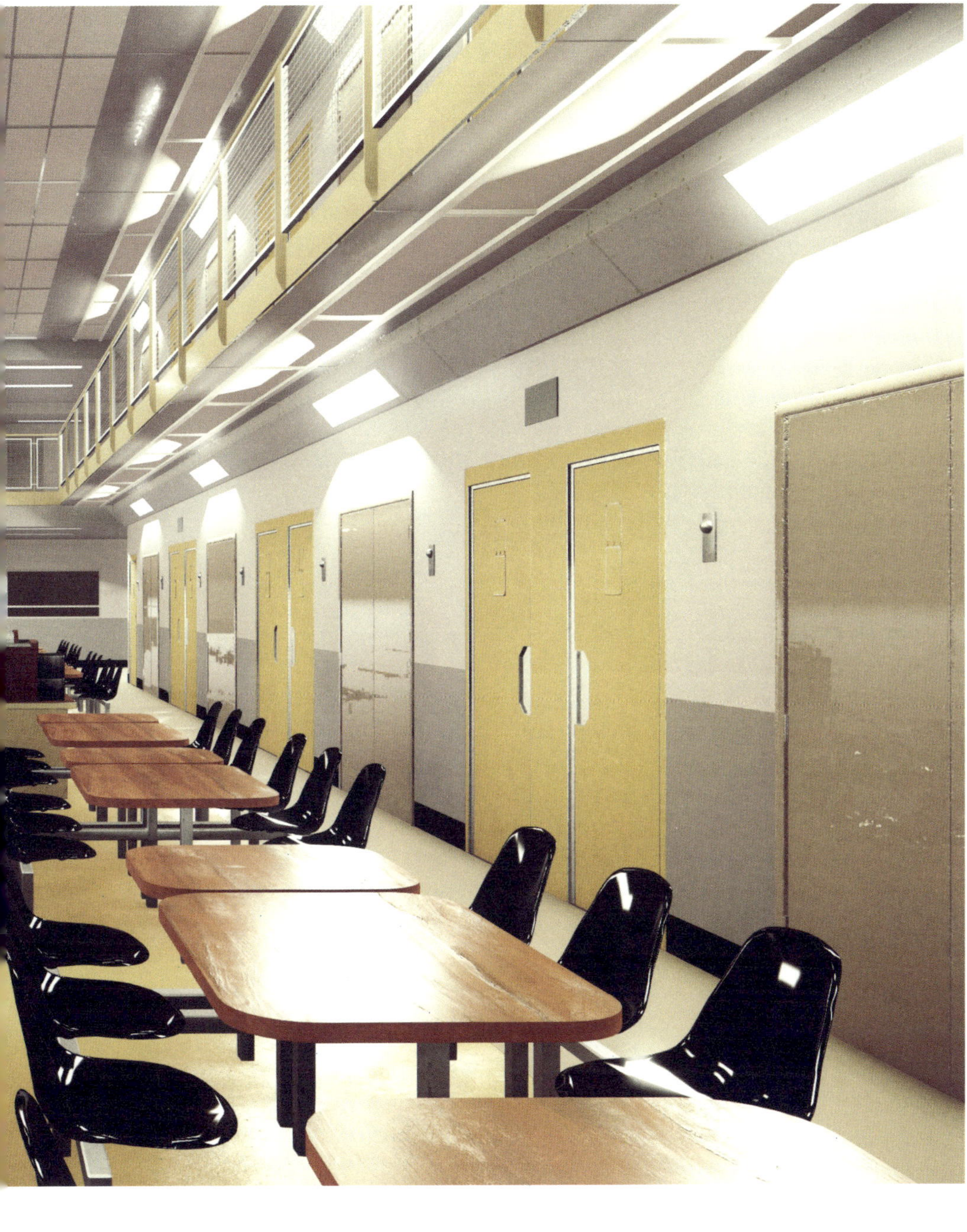

LW Multidisciplinary artists and thinkers such as Hito Steyerl, Harun Farocki, and James Bridle play a significant role in questioning—in both written and visual works—the vocabulary through which we conceive of the new technologies, images, and aesthetics. Bridle, for instance, chose the title "Apophenia" for a solo exhibition he did at Galleri Image (in conjunction with "WATCHED!" being shown at Kunsthal Aarhus in 2016).[13] "Apophenia" a psychiatric term describing the human tendency to perceive meaningful patterns within random data. In terms of alternatives to "seeing" the world from above, a scholar such as Nicholas Mirzoeff convincingly differentiates between "seeing" as a bodily sensory system and "visualizing" as an airborne technology to depict the world as an imperial and colonial space for war, for instance through photomaps and drones.[14] Another useful concept for grasping the discriminatory structure of the social surveillance assemblage from an intersectional perspective is Simone Browne's notion of racializing surveillance.[15] This describes technologies of social control in the form of practices, policies, and performances that produce norms pertaining to mechanisms of racial exclusion. → Fig. 9

ST For the most part, it seems that cyberspace gravitates to surveillance, from data-gathering to monitoring, rather than direct obstruction, insofar as cyberspace is operationalized as transnational, whereas physical space is bordered and any transgression of it is followed by indefinite incarceration. The problem of the tendency to anthropomorphize the drone is that it obscures the actual economic and political calculations of whose lives count and whose lives are grievable.

The personnel in Nevada drive home at the end of their shift, and while there may be psychological effects—as suggested by the depiction of a drone pilot in Omer Fast's video *5,000 Feet Is the Best* (2011)—there is nevertheless the assurance that the drone pilot will not be a war fatality, unlike the subcontractors, the mercenaries increasingly hired by the United States through private military companies in conflict zones. Not only is democratic accountability circumvented, since private military companies do not report to US Congress, but it also graphically demonstrates Judith Butler's differential distribution of precariousness and grievability in *Frames of War* (2009) regarding "whose lives are regarded as lives worth saving and defending, and whose are not."[16] As such, the claim that the "drone sees" makes invisible the material reality of war and surveillance, and the representational regimes from which it operates and that rationalize its operation. There is a link between Sweden's refusal of visas to the artists Salman Khan, Sajid Khan, and Wajahat Saeed and the US drone strikes on the FATA region—a linkage between the representational regime of drone strikes, which marks areas and people as "terror suspects," and the actions of the Swedish embassy as a proxy for the US drone pilot that repeats the perspective of suspicion, rejecting any other outcome. An alliance that suggests the integration of the algorithm with the human, the algorithm with the US drone pilot, and the algorithm with the Swedish embassy worker.

SB What you are describing clearly has to do with concepts such as political recognition and citizenship, which in the digital age of data mining are translated into the differentiation between signal and noise. As such, they are an essential part of pattern recognition in drone warfare, and also in surveillance. Louise, you mentioned the works of Hasan Elahi and Alberto Frigo, who, like others in your exhibition, not only work with self-tracking but also utilize vast collections of images and data for their works. How would you say phenomena such as big data are changing the idea of the archive and its potential representations—as artworks or otherwise?

LW Well, since the grand-scale projects by Elahi and Frigo are based on the continuous collection of data, their resulting archives are presented as dynamic online platforms.[17] And yes, this reflects how rather than conceiving of the archive as a static, privileged site of authoritarian knowledge and power, the machinic collecting of big data dramatically alters concepts of archival time and space. As network and cloud, "the archive" in principle works everywhere and all the time. However, the networked archive of stored everyday surveillance of course does not mean total transparency, or that the archived information is accessible to everybody and at any time-works such as those by Elahi and Frigo also point to the potentially antidemocratic use of private data in what Shoshana Zuboff has defined as the era of surveillance capitalism.[18] Similarly, certain events, subjects, and bodies are omitted from the archive—that is, censored or deliberately unseen—because they are perceived as unwanted, like, for instance, covert military actions, or victims of warfare and economic exploitation.

So if we want to try to understand how automated data-collecting and algorithmic information-sharing affect knowledge production and ultimately "truth," it is more urgent than ever to engage in critical investigations of "the archive," and here artists and activists continue to offer vital confrontations with and reimaginings of archival practice, where digitized data is represented along with embodied encounters and knowledge in order to make visible without exposing.

An important open archive of citizen journalism that I think we've all been referencing in our work is Lara Baladi's *Vox Populi: Archiving a Revolution in the Digital Age* (2011-), which offers counterimages to authoritarian surveillance and mainstream reporting of the revolution sparked by the 2011 protests around Tahrir Square in Cairo. Another prominent example of artistic and activist archiving of otherwise hidden or overseen data on contemporary warfare is Forensic Architecture, who gather information from multiple sources and media in order to create evidential image complexes of events such as drone strikes. This kind of forensic aesthetics is increasingly urgent in the current media climate of post-truth and alternative facts.

SB Yes, I agree. The work of Forensic Architecture is incredibly powerful and no doubt important. Their investigations into drone strikes (mainly in the FATA) have created archives that give visibility to drone strikes and thereby counter deniability. Also, testing different approaches and pointing to the pitfalls of the media available for counter-forensic approaches (such as satellite images that are calibrated at a resolution to hide both the human body and the impact of a drone's missile) is central to understanding how this technology works.[19] Nevertheless, I am struck by the surprising ease with which potentially positivist notions such as evidence have reentered critical debate, and I wonder how we can uphold a very clear stance against what you call the media climate of post-truth and alternative facts while also holding on to methods and experiences of uncertainty, double vision, and looking askew. What do you think?

ST I think you raise a crucial point, and insofar as the tension between a positivist notion of "evidence" and the desire to allow for uncertainty is conceived as an either/or argument, there is a failure to grasp what is at stake. If this tension is reconceptualized in terms of the priority of political interpretation, whereby a political perspective is not seen as some supplementary method but, as Fredric Jameson suggests in *The Political Unconscious* (1981), is "the absolute horizon of all reading and all interpretation,"[20] it becomes more a question of what constitutes a critical practice that is adequate to the conditions of contemporary life.

Donna Haraway, in her essay from 1988 "Situated Knowledges: The Science Question in Feminism and the Privilege of Partial Perspective," critiques the "god trick of seeing everywhere from nowhere"[21] and provides a useful reminder that the all-seeing, disembodied hidden eye naturalizes a partial perspective as a universal or total perspective. In this, Haraway's essay is not only prescient when read in the context of drone technology and algorithmic governmentality; in its emphasis on the determinate ideological parameters of a specific time and place, it is also a retrieval of human agency. Unlike the purposive narrative of "post-truth," which is to make the world unintelligible by denying any framework for understanding and interpretation, and in so doing to mask the question of power.

LW I agree that the notion of situated knowledge is seminal for what we're discussing, which in turn points to how one approaches the documentary genre, the medium of photography, as well as to how artistic practice and methodology can insert ambiguity into the understanding of surveillance and countersurveillance. Our three projects include works that are "looking askew" at authoritarian truth claims and the scientific "god trick," and which thus maintain skepticism toward the evidential through parody, mimicry, metaphor, appropriation, and paraphrase, while exposing misuses of power and proposing other modes of visibility. Eyal Weizman, for instance, emphasizes "forensis" as a methodology: "'a critical forensic practice' that includes both the production of evidence and the querying of the practices of evidence making."[22] This dynamic is ensured through the careful visual orchestration of a range of sources. Similarly, when working from an expanded notion of documentary photography, it is possible both to make evident the situatedness and to reach beyond the boundaries of the totalizing, single-authored statement. Here I am thinking of collaborative or multimedia projects, such as for instance Tina Enghoff's *Migrant Documents* (2011-2013) which comprises seven different ways of visualizing a group of Copenhagen-based migrants who are undocumented (and thus also deprived of legal and human rights), without exposing their identities. Some of her strategies include mimicry of—or to use your concept, Svea, "looking askew at"—various surveillance technologies as an indication of how the state monitors and governs its citizens and noncitizens. For me, Enghoff's practice strives to establish a civil space formulated and shared by photographer, photographed, and users, in opposition to the governing power—as Ariella Azoulay has notably defined it in her book *The Civil Contract of Photography* (2008).[23]

An effect of the increasing awareness of everyday surveillance or multiveillance is an insistence on the right to privacy and thus an unwillingness to be photographed, which John Roberts, among others, has problematized.[24] Because, how can urban signs of social injustice be documented? It is typically privileged citizens who are in a position to successfully claim privacy rights and take control in negotiations of voluntary and involuntary visibility. What are the available tools for the politically engaged photographer and visual artist?

> ST The remark on the desire to not be visible reminds me of the work of Lawrence Abu Hamdan, who traces how the right to silence as an inaugural moment of being placed in custody is withdrawn from asylum seekers in a bureaucratization of the voice that makes vowels and consonants legally accountable. Subjected to an "accent test" on the phone, an undocumented migrant's voice is submitted to a tribunal court to attest to a claim of country of origin that denies the lived contexts of migrant experiences.
>
> It therefore raises the question of the political effects of listening, of the voice and the earwitness, as a corollary of the political effects of seeing, of visibility and the eyewitness. I am curious about how listening factored in the curatorial choices for "WATCHED!" and "To See Without Being Seen," not least in terms of drone acoustics and sonic violence?

LW In "WATCHED!" sonic violence can only be said to have figured symbolically, as an underlying threat due to audio surveillance or the act of listening in. For instance, Meriç Algün Ringborg's *Which No One Will Ever See* (2012) referenced the spying and paranoia in Francis Ford Coppola's 1974 film *The Conversation*. The C/O Berlin version of the exhibition included Florian Mehnert's *Forestprotocols* (2013), an installation of twenty-two headphones hanging from the ceiling with recordings of anonymous conversations in forests. Sites of private leisure were thus turned "unsafe" by the eavesdropping artist, while also referencing both historical and present-day political ideals of the total transparency of security measures.

SB In the case of "To See Without Being Seen," we did not have any works that explored the sonic dimension of drone warfare. It is a crucial element, however, as studies such as "Living Under Drones" have shown that it is the constant humming of the drone that is experienced as the most harrowing.[25] It is the sound of the drone that transports the potentiality of the threat and thereby has a terrorizing and traumatizing effect. Also, no matter how important the visual element is, one should consider the drone as a sensing machine that not only works through various sensors but also affects all senses.

ST Through the research of artist Behjat Omer Abdulla for the exhibition at the Hasselblad Center, I became more acutely aware of the effects of drone acoustics. Behjat worked with a victim of an aerial bombardment in Daraa, Syria, who now lives in the largest asylum center in Sweden, Restad Gard, an hour from Gothenburg. Part of the terror of drone warfare is the sound of the drone. To use this sound in the three exhibitions would have replayed the sonic violence of drone warfare, and to do so would raise ethical considerations in terms of its effects on victims and survivors. From the artist's research at Restad Gard, what became apparent was how in fleeing the violence of aerial bombardment, civilians used drones to map routes to safety—so there is this use of the view from above as both a sight line to safety and military surveillance and targeting. It seems important to hold these two uses, this doubling of to see and not be seen, as a resource and threat, whereby civilians, in co-opting the view from above, are able to map routes in an effort to survive the violence. This is not in order to blunt arguments against drone warfare, but instead to understand the subversive potential of civilian use that retools a view from above in support of protest on the ground, and is therefore an important consideration in how the drone is understood and how war is archived.

LW Are there specific artistic methodologies that you would mention as examples of nuanced navigations between visible evidence and uncertainty, or between documenting the social world and caring for the integrity of precarious subjects?

SB First of all, I find it interesting and important to point out that throughout our conversation, questions of flight and migration, as well as the connected issues of border enforcements and population control, have come up time and again. Certainly, this has to do with drones not only being used to monitor borders but also having the effect of reducing human bodies to figures that barely register as human but are turned into numbers, patterns, or schematics. Earlier Sarah indicated this when mentioning that there is a link between the denial of visas—and hence the restriction of movement—and the targeting of people in certain frontier regions of the world, such as the FATA. I believe this is a point worth repeating, and you, Louise, have in a way already provided an artistic reflection on it by mentioning works that are bound up with issues of surveillance, biopolitics, migration, citizenship, and imaging technologies.

Second, I find the question of privacy and the visibility/invisibility divide interesting, because one can make the argument that, contrary to older forms of identity politics, the political agenda may no longer be so concerned with making visible and crafting specific images, but instead one should strive to become invisible and go unseen in order to be safe. However, this also makes (political) recognition difficult if not impossible, and it hinders the exchange of looks that is so pivotal to building relations. Plus, being invisible can significantly contribute to the denial of violence and its unleashing in wars that are often clandestine already. Yet I also realize that by arguing in this way, I am stuck in a similar binary, this time of the seen/unseen, which Sarah pointed out earlier in regard to the pitching of evidence and uncertainty against each other.

And this brings me to your question—which I guess also taps into the idea about the archives we work and think with. For me, the writings of Hito Steyerl about documentary uncertainty are still very important for thinking about the dynamic between realism, documents, and uncertainty.[26] Also, I find Trevor Paglen's approach to extremely detailed research into the US military's secret installations and infrastructures intriguing. He presents them as blurry photographs in which atmospheric conditions factor in a way that not only makes vision uncertain, but also opens up the realm of imagination due to their low definition. Yet, as I said before, I am also concerned by the imbalance of art being shown in the context of drones, because it reflects a predominantly European and North American view, which I am quite aware is also present in my answers here, because they are based on what I know and am aware of. Sarah's curatorial approach of working with partners in Cyprus and Pakistan was really important in its attempt to counter that imbalance of a predominantly Western view.

LW Returning, then, to the notion of the (w)archive, what are your thoughts on the archival meaning and effects of drone vision and imagery?

SB Although the drone is often described as a vision machine, it is actually far more of an archiving machine—that is, one of its main functions is the collection and transmission of vast amounts of data, not all of which is visual. This data is stored for later analysis and legal backing, but contrary to earlier wars—such as the Gulf War in 1990-1991, when images from the heads of cruise missiles were shown on television—it is not made public. Most of the combat footage we know was leaked and/or redacted. Due to this situation, there is quite a lot of speculation about the image quality that analysts and crews actually see on their screens. Furthermore, and in my opinion even more importantly, a dual situation of invisibility is produced. For not only is there a lack in images, but the classic category of the image also no longer holds. Drone images are operational images, and as such, they are invisible, contain central parts that are invisible, and/or are (almost) unintelligible. Trevor Paglen has spoken of an "invisible visual culture" of machine vision, and I find that a very apt phrase.[27] However much the drone may be about seeing or imaging, it may thus constitute an archive that is (at least partly) invisible and unintelligible.

Ways to address this archive can be manifold. For me, they mainly have to do with the archives we draw on in an attempt to make sense of the drone. One of these archives is art history. It comes into play, for instance, in the way Paglen references landscape photography of the American West, or color-field painting. Another example is the shadowy figures in Tomas van Houtryve's photographs, which simultaneously make me think of Weimar-era New Vision and Alberto Giacometti's ephemeral stick figures. These works, though, are very much about the military drone, and I wonder if we have to include commercial drones in the (w)archive in order to get a complete picture and attempt to understand what is going on or not?

LW Yes, and the references to art and photographic history also ensure a critical distance from an evidential positivism or a "looking askew" at conventional visuality paradigms. In the field of art probing issues of surveillance, we often see more explicit references to the history of photography as overview, classification, and control. One astute example is *Watchtowers* (2008), exiled Palestinian artist Taysir Batniji's photographic series of Israeli military watchtowers, which is inspired by Bernd and Hilla Becher's iconic typological inventory of European water towers. Some artists paraphrase the historical format of bertillonage (mug shots) to point to present-day criminalization, for instance of sexual minorities (in Charlotte Haslund-Christensen's *Who's Next*, 2013). Other artistic strategies are of course the employment of surveillance or spying technologies or aesthetics (Sophie Calle, Ann-Sofi Sidén), resulting in slightly grainy, blurry, and evocative imagery that precisely leaves room for doubt or double vision.

ST I think it is important to note how the drone distills a number of histories—technological, photographic, and military—which cannot be so readily disentangled. For the "Drone Vision" exhibition in Nicosia, Stelios Kallinikou took photographs from castles built between the late eleventh and early twelfth centuries in the Kyrenia Mountains, namely Kantara Castle, Buffavento Castle, and St. Hilarion Castle. Alongside this the artist documented the Royal Air Force station located in the Troodos Mountains, which, as the information leaked by Edward Snowden indicated, is a key military base for the interception of radio signals from the Middle East.

Thus, I would suggest that Paglen's "invisible visible culture" implicates the double aspect of the drone: the drone as infrastructure and motile camera, which renders the functional role of a castle or a watchtower symbolic. Moreover, in the temporal and spatial reach of the drone a different type of mapping is produced, one that intimately connects to the intensified, vertically layered reality of society that Stephen Graham describes in *Vertical: The City from Satellites to Bunkers* (2016) in which the rubric of "smart cities" overlaps with systemic data accumulation as a new genus of "surveillance capitalism."[28]

How then can we effectively disrupt the diffusion of image as data, and the cybernetic fantasies of the smart city, to expose the political economy of anticipatory securitization? Paglen powerfully exposes the installations, and as Svea indicates, he makes explicit the infrastructure, the new military urbanism of real-time data management and video analytics, while acknowledging the limits of "making visible" and the inescapably politico-ethical response to this opacity.

It does seem that artists are increasingly drawn toward a form of documentary, of forensis as methodology in order to counter the obfuscatory rhetorics of "post-truth," in part because surveillance and visualization are iterative processes in the production of fear and control. In this rethinking of the documentary form, notwithstanding the attendant problematics of the genre, Forensic Architecture have developed a pedagogic practice of critique and possibility, which revitalizes individual and collective responsibility and agency.

SB So how would you position your curatorial practice in regard to the archive as a practice, a mode of thinking and/or presentation? Would you say there is an archival impulse in your take on what the editors of this volume have dubbed the (w)archive?[29] And in what ways are we as curators and critics actively involved in shaping the archive and its various visibilities and invisibilities?

LW In terms of producing "alternative" knowledge by collecting traces left out of the official archives, you could say that an archival impulse is at play in several of the artistic approaches to the (w)archive. But what I find most intriguing in many of the works and artists in our projects is that they—in light of big data, digitalization, and new archiving machines' altered notions of visibility, temporality, and spatiality—point to the need for a critical rethinking of the conventional archive. What, where, and when is the (w)archive? My own curatorial practice had already been shaped by working in particular with queer art that criticizes and defies authoritarian, historical archives through virtuality, anachronicity, simultaneity, affect, and ephemerality—for instance, in the exhibition project "Lost and Found: Queerying the Archive."[30] The necessity of challenging the modes and ideologies of archiving is pressing not only in relation to the historical and political representation of queer bodies, colonized subjects, and racial and religious minorities, but also in relation to online presence and future archives in an increasingly multiveillant reality. As personally sensitive data is being shared, collected, and stored to an unfathomable degree, minority groups especially are vulnerable to exposure. Not only through leaks and deliberate misuse, but also authoritarian information exchanges, for instance at health care centers and border controls.

This brings me to the ethics of (re)presentation, which is also a matter we as curators need to constantly be aware of since we, as you suggest, are actively involved in shaping the archive by exhibiting, making public, and generating discussions. We are researching surveillance and (w)archive imagery, which is also appropriated by many of the artists we are working with. How—if at all—should we present such material? I am currently working on the conceptualization of an exhibition of photography from the interwar period, when the technical and scientific potentials of the medium were celebrated and employed in the establishment of new archives, from aerial surveys to criminal and biological typologies. Needless to say, the latter category was mostly taken without the subjects' consent and appeared in fascist and racist contexts. What potential contexts could allow critical displays and discussions of such imagery today, where their highly problematic historical use could teach us something about, for instance, current nonconsensual profiling, image circulation, and archiving? Working with the often sensitive and potentially harmful material that we do comes with a significant responsibility.

ST For me it was really important to commission new work, to activate research through a commissioning process that emphasized the geopolitics of place in order to grasp how the drone is understood across the subject fields of surveillance, warfare, and protest. Given that these questions are connected to the increasing datafication of society, there is therefore an attendant need to conceptualize a sociotechnical theory and practice of political agency. An emphasis that prompts careful consideration of the question of data, since it is as much an operational aspect of contemporary drone warfare as it is an operational aspect of the expansion of contingent labor, of the on-demand and gig economy managed through platform intermediaries.

The question of how curators and institutions might evolve to meet the challenge of the various visibilities/invisibilities cannot be separated from an engagement with the processes of datafication. This requires both an analytical and critical approach to emerging algorithmic governmentality and the corresponding uses of the power asymmetries of visibility/invisibility. One method whereby this might be realized is by thinking across vertical as well as horizontal geographies of power, and alongside this to critically examine the new emergent forms of visuality. As Hito Steyerl speculates in her 2011 essay "In Free Fall: A Thought Experiment in Vertical Perspective," the multiplication and de-linearization of horizons might produce "new tools of vision" which "serve to express, and even alter, the contemporary conditions of disruption and disorientation."[31] Steyerl provocatively suggests a positive consequence to the de-linearization of horizons, in which the vertiginous—in an echo of Theodor Adorno's description of vertigo[32]—produces a truth-telling.

This then seems to have a productive relationship with a broader decolonial project, in which the geographies and politics of simultaneity undermine and expose colonialist practice and thought. The curatorial choice to produce three exhibitions for "Drone Vision," with each exhibition presenting affective meanings and uses of drone technology pertinent to the specific geopolitics of Pakistan, Sweden, Cyprus, and regionally of South Asia, Scandinavia, and the Mediterranean, was such an effort, not only to link vertical geographies of place, politics, and image, but also to understand what insights, which otherwise might be lost in a more global analytic frame, emerge from emplacing arts research—or, as Louise succinctly expressed it, the what, where, and when of (w)archives—and to understand this as an politico-ethical response to our vertiginous times.

1. "To See Without Being Seen: Contemporary Art and Drone Warfare," Mildred Lane Kemper Art Museum at Washington University in St. Louis, USA, January 29-April 24, 2016; Svea Braeunert and Meredith Malone, *To See Without Being Seen: Contemporary Art and Drone Warfare* (Chicago: University of Chicago Press, 2016). "WATCHED! Surveillance, Art and Photography," Hasselblad Center, Gothenburg, Sweden, May 29-October 2, 2016, Kunsthal Aarhus, Denmark, October 14-December 31, 2016 (in collaboration with Galleri Image, Denmark, showing James Bridle, "Apophenia"), and C/O Berlin, Germany, February 17-May 21, 2017; Louise Wolthers, Niclas Östlind, and Dragana Vujanovic, eds., *WATCHED! Surveillance, Art and Photography* (Cologne: Verlag der Buchhandlung Walther König, 2016). "Drone Vision: Warfare, Surveillance, Protest," Hasselblad Center, Gothenburg, Sweden, Nicosia Municipal Arts Center in association with the Pierides Foundation, Cyprus, and Zahoor Ul Akhlaq Gallery, National College of Arts in Lahore, Pakistan, May 18-September 16, 2018.

2. We later reflected on our collaborative process in Svea Braeunert and Meredith Malone, "To See Without Being Seen: Critical Concepts and Curatorial Approaches Informing the Exhibition on Contemporary Art, Drones, and Surveillance," *Media-N: The Journal of the New Media Caucus* 13, no. 1 (2019): 39-56.

3. Grégoire Chamayou, *A Theory of the Drone*, trans. Janet Lloyd (New York: New Press, 2015); Byung-Chul Han, "Die Ethik des Drohnenkriegs," *Matthes & Seitz Berlin*, February 12, 2013, http://www.matthes-seitz-berlin.de/artikel/byung-chul-han-die-ethik-des-drohnenkriegs.html.

4. Kevin D. Haggerty, "Tear Down the Walls: On Demolishing the Panopticon," in *Theorizing Surveillance: The Panopticon and Beyond*, ed. David Lyon (New York: Routledge, 2006), 29.

5. Ibid., 39.

6. Dan Gettinger and Arthur Holland also raised this question (albeit from a slightly different point of view) in their presentation "Drone Art: What It Means, Why It Matters, and Where It's Going" at the conference "Drone Imaginaries and Society," University of Southern Denmark, Odense, June 2018.

7. These exhibitions included but were not limited to: "Heaven and Hell: From Magic Carpets to Drones," Foundation Boghossian, Brussels, Belgium, 2015; "Decolonized Skies," Apexart, New York, USA, 2014; "A Screaming Comes Across the Sky: Drones, Mass Surveillance and Invisible Wars," Laboral Centro de Arte y Creación Industrial, Gijón, Spain, 2014; "Visibility Machines: Harun Farocki and Trevor Paglen," Center for Art, Design, and Visual Culture, University of Maryland, Baltimore, USA, 2013; "Game of Drones: Von unbemannten Flugobjekten," Zeppelin Museum, Friedrichshafen, Germany, 2019.

8. Caren Kaplan, "Drone-O-Rama: Troubling the Temporal and Spatial Logics of Distance Warfare," in *Life in the Age of Drone Warfare*, ed. Lisa Parks and Caren Kaplan (Durham, NC: Duke University Press, 2017), 161-77.

9. Hito Steyerl, "A Sea of Data: Apophenia and Pattern (Mis-)Recognition," *e-flux Journal*, no. 72 (2006), http://www.e-flux.com/journal/72/60480/a-sea-of-data-apophenia-and-pattern-mis-recognition. The report by the *Intercept* is Cora Currier and Henrik Moltke, "Spies in the Sky: Israeli Drone Feeds Hacked by British and American Intelligence," *Intercept*, January 29, 2016, https://theintercept.com/2016/01/28/israeli-drone-feeds-hacked-by-british-and-american-intelligence.

10. Justine Smith, "Ouroboros and the Cycle of Violence: An Interview with Basma Alsharif," *Senses of Cinema*, no. 85 (December 2017), http://sensesofcinema.com/2017/feature-articles/basma-alsharif-interview/.

11. Victor Hasselblad, *Flyttfagelstrak* (Stockholm: Bonniers, 1935). Hasselblad's interest in photography stemmed from his early passion for ornithology and the desire to develop better cameras for photographing birds.

12. James Bridle, "The Machinic Sensorium," in *WATCHED!*, 244.

13. James Bridle, "Apophenia," Galleri Image, Aarhus, Denmark, 2016, http://www.galleriimage.dk/index.php/dk/2016/882-apophenia.

14. Nicholas Mirzoeff, *The Right to Look: A Counterhistory of Visuality* (Durham, NC: Duke University Press, 2011).

15. Simone Browne, *Dark Matters: On the Surveillance of Blackness* (Durham, NC: Duke University Press, 2015).

16. Judith Butler, *Frames of War: When Is Life Grievable?* (New York: Verso, 2009), 16.

17. For Hasan Elahi's *Tracking Transience*, see http://elahi.umd.edu/track/; for Alberto Frigo's *2004-2040*, see http://2004-2040.com/.

18. Shoshana Zuboff, *The Age Surveillance Capitalism: The Fight for a Human Future at the New Frontier of Power* (London: Profile Books, 2019).

19. See the section "Secrets" in *Forensis: The Architecture of Public Truth*, ed. Forensic Architecture (Berlin: Sternberg Press, 2014), 361-482; Eyal Weizman, *Forensic Architecture: Violence at the Threshold of Detectability* (New York: Zone Books, 2017).

20. Frederic Jameson, *The Political Unconscious: Narrative as a Socially Symbolic Act* (Ithaca, NY: Cornell University Press, 1981), 17.

21. Donna Haraway, "Situated Knowledges: The Science Question in Feminism and the Privilege of Partial Perspective," *Feminist Studies* 14, no. 3 (autumn 1988): 581.

22. Quoted from Eyal Weizman, "Notes of Forensis," in *Images of Conviction: The Construction of Visual Evidence* (Paris: Xavier Barrel, 2015), 234.

23. Ariella Azoulay, *The Civil Contract of Photography* (New York: Zone Books, 2008).

24. John Roberts, *Photography and Its Violations* (New York: Columbia University Press, 2014).

25. *Living under Drones: Death, Injury and Trauma to Civilians from US Drone Practices in Pakistan* (Stanford, CA: International Human Rights and Conflict Resolution Clinic, Stanford Law School, 2012), https://law.stanford.edu/projects/living-under-drones/.

26. Hito Steyerl, *Die Farbe der Wahrheit: Dokumentarismen im Kunstfeld* (Vienna: Turia + Kant, 2015).

27. Trevor Paglen, "Invisible Images (Your Pictures Are Looking at You)," *New Inquiry*, December 8, 2016, https://thenewinquiry.com/invisible-images-your-pictures-are-looking-at-you/.

28. Stephen Graham, *Vertical: The City from Satellites to Bunkers* (London: Verso, 2016).

29. On the notion of the archival impulse, see Hal Foster, "An Archival Impulse," *October*, no. 110 (Fall 2004): 3-22.

30. Mathias Danbolt, Jane Rowley, and Louise Wolthers, eds., *Lost and Found: Queerying the Archive* (Copenhagen: Nikolaj Contemporary Art Center, 2009).

31. Hito Steyerl, "In Free Fall: A Thought Experiment in Vertical Perspective," *e-flux Journal*, no. 24 (April 2011), https://www.e-flux.com/journal/24/67860/in-free-fall-a-thought-experiment-on-vertical-perspective/#_ftn13.

32. Theodor W. Adorno, *Negative Dialectics*, trans. E. B. Ashton (New York: Continuum, 1981), 33.

C SENSING WAR
Technologies, Intimacies, and Bodies

CRUEL INTIMACIES
Daniela Agostinho

SENSORIAL LABORS

In 2017 I walked into *Incoming* (2017), the immersive multichannel video installation by Richard Mosse, which was on display at the Barbican Centre's Curve in London. In many ways, the installation felt—and was intended to feel—like an assault on the senses. *Incoming* presents viewers with fragments of events along two major migration routes into Europe: one from the east, from countries such as Syria, Iraq, and Afghanistan, crossing Turkey and arriving in Europe on the shores of Aegean islands; the other from the south, from countries in the Sahel region such as Senegal, Mali, Nigeria, Niger, Chad, Sudan, Ethiopia, and Eritrea, through the Sahara Desert into Libya, where people attempt to cross the Mediterranean to reach Italy. These routes were captured by Mosse with a thermographic camera originally intended for military use, a camera that produces images by detecting thermal radiation, including the heat of human bodies, from as far as 30.3 kilometers away. Designed for long-range border enforcement, battlefield awareness, and search and rescue, the technology of this camera is part of the military-humanitarian complex that forms the European Union's dire response to the unfolding mass migration tragedy. It is sanctioned as a weapon under international law because it is used for long-range surveillance, and often connected to advanced weapons systems in order to lethally target enemy positions. It was this weapon that Mosse adapted and used to film the journeys of people from countries such as Syria, Iraq, Afghanistan, Senegal, and Somalia.

The film and panoramic images that compose the installation capture encampment structures and masses of tents, border police, boats at full capacity, and people of all ages in the most everyday moments of their lives, in internment or on the move. Mosse spent time in the refugee camps before photographing, and some of the people sheltered there helped him to arrange his shots.[1] But in the images displayed in the installation, these subjects are always seen at a distance, photographed from a perspective above eye-level that keeps those 30.3 kilometers somewhat perceptible, even though the subjects are seen up close through the thermographic camera.

In a note accompanying the exhibition, Mosse explains that "this powerful tool was not designed for storytelling and was never meant to be used aesthetically."[2] He further elaborates that "the work attempts to engage and confront the ways in which our governments and societies represent, and therefore regard, the refugee. *Incoming* is an attempt to use the camera against its intended purpose to create an immersive, humanist art form, allowing the viewer to meditate on the profoundly difficult and frequently tragic journeys of refugees."[3]

One could say that *Incoming* is a film not only about the technological sensorium of war—with its ever-expanding infrastructure—and the way it is used to track and target vulnerable populations, but also about the ways in which the senses of art publics[4] are solicited to interpret and respond to the ongoing effects of war and Empire. These are two ways in which the film represents and enacts an assault on the senses. By incorporating weaponized surveillance technology, the film portrays the ways in which the subjects most vulnerable to war, climate change, and immiseration are targeted and dehumanized by the perceptual system of military power. Simultaneously, the film intends to mobilize and rematerialize this dehumanizing apparatus into a "humanist art form," thus soliciting viewers' senses into a "humanitarian structure of feeling."[5]

My intention here is not to confirm how *Incoming* participates in humanitarian structures of feeling that compel those of us located in the Global North to respond to the "distant suffering"[6] presented to us by the media and the arts. At the same time, as I will later elaborate, I cannot purport to occupy a position outside of the sensorium that makes such structures of feeling possible. (This sensorium is the interiority or condition that we are in, and from which I write). As Asma Abbas has noted, liberal societies are sustained by an uneven distribution of pain between those who suffer and those who are solicited to redress that suffering.[7] The solicitations of empathy, sympathy, and compassion offered by humanitarian art forms thus confirm, rather than challenge, this uneven distribution of the labor of suffering. In other words, and in more materialist terms, the plight of others is not a mere topic or object of representation, but the very material condition that makes such aesthetic forms possible: suffering is endemic to liberal societies, and is therefore integral to the global sensorium that sustains such humanist art forms.

I therefore approach *Incoming* from a place of discomfort regarding how the suffering of Black and brown people is offered to me as "the raw material of white pedagogy and enjoyment"[8] and as "an instrument to facilitate the ethical responses of others."[9] In her book *In the Wake: On Blackness and Being* (2016), in a reflection on images of Black suffering, including those of transcontinental crossings across the Black global diaspora, Christina Sharpe writes that "these languages and the material conditions that they re/produce continue to produce our fast and slow deaths." As she reminds us: "This is true even though and when we find images of Black suffering in various publics framed in and as calls to action or calls to feel with and for. Most often these images function as a hail to the non Black person in the Althusserian sense. That is, these images work to confirm the status, locations, and already held opinions within dominant ideology about those exhibitions of spectacular Black bodies whose meanings then remain unchanged."[10] With this knowledge in mind, Sharpe asks what kind of ethical viewing might be possible in the face of these onslaughts, and rather than dismissing those images altogether, she sits with them to think through what they may call on her to do, think, and feel otherwise. In other words, Sharpe refuses the "terms of address" through which these images are circulated, and instead carves out a different space and practice to tend to the images and the subjects contained in them.[11] It is a process of imagining what escapes the frame, so as to deflect the humanitarian gaze and to unburden the subjects (and viewers) of that frame.

As one of the privileged viewers targeted by the Althusserian hail of such images, I am inspired by Sharpe's imagining beyond the frame, but also wary of the risks it entails. Seeing and engaging with a work such as *Incoming* is a form of participation in the structures of seeing and feeling that the work solicits from me. At the same time, I am compelled to ask if engaging with this work can activate other affective grammars beyond those directly requested from me.

In her writing on Black refusal and the work of Arthur Jafa, Tina Campt suggests that images of Black precarity solicit "affective labor." She uses the term "labor" to refer to "the work required to cultivate, maintain, articulate our relationship to black precarity" and "the effort required to position oneself in proximity to, or in a place of discomfort and, for some, potential complicity with, black precarity."[12] While Campt uses the term to refer to modalities of refusal that Black artistic practices might instantiate, I want to suggest undertaking this labor can be a way to work through (and against) the humanitarian structures of feeling that are proposed to us. Through these sensorial labors we can aim to look differently, and arrive at a different mode of engagement with the global (w)archive of violence.

What I wish to consider is the possibility of forging a relationship to this (w)archive beyond the affective dispositions in which it is presented to us. One of the reasons I find it important to "put in the work" is that the transformations of the war sensorium wrought by datafication have raised new ethical problems that need to be further investigated. While the critiques of humanitarian aesthetics are well known in relation to visual media such as photography and film, the rise of datafication has posed new questions for the senses.[13] With the conduct of remote warfare or "precision warfare," much of the violence of ongoing wars is now black-boxed in computational spaces, even if every now and then this violence leaks into publicity through the efforts of whistleblowers. This is also true for the tragedies unfolding across the Mediterranean. The sheer amount of information gathered by surveillance systems along European borders registers the numerous lives lost and imperiled at sea, but these data archives remain mostly inaccessible and thus sustain "regimes of unaccountability."[14] These opacities have put pressure on artists, activists, and open-source investigators to find ways to render these events visible and sensible, and we urgently need new vocabularies and practices to approach these archives with the care they require.[15] At the same time, datafication technologies have also brought war and violence up close—for one, in the way surveillance technologies enable an unequal perceptual proximity between sensor operators and targeted populations, as *Incoming* conveys, creating forms of "remote intimacy"[16] or "distance-intimacy."[17] Another form of proximity resides in the materiality of digital warfare, in how digital images have become weapons of war and how digital networks connect us much more densely with circuits of war practices. There is something to say about the technologies of war that also connect us across the globe in everyday digital engagements and thus create invisible infrastructural proximities. These simultaneous forms of distance and proximity rewire the global war sensorium in ways that impact our relationship to the archives of war. We are now more than ever in relationships of moral, affective, and material intimacy with suffering, and this calls for a reconsideration of how our senses are solicited by and implicated in the conduct of war and violence.

I propose to think through these moral, affective, and material intimacies through the notion of "cruel intimacies," in order to consider how the proximities afforded by digitization fold global spectators into the (w)archive of violence and conflict. These cruel intimacies form the very sensorial-material infrastructure through which global spectators see, feel, and respond to the suffering of others. Extending Campt's notion of labor, I also want to ask if a different ethical orientation toward this (w)archive might be "labored" from within the cruel intimacies that fold us into complicity.

The essay begins by working through *Incoming* to reflect on the global war sensorium that underwrites the premises of the work. While *Incoming* proposes to engage its viewers with the suffering of others by cultivating perceptual proximity with photographed subjects, I wish to shift attention to the sensorium that makes this perceptual proximity possible and how it gives us cause to reflect on the "cruel intimacies" that global spectators are always already implicated in. I then turn to Solmaz Sharif's book of poems *LOOK* (2016), which leads me to modulate my considerations of cruel intimacy to think through how a different affective grammar might be crafted from within the global war sensorium that folds us into relations of cruel intimacy. *LOOK* emerges as a companion in thinking about cruel intimacies, since it engages with the perceptual proximities afforded by remote technologies of war, while also claiming a space of radical intimacy from within the global war sensorium that brings into view other modes of ethical orientation beyond those solicited by humanitarian aesthetics. Ultimately, I suggest that the sensorial intimacy foregrounded by Sharif—premised on radical opacity, rather than on the transparency afforded by perceptual proximity—gestures toward a transformation of the senses that brings about other modalities of being with and tending to one another.

FROM DISTANCE-INTIMACY TO CRUEL INTIMACY

I begin by returning to the thermographic camera adapted for *Incoming* and how the 30.3 kilometer distance between photographer and subjects transforms the war sensorium. The thermal images that make up *Incoming* are emblematic of what Lisa Parks terms the "radiographic episteme," that is, the transformation of "imperceptible radiation into data that can be made productive within an information economy."[18] This radiographic episteme expands the war sensorium beyond the field of human vision: rather than capturing light and shadow, midwave infrared cameras record contours in heat. As Parks explains in relation to the drone's incorporation of infrared sensors, the detection of infrared radiation introduces a shift in the technologized perception of material reality. Thermal imagery is calibrated to visualize infrared emissions so that human bodies pop out in the visual field as white or black blotches of stasis or movement. Within this radiographic episteme, Parks notes, visual surveillance practices are extended beyond epidermalization,[19] as infrared imagery can be used to isolate people according to the energy emitted by their bodies, rather than by visual markers of racialization. For this reason, one might be led to think that this thermal episteme radically shifts the field of technological perception and how it registers embodied difference. However, even as it displaces the epidermal registers of ethnic and racial difference that are recognizable under visible light, infrared imaging reinforces already existing power hierarchies by monitoring and targeting racialized populations with much greater intensity.[20] Temperature data is extracted precisely so that it can be made operable within existing regimes of power.[21] Nicole Starosielski calls this "object-oriented thermal vision" exactly because it surfaces targets to be eliminated.[22] This radiographic episteme thus calls upon a racism that differentiates in advance who will be surveilled and targeted. In other words, racist differentiation is so immanent to the black-and-white infrared imagery of *Incoming* that it becomes its subject matter (it *is* its matter: it is enfolded in the very materiality of the infrared). That is to say, while this thermal imaginary reconfigures the senses beyond the field of human vision, it does not fundamentally challenge what we know about the senses as a racial formation.[23] The fact that thermal images capture heat rather than visible light does not change this.

This radiographic episteme integrated into *Incoming* points to how remote sensing technologies affect notions of perception, distance, and intimacy, altering the way one sees and relates to others.[24] This phenomenon of perceptual proximity afforded by remote sensing has been variously described as "remote intimacy"[25] or "distance-intimacy"[26] to refer to the experience of being both close and distant, in conditions that are unequal and premised on a "pragmatic co-presence."[27] Intimacy as a relationship of unequal proximity that enables violence is not a new development in the history of war and Empire. Postcolonial scholarship in particular has scrutinized the many ways in which the intimate domain figures in the making of racial categories, how it is managed as a tool of imperial rule, and harnessed as a mode of violence impressed upon colonized peoples.[28] Critical war studies have shown how these modes of colonial intimacy have been put to use as "a culturally informed strategy" of knowing, understanding, and ultimately defeating the enemy in the context of war.[29] In this respect, Laleh Khalili has noted that the gendering of intimacy produces the illusion that such a culturally and affectively informed strategy is softer, more "feminine," more "imbued with an understanding of the native."[30] This gendering renders the colonized visible and legible for the purposes of colonial administration, but does so through supposedly "humane means." Intimacy as a more humane strategy of knowing and controlling the enemy tracks with the practice of remote and precision warfare, which is usually described by war strategists as a more humane and ethical form of warfare, given that more precise surveillance and targeting supposedly reduce the number of civilian casualties. In many ways, the lethal distance-intimacy enabled by remote technologies has extended earlier inflections of the global in intimate spaces as modes of knowing and governing populations through data.

While *Incoming* intends to convert this lethal distance-intimacy into a perceptual opportunity for humanist proximity, by "turning the camera against itself," I want to suggest that we can approach the work in different terms, to think about the relationship of cruel intimacy that we are already in with these images. The cruel intimacy that I am proposing draws on Oraib Toukan's notion of "cruel images," on which she further elaborates in this volume.[31] For Toukan, cruel images are incapable of soliciting an adequate reaction to the plight of others: "I cannot make words come out and give them any of the weight that the subject being watched deserves."[32] One of the reasons for this inadequacy, Toukan notes, is that cruel images have become immanent to our everyday media environments. Cruel images appear on our phones and other digital devices; they pop up on Google image searches; they stream on our feeds, undistinguished from other, more pleasant and mundane images. The circulation of cruel images has become the very materiality of our digital sensorium, in such a way that we are always embedded in these images and sensorially implicated in the precarity they convey and are premised on. As global viewers connected through digital networks, we are differently exposed to them and participate in their algorithmic circulation through our everyday, semivoluntary digital engagements, which fold us into complicity.[33] "Cruel images," Toukan writes, "have tunnelled their way deep into the meninges of my brain, even when I have abstained from watching them."[34] We are always in relation with these images, even if we do not see them. What this means for the field of visual culture is that our relation to images goes beyond the level of representation (what images show and do not show), which has been central to the image wars of the early twenty-first century. Our relation to these images now also happens at an infrastructural level and through machinic processes that fold us into the materiality of their circulation. As media theorist Wendy Hui Kyong Chun noted in *Control and Freedom: Power and Paranoia in the Age of Fiber Optics* (2016), “wireless technologies open up the possibility of touch: of being constantly caressed or bombarded by the signals around us.”[35] According to Chun, the computers and devices that we tap on everyday put us in relations of touch with others, not in the metaphorical sense of “staying in touch,” but in sense that our tapping generates effects across networks that make us touch others, including those, as Kris Paulsen puts it, “who cannot touch us back.”[36] This is to say that our relationship to images of violence goes beyond the question of seeing or “looking away.” There is no turning away from these images, because we are already implicated in their circulation. They constitute the interiority that we live in and sense from.

The “cruel intimacy” that I point to here is therefore not a phenomenological experience exclusive to pilots or photographers using thermographic cameras, or to art publics made to inhabit these phenomenological experiences through an encounter with a video installation. Cruel intimacy translates the materialist realization that we are always implicated in—and in relationship with—the suffering of others through everyday engagements with the digital materiality that makes up our media environments and networked lives, and through our complicities with the material conditions that make suffering endemic to liberal societies. This cruel intimacy is thus the very affective-material infrastructure of our global sensorium. We do not need the “close-up at a distance”[37] to bring us any closer to the suffering and humanity of the dispossessed.

LET ME LOOK AT YOU: HAPTIC INTIMACIES

Cruel intimacy, by turning our attention to the ways in which we are always already implicated with one another through an affective-material infrastructure, also holds the potential to call for an ethical reorientation of the senses. In other words, the deep implication that cruel intimacy spotlights can also conjure a more textured experience of intimacy that binds subjects across time and space through ties that connect us more densely than the circuits of the global war sensorium allow for.

This modulation of intimacy is foregrounded in Sharif's book *LOOK*. The poems in *LOOK* are written from phrases taken from the US Department of Defense's *Dictionary of Military and Associated Terms*, beginning with the word of Sharif's title. According to this dictionary, "look" in mine warfare refers to "a period during which a mine circuit is receptive of an influence." As Sharif explains in a note, this dictionary is intended as a supplement to standard English dictionaries, and unclassified terms are added and subtracted depending in part on whether the terms are sufficiently integrated into standard English. She gives the example of the term "drone," which appeared in the 2007 version of the military dictionary but no longer appears in the 2015 version, likely as a result of "drone" fully entering English vernacular. In other words, Sharif explains, "the military definition is no longer a *supplement* to the English language, but the English language itself."[38] By using military terms as the material for writing, *LOOK* points to how the global war sensorium constitutes the condition from which writing is made possible. Sharif thus writes from this place of cruel intimacy in which war is folded into the materiality of writing, which in the book is signaled by the capitalization of seemingly ordinary words (SANCTUARY, SCALE, SCRIBING, SEARCH) that turn out to be imbued with military jargon. The title *LOOK* also points to how the entanglement between visuality and war permeates the book, in which military language is integrated into descriptions of vernacular visual material, from family photographs of an uncle in a military camp during the Iran-Iraq wars[39] to a VHS video of Sharif's father.[40] The usage of the term "look" thus suggests a sense of suspicion about looking as the venue of ethical engagement with others, or perhaps more precisely an acknowledgment that there is no looking as ethical engagement outside of the materiality of war that makes up the sensorium through which people look.

The modulation of domestic and romantic intimacy under this war sensorium is one of the recurring themes in the book.[41] In the opening poem, "LOOK," the conversations of lovers are pierced through by a thermal imaginary and the coded language of military drone operations:

Whereas years after they LOOK down from their jets
and declare my mother's Abadan block PROBABLY
DESTROYED, we walked by the villas, the faces
of buildings torn off into dioramas, and recorded it
on a handheld camcorder;

Whereas it could take as long as 16 seconds between
the trigger pulled in Las Vegas and the Hellfire missile
landing in Mazar-e-Sharif, after which they will ask
Did we hit a child? No. A dog. they will answer themselves;

Whereas the federal judge at the sentencing hearing said
I want to make sure I pronounce the defendant's name
correctly;

Whereas this lover would pronounce my name and call me
Exquisite and lay the floor lamp across the floor,
softening even the light.

Whereas the lover made my heat rise, rise so that if heat
sensors were trained on me, they could read
my THERMAL SHADOW through the roof and through
the wardrobe.[42]

In the poem, the body's erotic heat is juxtaposed with the thermal imaginary of military technologies, bringing into view the inflections of the global in intimate spaces. Drawing on the work of historian Sylvia van Kirk, who called for a focus on the "tender ties" of the intimate lives of Empire, Ann Laura Stoler has argued that the dense transfer points of power that generate such tender ties are sites of production of colonial inequities and therefore of "tense ties" as well.[43] In *LOOK*, such "tense and tender ties" are thrown into sharp relief by the juxtaposition of the erotic body and the surveilled body, which points to how the intimate is not merely a microcosm where power relations are inscribed. In *Haunted by Empire: Geographies of Intimacy in North American History* (2016), Stoler makes a clarification that is important in this context: "In these 'tense and tender ties' of empire, relations of power were knotted and tightened, loosened and cut, tangled and undone. These ties are not microcosms of empire but its marrow."[44] This marrow is evocative in this context, as it points to how the intimate, more than a domain or space on which power encroaches, is the very connective tissue that holds Empire together. This idea of marrow, of connective tissue, is also very clearly articulated in the poem "LOOK," where the intimate is foregrounded as the condition through which militarization and its technological infrastructures constitute the very sensorium from which one writes, sees, and feels. In this sense, the intimate is not only the domain of the domestic, the romantic, or the sexual upon which power is exercised, although it is also that; rather, the intimate is another term for the global war sensorium that connects us across space and time, the connective tissue through which we touch each other all the time.

Yet at the same time, the poem also points to how intimacy can be more than this by reclaiming a space and an affective experience not organized by surveillance and militarization:

> Whereas *ye know not what shall be on the morrow. For what is*
> *your life?* It is even a THERMAL SHADOW, it appears
> so little, and then vanishes from the screen;
>
> Whereas I cannot control my own heat and it can take
> As long as 16 seconds between the trigger, the Hellfire
> Missile, and *A dog,* they will answer themselves;
>
> Whereas *A dog,* they will say: Now, therefore,
>
> Let it matter what we call a thing.
>
> Let it be the exquisite face for at least 16 seconds.
>
> Let me LOOK at you.
>
> Let me LOOK at you in a light that takes years to get here.

In the gap between these final two verses, we can see how the poem solicits a different look from within the global war sensorium. While the poem acknowledges the pervasiveness of these conditions ("Whereas I cannot control my own heat and it can take / As long as 16 seconds between the trigger, the Hellfire / Missile, and *A dog*. they will answer themselves"), it also reclaims a space, an opening within those sixteen seconds where a different look can be called forth and activated. The poem thus introduces a distinction between the LOOK that governs the thermal screen—within which sixteen seconds elapse between the trigger pulled in Las Vegas and the Hellfire missile landing in Mazar-e-Sharif—and a look "in a light that takes years to get here." With this look that takes years rather than sixteen seconds, Sharif points to how intimacy can be conceived as more than the perceptual proximity afforded by militarized technology: intimacy here is precisely that which exceeds, even if it does not escape, the global war sensorium. Intimacy is therefore reinvented as the life lived *in spite of* this permanent surveillance of bodies, psyches, and language.

With this proposition, Sharif calls for a different conception of intimacy than that foregrounded in *Incoming*. While *Incoming* cultivates proximity with precarious subjects through remote technologies by turning the camera against itself, intimacy in *LOOK* is envisaged as the affective proximity one cultivates *in spite of*, not because of, those technologies. In other words, intimacy is to be attained not by bridging the perceptual gap of 30.3 kilometers, but by extending it further—light years further. The intimacy called forth in *LOOK* is therefore not a relationship of perceptual proximity, but rather one that cultivates radical illegibility. Because perceptual proximity is a vehicle of violence, *LOOK* deflects this desire for perceptual proximity and instead aspires to inscrutability, intangibility and opacity. This is a look that demands a sensorial transformation, it demands that the senses sense otherwise.

The poem therefore gestures toward what feels like a "warmer" conception of intimacy, in which the warmth of the erotic body exceeds, and remains illegible to, the heat signature captured by the thermographic camera. The erotic heat in the poem thus represents more than the close relationship between loving bodies, and rather pushes toward a "trans-corporeal" intimacy, that is, a mode of relationality that binds people across time and space.[45] At the same time, this erotic heat is also radically intercorporeal, in the sense that it acknowledges that our bodies are interconnected and implicated in one another, and that we therefore touch each other all the time in relations of vulnerability and complicity.

This touch that acknowledges our fundamentally interconnected nature calls for a different sensorium and affective grammar than that solicited by global war. Such a sensorial realignment resonates with what Tina Campt has eloquently termed "hapticity." For Campt, the haptic is a multisensorial modality of contact and relationality that includes but is not limited to physical contact (touching), visual contact (seeing), and psychic contact (feeling).[46] More recently, Campt has suggested that hapticity can also be a practice. The practice "to remain in relation to or in contact or connection with another. It is the labor of love required to feel across difference, precarity and suffering."[47] This being in contact and in relation to one another is not to be conflated with the empathy, compassion, or "feeling for" solicited by humanitarian aesthetics; rather, "it is the effort of feeling implicated or affected in ways that create restorative intimacy, how we feel with and through another in the absence of touch."[48]

Here I would like to slightly modulate this sense of hapticity to emphasize that even in the absence of physical touch we still touch each other all the time through the digital imbrications that establish touch between people across networks. As Chun reminds us, this networked hapticality makes us vulnerable to known and unknown others, and it implicates us in each other's lives. But it is also this networked touch of cruel intimacy that lays the foundation for more rich and imaginative ways of "living in/difference."[49]

The conception of intimacy foregrounded in Sharif's book, one that deflects perceptual proximity rather than embrace it, can inspire a model of contact and relationality in (w)archival times. Extending Campt and Chun, this conception of haptic intimacy prompts us to consider scale differently, in that it compels us to ask whether one can be intimate with the far away, across difference and incommensurability. This haptic intimacy might help us envisage modalities of affective proximity that connect us more densely across time and space without the proximity favored by lethal forms of distance-intimacy and by humanitarian aesthetics. Earlier I mentioned that throughout Sharif's book there is an acknowledgment that there is no looking as ethical engagement outside of the materiality of war that makes up the sensorium through which people may look. What Sharif intimates is that the haptic intimacy she points to does not exist outside of the war sensorium, but can exist in spite of and beyond it. Or as Chun puts it, the caressing and the bombarding occur through the same signals. This is to say that haptic intimacy as a mode of relationality emerges from within the cruel intimacies that implicate us in each other's lives in relations of vulnerability and complicity. This haptic intimacy is conjured from the condition of cruel intimacy that bonds us, and it is the result of a labor that transforms the senses and reorients the war sensorium toward haptic modalities of being with and tending to one another.

1. Max Campbell, "Richard Mosse's 'Heat Maps': A Military-Grade Camera Repurposed on the Migrant Trail," *New Yorker*, February 5, 2017.

2. Some of the footage captured by Mosse during this period was used in Forensic Architecture's investigation of an incident on October 28, 2015, when a migrant boat left the coast of western Turkey, heading to the closest European coast—the Greek island of Lesbos. The sea was rough, and the boat was old and overcrowded with more than three hundred passengers. It sank 280 meters beyond the maritime border into Greece, in European Union territorial waters, resulting in the deaths of at least forty-three people. It was the deadliest incident in a period known as the "long summer of migration," when over a million refugees and migrants attempted to reach EU shores by sea. Media reports at the time credited Frontex, the EU's border agency, and the Greek coastguard for having carried out a successful rescue operation. Forensic Architecture's analysis disputes this, and opens up possibilities for civil society groups to demand accountability for lives lost in the Mediterranean. See "Shipwreck at the Threshold of Europe, Lesvos, Aegean Sea," Investigations, Forensic Architecture, https://forensic-architecture.org/investigation/shipwreck-at-the-threshold-of-europe.

3. Richard Mosse, "Incoming," http://www.richardmosse.com/projects/incoming#.

4. By "art publics" I do not strictly mean art visitors, but the publics and counterpublics constituted politically by encounters and engagements with art forms, and the ways in which art forms position publics in specific epistemic positions.

5. Devika Sharma proposes the term "humanitarian structure of feeling" to describe an experience of spectatorship built not so much (or not only) on moral sentiments such as compassion, empathy, pity, or cynicism, but rather on a more ambivalent register of affectivity that indicates an unresolved response to humanitarian reason and the way that reason recruits viewers. Devika Sharma, "The Predicament of Spectatorship: Renzo Martens and the Humanitarian Image," in *Discursive Framings of Human Rights: Negotiating Agency and Victimhood*, ed. Karen-Margrethe Simonsen and Jonas Ross Kjaergard (New York: Routledge, 2016), 216-31.

6. Luc Boltanski, *Distant Suffering: Morality, Media and Politics*, trans. Graham D. Burchell (Cambridge: Cambridge University Press, 1999).

7. Asma Abbas, *Liberalism and Human Suffering: Materialist Reflections on Politics, Ethics, and Aesthetics* (Basingstoke: Palgrave Macmillan, 2010).

8. Saidiya Hartman, "Intimate History, Radical Narrative," *Black Perspectives*, May 22, 2020, https://www.aaihs.org/intimate-history-radical-narrative/.

9. Gil Z. Hochberg, *Visual Occupations: Violence and Visibility in a Conflict Zone* (Durham, NC: Duke University Press, 2015), 120.

10. Christina Sharpe, *In the Wake: On Blackness and Being* (Durham, NC: Duke University Press, 2016), 116.

11. Saidiya Hartman, "Review of Delia's Tears: Race, Science, and Photography in Nineteenth-Century America," *Journal of American History* 98, no. 2 (2011): 520-22.

12. Tina Campt, "The Visual Frequency of Black Life: Love, Labor, and the Practice of Refusal," *Social Text* 140, 37, no. 3 (2019): 26.

13. For a critical overview of these perspectives, see Sharma, "Predicament of Spectatorship."

14. Lila Lee-Morrison, "The Forensic Architecture Project: Virtual Imagery as Evidence in the Contemporary Context of the War on Terror" (paper, Virtual Zones of Peace and Conflict, Centre for Resolution of International Conflicts, University of Copenhagen, January 12-13, 2015).

15. We can look to Sophie Dyer's essay in this volume for an example of the effort to craft such vocabularies and practices through open-source investigation.

16. Hugh Gusterson, *Drone: Remote Control Warfare* (Cambridge, MA: MIT Press, 2017).

17. Cara Dagget, "Drone Disorientations: How 'Unmanned' Weapons Queer the Experience of Killing in War," *International Feminist Journal of Politics* 17, no. 3 (2015): 361-79.

18. Lisa Parks, "Vertical Mediation and the US Drone War in the Horn of Africa," in *Life in the Age of Drone Warfare*, ed. Lisa Parks and Caren Kaplan (Durham, NC: Duke University Press, 2017), 134.

19. On epidermalization and racializing surveillance, see Simone Browne, *Dark Matters: On the Surveillance of Blackness* (Durham, NC: Duke University Press, 2014).

20. On drones and racialization, see Lauren Wilcox, "Embodying Algorithmic War: Gender, Race, and the Posthuman in Drone Warfare," *Security Dialogue* 48, no. 1 (2017): 11-28; Keith P. Feldman, "Empire's Verticality: The Af/Pak Frontier, Visual Culture, and Racialization from Above," *Comparative American Studies* 9, no. 4 (2011): 325-41.

21. On thermal images and whiteness in *Incoming*, see Daniel C. Blight, "Incoming: Photography, Contemporary Art, Whiteness," *American Suburbx*, March 23, 2017, https://americansuburbx.com/2017/03/incoming-photography-contemporary-art-whiteness.html. See also Niall Martin, "As 'Index and Metaphor': Migration and the Thermal Imaginary in Richard Mosse's Incoming," *Culture Machine*, no. 17 (2019): 1-19.

22. Nicole Starosielski, "Thermal Vision," *Journal of Visual Culture* 18, no. 2 (2019): 147-68. Alongside the military history of thermal vision, Starosielski argues that there is another genealogy of this episteme, one of thermal landscape, whereby the environment is cast into regular and irregular zones structured by "thermal normativity." She calls these "zonal images" whereby what becomes visible is always already *abnormal*.

23. Here I recall Judith Butler's discussion of the videotape evidence used in the 1992 trial following the beating of Rodney King by Los Angeles police officers, which acquitted three of the four officers involved. Butler claims that "the visual field is not neutral to the question of race; it is itself a racial formation, an episteme, hegemonic and forceful," that determines in advance how a piece of evidence is seen and interpreted. Judith Butler, "Endangered/Endangering: Schematic Racism and White Paranoia," in *Reading Rodney King/Reading Urban Uprising*, ed. Robert Gooding-Williams (New York: Routledge, 1993), 15-22. As Niall Martin also argues in his reading of *Incoming*: "Mosse notes that the camera is colour blind, but it is colour-blind in the racialized sense because the thermal body as an object of concern, irrespective of its skin colour, is already black." Martin, "As 'Index and Metaphor,'" 9.

24. These alterations are particularly clear in testimonies by drone pilot whistleblowers who have come forward to denounce the effects of remote war. Working twelve-hour shifts six days a week, drone crews partake in an "endless loop of watching," shifting between visible light and infrared registers to get the best possible view. When the mission is to monitor a specific target, a sensor operator might linger above a single house for weeks. Those flying drone missions repeatedly state that they are not 7,500 miles away from their targets, but eighteen inches away—the distance from eye to screen. See Derek Gregory, "Deadly Embrace," *Kölner Geographische Arbeiten* 95 (2015): 110.

25. Gusterson, *Drone*.

26. Dagget, "Drone Disorientations."

27. Grégoire Chamayou, *A Theory of the Drone*, trans. Janet Lloyd (New York: New Press, 2015), 116.

28. Phanuel Antwi, Sarah Brophy, Helene Strauss & Y-Dang Troeung, "Postcolonial Intimacies: Gatherings, Disruptions, Departures," *Interventions: International Journal of Postcolonial Studies* 15, no. 1 (2013): 1-9. See also Ann Laura Stoler, *Haunted by Empire: Geographies of Intimacy in North American History* (Durham, NC: Duke University Press, 2006), 1-67; Lisa Lowe, *The Intimacies of Four Continents* (Durham, NC: Duke University Press, 2015).

29. See Derek Gregory, "'The Rush to the Intimate': Counterinsurgency and the Cultural Turn," *Radical Philosophy*, no. 150 (2008): 8-23.

30. Laleh Khalili, "The Uses of Happiness in Counterinsurgency," *Social Text* 32, no. 1 (2014): 26.

31. Oraib Toukan, "Cruel Images," *e-flux Journal*, no. 96 (2019), https://www.e-flux.com/journal/96/245037/cruel-images/.

32. Ibid.

33. Here I draw on Annie Ring's conceptualization of complicity in digital culture as "an unconscious folding-together into wrongdoing," a mode of everyday engagement with technology premised on a less conscious level than knowledge, as technology users engage in the habitual use of media that shape their bodies into archives of the networked world. Annie Ring, "Complicity," in *Uncertain Archives: Critical Keywords for Big Data*, ed. Nanna Bonde Thylstrup, Daniela Agostinho, Catherine D'Ignazio, Annie Ring, and Kristin Veel (Cambridge, MA: MIT Press, 2021), 87-98.

34. Toukan, "Cruel Images."

35. Wendy Hui Kyong Chun, *Control and Freedom: Power and Paranoia in the Age of Fiber Optics* (Cambridge, MA: MIT Press, 2006), 27.

36. Kris Paulsen, *Here/There: Telepresence, Touch, and Art at the Interface* (Cambridge, MA: MIT Press, 2017).

37. I borrow this expression from Laura Kurgan's *Close up at a Distance: Mapping, Technology and Politics* (New York: Zone Books, 2013).

38. Solmaz Sharif, *LOOK* (Minneapolis, MN: Graywolf Press, 2016), 95.

39. Ibid., 79.

40. Ibid., 39.

41. This point is also analyzed by Andrea Brady in her article "Drone Poetics," *New Formations* 89/90 (2017): 116-36.

42. Sharif, *LOOK*, 3.

43. Stoler, *Haunted by Empire*, 24.

44. Ibid., 3.

45. Stacy Alaimo, "States of Suspension: Trans-Corporeality at Sea," *Interdisciplinary Studies in Literature and Environment* 19, no. 3 (2012): 476-93.

46. Tina Campt, *Listening to Images* (Durham, NC: Duke University Press, 2017), 72.

47. Campt, "Visual Frequency," 43.

48. Ibid., 42.

49. Wendy Hui Kyong Chun, "Net-munity, or The Space between Us … Will Open the Future," *Critical Inquiry blog*, May 20, 2020. https://critinq.wordpress.com/2020/05/20/net-munity-or-the-space-between-us-will-open-the-future/.

A PROBABLE FEMALE, A PROBABLE CHILD
Civilian Casualties, Remote Monitoring, and Recognition Work in the Air War against ISIS

Sophie Dyer

BODIES

"You can't *see* through rubble," replied former British Royal Air Force (RAF) Commander Greg Bagwell when asked in 2018 by a British nongovernmental organization (NGO) if the military was doing everything possible to detect civilian casualties in the war against the so-called Islamic State in Iraq and Syria (ISIS).[1] Bagwell's logic was simple: if we cannot see the bodies, how can we know there *are* bodies? Yet the common-sense reply masks a number of difficult and unanswered questions that I want to engage with here about "seeing" and accountability in the war against ISIS, and more generally in the West's increasingly remote and air power-dominated military operations, and crucially, the role of NGOs as unsolicited observers.

To give some context, the United Kingdom joined the United States-led Coalition against ISIS soon after its formation in September 2014. By May 2018 the country's military had conducted nearly two thousand air strikes and was the second most active member of the Coalition after the United States.[2] Soon after Bagwell's comments, the British government admitted to its first "unintentional civilian fatality."[3] However, it did not say where or when this had occurred, making identification of the victim or their kin impossible. Months later, following a request by the NGO Action on Armed Violence, the UK Ministry of Defence released a new statistic: the RAF had killed or injured an estimated 4,315 ISIS fighters in Iraq and Syria. Implausibly, the number of civilians killed or injured remained the same: just one. If, by enlisting "the best available post-strike analysis," the British military could so accurately count combatant casualties, why could it not plausibly figure the civilian toll of war?[4] To put it another way: why could the military "see" certain bodies and not others?

Previously, the commander of the Coalition, US Army Lieutenant General Stephen Townsend, had responded to public allegations of civilian casualties with a different, possibly more telling logic. It was alleged that on March 20, 2017, a Coalition air strike had killed potentially dozens of civilian families sheltering in a former Bedouin school in the Syrian town of Al-Mansoura. During a call from Baghdad, Townsend informed a pool of journalists:

> We had multiple corroborating intelligence sources from various types of intelligence that told us the enemy was using that school. And we observed it. [...] We *saw* what we expected to *see*. We struck it. We *saw* what we expected to *see*.
>
> Afterwards, we got an allegation that it wasn't ISIS fighters. [...] It was instead refugees. [...] I'm not *seeing* any corroborating evidence of that. [...] Everything we've *seen* since then suggests that it was the 30 or so ISIS fighters that we expected.[5]

Townsend's claim was that he had not seen any civilians before or after the air strike; on the contrary, he had seen the ISIS fighters. While Bagwell acknowledged that the military could not see the bodies—which is to say, its vision was obstructed—Townsend would have us believe that what he saw was sufficient to make a judgment: no civilians, just ISIS fighters.

The assertion was proven terribly wrong. Over a year later, on June 28, 2018, the Coalition admitted to its error. Tens, possibly hundreds of civilians, mostly displaced families using the former school as a shelter, had been killed by the "deliberate" (planned) air strike. Officially, the military admitted to forty "unintentional" civilian deaths.[6] However, local sources, while not denying the presence of ISIS fighters, claimed that the air strike had killed hundreds of civilians, including women and children. The Coalition's figure of forty civilian deaths was taken from the findings of a ground investigation conducted by the US-based NGO Human Rights Watch. The investigation report by Human Rights Watch made clear that the actual death toll was "likely higher" because bodies were still under the rubble and many of those killed had been displaced from other areas, so were not known locally.[7]

Why did the civilian families go unseen and unaccounted for by the Coalition? Was Townsend's line of sight obstructed by the building and later the building rubble? Or given that he claimed to have seen "30 or so ISIS fighters," had he misidentified the civilians as combatants? What is certain is that Townsend's denial of mass civilian casualties at Al-Mansoura was consistent with the Coalition's position. Other military assessments of casualty allegations, self-congratulatory press releases, and government records tell a story of limited harm to civilians in a precision war fought against a "murderous" adversary. ISIS atrocities in the Middle East and overseas justified "annihilation tactics" and saw US Marines "fire more artillery rounds [in Syria] than any battalion since Vietnam."[8] In a response to further allegations of widespread civilian harm by NGOs, Townsend authored an opinion piece in an US magazine, entitled "Reports of Civilian Casualties in the War against ISIS Are Vastly Inflated." "I challenge anyone," wrote Townsend, "to find a more precise air campaign in the history of warfare."[9]

Despite such adversarial rhetoric and the Coalition's official position, the "systemic" not-seeing of civilians was identified as "the detection problem" in written evidence submitted to a British parliamentary inquiry in 2018 by a former senior advisor to the US State Department, Larry Lewis.[10] The detection problem described by the evidence is threefold: civilians were not being detected by the military before or after strikes, and when civilian casualties were identified, Coalition estimates were "very low in magnitude" compared with those of independent observers, namely journalists, NGOs, and the United Nations (UN).

WHO WERE THE "INDEPENDENT OBSERVERS"?

The only independent observer named in the body of evidence Lewis submitted to parliament is Airwars, a British civilian casualty monitor. Between 2017 and 2019 I worked as a researcher and advocacy officer at Airwars. In these roles, I followed the war at a distance from within a small team of Arabic language researchers (most of whom were from the Iraqi and Syrian diasporas), casualty assessors, investigative journalists, and volunteers. The organization was headquartered in London; however, my colleagues were spread around the United Kingdom, United States, the Netherlands, Turkey, and Iraq. As an advocacy officer, I worked with local reports of civilian casualties originating from Iraq and Syria, and routinely communicated with the Coalition to request investigations into new allegations.

Airwars was set up in 2014 by British investigative journalist Chris Woods. Previously, Woods had worked at the Bureau of Investigative Journalism, where he had run the Drone Warfare project, which tracked covert and often highly controversial US drone strikes in Afghanistan, Pakistan, Somalia, and Yemen. During the war against ISIS, Airwars became the only "independent" source for cumulative estimates of the numbers of civilians killed and wounded exclusively by the Coalition in Iraq and Syria.[11] Its findings were referenced in news articles, politicians' questions, and a classified US military study into civilian harm.[12] In previous conflicts, similar data had been collected via household surveys or from the records of morgues and hospitals. However, these had often offered only a "snapshot," usually after hostilities had ended. By contrast, on a daily basis my colleagues at Airwars searched social media and local news and spoke to regional monitors on the ground, collecting, grouping, and assessing reports of civilian deaths and injuries from air and artillery strikes to produce a rolling account of harm to civilians.

Our work was only possible because the war against ISIS was one of the first in history to be documented en masse by civilians, state militaries, and militants alike, all uploading content to the Internet in near real time. In 2014 in Iraq and Syria, the conditions were right for a groundswell of documentation from communities living inside ISIS-held territories. At the level of infrastructure, the regions had sufficient connectivity; at the level of code, social media was prevalent; and in the wake of the 2011 Arab Spring protests, an assortment of community-run pages, messaging nets, and citizen journalism websites had been set up to produce, share, and comment on local events.[13] These included Syrian news outlets and citizen-led media centers such as Shaam News Network, Euphrates Post, and the Syrian Media Action Revolution Team's news agency, as well as regional monitors such as the Violations Documentation Center and the Syrian Network for Human Rights, set up by government opposition activists in Syria and abroad. In the war against ISIS, two of the most widely known citizen journalism projects were *Mosul Eye* in Iraq and *Raqqa Is Being Slaughtered Silently* in Syria. Both were established in 2014 and covertly run by citizen journalists living in ISIS-controlled territories, at risk to and sometimes at the cost of their lives. Combined, the news outlets and blogs, social media pages and posts produced a collective, locally authored narrative of the war as it was experienced by civilians on the ground.

Poles Apart

By mid-2019, half a decade into the war through the territorial defeat of ISIS, the Coalition had conceded responsibility for 1,319 civilian deaths.[14] These casualties originated from just 315 incidents, and the figures included admissions of responsibility by individual member states such as the United Kingdom.[15]

The very existence of an official record was a novelty, and for that reason, under different circumstances, it might have met with applause instead of challenges to its integrity. During the US-led invasion of Iraq in 2003, and under public scrutiny, the US Pentagon had failed to produce a civilian casualty count. This changed in 2016 when an executive order from President Obama required the country's military to release public reports of civilian casualties resulting from its counterterrorism strikes. The 2017 National Defense Authorization Act contained similar requirements.[16]

Airwars's archive of civilian casualty allegations, however, contained documentation of a different, far bloodier war than that found in official records. By mid-2019 the NGO estimated that at least eight thousand to thirteen thousand civilians had been killed and many more wounded by Coalition strikes.[17] Significantly, the Airwars team had collected the names of more than 3,500 alleged victims.[18] Many of the names were descriptions of familial relationships, such as "wife of Manaf Hussein al A'thab," but nonetheless, unlike Coalition statements, they made the victims potentially identifiable.

During the first five years of the war, Airwars monitored an average of sixteen possible civilian deaths per day from Coalition strikes.[19] However, it was over two years before the Coalition established a Civilian Casualty Team and routinely published the outcomes of its assessments in monthly civilian casualty reports.

Once the Coalition Civilian Casualty Team was established in December 2016, Airwars became the source for over two-thirds of its investigations into possible civilian harm.

Judged side by side—as they were by the British Parliament and continue to be in Western media coverage of the war against ISIS—the Coalition and Airwars maintain two entangled but ultimately incommensurate accounts of the remote war. At stake was official recognition of the dead and injured by the Coalition and its member countries; compensation such as *ex gratia* (condolence or *solatia*) payments to victims and their kin; and, in the long term, a historical record of the war as it was experienced by civilians on the ground.

Working with Airwars's public archive and official records, what follows is an account of how local reports of civilian casualties were instrumentalized by activists in the West to counter official claims of no or low harm to civilians. I propose working with anticolonial and feminist critiques of vision and visual evidence: first to unpack the Coalition's multiple denials of civilian casualties, and second to address the serious ethical challenges raised by the emergence of civic remote monitoring projects. By "civic" I mean not military or state-run. In the case of Airwars, what did the project achieve and for whom? What new possibilities might this emergent form of activism and advocacy offer? To begin to answer these questions I turn to colonial-era records of aerial warfare, an activist history of civilian casualty recording, and contemporary exchanges between the Coalition, Airwars and Western media. In lieu of a conclusion, and departing from these examples, I end with notes toward a feminist and anticolonial remote monitoring. The questions that take shape—about history and memory, activism and archives, data and ethics—drive my essay as it moves between competing reports of civilian casualties to map their archival relations, which are also relations between sensed and sensing bodies.

MIS/SEEING

Townsend's claim—"we *saw* what we expected to *see*. [...] We struck it. We *saw* what we expected to *see*"—hints that what is at stake is not seeing but recognizing. I propose the term "mis/seeing" to describe the careless act of *seeing but not seeing*. I borrow this term from Black studies scholar Christina Sharpe's research into the "archives of disaster" of chattel slavery, where she uses it to describe the seeing-but-not-seeing of Black life across time.[20] Although Sharpe mentions "mis/seen" only once and in passing, the term captures the duplicity of misrecognition, albeit in a different sociohistorical context.[21]

In Sharpe's research, mis/seeing manifests in the ledgers of ships used to transport enslaved Africans to the United States. In these ledgers, sailors marked the dead or thrown overboard as "negro man, ditto, negro woman, ditto."[22] Sharpe charts this persistent logic of mis/seeing. In another archive and another example, a Getty Images photograph shows a young Black girl in the aftermath of the 2010 earthquake in Haiti with the word "ship" taped to her forehead, presumably marking her for evacuation by the US Coastguard. "The ledger that renders us illegible as human repeats, as does the ship," writes Sharpe in reference to the photograph.[23] For Sharpe, the ledger and the taped label index "at least a certain inability to see" the subjects they record.[24]

The mis/seen civilians who populate the official records of the war against ISIS are often barely legible or are conspicuous in their archival absence. They might be compared to the "ungrievable,"[25] "the uncounted,"[26] or the "made-killable."[27] If recorded at all, they are at minimum "civilian" and at most "probable female," "probable child," or "probable man." Following Sharpe, I want to know if attending to these records and their mis/seen subjects can "counter forgetting, erasure, the monumental, and that ditto ditto in the archives."[28]

It is useful to understand Sharpe's notion of mis/seeing in the context of feminist critiques of vision and visual evidence. In a 2016 article on the optics of drone warfare, gender studies scholar Lauren Wilcox argues that while drone technologies are supposed to remove issues of identity through a more-than-human assemblage of "bodies, technologies, signals, and images," gender and racial prejudice is instead "put into the service of the violence it enables."[29] Wilcox cites an essay by the feminist philosopher Judith Butler on visual evidence, specifically the videotape evidence used in the 1992 trial following the police beating of Rodney King in Los Angeles, which acquitted three of the four officers involved. In her analysis, Butler makes clear that "seeing" is not "a matter of direct perception as a means to truth but 'the racial production of the visible, the workings of racial constraints on what it means to 'see.'"[30] Critically, in Wilcox's and Butler's arguments, who or what is seen is contingent on who is seeing.[31]

Feminist theory has taught us that there are multiple ways in which bodies, and the violence done to them, can go unseen and unaccounted for: through being excluded, questionably present or fully present but unrecognized. It is in this racialized, gendered and otherwise polarized field of vision that NGOs, Airwars included, intervened. At the beginning of 2019, when Airwars relaunched its public archive of civilian casualty allegations to include media previously only available via the organization's internal research documents, it put online more than 3,900 images and videos, the majority of which were credited to sources on social media.[32] In the act, Airwars risked reproducing the same denials of civilian casualties it sought to address. In short, the archive risked being co-opted by the imaginary of a precise war. If so, how could the intervention be justified and under what conditions? Reflecting on her work with marginalized communities enduring violence, the US anthropologist Nancy Scheper-Hughes argues that "seeing, listening, [...] recording, can be, if done with sensitivity and care, acts of fraternity and sisterhood, acts of solidarity. Above all, they are the *work of recognition*."[33] The idea that recognition is work or more specifically, care work, resonates with Sharpe's call to counter the abandonment of certain lives with "another effort to try to look, to try to really see."[34] In view of the ethical challenges discussed here, can the same argument be made for the remote monitoring work undertaken by civil society groups such as Airwars? If practiced with care and sensitivity, can civilian casualty recording be understood as recognition work, as an act of solidarity?

REMOTE

What do I mean by "remote" when discussing remote monitoring? In monitoring as in warfare, I propose that being remote is a *position*, a *strategy*, and a *problem*. As a *position*, being remote means working at a distance, "with, by and through" local actors, which is itself a *strategy* of risk transfer (the deliberate and differential distribution of exposure to sources of harm). However, being remote is also a technical, methodological, and ethical *problem*, not least because it means having a restricted view—and when this is not enough, having to rely on others who are more proximate to the violence than you are to tell you what they see.

From the Coalition's perspective, the conflict was twice removed from the United States and its European allies, firstly through the formation of the Global Coalition against Daesh—a temporary entity of over eighty states and organizations—and secondly through the Coalition's partnerships with local forces. In Iraq the Coalition aligned itself with the government-run Iraqi Security Forces, and in Syria, for the most part, with the Kurdish-led Syrian Democratic Forces. With the exception of a small and unknown number of Special Operations, only local partner forces entered into close-quarters combat with ISIS militants. In return, the Coalition provided training and equipment, as well as intelligence and air and artillery support. The arrangement enabled a transfer of risk, in which local forces, and not the Coalition, absorbed many of the mortal and moral costs of war.[35] In an effort to break from the "heavy footprint" counterinsurgency campaigns of 2001 in Afghanistan and 2003 in Iraq, the Coalition against ISIS sought to work "with, by and through" local forces.[36] The phrase "with, by, and through" permeates military press briefing transcripts that stress the economy, efficacy, and collaborative nature of local partnerships. It was for these reasons, not reasons of geographical distance, that the military campaign was considered a "remote war" by the West. Other names given to this altered mode of war are "vicarious," "surrogate," and "liquid."[37] Common to all is the idea that without disengaging, the United States and the West in general had withdrawn, which is to say, had pushed war away.[38]

The Latin ancestor of remote, *removere*, means to "move back or away, put out of view." Its root, *movere*, means "to move." My sense of being remote from the war that I was monitoring at work—of being able to *put its violence out of view*—changed over time. Close to where I live in London is the Victoria and Albert Museum, a section of which was left unrestored after World War II bomb damage, as a monument to the building's survival. The museum's gouged stonework bears strong visual resemblance to the munitions-blasted buildings in contemporary Iraq and Syria. At work, I would routinely stare at buildings in images or videos of civilian casualties—it was part of my job to identify, as accurately as possible, their location, so as to "geolocate" the incident. The continuity between these images and the museum walls began to haunt me, for the reason that with it I could draw a line between twentieth-century air raids and twenty-first century "precision warfare." The longer I spent working with imagery from Iraq and Syria, the shorter the length of this line and the remoteness it symbolized became.

"What happens when we look at and listen [...] across time?" asks Sharpe in her book. "This looking," she writes, "makes ethical demands on the viewer; demands to imagine otherwise; to reckon with the fact that the archive, too, is an invention."[39] Beyond the world wars, a history of aerial warfare and its weaponization of the "view from above" is a colonial history.[40] Some of the earliest recorded air strikes were "punitive" raids carried out by the RAF in 1920s occupied Iraq. In the first seven months of 1920, the British War Office counted "no fewer than 25 cases of bombing from the air against Arab villages" in Iraq.[41] At eight o'clock in the morning on October 13, 1920, in an effort to quell an uprising against British colonial rule, the RAF "relentlessly bombed" and "pummeled [...] with artillery" several thousand Iraqis who had amassed near Al-Rumaitha to push back the colonial forces.[42] Records show that "air control" became a strategy of the British Empire.[43] Details of British colonial operations in Iraq are documented in the paperwork of the British War Office—telegrams, memoranda, financial accounts, munitions records, maps and architectural plans, service medals, and awards rolls—maintained in public view by the National Archives at Kew in London. In his 2015 essay "Decolonizing Knowledge and the Question of the Archive," Cameroonian philosopher Achille Mbembe notes "colonialism rhymes with mono-lingualism."[44] The National Archives at Kew present a contained, centralized, and monolingual archive of aerial warfare.

Preserved at least is the damning knowledge that "we" have been bombing Iraq since historical records of aerial warfare began. What would a civilian casualty archive look like that began with the British bombing of Iraq from 1920 to 1932 (under the

British Mandate), followed by entries for 1941 (the Anglo-Iraqi War), 1991 (the Gulf War), 1998 (Operation Desert Fox), 2001 (UK and US bombing targets near Baghdad), 2003–2011 (the Iraq War), and from 2014 to date (the Global Coalition against ISIS)? How would the category of "civilian" change over time? Could such an archiving project address, with the possibility of some form of redress, the *archival silences* that so often follow the deaths of civilians in war? Thinking with Sharpe, I propose that this looking back reorients the present problem of civilian casualty recording from a technological concern—about ever more powerful sensors, intelligent targeting systems, or battle damage assessments—to a set of social, historical, and archival urgencies.

MISSING

We can file civilian casualties under "missing data sets." Missing data sets, writes the Nigerian-American artist and researcher Mimi Onuoha, are "blank spots that exist in spaces that are otherwise data-saturated." They signify both a "lack" and an "ought," which is to say, the data does not exist, but it should. Onuoha has exhibited a filing cabinet filled with such missing data sets.[45]

Beyond war, there is a long history of civic and often collective efforts to document deaths that have been systematically denied, racialized, gendered, individualized, or otherwise suppressed: from the Names Project Memorial Quilt conceived in 1985 in San Francisco by the gay rights activist Cleve Jones, to the Trans Murder Monitoring project set up in 2009 to record the murders of "trans or gender-diverse people worldwide," to the #SayHerName social movement that began online in 2015 to "call attention to police violence against Black women in the US."[46] In these examples, recording the dead is understood as community activism or nonviolent protest. An influential precedent to Airwars's work was the Iraq Body Count project. Prior to Iraq Body Count, fatalities from the 2003 Iraq War were a missing data set. The monitoring project kept a count of "violent civilian deaths" resulting from the invasion of Iraq by a US-led Coalition. Publicly, the Pentagon reasoned that it never targeted civilians and so had no cause to try to count such deaths. Besides, it would be impossible, because the Iraqi paramilitaries fought in civilian clothes, the military was using civilians as human shields, and "anti-aircraft fire falling back to earth" caused civilian casualties, said a Pentagon spokesperson.[47]

There are only a few reasons for missing data sets, argues Onuoha. Most often, "those who have the resources to collect data lack the incentive," or those in a position to self-report perceive little benefit in doing so; alternatively, "the data to be collected resists simple quantification."[48] All three reasons could be said to apply to civilian casualty recording. Indeed, the UK public inquiry into the 2003 Iraq War concluded that collecting data on civilian casualties was beyond both its "scope and abilities."[49]

Like Airwars over a decade later, John Sloboda and Hamit Dardagan, who founded Iraq Body Count, identified a missing data set, and to a degree they succeeded in populating it.[50] However, lower levels of connectivity in Iraq in 2003 meant that the monitoring project was reliant upon professional news outlets and humanitarian reports rather than social media. By 2014, when Airwars was set up, other groups were already recording online and publicly available documentation of the war in Syria—notably the Syrian Archive, founded in 2011 by the Syrian activist Hadi Al Khatib. The Syrian Archive focused on possible violations of human rights laws: the project's classification system was derived from the UN Independent International Commission of Inquiry on the Syrian Arab Republic.[51] It also included civilian casualties from non-aerial warfare, and incidents alleged to have been perpetrated by the Syrian government.

Despite an apparent lack of incentives, Airwars chose to monitor all possible civilian casualties from Coalition strikes—including the vast majority of those considered to be legal collateral damage under international humanitarian law. Indeed, an analysis of Airwars data reveals that the most frequent number of casualties recorded per incident was one.[52] It is unlikely that these single-casualty incidents, which account for approximately 20 percent of incidents, violate the law. As a result, they are less likely to be registered by organizations—NGOs or the UN—with a focus on judicial forms of justice and accountability. Only if the incident repeats again and again, as it arguably does in the Airwars archive, might it be indicative of systemic harm and thus a possible breach of international humanitarian law.

Of course, the paradox is that these individual incidents must have been recorded in the first place to make such a legal argument possible.

The production of missing data is a political act that creates precious openings for advocacy work. Members of the Syrian Archive describe "acts of tagging, indexing, aggregating and defining of data and data categories" as "inherently political."[53] To put it another way, the production of missing civilian casualty data involves a string of decisions "where some values and interests are reproduced and others are not."[54] For instance, even a seemingly innocuous technical decision will delimit the data set and the future questions that can be asked of it. For civic civilian casualty monitoring projects, this ultimately means deciding whose lives and whose deaths to account for. If the goal of the project is to use its data sets or wider archive in advocacy work, then the question of which pathways to justice and accountability are open to it is a concern from the beginning. In short, the data set or archive must be created in the image of an as-yet-unrealized form of justice.

DISSONANCE

Distributed across websites, servers, and languages, the documentation of civilian deaths in the remote war against ISIS unfolded with a "radical dissonance." Radical dissonance is the "crazy-making" character of contemporary life, argues Butler: "Lives appear one way or the other only from specific historical perspectives."[55] As a result, "many people are highly regarded in one community that values their lives, and highly disregarded or abandoned in another social framework that considers their lives dispensable." This is what Butler calls an inequality of "grievability." Perhaps the most violent expression of this, she suggests, is collateral damage.

The US Department of Defense defines collateral damage as "unintentional or incidental injury or damage to persons or objects that would not be lawful military targets in the circumstances ruling at the time."[56] Two categories of collateral death are identified here. The first is "unintentional." For example, the civilian was unseen or "not observed" at the time of the strike.[57] The second is "incidental," which is to say that harm to civilians was foreseen and accounted for in a collateral damage estimate. In other words, the risk of injury or death to an unlawful target was predicted and judged proportional to the military advantage gained.

"Civilian deaths from collateral damage are not inevitable."[58] The US military set in advance an upper limit for its operations in Iraq and Syria. While the legal limits for collateral damage are codified in international law, in the United States and no doubt elsewhere, the ratio of civilian to combatant deaths deemed "acceptable" is a political judgment. During the war against ISIS, the US government recalibrated its Noncombatant Cutoff Value (NCV). The NCV "is kind of a cap on the acceptable number of civilian casualties," explained former US State Department advisor Lewis on a popular US news show. "In late 2016 that number was increased, so as you say the willingness to take risks to civilians, that risk threshold was increased."[59] Although the value is always secret, it is public that in 2016 the NCV in Afghanistan was zero. For US operations in Iraq and Syria, the NCV was likely "around 10" prior to the increase in late 2016.[60]

Denials

It took a full year of working with the military's monthly civilian casualty reports for me to realize that they gave descriptions of *how* casualties happened (e.g., killed by strike blast, killed by secondary explosion, entered target area after or just prior to the munition released, unseen at time of engagement, killed inside target building or target vehicle) but not *why*. Critically, "misidentification" was never mentioned, despite the fact that it was suggested as a major problem in a 2017 US military study into civilian harm.[61] The claim is made in the report's heavily redacted footnotes by two authors who disagree with its findings on positive identification. "CIVCAS [civilian casualties] primarily occur in one of two ways," the anonymized authors write. "The first is through Collateral Damage from an engagement with known enemy forces, where the effects of the engagement also impact nearby civilians; the second is through misidentification, where civilians are mistakenly believed to be enemy and are engaged because of that belief."[62] With regard to the war against ISIS, they note that "it is reasonable to suspect systematic undercounting of misidentifications" by the US military, and that "this may be particularly true given the more complex nature of the Mosul and Raqqa operations" in Iraq and Syria.[63] In other words, cases of mistaken identity may well be widespread; however, blinded by its initial error, the military is unable to detect them.

Against this backdrop, Airwars worked to fill the holes in public knowledge about civilian casualties. The organization funneled its limited resources into online searches for local reports of harm to civilians. The searches, mostly conducted in Arabic, comprised routine checks of known sources (news websites, blogs, social media accounts), followed up by advanced and reverse-image searches to identify new sources relevant to specific allegations. The biographical details of alleged victims accumulated in Airwars's private research documents: first names (*ism*), last names (*kunya*, occasionally tribal *nisbah*), ages, familial relationships, occupations, photographs of the deceased before the war. Cold, fleshy bodies that were never the intended subjects of precision warfare took form as data subjects, cached and latent.

Airwars's realization that these online sources were being erased came late. On social media, posts and pages, photographs and videos documenting civilian casualties were being removed without warning. The "takedowns" were the product of users flagging graphic, extremist, or otherwise inappropriate materials, combined with the human or algorithmic-led content moderation services provided by social media platforms. For example, YouTube claimed that it had removed "33 million videos in 2018, amounting to roughly 90,000 per day," while "Facebook removed roughly fifteen million pieces of content deemed 'terrorist propaganda' between October 2017 and October 2018."[64] Although the takedowns only involved social media, overall the lost sources included the websites of local media centers and news outlets erased for other reasons, such as unpaid hosting bills or the destruction of servers. Perhaps unsurprisingly, official records were no more stable. The Coalition press releases including strike reports and monthly civilian casualty reports were amended without record, and routinely purged from the US Central Command website. Only when its researchers noticed the mounting erasures two years into the war did Airwars begin to use a third-party archiving service. When tested in March 2019, 15 percent (48,839) of the original sources for civilian casualty allegations in Iraq and Syria linked to in the Airwars archive returned a 404 error message, indicating that they were offline. Some of these sources will have been archived elsewhere. However, Airwars's late response is testament to the fact that the organization never intended to maintain a public archive; rather, it saw itself as an independent real-time monitoring and advocacy project.

The takedowns amounted to another denial, in which civilians' experiences of war were removed from public view—discarded, often to the surprise of those who had uploaded them (see Dima Saber's essay in this volume). There is no scope here to engage meaningfully with the many issues around takedowns. However, it should be noted that debates among advocacy groups, governments, and social media platforms about what kind of content should be subject to removal, and how such judgments are made and by whom, are complex and ongoing.

Non-Credible Assessments

Poles apart, Airwars and the Coalition maintained two incommensurate records of the war and how it was experienced on the ground by civilians. And yet, their optics overlapped. From the beginning of the war, Airwars maintained a strained but nonetheless persistent dialogue with US Central Command and Coalition officials.[65] With no standardized or accessible procedure for Iraqis or Syrians to report allegations of civilian harm directly to the Coalition, the NGO positioned itself as an unsolicited mediator. From 2016, when the Coalition established a Civilian Casualty Team, Airwars submitted hundreds of civilian harm allegations. The Coalition responded by opening investigations, requesting further information, and sharing with Airwars the military grid reference coordinates for certain assessments. The outcome was further dissonance. The Coalition Civilian Casualty Team assessed three-quarters of the alleged incidents as "non-credible." In other words, it denied the incidents and widespread harm. Three generic reasons were given: "No Coalition strikes were conducted in the geographical area"; "insufficient information on the time and location"; "insufficient evidence of civilian harm." The first reason was given in half of all non-credible assessments. However, the thresholds for concession were unclear, even to Airwars, which was in direct contact with the Coalition Civilian Casualty Team. Terms such as "geographical area" were left undefined by the military, although a 2017 article in the *New York Times* suggested that it could be as low as "within 50 meters of a strike."[66] If the article was correct, this was well under the blast radius of some munitions. For example, the "minimum safe distance" from a Paveway IV 500-pound bomb (used in the war against ISIS) is 584 meters, according to US Department of Defense standards.[67] A standard artillery shell, which was fired in its thousands throughout the conflict, has a far lower safe distance but a "wide area effect" and an average margin of error of over 100 meters.[68] In an urban area this could mean a different building or street. A potential paradox existed: was the geographical accuracy demanded by the Coalition for civilian casualty allegations far greater than the spatial resolution of its own weaponry?

The second most frequently given reason for non-credible assessments was "insufficient information on the time and location," while the rest were dismissed on the vague claim of "insufficient evidence." A secret Pentagon document, obtained under the Freedom of Information Act by journalist Joseph Trevithick and published by Airwars in September 2015, shed some light on the kinds of evidence considered to be "insufficient" by the Coalition. The internal document tracks the assessment process of allegations of civilian casualties between August 2014 and May 2015. In one incident, related to an air strike in the area of Fallujah, Iraq, on December 21, 2014, the notes read:

> STATUS UPDATE: Approximately 10 minutes after the last weapons impact, a probable female and a probable child were observed on FMV [full-motion video] to walk through the target area. A probable male arrived and carried the child to a motorcycle and transported him to Fallujah hospital. The female walked to the road and lay down, and was not observed any further.
>
> INQUIRY RESPONSE: Assessed to be insufficient information to determine CIVCAS. The lack of urgency and the fact that the child walked apparently normally suggest that his injuries were not life threatening. There [were] no Iraqi allegations.[69]

The incident is dismissed on the basis of "insufficient information." Additionally, it is noted that the Australian Defence Force made an independent assessment and "reached a similar conclusion." However, the relative precision of the description of the subjects' movements jars with the lack of certainty about, or unwillingness to commit to knowing, their age and gender. Put another way, the document's standardized language indexes, as Sharpe might say, a certain inability to see the civilian subjects it records.[70]

Al-Mansoura

I want to end by returning to the air strike on the Bedouin school near Al-Mansoura in Syria, and to Townsend's wrongful claim that "we saw what we expected to see. [...] We struck it. We saw what we expected to see." What can we learn from the Coalition's denials and Airwars's remote monitoring?

On March 20, 2017, the Coalition air strike hit at the worst possible time: around midnight, when the families using the former school building as a shelter were asleep inside. The following morning, on social media, "the details and the deaths" (to echo Sharpe) fluctuated. A Facebook page called "Al-Mansoura in Its People's Eyes" reported by far the highest estimate: 420 civilians killed. In total, over thirty Facebook messages and twenty reports from other sources were archived, annotated, and assessed by Airwars. The victims' names lined the organization's research documents:

> Khalif Al-Ayto and his entire family, age unknown, male, killed
>
> Kitan Al'amash and his family, age unknown, male, killed
>
> Khaled Hasan al-Qadi, adult, male, killed
> A female, adult, female, killed
> Child 1, child, killed
> Child 2, child, killed
> (source said two or more children so number could be higher)
>
> Qasem al-Salama and his entire family, adult, male, killed
>
> Mohammed Jum'a Al-Hadid and his family, age unknown, male, killed[71]

The eventual list was seventy-two names long. Airwars's final casualty estimates ranged from forty (the lowest report) to 420 (the highest report).

In the days after the incident, the German newspaper *Süddeutsche Zeitung* broke a story that gave additional details, confirming that the air strike was "deliberate" (planned) as opposed to "dynamic" (unplanned, unanticipated, or in self-defense). In a secret meeting, the newspaper claimed, the German Defense Committee had been briefed that one of the country's Tornado aircraft had provided aerial imagery for a prestrike pattern-of-life analysis. A pattern of life is a "specific set of behaviors and movements" over time that can be used to identify targets or predict collateral damage.[72] The leaked details made it even harder to understand how the victims had not been identified before or afterward, and why the air strike had been planned for midnight, when civilian casualties would be highest.

In the timeline of how the incident was reported, Townsend's denial of the civilian casualties came a week later, on March 28, 2017. Shortly after, on March 30, the UN recognized reports of mass casualties and condemned the air strike. Three months later, on July 7, in its monthly civilian casualty report, the Coalition reaffirmed Townsend's initial assessment: "March 20, 2017, near [Al-Mansoura], Syria, via social media report: After [a] review of available information and strike video it was assessed that there is insufficient evidence to find that civilians were harmed in this strike."[73] The Human Rights Watch field investigation and subsequent report—which identified forty named victims, including sixteen children and fifteen women—was published at the end of the summer, in September.[74] It then took a full year for the UN to release its estimate of "at least 150" civilian deaths and to conclude that the Coalition had "failed to take all feasible precautions to protect civilians" and thus was "in violation of international humanitarian law."[75] The Coalition did not offer a public response. Instead, two months later on June 28, 2018, it revised its initial assessment to concede forty civilian deaths.[76]

Airwars collected, assessed, translated, and republished local reports, months before a ground investigation was possible and a full year before the UN released its findings. Critically, in the immediate aftermath of the air strike, the organization's remote monitoring prioritized the experiences of those most proximate to the violence. Indeed, half of all the sources it lists appear to be local and are dated March 21, the day after the air strike. As a result, the Airwars archive maintains a fragmentary record, which preserves in view the many ambiguities, internal conflicts, and gaps in information produced by remote monitoring.

The wide-angle view afforded by the Airwars archive makes it hard to dismiss individual casualties as isolated, or incidents as anomalous. The organization's continuous monitoring since 2014 means that the record for Al-Mansoura is embedded within a rolling account of civilian harm. On March 20, 2017, the day Al-Mansoura was struck, Airwars recorded an additional twelve possible incidents of civilian harm from Coalition strikes—five in Iraq and seven in Syria—almost all involving multiple fatalities. If we think with Sharpe, it is not the details and the deaths that repeat, but rather the persistent conditions of visuality under which civilian lives are mis/seen.

NOTES TOWARD A FEMINIST AND ANTICOLONIAL REMOTE MONITORING

I have argued that civilian casualty recording is a social, historical, and archival urgency—one that there are few incentives to address. For Western NGOs, the work is resource-intensive: reports of civilian casualties are often limited, conflicting, and hard to authenticate; online documentation is vulnerable to erasure; and legal pathways to justice and accountability are largely foreclosed. Moreover, the civic remote monitoring projects that attend to this urgency risk remaking the detached "colonial optics"[77] that made-killable the very lives they seek to record. In other words, they risk enacting more violence.

Under these conditions, choosing not to look, to turn away, might be an ethical or indeed moral response—if it were not for the groundswell of online documentation that transforms such a decision into an act of abandonment. Remote wars fought with "our taxes" are a business that "we" cannot easily divest ourselves from, regardless of whether we agree with the reasoning behind them. Indeed, it is a privilege if this long-worn complicity feels abstract.[78]

In the modified definition of mis/seeing I have developed, I include the military's persistent problem of misidentification. However, following Sharpe, I also include civilians that, in the official records of the West's war against ISIS, go unseen, barely seen, or seen too late. In Butler's paradigm of grievability, they might be described as either "questionably alive" or "living figures of the threat to life."[79] As such, their deaths are not marked or duly noted as lawful targets. If mis/seeing is at stake, a pertinent question is then: how can civic remote monitoring projects do recognition work differently? To put it another way, under what conditions can recognition work become "a counter to abandonment, another effort to try to look, to try to really see"?[80]

I propose imagining a civilian casualty recording project that is informed by the work of Iraq Body Count, the Syrian Archive, Airwars, and others, but departs from it to rethink remote monitoring on explicitly feminist and anticolonial terms. Such a project would be a move toward a "radical equality of the grievable."[81] What follows is not an exhaustive list of attributes or concerns, but rather notes toward a feminist and anticolonial remote monitoring.

Let a Feminist Ethics of Care or "Radical Empathy" Inform Decisions

Remote monitoring is defined by gross asymmetries of power, risk (exposure to physical or psychological harm), and reward (financial, reputational, or otherwise) between the monitor and those who populate monitoring as the subjects or producers of documentation ("civilian witnesses," citizen journalists, anonymized activists, or regional monitors).[82] These asymmetries extend in more nuanced ways to the composition of the teams conducting the monitoring work. A feminist remote monitoring project must begin by asking: how can the needs and experiences of those most proximate to the violence, and therefore exposed to the greatest risks, be prioritized?

For instance, how accessible or useful are the project's findings to the subjects or producers of the documentation? A similar question is posed by the US archival scholars Michelle Caswell and Marika Cifor, who call for a "feminist ethics, that centers on *radical empathy* and *obligations of care*" to be considered alongside a human rights framework.[83] In their view, while human rights frameworks focus on the rights of the individual, feminist ethics of care stress the relations between the people and larger communities behind the archive or findings. For Caswell and Cifor, "empathy is radical if we allow it to define archival interactions even when our own visceral affective responses are steeped in fear, disgust, or anger."[84] Letting radical empathy into decision-making requires reimagining the relationships among remote monitors, producers of the documentation, subjects of the documentation, users of the archive, and larger communities as a "web of mutual responsibility."[85]

Practice a Modified and Modest Remote Monitoring

A modest and modified remote monitoring is an argument against the need for higher resolution imagery and more powerful hyperspectral sensors. The British geographer Derek McCormack proposes a "modified and modest" remote sensing that is not reducible to "techniques of elevated distancing via imaging devices."[86] By modest, McCormack means a remote sensing that is sympathetic to the fact that it is "never merely an act of recovery"; rather, "it is always haunted by the prospect of that which cannot be sensed, by the limit of its own spectral logics."[87] To abridge McCormack's words, a modified and modest remote sensing is:

1. More than visual: insofar as it involves sensing, this sensing takes place through multiple registers—including vision but also touch, sound, and movement;

2. More than the comprehension of spatial data: it is also a matter of comprehending how the afterlives of specific events persist with variable duration and intensity in a process that takes place at a range of sites;

3. Not reducible to the practice of representation in which words and worlds are separate;

4. Never self-evident: it is a move against the privileging of either affectivity or materiality as a way of realizing "dreams of presence."[88]

I propose a modest and modified remote monitoring that befits the current shift in human rights investigations away from satellite imagery analysis, toward the unglamorous and intimate task of online searches for camera phone media, personal messages of condolence, and status updates. Such an approach values the "poor image" that has been "uploaded, downloaded, shared, reformatted, and re-edited"[89] and privileges its "partial perspective."[90] Indeed, this circulation is evidence of the web of social relations behind the project.

Stretch the Meaning of Real-Time Monitoring

Following Sharpe's ethical demands and the provocation "to imagine otherwise; to reckon with the fact that the archive is, too, invented,"[91] I propose that such a project might stretch the definition of real-time monitoring to look back as well as forward, so as to address the archival silences that persist around civilian casualties and to situate its work within a colonial history of "air control" that ghosts the present. Only under these conditions can the democratization of the archive, through the inclusion of civilian witnesses and local reporting, become the decolonization of the archive.

Design for Ambiguity

A feminist and anticolonial remote monitoring project must design for ambiguity (unknowns, internal conflicts, and missing bodies) and "build dissent" into its workflow, from its monitoring work to the communication of its findings or construction of a public archive.[92] Working with, not against, ambiguity is a recognition that being remote means having a restricted view and relying on others to tell you what they see, hear, or more broadly experience. This means unsettling established ideas of who in the project is an expert and who is a monitoring subject,[93] as well as problematizing the inherently normative language of authentication, in which a source or piece of documentation is either authenticated or not, included or excluded from the project's findings or archive.

The British cultural theorist Clare Birchall makes a comparable argument for "staying with the secret" in light of the "Snowden event" (the massive leak by Edward Snowden of US National Security Agency documents), so as to allow for a "a radical political response" instead of a rush toward revelation at the risk of normalization and false reforms—what Birchall, calls "containment strategies."[94] An example emerging from civilian casualty recording is greater transparency by militaries and their governments without greater accountability. Birchall advocates for focusing on the "*aesthetics* of the secret," that is to say, the conditions of visuality that make it possible, which include "space, time, the visible, the sayable, the audible, and political experience."[95] Following Birchall, I propose that designing for ambiguity resists the configuration of civilian casualties as a "rhetorical problem subject to legal tweaks" or as an "entrenched component" of remote warfare that elicits the response "you can't see through rubble."[96]

Make the Work Sustainable

"Caring for myself is not self-indulgence," wrote the African American lesbian poet, librarian, and activist Audre Lorde, "it is self-preservation, and that is an act of political warfare."[97] Presently, civilian casualty recording and other types of remote conflict monitoring require workers, and often volunteers, to pore over the documentation of violence—to watch it, hear it, read it.[98] Over time, repeated exposure can lead to vicarious trauma, "a process of change resulting from empathetic engagement with trauma survivors."[99] Vicarious trauma is a truly intersectional issue: my experience as a white cis university-educated woman will be different than yours. Among the many questions the issue raises is: how can the work be made sustainable for everyone—especially for workers or volunteers "who may have already experienced trauma themselves, generationally or have a personal connection to the subject of an investigation"?[100]

Provide Aftercare for Afterlives

Applying a feminist ethics of care to remote monitoring means reassessing what constitutes care work and how that work is valued. Sharpe offers a definition of care as "repair, maintenance and attention."[101] In a civilian casualty recording project, repair, maintenance, and attention might mean among other things taking the time to clean data, update records, generate backups, and mend code, as well as resourcing the upkeep of servers and other hardware long after the monitoring work has ended.

Acknowledgments

The section "Notes toward a Feminist Remote Monitoring" uses ideas and references developed with Gabriela Ivens for the article "What Would a Feminist Open Source Investigation Look Like?" published in the inaugural issue of the journal *Digital War*.

I owe a debt of gratitude to Sasha Engelmann for the gift of Christina Sharpe's *In the Wake: On Blackness and Being*, roving conversations, and disciplined feedback. I am grateful to those who so generously reviewed the chapter (in alphabetical order): Matthew Battles, Lauren Gould, Alex Hopkins, Lorenzo Pezzani, and Chris Woods. Also to Lizzie Malcolm, Samuel Oakford, Dan Powers, Eeva Sarlin, and Abdulwahab Tahhan for their assistance during the research process. I thank Susan Schuppli for recommending me to this book's editors, who were so trusting. I am thankful to Nicola Locatelli for the books, patience, and encouragement.

1. Drone Wars UK, "Interview of Air Marshall Greg Bagwell by Chris Cole, Drone Wars UK," January 2018, https://dronewars.net/interview-of-air-marshall-greg-bagwell-drone-wars-uk/, my emphasis. Bagwell made clear that his position was not the same as the government's: "The 100% claim [of zero civilian casualties from British air strikes] and the incessant pressure on its defence has frustrated me. I'd rather we said we make every effort and that we strive for 100% perfection but can never be sure with absolute certainty, despite every effort to try. Standing up and saying we are 100% perfect on this, who is going to believe that?"

2. By 2020, France's artillery strikes made it the second most active member of the coalition, moving the United Kingdom to third place.

3. Gavin Williamson, "Counter-Daesh Operations: Written Statement HCWS665," May 2, 2018, http://www.parliament.uk/business/publications/written-questions-answers-statements/written-statement/Commons/2018-05-02/HCWS665/. The admission of a single civilian casualty was made on May 2, 2018, by the Secretary of State for Defence, Gavin Williamson. At the time, the United Kingdom had launched 1,600 air strikes. One air strike can refer to multiple weapons launched from different aircraft aimed at multiple targets within the same area.

4. Action on Armed Violence, "RAF Claims 4,315 Enemies Killed and Injured in Syria and Iraq, with Just One Civilian Casualty," March 7, 2019, https://aoav.org.uk/2019/raf-claims-4315-enemies-killed-and-injured-in-syria-and-iraq-with-just-one-civilian-casualty/.

5. Stephen Townsend, "Department of Defense Briefing by Gen. Townsend via Telephone from Baghdad, Iraq," US Department of Defense, 2017, https://www.defense.gov/Newsroom/Transcripts/Transcript/Article/1133033/department-of-defense-briefing-by-gen-townsend-via-telephone-from-baghdad-iraq/, my emphases.

6. CJTF-OIR, "CJTF-OIR Monthly Civilian Casualty Report June 2018," Operation Inherent Resolve, June 28, 2018, https://www.inherentresolve.mil/Media-Library/Article/1562215/cjtf-oir-monthly-civilian-casualty-report/.

7. Human Rights Watch, "All Feasible Precautions? Civilian Casualties in Anti-ISIS Coalition Airstrikes in Syria," September 24, 2017, https://www.hrw.org/report/2017/09/24/all-feasible-precautions/civilian-casualties-anti-isis-coalition-airstrikes-syria.

8. Barack Obama, "Remarks by President Obama and President Hollande of France in Joint Press Conference," Obama White House Archives, November 24, 2015, https://obamawhitehouse.archives.gov/the-press-office/2015/11/24/remarks-president-obama-and-president-hollande-france-joint-press; James Mattis, "Transcript: Defense Secretary James Mattis on 'Face the Nation,'" *CBS News*, May 28, 2017, https://www.cbsnews.com/news/transcript-defense-secretary-james-mattis-on-face-the-nation-may-28-2017/; Shawn Snow, "These Marines in Syria Fired More Artillery Than Any Battalion Since Vietnam," *Marine Corps Times*, February 6, 2018, http://www.marinecorpstimes.com/news/your-marine-corps/2018/02/06/these-marines-in-syria-fired-more-artillery-than-any-battalion-since-vietnam/.

9. Stephen Townsend, "Reports of Civilian Casualties in the War against ISIS Are Vastly Inflated," *Foreign Policy*, September 15, 2017, https://foreignpolicy.com/2017/09/15/reports-of-civilian-casualties-from-coalition-strikes-on-isis-are-vastly-inflated-lt-gen-townsend-cjtf-oir/.

The US Air Force defines precision as the ability to "apply selective force against specific targets and achieve discrete and discriminant effects." In other words, precision is more than striking a target with pinpoint accuracy; it means knowing that target, and mitigating harm to anyone or anything in its vicinity. United States Air Force, "Core Competency: Precision Engagement," Air University, http://www.au.af.mil/au/awc/awcgate/global/competencies/precision.htm.

10. Larry Lewis, "Lesson from Mosul and Raqqa: Next Time, Do 'Everything Possible' to Reduce Civilian Casualties," UK Houses of Parliament, 2018, http://data.parliament.uk/writtenevidence/committeeevidence.svc/evidencedocument/defence-committee/uk-military-operations-in-mosul-and-raqqa/written/86187.pdf.

11. The Syrian Observatory for Human Rights produced estimates for civilians killed exclusively by coalition actions in Syria. Syrian Observatory for Human Rights, "Five Years of International Coalition Involvement in Syria: One-Third of the Country and 70% of Oil and Gas Are under Its Control, While Thousands of Victims and Violations Awaiting Investigation," February 10, 2019, https://www.syriahr.com/en/142551/. Other civilian casualty estimates were for all belligerents, including, among others, the Syrian government, ISIS, and Russia.

12. The US military's 2018 study on civilian casualties, commissioned by General Joseph Dunford, chair of the Joint Chiefs of Staff, was published on April 17, 2018, but classified "SECRET/NOFORN" (no foreign nationals). However, a redacted version was obtained through a Freedom of Information Act request by the journalist Missy Ryan, and published by the *Washington Post* on February 4, 2019, https://www.washingtonpost.com/world/national-security/after-bloody-insurgent-wars-pentagon-launches-effort-to-prevent-civilian-deaths/2019/02/04/ce5386d8-7fec-4fcf-9cda-60e06b638115_story.html.

13. Eyal Weizman, "Open Verification," *e-flux Architecture*, June 18, 2019, https://www.e-flux.com/architecture/becoming-digital/248062/open-verification/.

14. CJTF-OIR, "CJTF-OIR Monthly Civilian Casualty Report June 2019," Operation Inherent Resolve, June 28, 2019, https://www.centcom.mil/MEDIA/NEWS-ARTICLES/News-Article-View/Article/1890275/combined-joint-task-force-operation-inherent-resolve-monthly-civilian-casualty/.

15. The creation of a single coalition tally for civilian casualties was strategic. In late 2016, likely frustrated with their allies' refusal to concede responsibility for eighty civilian deaths from non-US actions, the United States moved to form the Coalition Civilian Casualty Team. While consolidation standardized the assessment process, it cut transparency. Umbrella reporting in the name of the coalition meant that future admissions of civilian harm no longer required the country responsible to be named. The move enabled the United Kingdom, France, Australia, Belgium, and the Netherlands to maintain a record of no or very low civilian harm, and the United States to stop confirming responsibility for the civilian casualties it caused. Sam Oakford, "The U.S. Is Helping Allies Hide Civilian Casualties in Iraq and Syria," *Foreign Policy*, May 26 2017, https://foreignpolicy.com/2017/05/26/america-helps-europe-conceal-its-civilian-casualties-in-iraq-and-syria/. The eighty "not previously announced" deaths were quietly published on April 30, 2017, without explanation or further detail.

16. Lewis, "Lesson from Mosul and Raqqa."

17. In Airwars's assessment for the first half of 2019, the NGO estimated "based both on its own assessments, and events confirmed by the US-led alliance, that a minimum of between 8,175 and 13,051 civilians are likely to have died as a result of Coalition actions." Alex Hopkins, "Airwars Six Monthly Assessment: January-June 2019," Airwars, August 2019, https://airwars.org/report/airwars-monthly-assessment-june-2019/.

18. Airwars, "Civilian Casualties Archive," 2019, https://airwars.org/civilian-casualties.

19. "Over 1,670 days of conflict (From Aug. 8, 2015 to Mar. 5, 2019) Airwars identified 2,790 alleged US-led Coalition casualty events in Iraq and Syria, corresponding to maximum of 28,000 non combatant fatalities-an average of 1.7 alleged incidents (or 16 alleged non combatant fatalities) per day." Airwars, "Civilian Casualties Archive."

20. Christina Sharpe, *In the Wake: On Blackness and Being* (Durham, NC: Duke University Press, 2016), 51.

21. Ibid., 51.

22. Ibid., 51-52.

23. Ibid., 47.

24. Ibid., 49.

25. Judith Butler, *Frames of War: When Is Life Grievable?* (London: Verso, 2009).

26. Azmat Khan and Anand Gopal, "The Uncounted," *New York Times*, November 16, 2017, https://www.nytimes.com/interactive/2017/11/16/magazine/uncounted-civilian-casualties-iraq-airstrikes.html.

27. Eve Tuck and C. Ree, "A Glossary of Haunting," in *Handbook of Autoethnography*, ed. Stacy Holman Jones, Tony E. Adams, and Carolyn Ellis (Walnut Creek, CA: Left Coast Press), 639-58.

28. Sharpe, *In the Wake*, 59.

29. Lauren Wilcox, "Embodying algorithmic war: Gender, race, and the posthuman in drone warfare," *Security Dialogue* 48, no. 1 (September 2016): 11.

30. Judith Butler quoted in ibid., 20.

31. These arguments about visibility and race resonate with an existing body of feminist work addressing ways of knowing and ways of seeing. However, this chapter focuses on registers of mis/seeing in the specific context of aerial conflict. See Donna Haraway, "Situated Knowledges: The Science Question in Feminism and the Privilege of Partial Perspective," *Feminist Studies* 14, no. 3 (1988): 575-599.

32. There were 3,135 images and 824 embedded videos, associated with 2,849 possible incidents of civilian harm from US-led coalition strikes in Iraq and Syria, published on the Airwars website before January 1, 2019.

33. Nancy Scheper-Hughes, *Death without Weeping: The Violence of Everyday Life in Brazil* (Berkeley: University of California Press, 1993), 28, my emphasis.

34. Sharpe, *In the Wake*, 117.

35. See Costs of War Project, "Costs of War," Watson Institute for International and Public Affairs, Brown University, https://watson.brown.edu/costsofwar/papers/summary.

36. Patrick M. Shanahan, "Statement from the Acting Secretary of Defense on Territory Once Held by ISIS," Department of Defense, 2019, http://www.defense.gov/Newsroom/

Releases/Release/Article/1793772/statement-from-the-acting-secretary-of-defense-on-territory-once-held-by-isis/.

37. Thomas Waldman, "Vicarious Warfare: The Counterproductive Consequences of Modern American Military Practice," *Contemporary Security Policy* 39, no. 2 (2018): 181-205; Andreas Krieg and Jean-Marc Rickli, "Surrogate Warfare: The Art of War in the 21st Century?" *Defence Studies* 18, no. 2 (2018): 113-30; Jolle Demmers and Lauren Gould, "An Assemblage Approach to Liquid Warfare: AFRICOM and the 'Hunt' for Joseph Kony," *Security Dialogue* 39, no. 2 (2018): 1-18.

38. "Liquid warfare," a term proposed by Dutch conflict scholars Jolle Demmers and Lauren Gould, highlights more than other terms the protean way of waging war that mutates legal norms and successfully diffuses responsibility for its dirty effects among broad political and military alliances. Gould and Demmers draw attention to how the liquid state of contemporary warfare can confuse Western publics into "indifference, and, importantly, those at the receiving end of the violence are unable to hold governments to account." In this way, "war is rendered invisible and normalized." Demmers and Gould, "An Assemblage Approach to Liquid Warfare," 2.

39. Sharpe, *In the Wake*, 51.

40. The first bomb dropped from a heavier-than-air aircraft was by the pilot Lieutenant Giulio Gavotti, over Italian-occupied Libya in November 1911. It is notable that after Iraq and Syria, Libya was the third country Airwars' monitoring work covered.

41. Winston Churchill, "Memorandum by the Secretary of State for War: Situation in Mesopotamia," National Archives, 1920, https://discovery.nationalarchives.gov.uk/details/r/D7736189.

42. James Corum, "The Myth of Air Control: Reassessing the History," *Aerospace Power Journal* 14, no. 4 (2000): 64-77. According to historical accounts, "the British suppressed the rebellion but at a cost of 1,040 killed and missing soldiers and 1,228 wounded—not to mention an estimated 8,450 dead Iraqi rebels." Ibid., 64.

43. Ibid.; Mark Jacobsen, "'Only by the Sword': British Counter-Insurgency in Iraq, 1920," *Small Wars & Insurgencies* 2, no. 2 (1991): 323-63; David Lee, *Flight from the Middle East: A History of the Royal Air Force in the Arabian Peninsula and Adjacent Territories 1945-1972* (London: Ministry of Defense, Air Historical Branch, Her Majesty's Stationery Office, 1980).

44. Achille Mbembe, "Decolonizing Knowledge and the Question of the Archive," *Frame* 15, no. 1 (2016): 36.

45. Mimi Onuoha, "Missing Datasets," Collaborative Version Control, *GitHub*, January 25, 2018, http://www.github.com/MimiOnuoha/missing-datasets.

46. The AIDS Memorial Quilt, "National Aids Memorial," http://www.aidsmemorial.org/theaidsquilt-learnmore; Trans Respect versus Transphobia Worldwide, "Trans Murder Monitoring," http://www.transrespect.org/en/research/trans-murder-monitoring/; African American Policy Forum and Center for Intersectionality and Social Policy Studies, "Say Her Name: Resisting Police Brutality Against Black Women," African American Policy Forum, 2015, https://aapf.org/sayhernamereport.

47. Associated Press, "AP Tallies 3,240 Civilian Deaths in Iraq," 2003.

48. Onuoha, "Missing Datasets."

49. Iraq War Inquiry, "The Report of the Iraq Inquiry: Section 17 Civilian Casualties," National Archives, July 6, 2016, http://www.webarchive.nationalarchives.gov.uk/20171123123908/

50. Between 2003 and 2012, Iraq Body Count recorded 105,052 to 114,731 violent civilian deaths.

51. The Independent International Commission of Inquiry on the Syrian Arab Republic was set up in 2011 by the Office of the United Nations High Commissioner for Human Rights in response to massacres and other unlawful killings, arbitrary arrests and unlawful detentions, and hostage-taking.

52. This is the mode for both maximum and minimum civilian casualty estimates in Iraq and Syria between 2011 and mid-2019.

53. Jeff Deutch and Hadi Habal, "The Syrian Archive: A Methodological Case Study of Open-Source Investigation of State Crime Using Video Evidence from Social Media Platforms," *State Crime Journal* 7, no. 1 (2018): 46–76.

54. Civic Laboratory for Environmental Action Research, "Citizen Science," https://civiclaboratory.nl/citizen-science/. The Civic Laboratory for Environmental Action Research is a feminist anticolonial lab based on the island of Newfoundland, Canada.

55. Judith Butler, "My Life, Your Life: Equality and the Philosophy of Non-Violence" (Gifford Lecture Series, Glasgow University, October 1, 2018).

56. United States Department of Defense, "DoD Dictionary of Military and Associated Terms," 2019.

57. CJTF-OIR, "CJTF-OIR Monthly Civilian Casualty Report September 2017," Operation Inherent Resolve, September 1, 2017, https://www.inherentresolve.mil/Media-Library/Article/1297778/cjtf-oir-monthly-civilian-casualty-report/.

58. Nick McDonell, "Op-Ed: Civilian Casualties Are Not Inevitable. The Military Sets an Acceptable Number in Advance," *Los Angeles Times*, March 31, 2017, https://www.latimes.com/opinion/op-ed/la-oe-mcdonell-civilian-casualties-ncv-20170331-story.html.

59. PBS News Hour, "The US Military Has a Number of Civilian Casualties That Is Deemed Acceptable. Has That Number Changed?" Public Broadcasting Service, December 31, 2018.

60. Nick McDonell, *The Bodies in Person* (New York: Blue Rider Press, 2018), 137.

61. US Military, "Civilian Casualty (CIVCAS) Review: Executive Summary (Declassified Version)," 2018, https://games-cdn.washingtonpost.com/notes/prod/default/documents/e39c5889-6489-4373-bd8e-ac2ca012e03d/note/6c60bba4-5781-4874-acdf-87e199f6e31b.pdf#page=1.

62. Ibid., 6.

63. Ibid.

64. Electronic Frontier Foundation, Syrian Archive, and Witness, "Caught in the Net: The Impact of 'Extremist' Speech Regulations on Human Rights Content," Electronic Frontier Foundation, 2019, https://www.eff.org/files/2019/05/30/caught_in_the_net_whitepaper_2019.pdf.

65. Airwars engaged with US Central Command and, from 2016, with Combined Joint Task Force-Operation Inherent Resolve when its Civilian Casualty Team was formed.

66. Khan and Ghopal, "The Uncounted."

67. Minimum safe distances are calculated based upon the net explosive weight of the munition and a k-factor of 328, the "absolute safe distance" standard used by the US Department of Defense. Department of Defense, "K-Factor," *Defense Acquisition University*, http://www.dau.mil/cop/ammo/DAU%20Sponsored%20Documents/K%20Factor.pptx.

68. Amnesty International, "War of Annihilation," 2018, https://www.amnesty.org.uk/files/reports/War%20of%20annihiliation%20report.pdf. A standard artillery shell fired from an M777 howitzer (a 155-millimeter thirty-nine-caliber towed gun) has an average margin of error of over 100 meters.

69. US Centcom, "Iraq/Syria CIVCAS Allegation Tracker," Airwars and Australian Broadcasting Corporation, 2015.

70. Sharpe, *In the Wake*, 49.

71. Airwars, "Civilian Casualties Archive," www.airwars.org/civilian-casualties/cs598-march-20-2017.

72. Patrick Biltgen, Todd S. Bacastow, Thom Kaye, and Jeffrey M. Young, "Activity-Based Intelligence: Understanding Patterns-of-Life," *State and Future of GEOINT* (2017): 24.

73. CJTF-OIR, "CJTF-OIR Monthly Civilian Casualty Report July 2017," Operation Inherent Resolve, July 7, 2017, http://archive.md/PrPi2.

74. Human Rights Watch, "All Feasible Precautions?"

75. UN Commission of Inquiry on Syria, "Amid the Ruins of Ar-Raqqah and Dayr al-Zawr, Calls for Justice and Accountability by Victims and Families Must Be Urgently Addressed," Office of the United Nations High Commissioner for Human Rights, 2018, https://www.ohchr.org/EN/NewsEvents/Pages/DisplayNews.aspx?NewsID=22766&LangID=E.

76. CJTF-OIR, "CJTF-OIR Monthly Civilian Casualty Report June 2018."

77. Sharpe, *In the Wake*, 124.

78. Adrienne Rich, "Notes toward a Politics of Location" (1984), in *Blood, Bread, and Poetry: Selected Prose 1979-1985* (New York: W.W. Norton & Co., 1994), 210-31.

79. Butler, *Frames of War*, 8.

80. Sharpe, *In the Wake*, 117.

81. Butler, "My Life, Your Life."

82. Zara Rahman and Gabriela Ivens, "Ethics in Open Source Investigations," in *Digital Witness: Using Open Source Information for Human Rights Investigation, Documentation, and Accountability*, ed. Sam Dubberley, Alexa Koenig, and Daragh Murray (Oxford: Oxford University Press, 2020) 249-70; Christof Heyns, "Report of the Special Rapporteur on Extrajudicial, Summary or Arbitrary Executions," UN Human Rights Council, 2015.

83. Michelle Caswell and Marika Cifor, "From Human Rights to Feminist Ethics: Radical Empathy in the Archives," *Archivaria*, no. 81 (2016): 24, my emphasis.

84. Caswell and Cifor, "From Human Rights to Feminist Ethics," 25.

85. Ibid., my emphasis.

86. Derek McCormack, "Remotely Sensing Affective Afterlives: The Spectral Geographies of Material Remains," *Annals of the Association of American Geographers* 100, no. 3 (2010): 651.

87. Ibid.

88. Ibid.

89. Hito Steyerl, "In Defense of the Poor Image," *e-flux Journal*, no. 10 (2009), https://www.e-flux.com/journal/10/61362/in-defense-of-the-poor-image/.

90. Haraway, "Situated Knowledges."

91. Sharpe, *In the Wake*, 51.

92. Catherine D'Ignazio, "What Would Feminist Data Visualization Look Like?" *Medium*, January 22, 2017, https://medium.com/@kanarinka/what-would-feminist-data-visualization-look-like-aa3f8fc7f96c.

93. Rigoberto Lara Guzmán and Sareeta Amrute, "How to Cite Like a Badass Tech Feminist Scholar of Color," *Medium*, August 22, 2019, https://points.datasociety.net/how-to-cite-like-a-badass-tech-feminist-scholar-of-color-ebc839a3619c.

94. Clare Birchall, "Aesthetics of the Secret," *New Formations*, no. 83 (2014): 26.

95. Ibid.

96. Ibid., 28.

97. Audre Lorde, *A Burst of Light and Other Essays* (Mineola, NY: Dover Ixia Press, 2017), 130.

98. Sophie Dyer and Gabriela Ivens, "What Would a Feminist Open Source Investigation Look Like?" *Digital War* 1, no. 1 (2020).

99. British Medical Association, "Vicarious Trauma: Signs and Strategies for Coping," December 7, 2018, https://www.bma.org.uk/advice/work-life-support/your-wellbeing/vicarious-trauma.

100. Dyer and Ivens, "What Would a Feminist Open Source Investigation Look Like?"

101. Sharpe, *In the Wake*, 131.

(TOURING)
Oraib Toukan

1. If cruel images have a sound, then a scene in Omar Amiralay's film *Plate of Sardines—or, The First Time I Heard of Israel* (1997) captures it masterfully: the hollow footsteps of the director Mohammad Malas walking through ruin and destruction. A slow and reluctant stride that happens after total destruction—on grit, on crushed concrete and rubble, on dry, coarse dirt and brittle gravel.

2. When pace and material suddenly become audible, they become readable. In hearing pace, we can read feelings and decipher the material of what once was. We can imagine disgust felt, or wonder witnessed. The sound of stepping on rubble is cinematic in itself, because it has that crisp and clear quality of "true" Dolby stereo. Similar to the true fear felt when watching the "hero" climb the stairs of an abandoned house in a gripping horror film—except you, "a local," are suddenly illuminated on the screen of that cinema, and the rubble resounds a little differently when it's your home being projected.

3. In 1974, Mohammad Malas filmed the actress Naila Al Atrash, frantically treading the rubble of the ruined Syrian town of Quneitra for his film *Quneitra '74*.[1] Twenty years later, Amiralay asked Malas to walk on the same rubble for the abovementioned scene in Amiralay's film.

4. Quneitra was a trophy for cruelty and might. Israel returned it to Syria entirely destroyed months after the October 1973 War—and seven years after occupying it during the 1967 War. And Syria, too, had preserved it, destroyed, like a pickle left to ferment. Malas, himself from Quneitra, had returned there in 1974 with hundreds of citizens, refugees, and international reporters on a state-sponsored

tour to see "first hand" the condition it was in. Malas was working for Syrian Television at the time and used this footage in a remarkably self-reflexive twenty-minute piece on the cruelty of filming tragedy itself: the way touring ruin can resound.

5. *Quneitra '74* opens with a stream of people walking, crying, reuniting with one another. Three dramatic cross-cuts move from a close shot of a photographer with a long Nikon lens winding his lever, to stills of demolished architecture, and back to the lever. The faint patter of a woman's feet can be heard running across a ghost town, looking for her house. We eventually realise she is actually running away from us—from the camera chasing her, from our gaze. Only then do the opening credits begin, passing on a still frame of her staring right back at us, as though addressing us in respite, in shame, for looking at her tragedy, for making her feel that she was being seen. We nevertheless continue to watch her. We watch her look for all that remains of her home. We watch her find a neighbor who appears to have never left. We watch her attempt to reconstruct what seems to be her house from rubble. In the end, we watch her clean a small, sharp piece of glass stuck to the window pane of the remnants of this house. She looks to see what's on the other side of this piece of glass, but then she catches a reflection of herself. And, as though deciding to forget it all, she closes the tattered window upon hearing the sound of war in the distance.

6. The town of Quneitra remained haunted until 2014, when it became a base for the Syrian resistance; disaster tourists now flocked to the other side of the border, on the Israeli side, to take in the look and feel of battle just two kilometers away in Syria.

7. In the poem "Standing Before the Ruins of al-Birweh" Mahmoud Darwish returns to the village he and his family fled from when he was around six years of age. Al-Birweh was occupied and depopulated by Israeli forces in 1948, and a year later a kibbutz was established on its ruins, right outside of Acre.[2] In the poem, Darwish treads this territory, wavering between two different gazes, that of a foreign correspondent and that of a tourist. He writes:

The journalist interrupts my secret song:
Do you see that dairy factory behind that strong pine tree?
I say: No, I only see the gazelle at the window
He says: What about the modern roads on the rubble
of houses?
I say: No, I don't see them
I only see the garden under them
and I see the cobweb[3]

8. The foreign correspondent sees the landscape in terms of what's absent from the scene, while the tourist is inspired, moved, and awakened because of this absence. The figure of the local in Darwish's poem is unconditionally a foreigner to the place. The local has been silenced. One must therefore "hear" the cruelty of the landscape, and be able to read the signals and signs of what once was: modern roads on the rubble of native architecture, a dairy factory on native plants.[4]

9. Who exactly is considered "local" in tragic times? How do we navigate images in a way that we can begin seeing "I" and "other" as more than elements of the gaze, but, in terms of the prerogative of who has the right to call herself local when representing a cruel event? This is different to a critique of "radical tourism" of the revolution as explored by Hans Magnus Enzensberger in 1974,[5] or leftist internationalism toward and for Palestine as summed up in a few of Jean-Luc Godard's films from 1973.[6] Or its opposite: complete immersion—for example, in Jean Genet's *Prisoner of Love* (1986), which, as Esmail Nashif put it, "is probably the most vivid account of being with the Palestinians but not of them."[7]

10. During the 2006 Israeli bombardment of Beirut, an image by a photographer named Spencer Platt roamed the Internet depicting five young Lebanese in a red convertible driving through the destroyed Haret Hreik neighborhood during the July war.[8] We see four women with oversized sunglasses, clear skin, wearing tight, clean white T-shirts and black tank tops, being driven in a Mini Cooper by a male with equally big glasses. We see a pocket tissue close to one of the women's nose, possibly blocking a stench, another woman with her mobile phone raised up to film, with a half-smile or nervous

frown. The background stands behind them in a slightly shallow depth of field. The image feels somewhat like a collage, because the perfectly exposed chrome details of the car do not seem to fit the ruins around them. In that background, however, one can still decipher what once was: large objects that seem to once belong to a cityscape, like a rooftop water boiler, an advertising banner, a more modern water boiler, among more rubble and busy and distracted people on their phones—and one man who stares at these women. The women, however, cannot see him, because they are facing us, the spectators, presumably fascinated by what seems to be a theater of ruin behind the photographer's field of view.

11. Platt took the photograph for Getty Images, and it was this particular shot, and not the many that represented the total destruction behind the position of Platt's camera, that won the 2007 World Press Photo of the Year. In the words of the jury, it had "the complexity and contradiction of real life, amidst the chaos."[9] Platt's lure though to this frame and not the traumatic one his subjects were taking in, is a disaster-tourist trap. Because he framed the gaze of non-veiled women as a necessarily "outsider" gaze: the viewpoint of Westernized-looking elites flocking to a distant Shiite-majority neighborhood to look at their demise. Counterintuitively, class becomes the perpetrator here, and not the violent condition of that war.

12. Although the women look like they were on a test-track ride in a simulated excursion to view the future in Florida's Epcot Center, the reality was in fact as present as it can get: the women were indeed from this neighborhood and were returning home for the first time after fleeing it, to look for traces of their community.[10] The cruelty is that they were locals touring their own tragedy. The driver was the brother of the distressed woman holding up the phone, and the woman in the front seat was their sister. The two other women worked in a hotel in a safer part of Beirut that hosted these siblings and other refugees for free.[11] Perhaps the photographer, himself the outsider touring the neighbourhood the morning after a raid, might have turned his lens back at the real crime behind him had the women been wearing head scarves.

13. In a letter addressed to the readers of *Photographic News* in 1859, a British photographer by the initials C. A. wrote, "I am a stranger in a strange land."[12] C. A. introduced himself as a tourist in Algeria seeking warm weather and a few photographs to take home. One morning, while wondering about the "Frenchified appearance of everything," he encountered the superstructure of a scaffold for public executions. The beheading of a group of "Arab natives" was scheduled for the next morning. He then pondered, "If I could get permission to establish my [camera] apparatus in a suitable position, the execution would form the subject of an interesting photograph."[13] In both a word of warning and a question addressed to fellow European adventurers, who like him may "wander amongst a half-civilised tribe in search of food for the camera,"[14] he presented a very particular problem:

> The criminals were not brought on the scaffold together, but led up one at a time. The first was the sheikh, who seemed perfectly indifferent to his fate. So rapidly was he bound to the plank and thrust under the axe, that I had barely time to insert the plate-holder and get the instantaneous movement into order before the sharp edge descended, and his head rolled into the basket. This picture was quite successful, and so was the second, but the third presented a dim appearance, the fourth was nearly, and the fifth and six were wholly, invisible. How to account for this I know not, unless the atmosphere around the scaffold became in some way affected by the blood, the odour of which was distinctly perceptible to me. Perhaps some of your readers may be able to suggest the reason.[15]

14. In detached detail, C. A. presents a predicament—namely, that he seems to have lost his subject. Why this has happened is unclear: it could be from the "distinctly perceptible" odor of blood as he explains it, or from some other mystical force, like the referents ("native Arabs") who seem to have ascended their image. By the fifth and sixth plate, his subjects left the photograph altogether, leaving it "wholly, invisible." In artist and writer Jalal Toufic's terms, this was perhaps an immaterial "*withdrawal* of what we think is still there":[16] the photographic plate was materially present, but

its content was immaterially withdrawn in the same moment.[17] Incidentally, it is because of this sudden absence or unavailability of the image that the story was revealed and not buried with the dead—both in his letter to the journal for technical advice, and later in our unearthing of his predicament through archival issues of this weekly. And it is because the image withdrew that we ultimately learned about this tourist's attempt to photograph a colonial French administered beheading of native Algerians for one Algerian's looting and attempted murder of a French settler.

15. What's more astonishing here is C. A.'s normalized and anaesthetized tone in describing the beheading. His distance feels like the "innocent whistle" in the thriller genre, the one typically pointing to the unsuspected killer. In Quentin Tarantino's *Kill Bill* (2003), for example, Elle whistles her way through the hospital dressed up as a nurse, before seeking to inject poison in the Bride while the latter is comatose. This mind-blowing tune was supposedly borrowed from Bernard Herrmann's score for the 1969 British thriller *Twisted Nerve*. But it's also the opening tune of Kais al-Zubaidi's 1972 documentary, *Testimony of Palestinian Children during Wartime*. In what became an audio version of a mise en abyme, this tune continues to travel verbatim into phone ringtones in film scenes or advertisements.[18] This may be because the tone really does somehow "ring" true (or has come to ring "true") to the image of the voyeur, the creepy onlooker, the wanderer in a context not her own: the one who takes the crime to another level. In C. A.'s case, an obscene desire to capture an image of the native Arab in the form of a decapitated head. C. A. dehumanized the "native" to the extent of objectifying his body parts to whole, round objects worthy of photographic transfer (like a still life of, say, a basket of fruit, but with a decapitated head landing into that basket instead). These "wholly, invisible" images implicate the photographer further by subverting the topic of conversation from the thing being photographed to why this tourist would set his camera upon such gore in the first place.

16. Luckily, C. A.'s image left *nothing* in its material realization. Because gory images, in the end, reveal nothing. They end up saying "nothing happened" when a lot did, by showing too much and

revealing very little. Etymologically, the meaning of "gory" stems from gore: dirt, filth, as well as dung, muck, filth (from Dutch, Swedish, and German variations).[19] Gore is also "thick, clotted blood": blood that could render a picture invisible, all the while delaying the conclusions we can make from it—in exactly the same sense that a latent image will reveal itself later. Clotting in itself is embedded into the mechanism of how a filmic image behaves. In the same way, silver halide crystals lie on film as emulsion waiting to see the light of day. Once exposed to it, they subtly thicken and clot, and draw what they have seen from that light. Still sensitive but now exposed, they lie dormant in varying densities waiting to appear.

17. But what if the disaster tourist, the scavenger, the vulture that arrives the day after death is the culturati coming to make sense of the crime? In the same poem, "Standing Before the Ruins of al-Birweh," Darwish concludes, "For every home to be stormed by the wind, there is a rhyme."[20] What better way to raise that rhyme than through the mediation of a camera. The detached, exclusive experience of looking into a viewfinder can soothe, deflect, and pacify in the darkest of times, and in fractions of seconds—a much quicker fix than any other medium. But that comfort is reserved only for the person behind the viewfinder.

18. Perhaps the local should have not only the prerogative to represent the cruel image, but also the exclusive rights to it. And so suddenly, it's a privilege to be the local of a cruel event. Because s/he, of all people, *knows* the "aura" of that image.[21]

19. The 1973 war that both Amiralay and Malas refer to was a twenty-day battle in October of that year, when Syria and Egypt coordinated attacks from both sides of their borders with Israel on Yom Kippur to regain the territory they lost in 1967. In the middle of this short war, Susan Sontag traveled to Israel from New York and produced *Promised Lands* (1974), one of four films she directed over the course of her career. The film is about Israel perceived through its signals and signs, but it is also a reflection on war in general, and in its most decontextualized form. Critical reviews bashed it as presenting an entirely "touristic gaze" of Israel, and the film was banned altogether in Israel. [22]

20. *Promised Lands* is somewhat banal in comparison to the potential of the subject matter. It belongs to a genre of films, from Chris Marker's *Description d'un combat* (1960) to Pier Paolo Pasolini's *A Visit to Palestine* (1965), that crash-landed on the Palestine/Israel landscape with great intrigue, and departed with demystified disenchantment.

21. What stands out so starkly in *Promised Lands* though, and surprisingly the least mentioned aspect in critiques of it, is Sontag's incredibly voyeuristic gaze at the scorched human body. Within the first nine minutes of this ninety-minute film, Sontag shows variations of a shot of a charred body lying in the desert like a found carbon sculpture: arms across chest, and legs bent wide open like a dead bird displaying itself for a vulture. The only thing that remains decipherable, and the only thing, it seems, that can survive a war intact, are the soldier's combat boots. Sontag returns to this exact shot in another sequence and twins it with a shot of another body whose legs are spread as far apart as a scarecrow's arms. She then cuts to a horrifically close and somewhat lengthy shot of a face more gruesomely burned than the combat face mask protecting it. An Arabic notebook lies on the ground of this scene.

22. Sontag does not really represent the Arab in this film. After all, as Hanan Toukan puts it in a 2012 essay on the film, "This was a period when the 'Palestinian,' and the very idea of 'Palestine,' was either non-existent or simply a synonym for 'terrorist' in mainstream Western (especially American) society."[23] To Sontag, a native person does indeed exist, but it seems to only be the Bedouin or the villager she films from a distance.

23. One can't help but wonder if Sontag would have included these scorched shots had they been corpses of non-Arab soldiers—granted that she is genuinely and wholeheartedly commenting on the total dehumanizing condition of war to the extent that it destroys the physical appearance of being human.

24. Perhaps the intensity of Sontag's writing in her landmark book *On Photography* (1977) came from having experienced the cruel image to record some of the acute realizations she made on the aesthetic and moral problem of photographing suffering. From

having had the impulse to tour disaster in a distant locale in order to inscribe it in celluloid. Put differently, perhaps the insightfulness of *On Photography* came from a practice, from someone engaging with the moral force field of making decisions on behalf of images. Capturing, handling, treating, editing, and distributing a cruel image captured in a distant locale. Ironically, the 1974 *New York Times* review of *Promised Lands* mocks her in the closing paragraph: "Perhaps [it] should have been a book instead of a film."[24]

25. Sontag did release the first version of her essay "In Plato's Cave" (at the time titled simply "Photography") in the *New York Review of Books* in October 1973, which seems to coincide with her time in Jerusalem. This particular essay became the introduction to *On Photography* and opened up a series of pivotal writings that eventually culminated in that book. She wrote, "The camera doesn't rape, or even possess, though it may presume, intrude, trespass, distort, exploit, and, at the farthest reach of metaphor, assassinate—all activities that, unlike the sexual push and shove, can be conducted from a distance, and with some detachment."[25]

26. Distance is not only about detachment and degrees of separation from the cruel event but also about who has the right to capture the cruelties of that war. Sontag was, after all, a Jewish-born intellectual, clearly and sincerely grappling with representations of and distance to a "conflict" she toured and could not entirely decode or identify with. Sontag's son, David Reiff, could not find specific notes on the filming of *Promised Lands* in her diaries from the period.[26] However, in an entry from October 12, 1973, during the war, she does log an evening in Jerusalem that she and David spent with Gershom Scholem, a historian of Jewish mysticism (and a friend of Walter Benjamin, who parted ways with him on a few matters, including Benjamin's discomfort with Zionism).[27] Reading this diary entry, one can just imagine the inspiration drawn from making sense of the connection between these intellectual figures—maybe even over a drink on a beautiful, breezy early autumn evening in Jerusalem. Akin to Darwish's tourist who can "only see the gazelle at the window," Sontag apparently shares these inspirations at a dinner party upon her return home. She writes in the next diary entry, "Hannah Arendt said that Benjamin was the only person Scholem ever really

loved (the evening at Lizzy's [Elizabeth Hardwick] house last week in NY)."[28] Such is the cruel irony of disaster tourism. Breezy evenings with the local intellectual come at the end of a "field day" filming a native, or a corpse or two. Fittingly, Sontag concludes her long sequences of cemeteries in *Promised Lands* with a fixed shot of a tombstone that reads: "His last message: No more wars for me."[29]

***

27. Technology has continued to valorize the phenomenon of war tourism and facilitate the proliferation of image souvenirs. If anything, it has memorialized the figure of the disaster tourist. One can tour total ruin in virtual-reality apps that gamify its cruel details. One can play and replay drone footage of ruined cities that have never been visited. If not edit, color correct, and add text to this footage for the next share. Like phantoms, cruel images lurk, rearing their ugly heads after each disaster, waiting to be toured like an archaeological ruin liberated from the weight of history. At best, in curious guidebooks.

28. A book called *Bloody Britain*, published by the Automobile Association of Great Britain in 2002, traces travel itineraries to locations in Britain with the "bloodiest" histories.[30] Flipping through it feels like handling an IGCSE biology book, except that the color-coded titles, text boxes, maps, and locations are interjected with descriptions of unpleasant details set in huge typefaces. In the Staffordshire section, for example, a twenty-four-point-size font reads: "They chased them for 2 miles, slashing and slaughtering as they went, until around 2,000 mutilated Lancastrian corpses littered the Shropshire fields." (Note that the least obscene paragraph found has been quoted.)

29. Luckily, nations can and do cleanse and distance themselves from all their gore. With enough distance, they can propel a Mini Cooper down rolling hills, with a Labrador Retriever and Wellington boots in tow, in a search for gore that ends with a splendid Sunday roast.

Oxford, July 2018

1. The scene in Amiralay's film is a reference to *Quneitra '74*.

2. Sinan Antoon, translator's note to Mahmoud Darwish "Standing before the Ruins of al-Birweh," *Jadaliyya*, March 13, 2011, http://jadaliyya.com/Details/23789.

3. Darwish, "Standing before the Ruins of al-Birweh."

4. Darwish. See also the Israeli organization Zochrot and their walking tours on reading the "signs" of obliterated villages.

5. Hans Magnus Enzensberger, "Tourists of the Revolution," in *The Consciousness Industry: On Literature, Politics, and the Media*, trans. Michael Roloff (London: Continuum, 1974).

6. See Irmgard Emmelhainz, "Geopolitics and Contemporary Art, Part I: From Representation's Ruin to Salvaging the Real," *e-flux Journal*, no. 69 (January 2016); and Irmgard Emmelhainz, "Between Objective Engagement and Engaged Cinema: Jean-Luc Godard's 'Militant Filmmaking' (1967-1974), Part I," *e-flux Journal*, no. 34 (April 2012).

7. Esmail Nashif, *Palestinian Political Prisoners: Identity and Community* (London: Routledge, 2008); Jean Genet, *Prisoner of Love*, trans. Barbara Bray (New York: New York Review Books, 2003).

8. See the description of Platt's photograph and a description are published on the 2007 World Press Photo Contest website, https://www.worldpressphoto.org/collection/photo/2007/daily-life/spencer-platt.

9. "Award-Winning Photo Draws Criticism for Subjects," NPR, March 2, 2007, https://www.npr.org/templates/story/story.php?storyId=7684938?storyId=7684938&t=153615332238.

10. Ulrike Putz, "Catering to a Lebanese Cliché: World Press Photo Mix-Up," *Spiegel Online*, February 28, 2007, http://www.spiegel.de/international/catering-to-a-lebanese-cliche-world-press-photo-mix-up-a-469070.html.

11. Ibid.

12. William Crookes, ed., *The Photographic News*, September 5, 1859, 6.

13. Ibid.

14. Ibid., 7.

15. Ibid., 6.

16. "Walid Raad & Jalal Toufic: The Withdrawal of Tradition Past a Surpassing Disaster," Art & Education announcement, January 18, 2007, https://www.artandeducation.net/announcements/111510/walid-raad-amp-jalal-toufic-the-withdrawal-of-tradition-past-a-surpassing-disaster.

17. Jalal Toufic, *Forthcoming* (Berkeley, CA: Atelos, 2001). See also Mark Westmoreland, "Catastrophic Subjectivity: Representing Lebanon's Living Dead," *Alif: Journal of Comparative Poetics*, no. 30 (2010): 176.

18. Pete R, "Twisted Nerve," Quentin Tarantino Archives, May 28, 2007, https://wiki.tarantino.info/index.php/Twisted_Nerve.

19. *Online Etymology Dictionary*, s.v. "gore," https://www.etymonline.com/word/gore?ref=etymonline_crossreference#etymonline_v_9058.

20. Darwish, "Standing on the Ruins of al-Birweh." See also the posthumous collection it was published in, *La Uridu Li-Hadhihi al-Qasidati an Tantahi* [I don't want this poem to end] (Beirut: Riyad al-Rayyis, 2009).

21. But, again, what does this make of non-locals like Jean Genet, who was made to feel like a local in the Palestinian communities he lived with, and vice versa?

22. See Ella Shohat's introduction to the film in *Israeli Cinema: East/West and the Politics of Representation*, 2nd ed. (New York: I. B. Tauris, 2010). See also Hanan Toukan, "Grappling with Israel: From Sontag to Lacan and the Maoists in Between," *Jadaliyya*, September 3, 2012, http://www.middleeastdigest.com/pages/index/7176/grappling-with-israel_from-sontag-to-lacan-and-the.

23. Toukan, "Grappling with Israel."

24. To be more precise: Nora Sayre concludes, in her *New York Times* review, "Moments have been filmed with such confusion that we can't respond to (this) suffering—indeed, suffering's hardly conveyed in 'Promised Lands.' Because the movie is dull and badly organized, the war is made to seem unreal. Unlike Claude Lanzmann's very fine documentary, 'Israel Why,' which was shown at the 1973 New York Film Festival, the Sontag film won't increase your understanding of Israel. Perhaps the latter should have been a book instead of a film." Nora Sayre, "Susan Sontag's 'Promised Lands': Treatment of Israel Is at Screening Room," *New York Times*, July 12, 1974.

25. Susan Sontag, *On Photography* (New York: Farrar, Straus and Giroux, 1977), 13.

26. Susan Sontag, *As Consciousness Is Harnessed to Flesh: Journals and Notebooks,1964-1980* ed. David Rieff (London: Penguin, 2003), 367.

27. See Scholem Gershom, *Walter Benjamin: The Story of a Friendship* (New York: New York Review Books, 2003).

28. Sontag, *As Consciousness Is Harnessed to Flesh*, 368.

29. The sequence appears at 1:27 minutes in Susan Sontag's *Promised Lands* (1974).

30. Mike Ivory, *Bloody Britain: A Guide to the History of Murder, Massacre and Mayhem* (London: AA Publishing, 2002). More representative titles of their publications include *50 Walks in the Cotswolds* and *Britain's Best Bed & Breakfasts and Country Inns*, etc.

THE SUBVERSIVE BODY
Aimée Zito Lema

The Subversive Body, an installation and performance, uses as its starting point images of revolutionary and guerrilla movements from dictatorial periods in Argentina between 1966 and 1983, culled from the Argentinean National Archive (Argentina Archivo General de la Nación Dpto. Doc. Fotográficos). The original archival images have been rephotographed, focusing primarily on bodily gestures. Close-up and abstracted, the images become condensed traces of physical resistance against political horror. The imagery is printed in black and white on large pieces of paper that have been shaped and stiffened into a new corpus, the mold for which was the artist's own body. Once paper has taken a certain form, the fiber "remembers" this information, resulting in a sculpture that has a "double memory": it recalls a shape as well as a historical event. The work addresses questions in relation to corporeal memory and the traces that sociopolitical conflicts leave behind, ones that can be passed on (often in the form of trauma) from one generation to another.

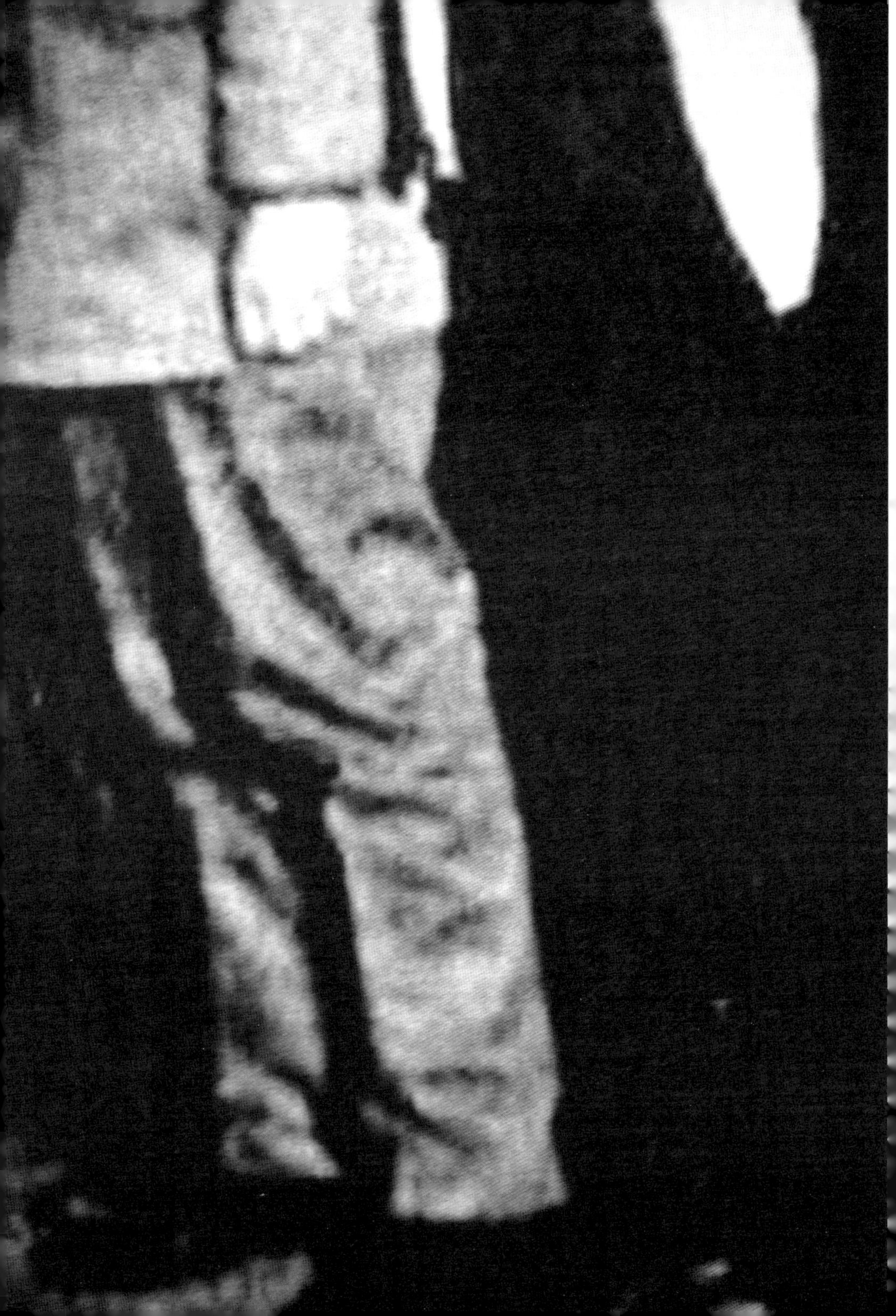

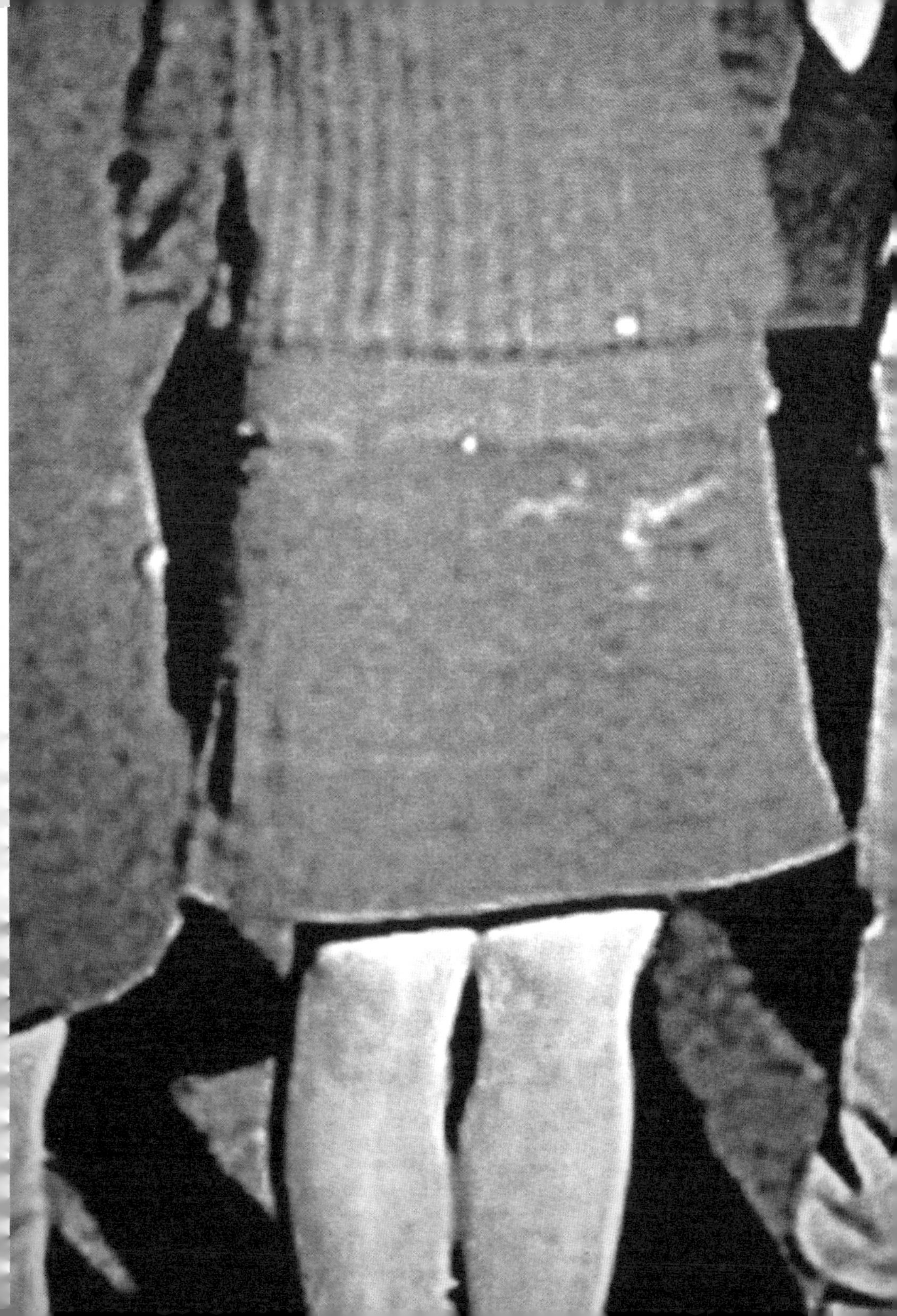

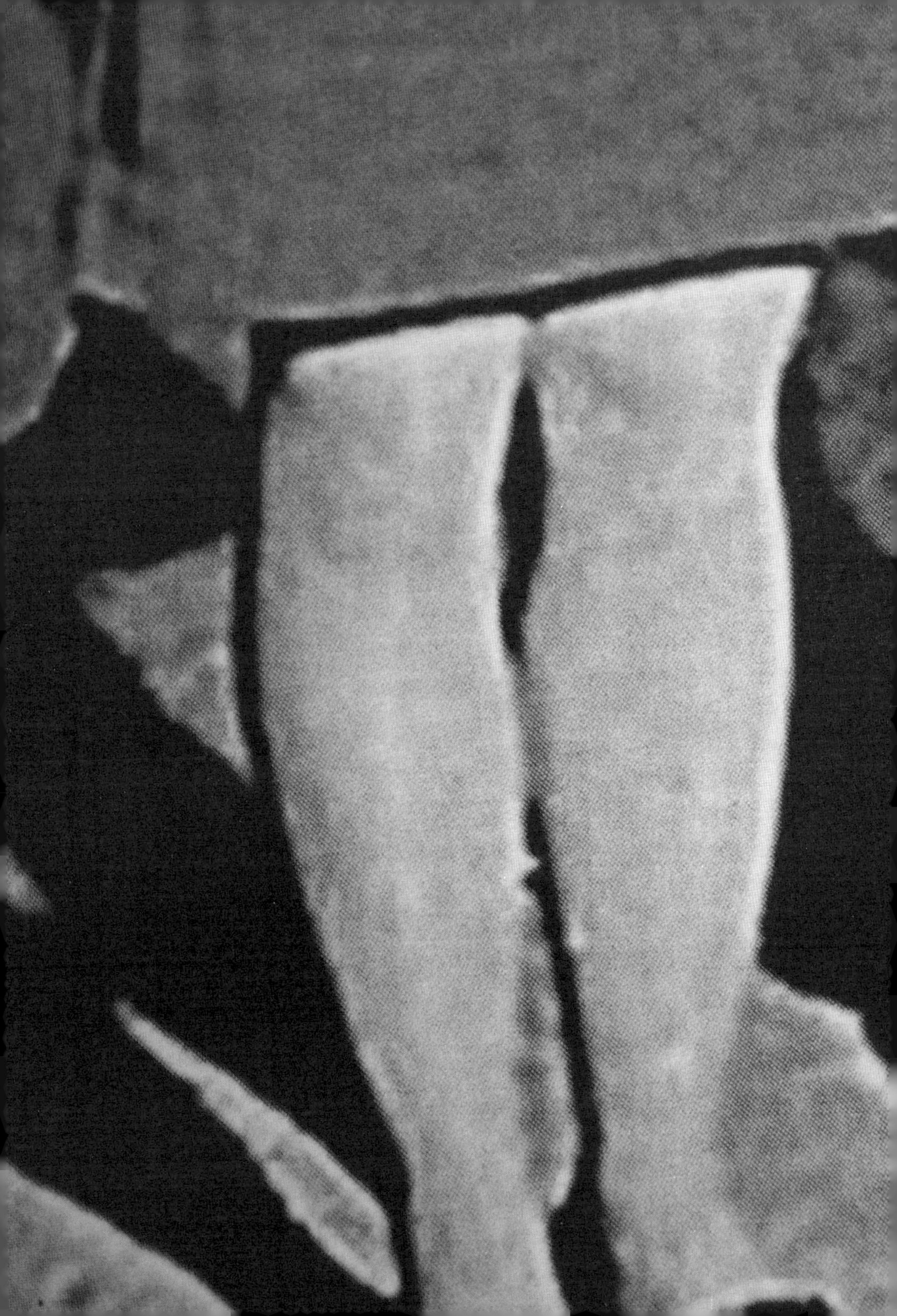

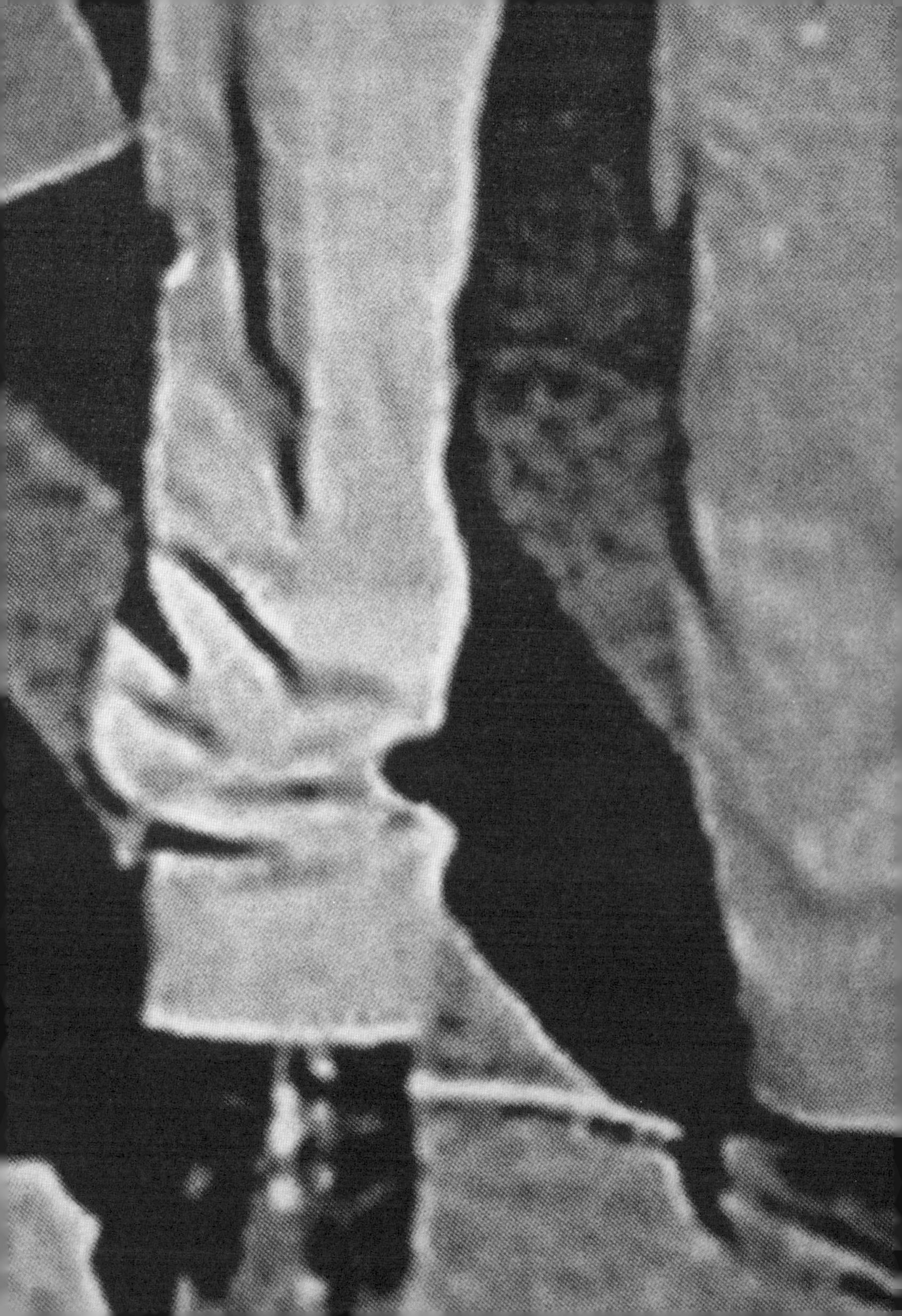

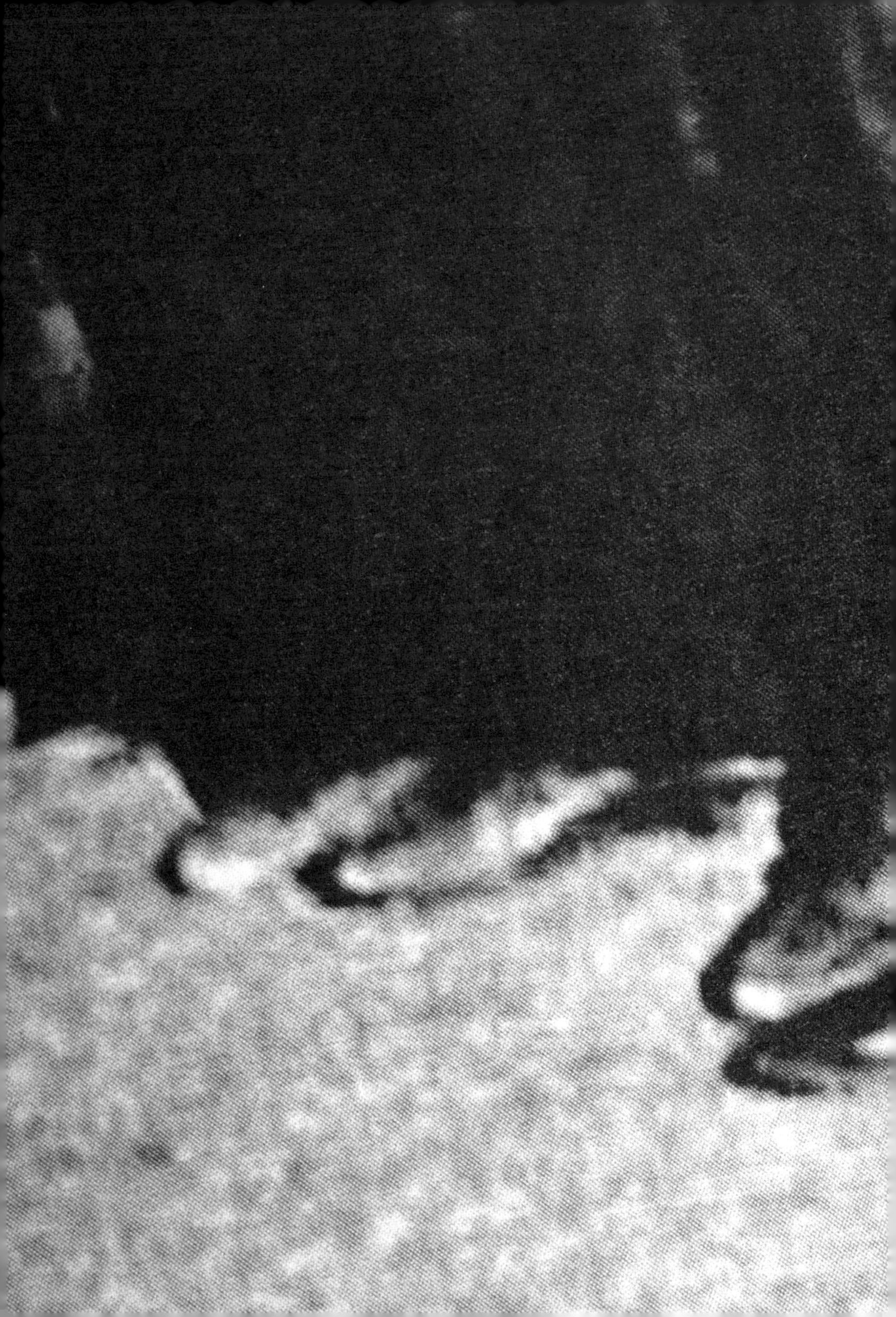

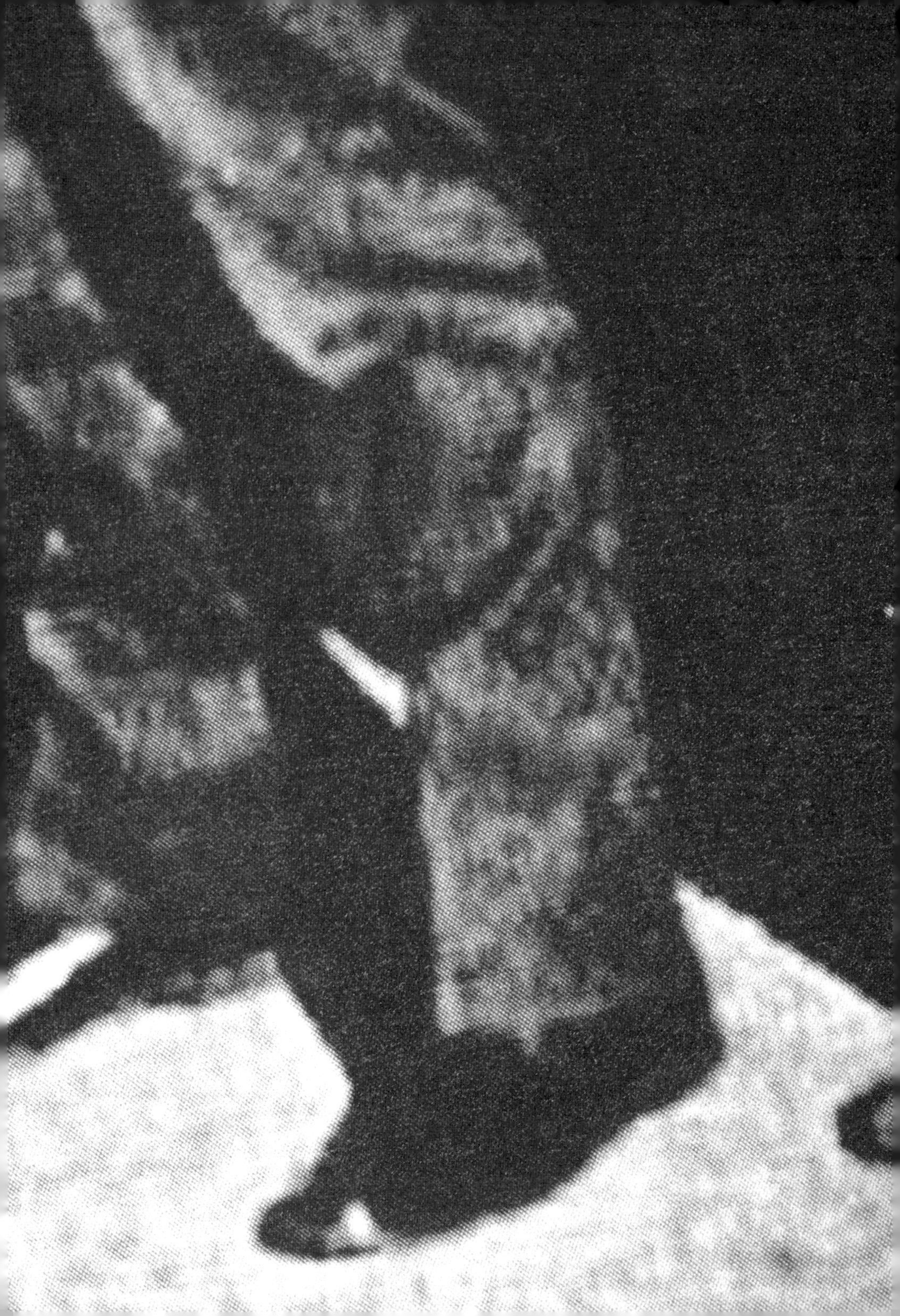

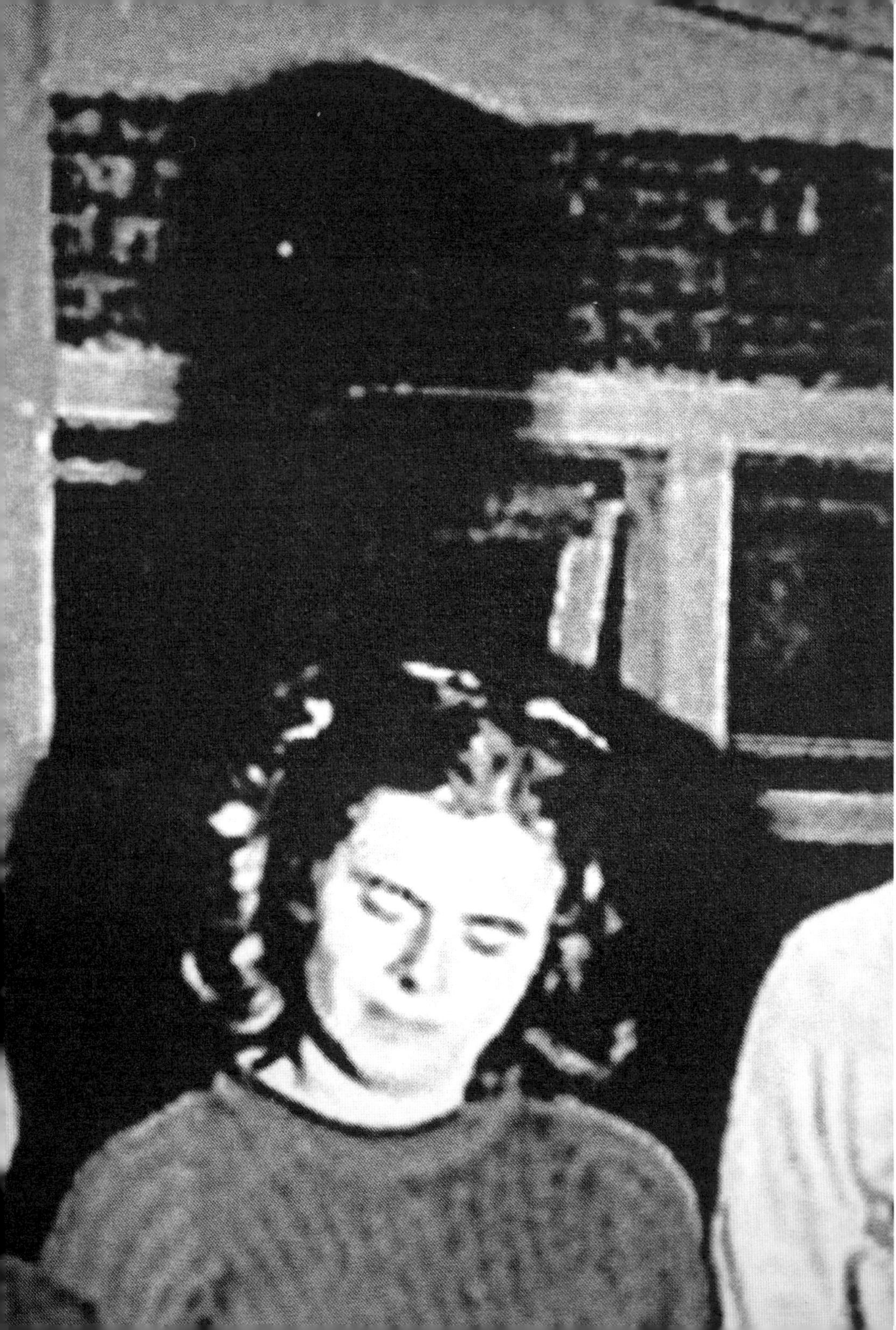

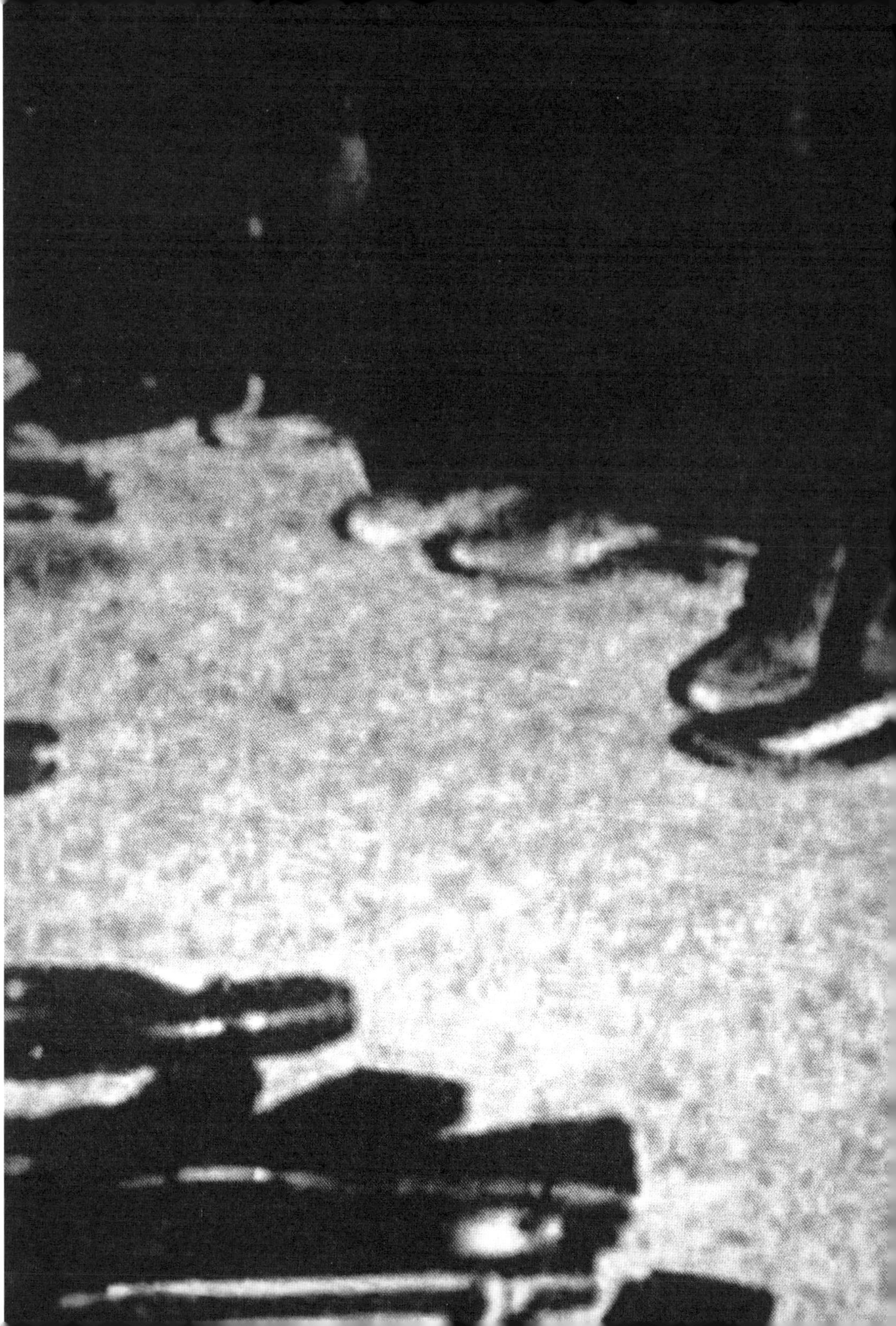

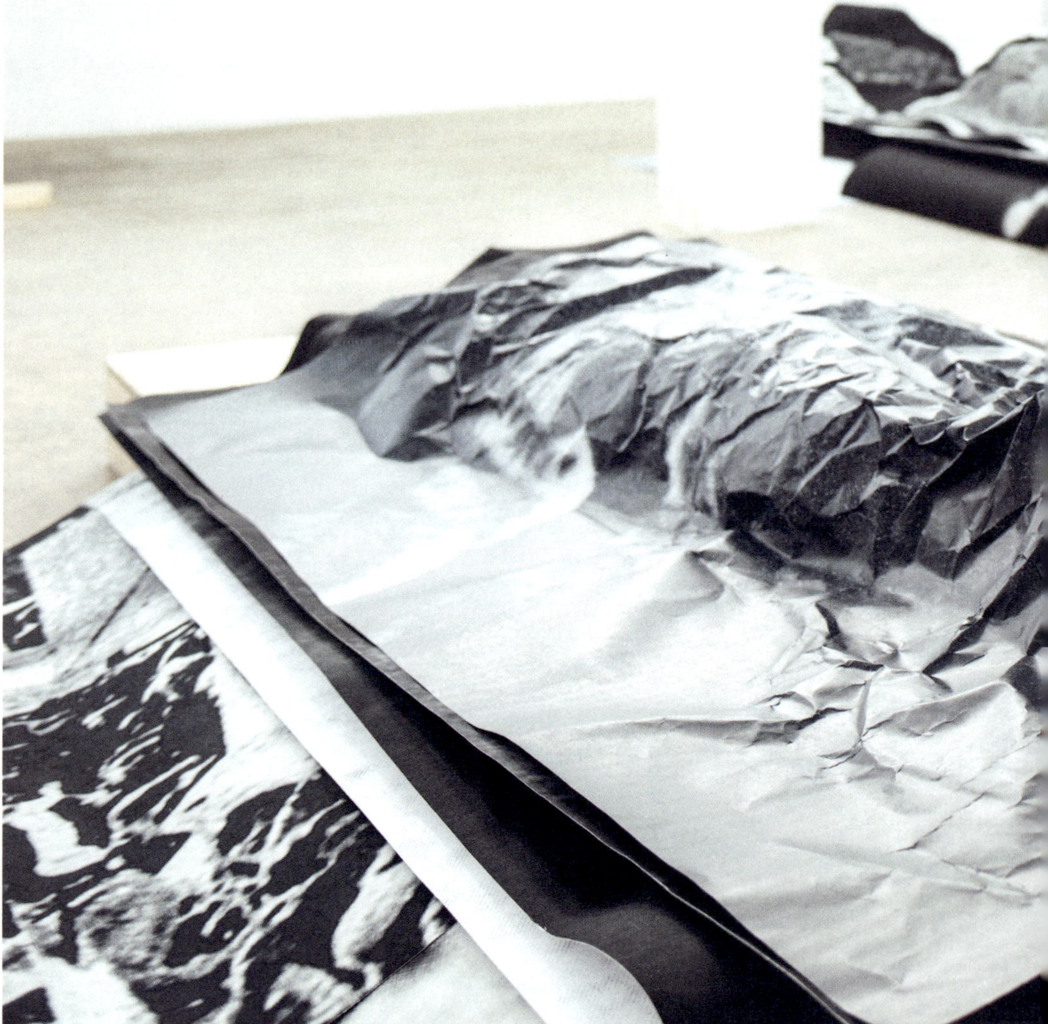

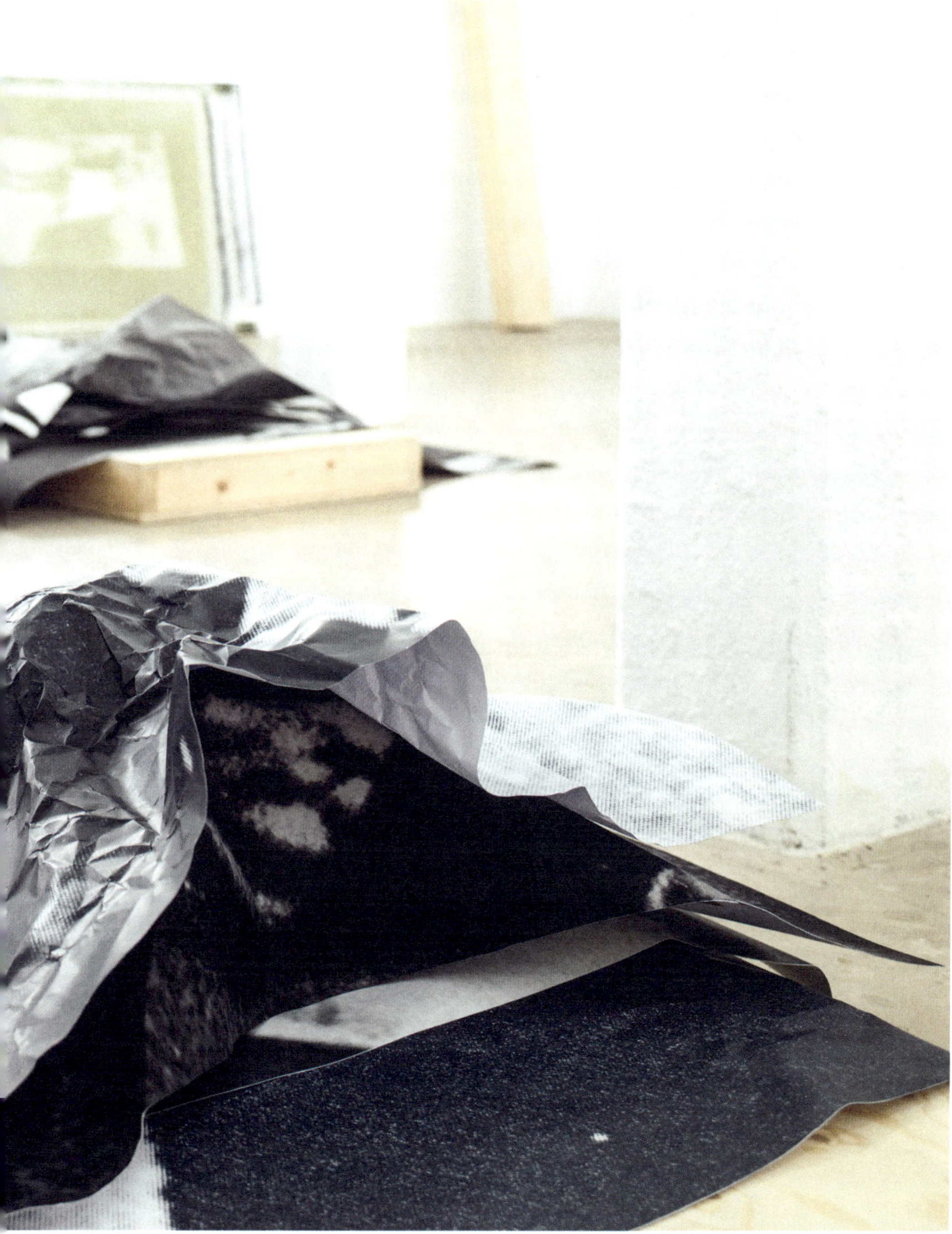

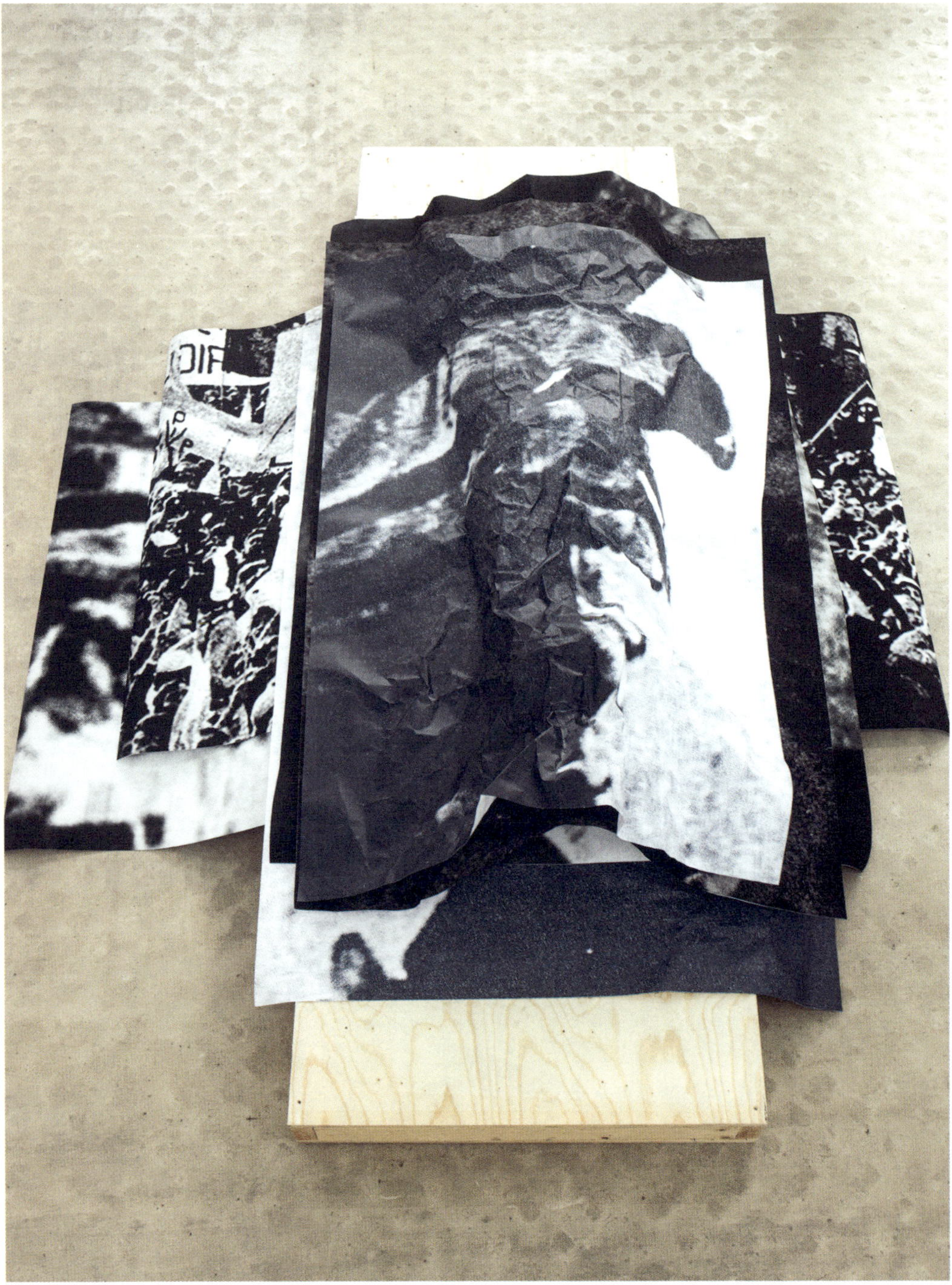

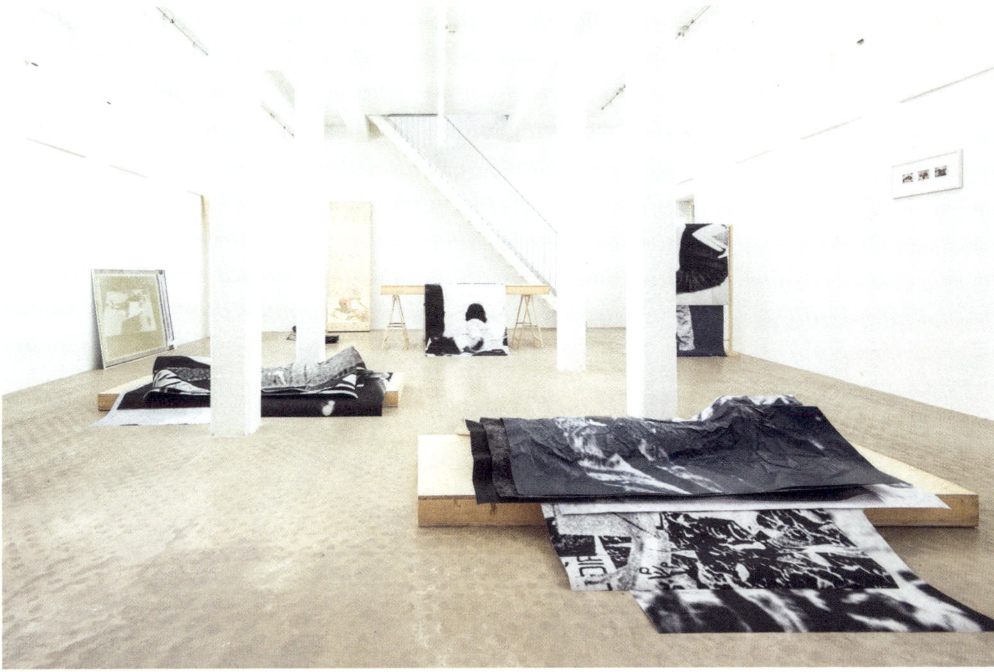

Images on pages 272–79 depict the Trelew Massacre, a mass execution of nineteen political prisoners, militants of different Peronist and left-wing organizations, by the military government of Argentina. Of the nineteen militants, sixteen were killed and three survived but were subsequently captured and "disappeared." The massacre took place on the morning of August 22, 1972, at the Almirante Marcos A. Zar base of the Argentine navy near the city of Trelew, in Patagonia. The prisoners were recaptured after an escape attempt and subsequently shot down by marines in a simulated escape attempt.

ARCHIVES OF THE FLESH
Reenacting Memories of Torture
Sofie Lebech

Fig. 1 ←

EXTRACTS FROM THE PERFORMANCE
This Is for Her: Prologue and Part I

Prologue

I We want her to describe the pain.
We want to understand why.
We want to know.
We *want* to know.
In the beginning we want to see.
After a while we are not so interested.
It's the old discussion of looking or not looking.
Some say we should look.
Some say we should look away.
We need a clean victim.
We *need* a clean victim.
We want her to be more precise.
Please be more precise!

You The cell is very small. The walls are gray. They are made out of concrete. There is a window. But it is placed so high up that it is impossible to look out. Sometimes dust comes in through the window. Outside, the streets lead to the city and the tourist attractions. Perhaps the pyramids, perhaps the Holiday Inn, with its bullet holes and bomb craters, perhaps the Great Wall or the Wailing Wall. It's incredibly far away.

I We are not saying anything about nationality. Or race. We are not saying anything about outsourced torture. We are just saying that it's far away from us.

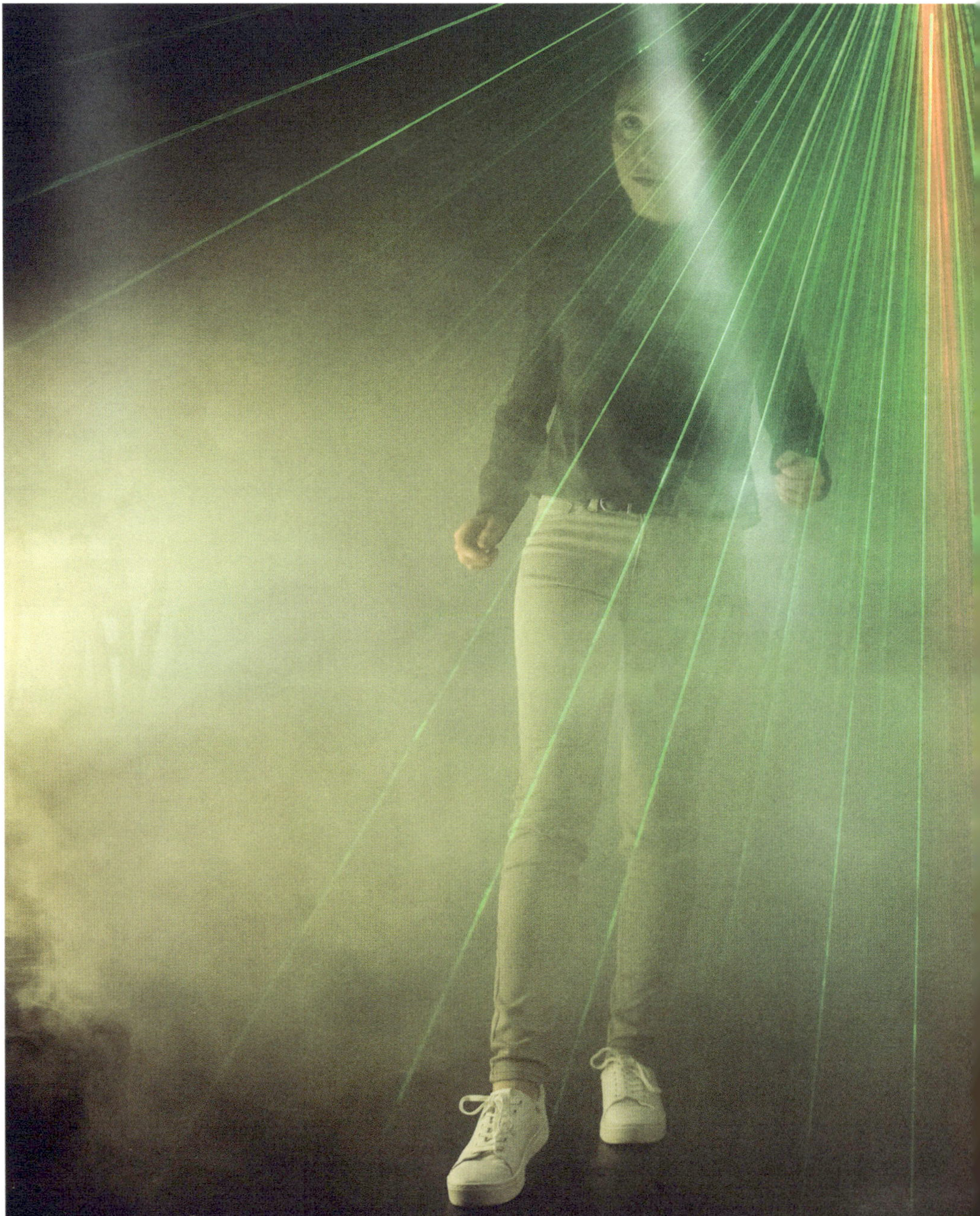

Fig. 1 Sofie Lebech, *This Is for Her*, 2017

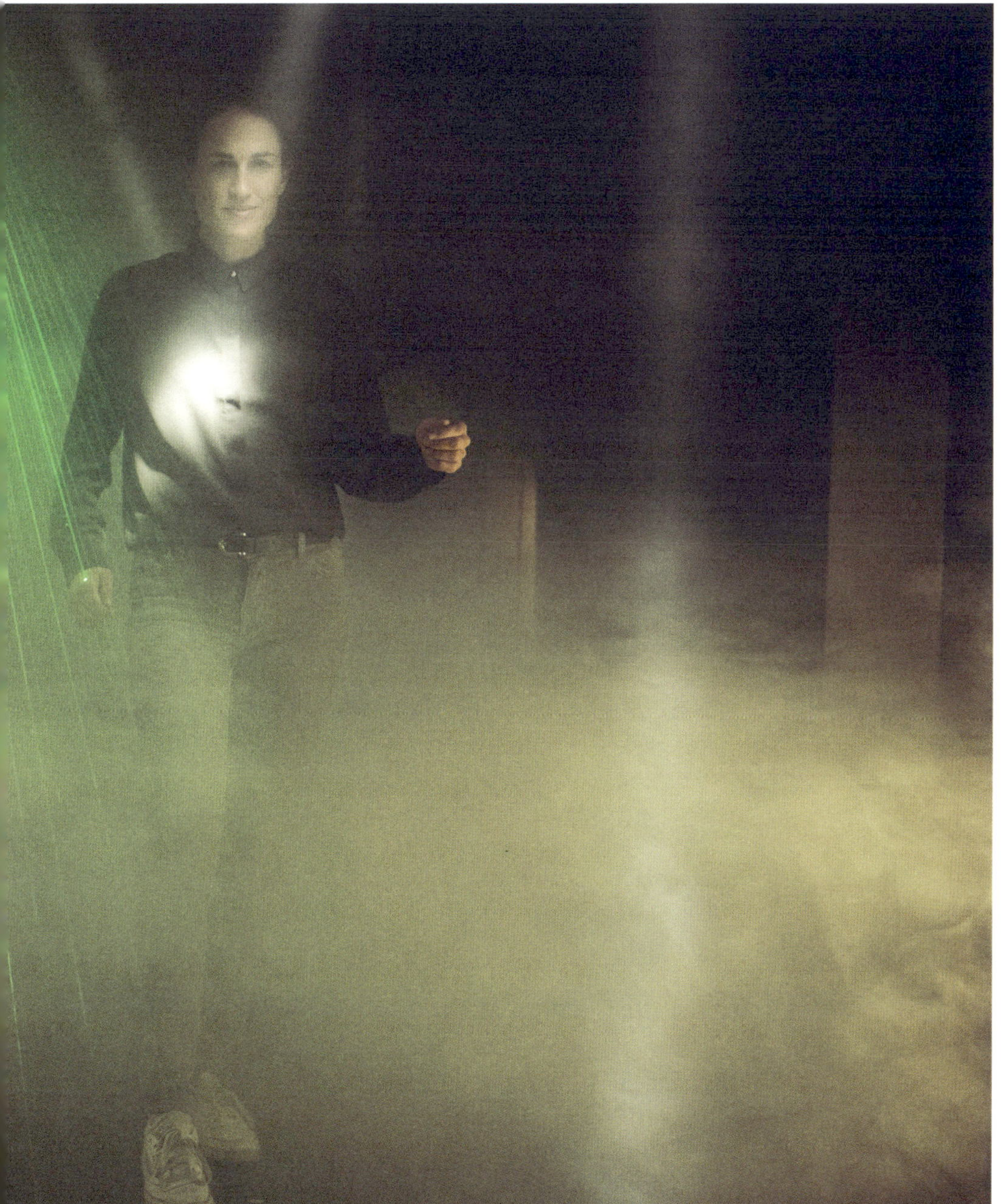

You It is incredibly far away.

I We are just saying that the history is different there.

You The history is so different there.

I And the architecture is different.

You The architecture is very different there with features of French or British colonialism.

I But never Danish.

You No, never Danish.

I There is the victim, and there is the perpetrator.

You *This is for her.*

Part I. Argentina: The Dirty War, 1974-1983

I There was something about the atmosphere that reminded me of a theater. Everything inside and outside the prison seemed very staged. Almost as if an audience was seated in the darkness. The police destroy. The army destroys. In the theater you create something. When you do that performance, it has to be good. Important. It has to make people listen. It must never happen again. It was for fun. It happens all the time. It happens and happens and happens. Soon it will happen here too; perhaps it has already begun.

Are you recording this?

At the time I was teaching philosophy at the university. It was during the dictatorship, *Guerra Sucia*—the Dirty War—from 1974 to 1983. Thirty thousand people disappeared. I opposed the government, so they arrested me. First, I was given warnings; they said I had to support them and make my students support them. If not, I would be punished. They were serious. One night they took me, and for more than a year they tortured me. But then I escaped. That's a story I can tell you later.

I was with my son when they arrested me. He was two. We were walking along the street when a group of policemen came toward us. They knew who I was. They didn't come to our home. They didn't warn me. They just grabbed me off the street with my son. He clung to me. They took us to the police station. He was afraid. Being there with him was horrifying. That evening they also arrested my husband. I never saw him again.

They told me to support the dictatorship, but I said, "No, I'm against it." They told me they would show me who I was dealing with, and they hit my son—a two-year-old—and blood ran from his nose. I said, "Hit me, not him." And they said, "No, we will hit him, so you understand why you must support us." After a few hours they started torturing me.

Some days later they came to take him away. They said they would take him to my family. I didn't know if they were telling the truth. They were. He ended up living with my in-laws. I saw him again two years later, but he didn't recognize me. He didn't want to be with me. He ran away from me.

I was moved to a new place. We drove through the city, I couldn't see anything, but soon I found out where we were. It was the military academy. The soccer World Cup was taking place in Buenos Aires that summer. The main stadium was, *is*, located close by. We could hear the matches. The shouts of joy. People singing in the streets. We could hear where we were. And we could smell it too. You never forget the smell of people; shit, piss, sweat, fear. The taste of tears. First, they run; then they just stick to your skin. It's dirty; you can't wash, the dust sets in.

We were under the roof. It was summer, and some days it felt like we were burning up. They weren't real cells. Rather, small compartments. They were 2.5 meters long, seventy-five centimeters wide, and one meter high. Like coffins. We were the living dead. ~~Sometimes we were left in the coffins for days, lying handcuffed in our own piss with hoods covering our faces.~~[1] We were able to sit or lie down. It was dark. We tried communicating by banging on the wooden walls, but they played the radio very loud, so we could only hear the knocking when there were small gaps in the broadcast. If you needed the toilet, you had to call for the guard. Sometimes they came, other times they didn't.

During winter it was cold. I didn't get blankets. Only sleep and torture. Sleep and torture.

The cells for pregnant prisoners were on the same level. They were moved there when they were seven or eight months pregnant. They gave birth in the military hospital. Then they came back, and later they disappeared. We never saw the babies. ~~I was so lucky not to give birth in prison~~. Much later we found out that the babies were adopted by childless army couples, or couples who supported the army as part of the government's "reorganization process." They said the children were not to blame for their parents' mistakes, their misconceptions. The children were never told. Imagine that. Imagine growing up with people who support the system that killed your parents.

Do you know the Abuelas de Plaza de Mayo? They are the grandmothers of the adopted children. They began searching for their grandchildren in the late 1970s. They knew that their daughters were pregnant when they were taken. They believed that their grandchildren were alive somewhere. And they were right.

Did they have a plan? I don't know. I don't know whether they intended to release us at some point or whether our death sentence had already been passed. Sorry, can I do that again? Was there an overall plan? I don't know. I don't know if they intended to release us at some point, or if our death sentence had already been passed. We knew nothing. Were we going to be tortured? Today? Tomorrow? Would we disappear completely? During the dictatorship five thousand men and women went through the military academy. Only two hundred survived. I survived. It was located in the city. That's hard to understand. People walked past it every day on their way to work.

We were tortured in the basement... it was divided into smaller rooms. One was named the "egg tray"—the walls were lined with egg trays to muffle the screams. Why do you always get tortured in the basement? Is it so people can't hear you? Or is it because the perpetrators want to be far from heaven and closer to hell?

In the beginning it was all the time, every day, every hour, every minute, interrogation and torture. There were many kinds of torture. There was something we called football torture. You are the ball. Sometimes they hang you from the ceiling.

Sometimes they give you an electric shock. They chain you up, cover your head with a hood, and give you an electric shock. We called that one the opera torture. The sound in your head. Some people were given enough morphine to become addicted, and then the morphine was taken away from them. There was a lot of pain. But… it's complicated.

When I speak about it, it happens again. I see their faces. I hear their voices. I feel their bodies. You want to know what is coming for you in the darkness. Clothes offer no protection. They can be ripped to pieces. There is physical torture, and there is mental torture. You wait. They come to humiliate you. They laugh at you. They pick you up at night and take you to a place of execution. They cover your eyes and start shooting and you think: Now, I'm going to die. But they don't kill you.

On Wednesdays the whole place was on edge—almost quivering. It was the day people disappeared. ~~We hoped they had been released but knew they probably weren't~~. The prisoners were selected at 5:00 p.m. They were told they were being transferred to a normal prison in the south of Argentina. But they were drugged and thrown out from airplanes into the Atlantic or the Río de la Plata. Later, the bodies were found washed up on the beaches.

What is the worst thing about torture? The worst thing is that your life totally depends on another person—the perpetrator. You are tortured. You see others being tortured. You notice people disappear. You think they have died, but you don't know. *Not knowing* is torture. I didn't know what had happened to my husband, to my son, and I didn't know if they knew that I was still alive. They told me several times that they would release me if I supported them, but I didn't trust them. I believed that once I gave in, I would disappear too. If you are tortured, you remain tortured. It never goes away.

I witnessed some of my students being raped. I didn't want to watch, but they forced me to. They wanted names. Who would I betray? What should I say? They told me they would kill them. I didn't know what to believe. Kill young students? ~~The students were furious when the military junta seized power~~. At the beginning no one believed they could be killed for political resistance.

The information was not important to them. The torture was. ~~From time to time they'd let people go just so the outside world would get to know about what was happening behind the walls what could happen if you were politically active.~~ They wanted to demonstrate their financial and military power. The ones who were taken were just the visible people. The armed activists were invisible. They lived underground and carried weapons and poison to take if they were caught. Of course, many of them were taken, but a lot of the people who were taken were intellectuals, students, or union members. My husband and I were members of a leftist organization—back then we were all leftists—he was a union rep and handed out fliers. That's all it took.

Of course, I also knew people who went further. My best friend became a militant. We went to university together in the late 1960s. We studied medicine. He wanted to be a psychiatrist. I wanted to be a surgeon. He wasn't political at all, but I took him to a meeting. Somehow, he got involved with one of the militant groups, Montoneros, and he advanced very quickly. *He* began carrying weapons. I changed to philosophy and started teaching after I graduated. He had to flee with his wife and child when the regime started tightening the grip in the mid-1970s. Later they returned, thinking it was safe. Then they were taken.

If I had to describe the country back then... There was an atmosphere that terrified people. When you saw the army or the police, you panicked. Torture is an effective way of controlling the population. I remember an incident when I was on the train and noticed my brother's friend sitting across from me. He looked away. He avoided my gaze, so I didn't greet him. Back then you didn't want to be associated with someone in the danger zone. You never knew what might trigger an arrest.

If you want, I can tell you how I escaped. If not, I won't.

At some point I was admitted to the military hospital with an infection. The treatment wasn't very good, and I was in a lot of pain. I knew they'd kill me; they just weren't going to kill me yet. One month later they picked me up for interrogation. The interrogation took place in an ordinary room at the hospital. They beat me harder than ever before. Tore hair from my scalp. Burned me with cigarettes. After that I couldn't stand the smell of smoke. I had lost twenty kilos and was just a bag of bones.

They said they would kill me. I said nothing. It was as if they had become bored of torturing me. They dragged me into the courtyard. One of the guards stayed with me. He seemed very tired and said, "Wait here, we are going to kill you." I said okay and closed my eyes. When I opened them, he had disappeared into the building. So I ran. Away. They must have thought I couldn't move any more, that I had stopped resisting. I wasn't even handcuffed.

The military academy borders the railway. The area is just surrounded by a wall. I ran to the wall and climbed on top of a wagon to get across. I made that decision in ten seconds and managed it in twenty. It was completely impossible, but I did it. I got out. No one saw me. I ran along the railroad, two or three kilometers, until I saw a white house. I knocked on the door, they opened, and I said that I had run away, that I had been tortured and that they would kill me. They let me in. They arranged a truck ride for me... sorry... they arranged a truck ride for me out of town that very evening. I was so lucky. When you survive, you can't understand. Why me?

The next couple of weeks we drove north until we arrived at the Brazilian border. Brazil was also a dictatorship, but it was much safer for us than Argentina. There I met others in exile. Most of them coped by doing odd jobs. No one ever tells you that it's really expensive to live in exile. If you don't have something to sell or some money with you, you immediately become part of the exile underclass. That's why many people went back home, risking their lives. And this is how I was able to send word to my family. I waited and waited. One day my in-laws arrived with my son. They told me that my husband had disappeared, and they gave me money to travel further away with my son to safety. I never discovered what had happened to my husband. I know when and where he was taken. That's all.

I suffered for a long time. The days were light and heavy at the same time. It's like the tide. In Spanish we call it *la marea*. Marea means both dizziness and the tide. That's how it is. The pain comes suddenly and then withdraws. You are dizzy in life. You are afraid of falling and never being able to get up again. Death is not pain. We fear death, but really it is the end of pain. That's the attraction of suicide.

Yes. I wanted to kill myself. Many times. Sometimes it comes back. Imagine if you suddenly committed suicide after all these years. Would it be a waste not to have done it earlier? ~~All the times you wanted to, but didn't~~. Or is it enough to live as long as you possibly can? I often wonder why people commit suicide after the worst is over. After the torture, after the war, after the winter—in times of peace. The biggest choice is to continue living. To hold on. To move on to become a person again.

Having a child can't save you. When the pain comes, nothing can save you. But it gives hope. Love and pain are parallel emotions. I have a photo of my son in the bath... smiling... You may love the child, but it doesn't take the pain away. My son has been destroyed. What happened continues inside. He feels like his identity has been taken away. That history has robbed him of the possibility of having a normal life and a family. His entire life is shaped around the loss of his father. It's easier for me. I survive by remembering. The worst is ignorance.

Torture breaks you down physically and mentally. They take your mind and your body away from you. I was healthy before, and sick after. They hit me on the head so many times that something broke inside. I stop breathing when I sleep. I had an operation, but I still have to use a mask. Sometimes I have nightmares. I'm back in prison. I'm trying to escape but I can't. I don't know what to do, and suddenly I wake up.

I went back once. The buildings are still there, like monuments. There are ghosts everywhere. So many people disappeared. I don't believe for one second that it was only thirty thousand. People don't talk about it. They say it's important to remember, but they don't talk about it. I visited my friend's sister. She lives in the countryside. Down south. She is still hiding. She showed me her gun and said, "This time they are not going to get me." *Nunca terminamos de salir.* It may be over, but we'll never escape.

Who is to blame? Personally, I think the Minister of Finance and the senior figures in the army. The blame is political and economic. I often wonder who was in the army. Who was the soldier? Who was the policeman? I didn't know anyone. My friends didn't know anyone. But it can't be true that no one knew them. Were they just shadows? I *refuse* to blame individuals. But I'm tempted. I believe you can say no. You *can* say no. ~~No. No. No~~.

If we should stop here? It's up to you.

FRAMING *This Is for Her*

This Is for Her is a performance about torture and therapy. The dramaturgy of the performance follows a three-part structure. The first part (printed here) is a solo documentary monologue in which I reenact interviews I conducted with survivors who lived through the disappearances in Argentina during the *Guerra Sucia*, the Dirty War, a period of state terrorism between 1974 and 1983 when more than thirty thousand people were tortured and disappeared.[2] In the second part I reenact the Abu Ghraib photos through bodily gesture and language, and I reflect on the use of torture in armed conflicts far away.[3] In the third part I discuss the effect of therapy on the victim of torture and the soldier coming home from war.

The performance premiered at the Danish theater Faar 302 in 2017, and I wrote, staged, and performed the piece myself together with another performer. The performance was part of my artistic PhD project *Thinking with Performance: Research-Based Aesthetics in Times of Conflict and Crisis*, in which I examine how to critically think with performance. I argue that research-based performance uses research to respond to conflict and crisis and to create spaces for thinking where artist and audience can reflect on the represented material. Throughout the PhD project, my situatedness as a Western artist-researcher became clear and raised questions about how to artistically represent crises and conflicts. Who has the authority or right to name a crisis? How could I avoid defining and confirming the power structures that I sought to examine? And how did I decide to focus on one specific place and crisis rather than another?

In the making of *This Is for Her*, I used different research strategies such as interviews, theory, and historical documents focusing on the Dirty War in Argentina, the Abu Ghraib photos, and different forms of therapy for victims of torture and soldiers. Importantly, I was situated as an observer, a bystander, a witness to people and events in radically different contexts than my own. My situated position was complex regarding my choices. For instance: what is the cross-reference between Argentina and Abu Ghraib? I was aware of the importance of the specific cultural context, but what I was seeking to do was to make connections between globalized power structures, as with my analysis of the complex relationship between victim and perpetrator, or my reflections on how to reenact the photos from Abu Ghraib. In each part of the performance I sought to examine the recurring system of torture and the logics of power between victim and perpetrator on a structural and interpersonal level.[4]

I did not want to make a documentary. I wanted to focus on structures of violence. I used interviews with researchers, victims, anthropologists, and therapists to analyze the mirroring between torture and therapy and how in each of these instances humans, systems, and techniques circulate. I was interested in the arbitrary mirroring between the retellings of a narrative—the acts of testifying—in the torture situation, in the therapy room, and in the performance room. In this essay I will trace testimony as a figure that travels between the people I interviewed, the script, the performance, the audience, and how in each of these instances a new layer of testimony arises, creating a written, spoken, and embodied archive that exists both then and there and here and now in the theater.

Geographical Clarification

The performance marks a historical and geographical movement from Argentina (victim) to Iraq (perpetrator) to Denmark (therapy). I link these three seemingly disparate geographies in order to discuss Denmark's different engagements with or positions in relation to torture. In the late 1970s and early 1980s, Denmark accepted many political refugees from South America, and in 1982 Dignity (the Danish Institute against Torture) was founded in order to provide specialist treatment to victims of torture. Now the situation is radically different: many of the torture survivors are refugees from war zones in the Middle East—for instance Iraq, where Denmark was part of the US-led coalition's military operations from 2003 to 2007. I wanted to examine this complex shift, from helping refugees fleeing South American dictatorships, to helping refugees fleeing conflict zones where Denmark is involved. In the second part of the performance, I chose to focus on the photos from Abu Ghraib because of the disturbing theatricality of the photos.[5]

In the first part of the performance, I chose to focus on Argentina because it gave me the opportunity to observe the durational affect and effect of torture, and how the trauma is still unfolding in the country now, forty years later. I also have a strong personal attachment to Argentina because I lived in Buenos Aires for several years. Thus, the different geographical and historical contexts, which may at first appear arbitrary, served for me as a way to examine Denmark's various stances on the question of torture and therapy. I was aware of the constant risk that I would just touch, but never really engage with, the people and places that I encountered, not least because of my limited funds and time to stay with the trouble.[6] This dilemma affected my choice to focus on how the audience and I relate to the representation of torture and therapy, rather than making an account of torture in Iraq or Argentina.

The Relationship between Torture, Therapy, and Performance

During the artistic research process, I became interested in the parallels between the interrogation room and the therapy room. In both rooms, the victim is asked to tell her story—of course, to very different people and with very different intentions. The interviews I conducted were important not least because they pointed to
Fig. 2 ← the interview dimension of both torture and therapy. The torture situation and the therapeutic situation involve a meeting between two or more people, and both interrogation and therapy are structured around questions and answers. I found it paradoxical that torture and the treatment of torture unfold within mirroring frames of questions and answers between two persons. Further, I began reflecting on the frames of the interview between an artist and an interviewee, and the frames of the performance situation where spectator and performer meet.[7]

I wanted to examine how the moment of torture stretches into the future when it is retold in different contexts. The torture moment is a punctual event that anticipates the future. When it is retold in a performance, we might talk about a scripted retelling of that event that repeats and transforms the event again and again. In the performance, the performer enacts a scripted version of the past, or of the past past: the retelling of

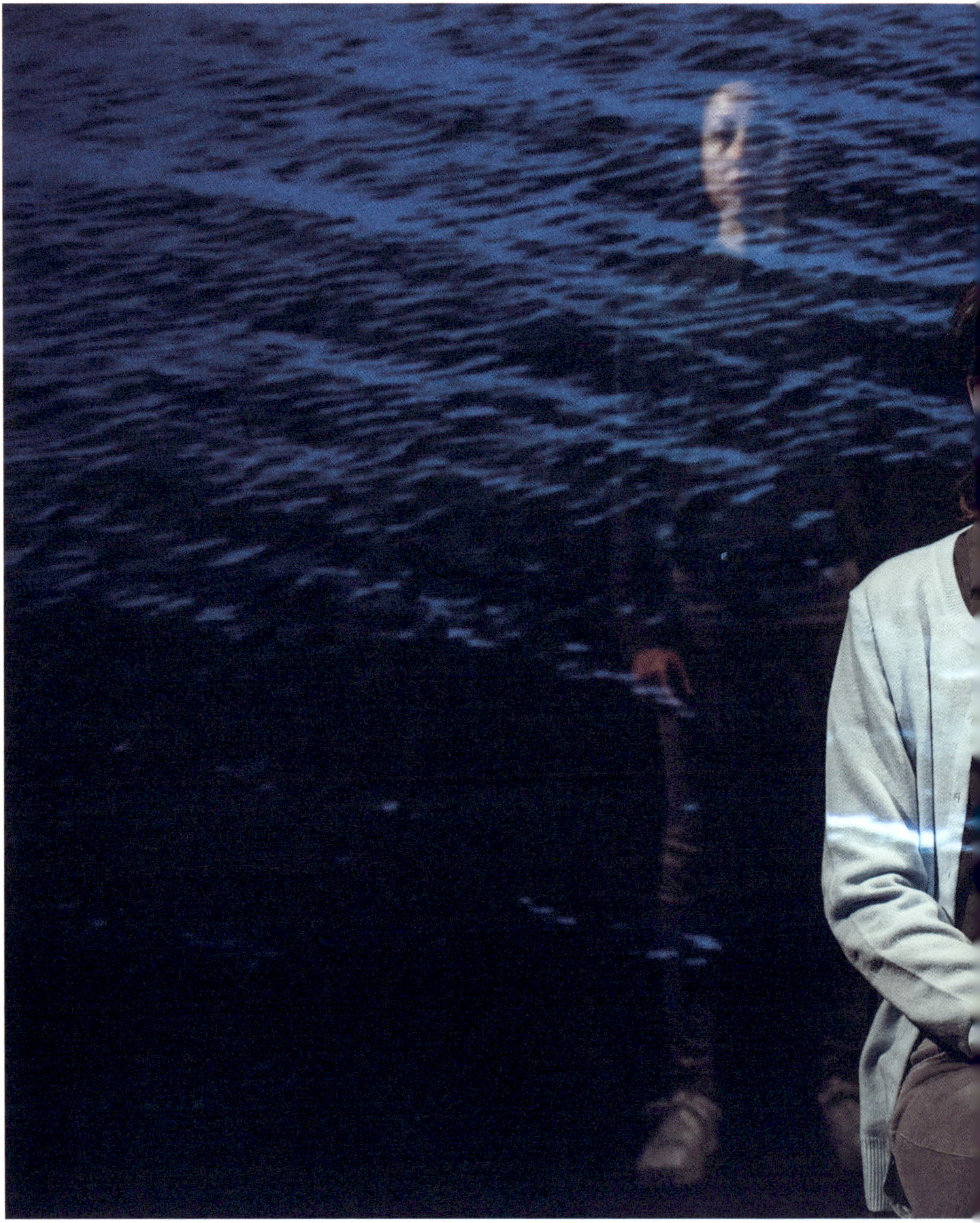

Fig. 2 Sofie Lebech, *This Is for Her*, 2017

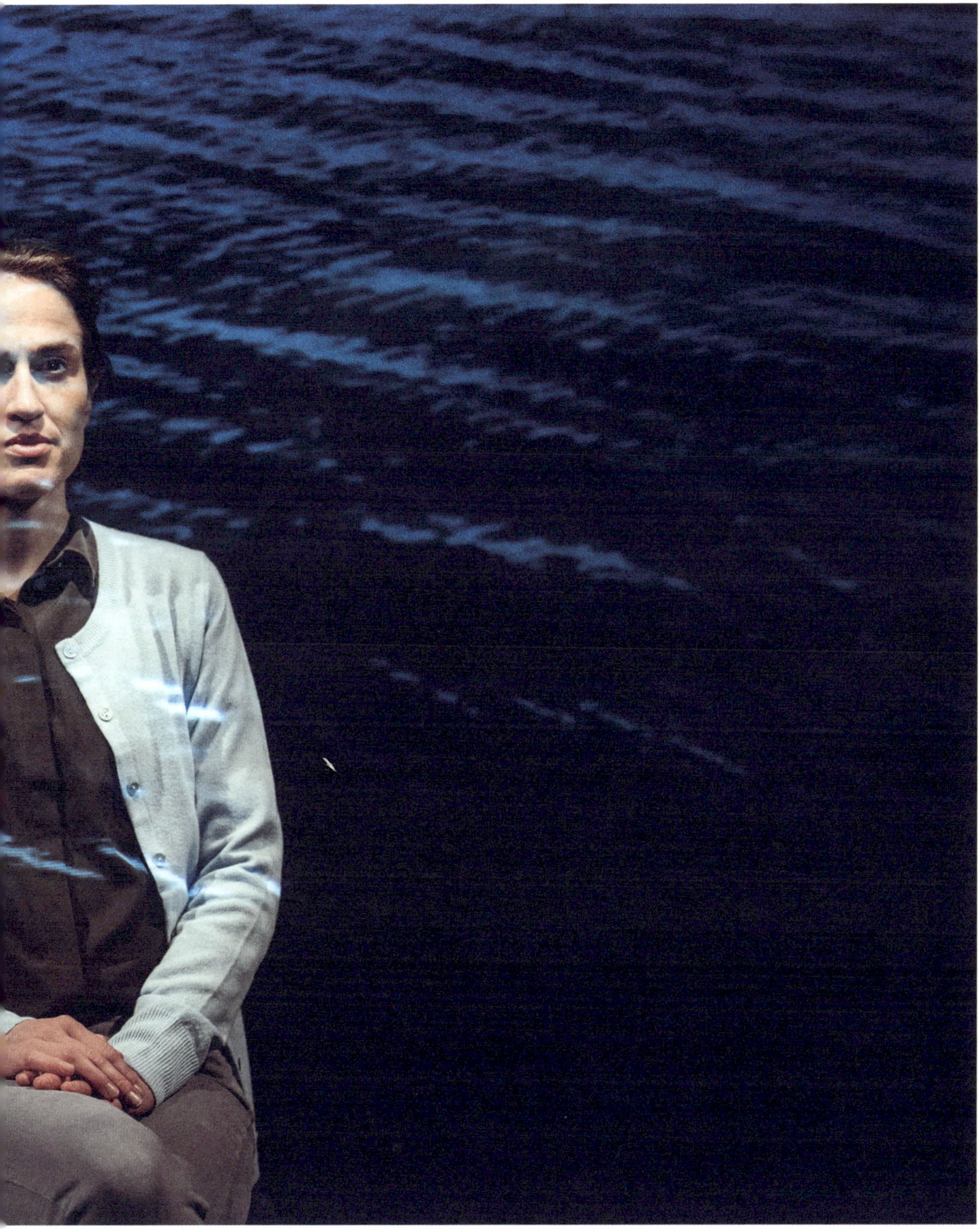

an interview with a survivor retelling the event of the past. Further, the retelling of the script already anticipates a possible repetition in the future. Retelling takes place between past, present, and future, and places the spectators in a position where they are witnessing the testimony of an event that took place and will take place again. The spectator becomes a co-testifier.

I use retelling and reenactment to reflect on the durational affect and effect of torture. Torture does not disappear but endures, on a personal as well as a state level. Victims often have to retell a simplified script about their torture moments—when they seek asylum, when they get therapy later, and when their testimony appears in a performance about torture and therapy. *This Is for Her* contains some narratives and excludes others. It does not claim to unmask the complexity of the individual narrative of torture. Rather, it points to testimony as a durational event that travels back and forth between the torture situation and the therapy room. In performance situations, these past sites and states of mind can be reactualized by the performer and the spectator.

Artistic Choices

The monologue is based on four interviews conducted in Argentina, with Susana Bogey, Felipe Vallese, Berta Mirabella, and Carlos Gavarotto.[8] Felipe is the son of one of the first people to disappear. Berta was an activist and did political theater as resistance to the military junta. Carlos was a member of one of the militant groups, Montoneros, during the dictatorship. Susana was a union member and was tortured for thirteen months in prison, where she tried to commit suicide. Her husband disappeared. For me, she is the testimony, but I can still pinpoint from whom the different elements of the monologue come.

In a performance I decided that a testimony does not have to be accurate, unless it is part of a historical narrative or court proceedings. I turned the different testimonies into one voice. I turned the survivors into a female representative. I added philosophical, fictional, and poetic details to the account, and used elements from a number of informal conversations I had had with people in Argentina and Denmark about the experience of torture. All of this adds up to a momentary "performative truth" onstage where the performer's and the spectator's reactions to the representation of the testimonies are a way of bearing witness.

Why did I choose to edit the interviews down to one cohesive monologue? Should I have chosen to reenact one interview at full length? Working with personal and sensitive material, I confronted several artistic and ethical dilemmas. I tried to avoid projecting a universal idea of the "the victim of torture" by clearly combining the voices of several victims/survivors. Further, I was challenged by the fictitious character of my research material, which several times underlined the subjective nature of memory: the people I interviewed gave me contradictory statements, remembered something and then did not remember, and told me things that I found hard to believe. Does it matter if they were telling the truth? Not for me. It was all part of the testimony's momentary truth. I was aware that I am an artist-researcher, and as such I do not have the interviewing skills of an ethnographer or therapist, so I never pushed the interviewees.

I wanted to create a coherent narrative that the spectator would be willing to listen to—a testimony that could be heard. However, I do regret that I did not show the constructed nature of the testimony at the end of the performance by giving the last word to the people I had interviewed in a video projection, as I had first intended. Instead, the performance ended with a scene that, inspired by Elaine Scarry's concept of torture as the unmaking of the victim's world, explored the continuing invisibility of the survivor in the country where she has sought asylum.[9]

Testimony as Durational Event

Watching a performance is an act of bearing witness. In her 1992 book *Testimony: Crises of Witnessing in Literature, Psychoanalysis, and History*, Shoshana Felman proposes that writing literature and reading literary texts can be understood as bearing witness.[10] Literature can be "considered events of speech," and its testimony can be "understood as a mode of truth's realization beyond what is available as statement."[11] Following this thought, I want to suggest that the interview that the artist carries out with the victim is a performative speech act in which the victim's testimony resonates with the artist's testimony enacting itself in the performance. In the moment of the interview, the survivor meets a listener, and in the future artistic representation there will be a second listener: an audience. If we assume that the performance is a testimony, we might say that the spectators are witnessing a three-layered testimony including the interviews, the written text, and the performance. The interviews are testimonies, the script testifies to the interviews, and the audience witnesses the performance of the script and the bodily reenactment of the interviews.

My understanding of testimony as a durational act that exists in the performance space, the interview situation, and the original scene of violence is strongly influenced by Rebecca Schneider's ethics of call and response. In *Performing Remains: Art and War in Times of Theatrical Reenactment* (2011), Schneider demonstrates the entanglement between reenactments and time through a reading of the Abu Ghraib photos.[12] She argues that the images are not only records of war, torture, and abuse, but can also be read as durational events that exist both then and there and here and now. In the performance I worked both with retelling the testimonies of torture and with reenacting the photos from Abu Ghraib, in order to understand these moments of violence as something that we continue to witness and something that continues to call for account. Further, I wanted to explore whether performing testimonies onstage of past events of torture combined with the braiding of different geographical contexts related to torture could be a way of viewing events as something that exists both then and there and here and now.

Schneider's argument makes it possible to connect nonartistic events such as torture and therapy with the performance space, because the original event is enacted in the performance space and calls for account. Here, it becomes important to see how the performer's embodiment of the testimonies creates a human archive of the event: how gestures, intonations, and physicality make the performer and spectator revisit the original testimony.

In the monologue, I bring together the voices of several persons who reflect on their lived realities during the dictatorship. Onstage I performed the textual testimony of the interviews: I tried to speak like the interviewees, to repeat their long silences, their sudden broken language, and outbreaks of emotion before continuing the account. I tried to remember and reproduce the persons' gestures and intonations, thus creating a human archive of embodied testimonies. It may be controversial to call the reenactment of several interviews in one monologue "a human archive of embodied testimonies." However, as Schneider suggests, the temporality of theater is always vexed when it comes to reenactment. A script is posited toward a future reenactment, and as such it is a preenactment. Reading a script as a preenactment of a reenactment seems complicated, of course. But what I am trying to argue here is that this complexity has to take place if we are to touch the incomprehensible problem of violence in torture.

Bearing witness is a performative act in the interview, in the written text, and in the performance. The monologue is my testimony of the interviews. It is not a retelling with documentary reference to reality,[13] but rather a retelling of researched and reflected material framing and doubling a lived reality: an archive of voices, bodies, and words embodied in a performative testimony.

1. The crossed-out sentences reveal how I continuously edited and changed the script. Further, I used the crossed-out sentences to refer to the erasures in Mohamedou Ould Slahi's *Guantánamo Diary* (Edinburgh: Canongate, 2015) and in "The Committee Study of the Central Intelligence Agency's Detention and Interrogation Program," 2014, https://fas.org/irp/congress/2014_rpt/ssci-rdi.pdf). In the performance these references were made visible by repeated blackouts.

2. The term *Guerra Sucia* was used by the military junta, which claimed that a war was necessary to maintain social order and eradicate political opponents, although this war included torture, rape, and killings. Importantly, the term has been questioned by nongovernmental human rights organizations, and by organizations such as the Abuelas de Plaza de Mayo (Grandmothers of the Plaza de Mayo), because it suggests that a civil war was going on, justifying the killings and the state terrorism that took place during the dictatorship. Arguably, the term has affected the narrative of the dictatorship. See also Diana Taylor, who examines the Dirty War in order to analyze how national identity is shaped, gendered, and contested through spectacle and spectatorship. Diana Taylor, *Disappearing Acts: Spectacles of Gender and Nationalism in Argentina's "Dirty War"* (Durham, NC: Duke University Press, 1997).

3. In April 2004, CBS News published the Abu Ghraib photos, showing a series of human rights violations committed by personnel of the United States Army and the Central Intelligence Agency in the Abu Ghraib prison in Iraq. The violations included physical and sexual abuse, torture, rape, and murder. The Bush administration avoided using the word "torture" and consequently referred to the actions as "abuse" or "humiliation." However, subsequent investigations stated that such torture did not occur as a set of isolated incidents at Abu Ghraib but happened in several US detention centers in Iraq, Afghanistan, and Guantanamo Bay. See "The Committee Study of the Central Intelligence Agency's Detention and Interrogation Program," https://fas.org/irp/congress/2014_rpt/ssci-rdi.pdf.

4. As Elaine Scarry has forcefully discussed in *The Body in Pain*, it is hard to comprehend how torture is possible on a structural level—how societies can pretend or even believe, for instance, that it is intelligence-gathering rather than torture that is taking place. Elaine Scarry, *The Body in Pain: The Making and Unmaking of the World* (New York: Oxford University Press, 1985).

5. There have been cases of direct Danish involvement in torture. On September 13, 2011, the Danish Ministry of Defense was put on trial over Denmark's responsibility for a very heavy-handed capture of civilian Sunni Iraqis in 2004 during Operation Green Desert. They were surrendered to the Iraqi Shia police, despite the fact that the Danes knew that the Iraqi police used torture. See "Irak tortursager" [Iraq Torture Cases], http://iraktortursager.dk. The case has not had much media coverage in Denmark, and the Ministry of Defense tried to bring it to a close. See "Staten brugte 6 millioner kroner på at stoppe torturofres erstatningssag" [The State Spent 6 Million Kroner to Avoid Being Sued for Compensation by Victims of Torture], *Politiken*, November 6, 2016.

6. Here we may think of Hal Foster's critique of what he calls "the artist as ethnographer." The scenario is this: an artist is flown in to engage with a chosen community, but there is not enough time or money to actually interact with the community, there is no critique of the relationship between participants and observer, and the

community is not affected. Hal Foster, "The Artist as Ethnographer?" in *The Return of the Real: The Avantgarde at the End of the Century* (Cambridge, MA: MIT Press, 1996), 302-9.

7. Most theater has the structure of a meeting without being a dialogue. However, a number of performance artists try to center the artistic experience on the meeting and, by doing so, try to negotiate the public sphere in new ways. Examples are immersive performances made by performance collectives such as the Danish SIGNA, in which the audience inhabits the performance space with the performers, for a limited time frame or for the whole performance period. See "SIGNA," https://signa.dk/. For more on immersive theater, see Josephine Machon, *Immersive Theatres: Intimacy and Immediacy in Contemporary Performance* (Basingstoke: Palgrave Macmillan, 2013).

8. Interviews conducted March 6-20, 2017, by producer René Kruse, assistant Agustina Barzola Würth, and me.

9. In *The Body in Pain*, Scarry analyses the difficulty of expressing physical pain and the political and perceptual consequences of this difficulty. Physical pain inflicted by authorities leads to the unmaking of the victim's world. The making of the world, on the other hand, becomes possible through human creation as language, culture, or art.

10. An example is Elias Canetti's book *Kafka's Other Trial: The Letters to Felice* (London: Penguin Classic, 2012), which can be understood as a testimony. Kafka's letters to his fiancée Felice represent a textual testimony of life, and Canetti's reading of Kafka makes him a witness to Kafka. Shoshana Felman and Dori Laub, *Testimony: Crises of Witnessing in Literature, Psychoanalysis, and History* (New York: Routledge, 1992). Likewise, Cathy Caruth has examined how the memory of traumatic events is not only to be understood through conscious understanding, but can also be approached through literature. Cathy Caruth, *Trauma: Explorations in Memory* (Baltimore: Johns Hopkins University Press, 1995).

11. Felman and Laub, *Testimony*, 2.

12. Rebecca Schneider, *Performing Remains: Art and War in Times of Theatrical Reenactment* (London: Routledge, 2011).

13. For more on how we may understand the "documentary reference to reality," see Stella Bruzzi's article on the use of documentary images in legal procedures. Stella Bruzzi, "Narrative, 'Evidence Vérité,' and the Different Truths of the Modern Trial Documentary," in *Documentary across Disciplines*, ed. Erika Balsom and Hila Peleg (Cambridge, MA: MIT Press, 2016), 252-79.

D EVIDENTIARY AESTHETICS Documenting, Witnessing, Redressing

THE IMPERIAL CONDITION OF PHOTOGRAPHY IN PALESTINE

Archives, Looting, and the Figure of the Infiltrator

Ariella Azoulay

The imperial *document* was invented as the correlation between pieces of written paper, violent actions, and manufactured realities.[1] Actions are assumed to stem directly from documents, similarly to the way a blueprint or a template testifies to the craft of a carpenter or a mason. Documents such as the respective Declarations of Independence of Israel and the United States consist of violent campaigns conducted as sets of authorized actions inscribed on paper to posit "independence" as a fait accompli, a milestone assumed and cited in historical narratives of culture and politics in the now sovereign United States or Israel. Through such imperial documents, circulating globally and stored in archives, people can become slaves, material worlds can become individual actors' property, and states can be formed.[2] With the invention of the imperial document, an arena of "international" legitimate state actors—whose recognition of these documents is what endowed them with such status—was invented. Thus, with the same stroke, the struggles of local and indigenous people against the creation of these new statuses and states are expunged from acceptable narratives, their traces fragmented, and their memories forced to take the shape of alternative narratives.

Through the institution of the archive and its army, a concerted effort is invested in making this correlation between documents and violence, exercised as authorized actions, appear obvious. Imperial acts, withdrawn from the political space in which they could be challenged, are thus always already institutionalized, framed, and insulated.

Since March 2018, tens of thousands of Palestinians caged in the Gaza Ghetto have participated in the Great March of Return to their homeland. This is not a march in the sense of a singular procession, a progressive movement from one point in space to another. It is rather a *marche arrière*, an attempt to reverse the forced march forward that was imposed when the violence against their ancestors reached a point where a series of documents could attest to the existence of a different state in their homeland, to the existence of a border where there was none, and to their status as stateless. In other words, the archive was made full of internationally recognized documents that disaffiliate them from the present, and render them, and their claims, to an improvable past. Marching against the command inscribed in these documents or in these borders, they reenact a worldly sovereignty that was denied to them. Aware of the presence of Israeli snipers ready to shoot at them, they approach the border as if shouting "kill me if you wish." And Israeli Jewish young men—who were born subjects of this state, were born to recognize the power of their state to instate realities and to make them executioners of others—shoot. Against tacit claims asserted by international laws and treaties, the Palestinians seem to claim "as long as we are alive, we misrecognize the 'proper place' assigned to us by these documents and this border. We do not acknowledge the disappearance of Palestine that they proclaim. We are Palestine—kill us if you wish." The Great March of Return is not only a matter of defiance; literally and physically, it potentializes history, keeps these claims—constantly under threat to be made past-present, ensures that they have not and can never be buried, even as many bodies are buried.

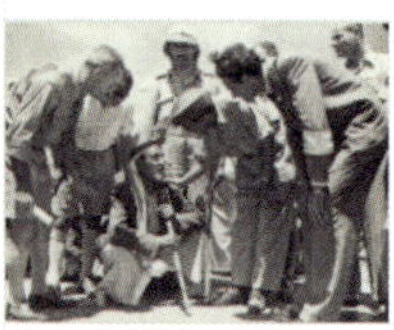

PALESTINE

Kfar Yona, premières lignes juives. Un ancien prisonnier de guerre est interrogé en présence d'un délégué du CICR.
De gauche à droite : commandant du secteur juif; ancien prisonnier de guerre; capitaine commandant du secteur irakien (portant un casque); autre capitaine irakien; Jean Courvoisier, délégué du CICR.

V-P-PS-N-00004-2677
public

1949

© CICR/

Fig. 1 Screenshot of a low-res image from Palestine, 1949, viewed at the International Committee of the Red Cross (ICRC)

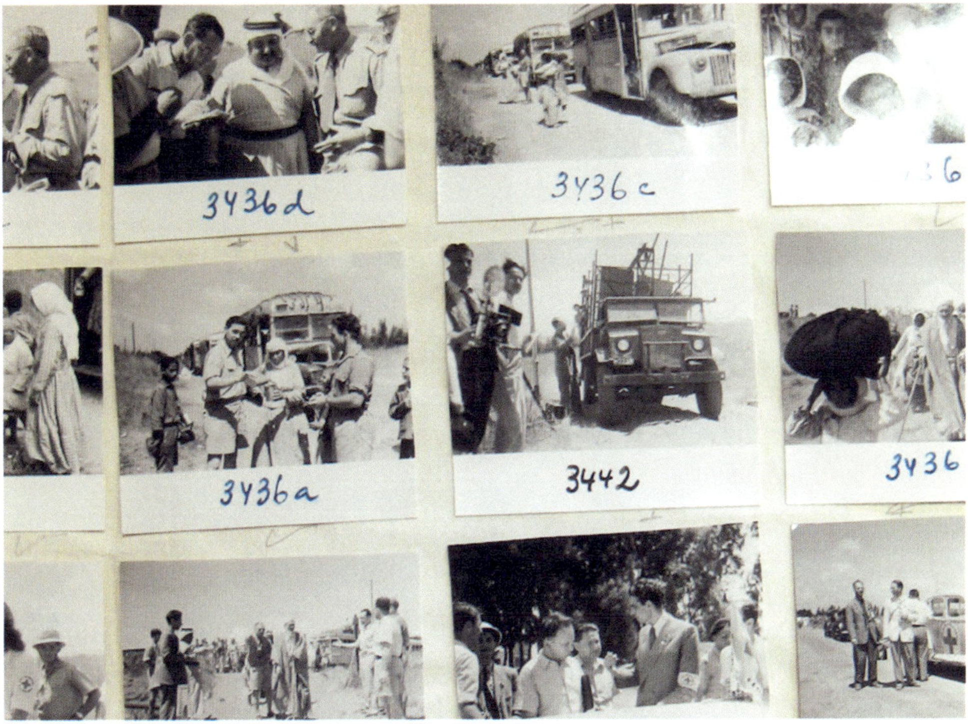

Fig. 2 Screenshot of album pages from photographer Beno Rothenberg's series of photographs taken in Palestine, 1949, titled "Arab women from Tantura going to Jordan," from Non-Imperial Archive (NIA)

I shall return to the Great March of Return at the end of this text. Situating the origins of this drama in 1948 is at the heart of this essay. Here is a screenshot of a photograph, one of twenty-five images that I selected from the archives of the International Committee of the Red Cross (ICRC) and was not authorized to include in an exhibition I curated several years ago. In the archive, this photograph of an elegant elderly man is captioned: "Kfar Yona, Jewish front line. A former prisoner of war is interrogated in the presence of a delegate from the ICRC." When I first saw the photograph, I recognized some of the figures from other images kept in Zionist archives. I knew, even before examining the photograph more closely, that this old man was not, and could not be, a prisoner of war. Young men aged

Fig. 1 ←
Fig. 2 ←

between fifteen and forty had been the first to be removed from their communities. This guy had stayed behind with the women, children, and other men of his age group. Relating to him as an embodiment of a neutral category—prisoner of war—reflected the way that agents of the ICRC, either on the ground or in the archive, interacted with the subject's actions, or more accurately, with his avoidance of action, with the embarrassing situation that he created by not moving on as expected, and in front of the cameras. The expulsion was supposed to keep going. Contrary to many other operations of the expulsion of Palestinians conducted during the years 1948–1949, this one in particular was open to photographers and international organizations such as the ICRC, since it was conducted under the aegis of the normative category of post-World War II "repatriation" when millions were forcibly displaced in Europe.[3] Palestinians who were deported from their homes during these years could not be repatriated to their homes elsewhere, as Palestine was their homeland. It was only with the creation of an imperial sovereign nation-state—Israel—endorsed and recognized by the United Nations, an organization whose aim was to standardize the political imaginary, that terms such as "partition" and "repatriation," whose implementation uprooted people from their worlds, could be used as neutral markers of policy. These terms are used factually in the captions of several photos taken in Palestine during such uprooting operations. At this particular expulsion, approximately two thousand Palestinians of Arab origin—mostly women, children, and elderly people—were left with little choice but to sign papers proving that they had agreed to be evacuated to Jordan as part of "family reunification" (their relatives having already been expelled a few months earlier, or incarcerated in labor camps).[4] Out of the two thousand women destined for "transfer" through this kind of expulsion, conducted "willingly," about eight hundred refused to evacuate in spite of being threatened by the Jewish forces.[5]

What lies were these women told in order to make the term "repatriation" sound plausible? What kind of pressure was put on them? To which types of violence were they exposed so that they would give their consent to leave not only their homes—they had already been forced to leave those when they had been evacuated from Tantura—but now also their country? In the absence of photographs from this phase, we cannot say much about the means employed to obtain the women's consent, nor about the fate of those who refused. We can only say that this preparatory phase had to be concluded before the scene was opened to photographers, who were invited to affirm with their cameras the success of the repatriation operation. Convening a sort of press conference in the field was not about those who refused, nor was it an opportunity for the expellees to showcase their demands. At the Israel State Archives, photographs of the same event are classified under the handwritten caption of another photographer, Beno Rothenberg: "Arab women from Tantura going to Jordan." Rothenberg, like the Israeli journalists who attended the expulsion, knew that the expellees were not inhabitants of Fureidis, from where they were now being expelled, but rather had already been expelled from Tantura.[6] Rothenberg's caption played a pivotal role in understanding that this expulsion was actually a second expulsion. Included in this category of "women" were elderly men and children; at this point, military-age men from Tantura had already been either incarcerated or massacred.[7]

In front of the cameras and representatives of the international community, unexpectedly, and outside of any protocol that was prepared for this occasion, this elderly man dares to stop, to withdraw "his consent" to leave his home, and ceases to move. Halting precisely where many cameras are present, he threatens to spoil the orchestrated spectacle of nascent imperial nation-states' inhabitants—in this case, Arab Palestinians—"leaving of their own will." Not much work is required in order to argue that were he a prisoner of war, representatives of various nongovernmental organizations and military forces would not be seen gently gesticulating around him, trying to find the right words and gestures to force him, without direct violence, to accept his fate, respect the consent form he signed, and leave his homeland of his own free will, forever. Yet, rather than relating to this caption, written during a violent campaign, as a caption that may be open to revisions, the ICRC requires its workers to protect the caption from modifications and preserve it as if it were fused with the photograph forever. The photograph, their policy states, can only be shared with others on the condition that it is accompanied by the ICRC's caption alone. As I already mentioned, my request for permission to include the photograph in an exhibition was denied. Hence, rather than showing this photograph, I can share with you its substitute, its placeholder—not a photograph, but what I call an unshowable photograph. This denial of permission had nothing to do with what is in the photograph, which is still accessible in the ICRC archives. Nor did it have to do with me, since their personnel could not have known in advance what I planned to write. Rather, it was about my stated intention to append a caption of my own to the ICRC's. It was about questioning the way that the photograph endured in the archive through language that made this man a prisoner of war, and the entire operation one of repatriation, return to a *patrie*, while it was actually a transfer from one's homeland. → Fig. 3

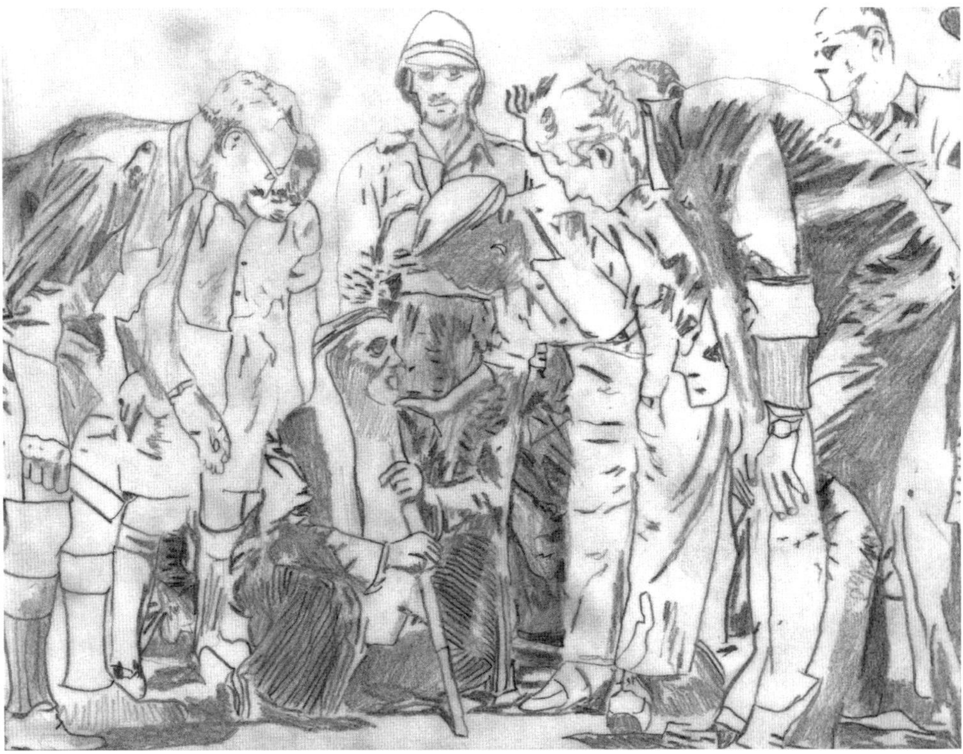

Fig. 3 Unshowable photograph, from NIA

The ICRC's implied anxiety, however, was not ungrounded. I did indeed intend to study those photographs together with my companion—the photographed person—even if, according to the archive, our worlds as well as our political roles were meant to be kept apart. Looking at photographs of plight together with the photographed persons redefines what one ought to see in the photograph—not only the plight, but what preceded it, was destroyed by it. Thus, looking at the photograph of this man, taken at the moment he was forced out of his homeland, I invite you to also see the wealth of which he was dispossessed at that very moment—the material culture of Palestine in which he had his place, in which recognized himself, and in which his place was secured. Just think of the different kinds of Palestinians' archives that were plundered and incorporated into the new state of Israel built on the ruins of Palestine, and the material culture on which it was built, and the protection that such archives—irreducible to the documents preserved in them—provided. Under the imperial ideology of monoculture, the archive was shaped as a container of items of one type—documents—and these started to have a life of their own, detached from the communities of which they were or could be part. In other words, for the sake of the document, many things could be destroyed. Thus, when I am relating to the protection that different kinds of archives provide to their communities, I am not relating to discrete documents as legal proofs of ownership or identity, but rather to their being in the world, part of it—what Hannah Arendt calls "worldliness."

Since this man was deported not alone but together with hundreds of thousands of other Palestinians, the moment of his deportation was also the moment when Palestinian archives lost the protection of the people—that is, Palestinians themselves—who recognized their existence as meaningful and hence in need of protection. Their transfer was the moment when archives, libraries, landscapes, crafts, tastes, food, etc., became vulnerable to looting. His expulsion, and the foreclosure of his refusal to be expelled, is sanctioned by the looting of Palestinian archives and the entitlement of Israeli Jews to study Palestinian culture in and through archives, in the absence—or in the differential presence—of Palestinians and their archives. With the mass expulsion of Palestinians, their archives were partially destroyed, and partially converted into a pile of appropriable segments by the newly established sovereign state and the international organizations that collaborated with it. Nothing of this drama, which is the heart of the story, is meant to be archived through the imperial categories used by nation-states. Sovereign nation-states are predicated on archives that they shape in correspondence with the violent policies they pursue toward segments of populations. This is epitomized in the way that they force these populations to be governed by them but they do not relate to them as part of the body politic of the governed. In the demographic fantasy of the nation-state, the body politic consists of governed citizens belonging to a particular race or ethnos, and expulsion is one of the major means to shape the body politic.

I was born an Israeli citizen of Jewish origins. When I started to understand the role this citizenship played in keeping Palestinians outside of the image of the body politic of the governed, in order to legitimize a political regime of which they were not part, I decided to refrain from going to archives in Israel where such images are preserved without my companion. My companion, a Palestinian who refused to be expelled from his homeland, was denuded of his life within a community and made a vagabond, then a dweller in a refugee camp, and soon after an "infiltrator," until another brutal category was made his: that of a stateless person, carrying only flimsy travel documents or no documents at all, holding none of the papers without which one can hardly move between nation-states' gates. It is only when one forgets to conceive of one's citizenship as unrelated to the violence of the state—as a citizen is taught from birth—that one can continue to enter the archive, as a matter of fact and of civil status. Asking about this man and his like in an imperial archive cannot be assumed to be a simple procedure of research that involves asking for information, since the institution of the archive takes part in the transformation of Arab Palestinians from inhabitants of their country into a threat to the regime (including its archives), and of Israeli Jews into rightful citizens. The free movement of Israeli citizens to the archive is inseparable from the ban and restriction of Palestinians from such movement. Going to the archive with him is making sure that his understanding of the meanings of expulsion, body politic, citizenship, accountability, rights, worldliness, etc.—encapsulated in his firm presence there, kneeling and holding his stick as an anchor in the ground to which he belongs, and rejecting these men's threats and pleas calling on him to move on—are not dismissed as something else, but rather enhanced and foregrounded as a gesture of opposition that, against the massive military operation of controlling the image that would be generated of the destruction of an entire culture, was nonetheless captured. The fact that this is one of the rare accessible photographs (so far, at least) of such a gesture testifies not to the Palestinians' failure to oppose the destruction of their world, but to the degree to which the apparatus of a totalitarian regime made even the possibility of the existence of such gestures unimaginable for several decades.

Exploring the archive with a Palestinian companion has become part of my archival routine, a constant attempt to make our actions coincide in space and time, even though he is still forced to live outside of the body politic of which I am a part. It is not the fact that he is no longer alive that keeps him outside of the body politic, but the fact that his gesture of refusing to leave Palestine dates from more than seventy years ago, and the state invests much violence in colonizing the minds of its citizens to see it as obsolete. The temporality and spatiality imposed and epitomized by imperial archives doom his claims to appear either as over or as always coming from a post-ness and an outside that mark his grievances as violations of the law, and mine as at best expressions of solidarity with his ancient plight. Only as co-citizens of a nonimperial imagination can we enter the archive together, share in common those claims to stop the ruination of Palestine that became "his" claims, and together reject differential citizenship and its implication in the perpetuation of violence against those whose belonging to the body politic was denied by their displacement beyond the state's borders. It was only in his presence that I could rewrite several versions of this and other sentences until I was able to force the language to be articulated outside of the imperial temporality and spatiality and to be molded in the affirmative, accounting for his belonging to the body politic.

Entering an imperial archive with a Palestinian companion is part of unlearning imperialism and having access not to what is *in* the archive, but to this invaluable option of thinking and seeing in a nonimperial way and participating in the actualization of nonimperial archival modalities. Compared with citizens who for years have been brainwashed by the imperial state, my companion had less to unlearn about the past and the struggle with political lies in order to disclose, from underneath the ICRC language, that he was not a prisoner of war, and that even if he gave his consent under threat to be uprooted from his home, this formal consent was achieved against his will and against any common sense—it was from start to end an act of sheer violence, and not an agreement based on an acceptable exchange.

Let me pause now and ask: what is an archive?

In his influential 1995 book *Archive Fever*, Jacques Derrida analyzes the archive and reveals its secret: violence, "the violence of the archive itself, *as archive, as archival violence*."[8] He starts with the figure of the archon, the guardian of documents, the sentry: "The archons are first of all the documents' guardians. They do not only ensure the physical security of what is deposited and of the substrate. They are also accorded the hermeneutic right and competence. They have the power to interpret the archives. Entrusted to such archons, these documents in effect speak the law: they recall the law and call on or impose the law."[9] The archon is the first of the three pylons supporting the archive. The law, as Derrida argues in this passage, is the second, and the Greek *arkheion*, the house, the place, is the third. In locating *arkhe*, as both "commencement" and "commandment," at the conceptual core of the archive, Derrida alternately places emphasis on documents and on the law. "To be guarded thus," Derrida continues, "in the jurisdiction of this *speaking the law*, they [the documents] needed at once a guardian and a localization."[10] This conflation between law and documents is troubling, and is made possible only when the internal machination of the archive is centered on the "core" of the archive, the essence that the philosopher can grasp only when the noisy presence of people is removed, what Derrida calls its "topo-nomology," "without which no archive would ever come into play or appear as such." Derrida's account of the archive is schematic and abstract. The documents that "needed" their guardian and localization are depicted as the focal points of the archive. Derrida's own intervention in the archive does not leave its impression in this schematic depiction; he remains external to the mechanism of the archive, a guest who comes after its constitution. Such external observation of *how the archive works* could not be obtained were Derrida not being lured, seduced by the sentries to look at their work from the outside, to track down the borders they set and the fences they erect, and by doing so to acknowledge the law they legislate. After all, part of the sentries' work is to fool the one who stands at the archive's entrance and make him or her believe that they, notwithstanding the law they guard, were there before. Yet, in turn, Derrida tries to fool the sentries, writing that, "in an enigmatic sense, [...] the question of the archive is not, we repeat, a question of the past. [...] It is a question of the future, the question of the future itself, the question of a response, of a promise and of a responsibility for tomorrow."[11]

Certainly, something is wrong with the temporality of the archive, and with its announced mission to serve as a guardian of the past. Achille Mbembe locates the problem in the archive's desire to forget and liquidate the past, while Derrida performs this desire even as he detaches the past from the future, without providing any argument to sustain such a separation: "The question of the archive is not, we repeat, a question of the past. [...] It is a question of the future."[12] This claim is similar to the positing of a new beginning that disrupts the oppressive past—a positing that has become commonly identified as the revolutionary gesture par excellence, rather than recognized as an imperial gesture whose license to destroy cultures is grounded in the phantasy of a new beginning. The notion of a radically new beginning, inherited from the major eighteenth-century revolutions, is inseparable from the violent formation of a body politic based on operations of subtraction and addition and whose members are differentially ruled. This means that those who are dispossessed in the process are made unqualified for reparations, restitution, and compensations. This disruptive temporality stands at odds with people's modes of negotiating the time of the archive, which are never a matter of aspiring for a new beginning but rather always a rejection of and negotiation with the archive's mission of isolating historical actions and foreclosing interactions with them—in effect, the archive's mission of stealing common time by making people's claims disappear for varied durations before they are permitted to reemerge publicly. Co-citizens' concrete actions in and interactions with the archive—their insistence on their right to continue to engage with that which was removed from the course of events that shape the common—can be substituted for an abstracted past and an engineered future only in an approach to the archive, exemplified by Derrida's text, that relegates these co-citizens to a place outside the archive, labeling them external users if it asserts their presence at all. No less than through the documents it preserves, the archive's operation is conducted through the way it rules over governed populations. Consequently, it is not only an interest in documents that brings people to interact with archives, but also the way they are ruled by archives, sometimes through documents, sometimes in their absence.

By assuming the presence of the guardians in the archive as original, preceding that of others conceived as contingent users whose presence is incidental and secondary to its operation, the philosopher makes himself complicit with the guardians, denying the interactions of others, including himself, with the guardians and the rules—interactions that often consist in refusing to hand over some documents, smuggling others out of the vicinity of the archive, copying them illicitly, and sharing them randomly with others, even selling them for a profit. Yet if one chooses not to ignore these others and instead becomes their companion, rather than relating to the archive as an accomplished place of the law with incontestable archons, the first thing that becomes clear is that the archive is not a place but a threshold. When the archive is seen as a threshold, it is no longer possible to prioritize the archons' pretension to be guardians of a consummate sovereignty over the living reality of masses of deprived and dispossessed groups of co-citizens that constantly challenge the law that was made to preserve their dispossession and deprivation. At the archive's entrance, the question "what is an archive?"—a place or a threshold, a depository of documents or an apparatus of rule, an accomplished law or contested violence—is essential if one wants to avoid siding with the guardians and looking inward, thus viewing those dispossessed by the archive solely through their presence in the documents preserved inside it, that is, looking for them under categories provided by the differential sovereignty the archive was made to serve, categories such as "infiltrators" or "refugees." Those who continue to be dispossessed by the archive and forced to embody political categories such as "infiltrators" do not expect to find in it a remedy in the form of an apocalyptic leap into a future, such as the one Derrida depicts when he writes, "If we want to know what [the archive] will have meant, we will only know in times to come [...] a spectral messianicity is at work in the concept of the archive."[13] My Palestinian companion's refusal to inhabit the figure of the infiltrator is not an expression of a spectral messianicity, but rather a rejection of the violence enforced on Palestinians' bodies and a persistent call that denies their classification in a past detached from what came after and a future made into an a priori law whose meaning is still to be revealed.

When this person or his peers sought to return, the category of "infiltrator" was attached to their bodies. This category—which denied their present grievances, and relegated them either to a completed past that could not be reversed or to a future beyond reach—is a constitutive element of the differential sovereign regime that was created in their country; it is a relative of the category "undocumented," and in accordance with the international legal language of empire. The category "infiltrator" was made perceptible and legible to security agents at borders and front lines, who read in it a set of instructions—interrogate, arrest, harass, expel, or execute—that also became legible to citizens. One does not have to look for orders to read it in this way in the archive; one can view photographs taken at the border out of which these orders can be reconstructed. The violence these agents exercise against those who were until recently their co-citizens eventually produces masses of archival documents that scholars are interpellated to explore. The archive lures scholars to comply with the imperative to look for infiltrators *in* photographs and documents, where their images, manners, habits, and modes of infiltration can be viewed and studied carefully. In the archive, the legibility of the category of the "infiltrator" is acknowledged and confirmed as an object of knowledge accessible to citizens.

Deciding to enter the archive only with my Palestinian companion—obviously an impossible goal—and actually dwelling in its threshold, not being able to enter, enabled me to state, without consulting any document, that the infiltrator allegedly captured in the photos thus captioned *does not exist*. As I work in his company, he ceases to be—or actually cannot become—an object of knowledge, and together we inhabit a continuous present in which state agents try to force a Palestinian who resists the authority of the state to expel him from his homeland to be an "infiltrator," to be perceived as an embodiment of this category. In his company, the interpellation directed at Israeli Jewish citizens to recognize Palestinians in these documents dealing with infiltrators cannot be brought to completion, since it is not about granting him a right to return as an expression of progress, generosity, humanitarianism, or going forward, but about recognizing his refusal to be expelled to begin with as a refusal that has never ceased.

My assumption—the infiltrator does not exist—is an onto-political assertion that the archive cannot confirm or refute, since the archive is one of the sites where infiltrators are fabricated against their will, and it is invested in affirming their existence. Similarly, the existence of "infiltrators" cannot be confirmed or refuted by the presence of photographs in the archive that are classified under this title and caption. Rather than reading such photographs as representations or evidence of infiltrators, I use them as an opportunity to ask: what are the photographic and archival conditions for the fabrication of the infiltrator? Being a product of violence, the infiltrator should not be studied as such—that is, as an object of knowledge that can be tracked down *in* documents—but rather in relation to the citizen, who, in being differentiated from the infiltrator, participates in the latter category's fabrication. Hence, the claim that the infiltrator does not exist is equivalent to the claim that citizenship is a light weapon that coerces people to embody outrageous political categories. The persistence of the figure of the infiltrator, I argue, is evidence of the ongoing violence and dispossession embedded in the institutions of citizenship, archives, and scholarship in places where such a category has been naturalized into the discourse.

Relating to the archive as a document-centered institution driven by concern for a discrete past, as we do when we consult the documents an archive holds, elides the violent military as well as ideological and political campaign that must take place inside and outside the archive, often even outside the country, to maintain the perception of the archive as a professional institution in charge of preserving the past. Statements that express shock at the poor maintenance of negatives and documents that have "historical value," important as these artifacts might be, uphold the idea of the archive as a site of historical preservation, rather than as one of the major ruling apparatuses of a regime-made disaster that operates by secluding forms of life, often through looting and confiscation, and showcasing them as history.

Slightly differently from scholars such as Gish Amit on the robbing of Palestinian libraries, Aron Shai on the involvement of the Israel Antiquities Authority in the destruction of Palestinian villages, or Rona Sela on looted collections of photographs in the Israel Defense Forces archive, all of whose work is based on exposing classified documents that have been stored in archives for decades,[14] I am more interested in the looting that takes place in full sight—in floodlit arenas, even. These public spectacles, involving the private or semi-private seizure of trophies, are essential elements in training Israeli Jewish citizens not to see the violence of which they consist. Rather than acting as one who "unearths" the looting of Palestinian archives and scientifically reconstructs these events from archival documents that have been declassified after an abominable delay and in which one can find plans for looting explicitly written—an approach that would give more weight to archival documents than to people's grievances, testimonies, and photographs that are not classified and hence do not have to be discovered—I prefer to explore the regime-made disaster as it manifests itself openly, on the surface, in the aftermath of brutal interventions. Learning from and with Palestinian companions, I cannot fail to perceive the different instantiations of looting as limited to the expropriation of documents; rather, I see how these acts of plunder become central to the form of rule that governs us—Arabs and Jews—together, and imposes limits on our capacity to imagine and inhabit time and space differently than along the dividing lines of differential sovereignty. This companionship becomes a way to engage with one another outside the form of our respective roles in the theater of differential sovereignty.

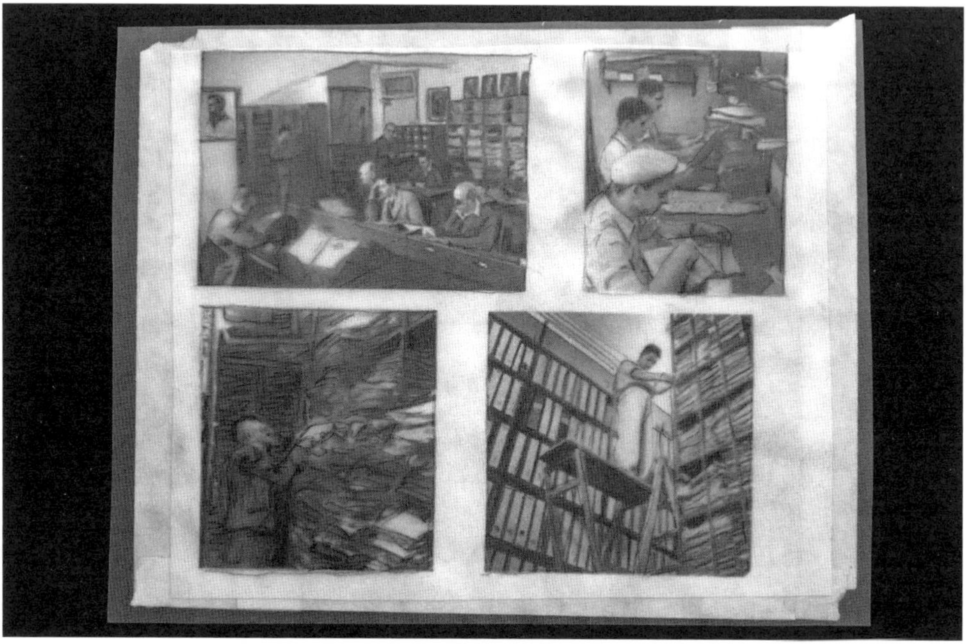

Fig. 4 Zionist Archive, Jerusalem, web page screenshot, from NIA

Photographs of looting, and looted photographs that no one considered classifying, can—and should—teach us about archives, archival procedures and laws, and archivists and their field of expertise. Looking at certain photographs from the peak of the war the state of Israel has waged against those it made into "infiltrators"—namely, photographs taken by soldiers and shared publicly on digital platforms—we can learn about the ways photographs are handled, the body language of expropriation and appropriation, the ceremonies of taking trophy pictures, and the judgments soldiers make about the meanings and uses of photographs as incriminating evidence of enemy aspirations, as confidential or dangerous material, or as signs of cultural hierarchies and distinctions. The looted materials are sorted according to the military needs, general and particular interests, and short- and long-term public-relations concerns that guided the soldiers in deciding which documents they would take with them and which they would leave behind, in the latter case manifesting their lack of interest in them and their poor value. Some recurrent gestures, which are visible in many of the images taken at sites of looting but seldom discussed as constitutive of the archive, deserve attention and inclusion into our understanding of what an archive is. Here is a clear gesture of ostentatious disregard for Palestinian Fig. 4 ← archives, the role they play in the social fabric, the labor invested in them, the impact of time on them, and their modes of caring for Palestinians' past, for their documents, records, or modes of organization. This sight is the outcome of a series of gestures that directly contradict the image of meticulous archival labor that the Zionist archive foregrounded as the expression of its mission and mode of operation. This dimension of disregard, vandalism, damage, desecration, and havoc, although it coincides with the act of plunder, is not its by-product, but rather is an operation in itself, having its own goals vis-à-vis citizens and those who are governed as noncitizens. The piles of papers are thrown on the ground in complete disorder, and those that are demonstratively trashed testify to the soldiers' authority to act as archivists, determining the value of documents and deciding their fate. The destruction is produced according to calculated decisions whose aim is to show publicly that Palestinians are unable to protect their own assets, and thus to provide the justification for a "rescue" operation for records that will be deemed valuable for what is in them when brought "back home" with the soldiers. Documents are sorted during (or sometimes after) military operations by those who are not recognized as archivists but act as such, already within the relevant institutions, as well as by recognizable archivists and librarians who handle them with the proper professional care and scientific attention. Some materials, with or without army commanders' agreement, are taken out of the national booty and put into the realm of private individuals, serving as personal souvenirs through which family members are socialized into the theater of looting.

Fig. 5 ← Here is an archivist. Although he does not wear gloves and does not look like any of the familiar archivists who welcome us in state archives, there is no reason to deny that much of the material we consult in state archives around the world is procured in a similar way. In his hand he holds a bunch of photographs. Together with several other photos, this one was uploaded by former soldiers to the website of their military unit, demonstrating with evident pride

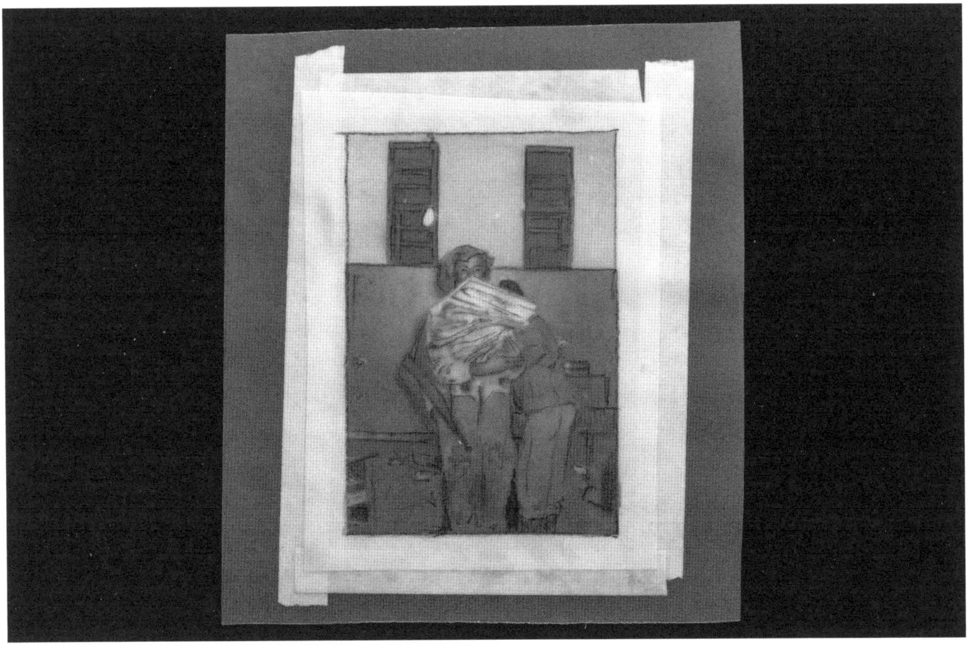

Fig. 5 Unshowable photograph, The Bnot Yaacov Bridge Customs House, "Customs House Sa'ir Operation," October 22, 1955, from NIA

that soldiers were authorized to handle photographic collections. The mission of Unit 101 was to pursue "infiltrators" before or after they crossed the border into Israel. Until 1956, this unit was responsible for what were called "retaliation operations," but as can be seen on their website, a considerable component of these operations was the looting of documents, including photographs.[15] In the next photo, probably taken during a nighttime operation, several soldiers crowd around a number of small photographs held by one soldier. This soldier shows the photographs to his unit mates, and passes some of them over to the soldier standing next to him. The soldiers whose attention is focused on the photos seem rather amused by what they see. We cannot know what is in these photos, or whether they are personal or official. We can tell, though, that looking together at looted photographs—photos seen without permission from and in the absence of their owners—is a bonding moment, forming the bond of accomplices who have the power to transform a crime into an acceptable act. The soldiers' → Fig. 6

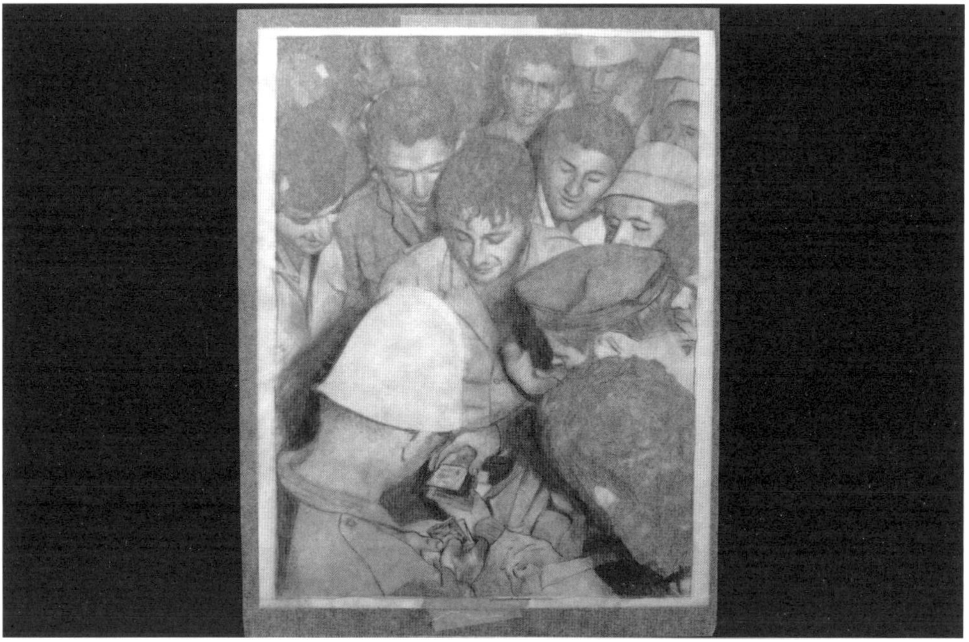

Fig. 6 Unshowable photograph, "Arik and Davidi checking documents and pictures found at the outpost near the Customs House," from NIA

way of holding their photographic booty arouses reasonable suspicion that not all photographs were deposited in archives, and that some—reaching military offices that found them neither incriminating nor valuable—were trashed instead.

Fig. 7 ← Here is another photo, from "Operation Volcano" at the Sabha outpost in Gaza, in which a soldier poses with his booty, probably after his return from the military operation to judge from his posture, the full daylight, and the skyline reminiscent of a Jewish settlement. He presents to the camera Jamal 'Abd al-Nasir's portrait printed at the center of a kerchief as incriminating evidence that Egyptians, and perhaps even Palestinian refugees in Gaza, adore their leader.[16] It is worth mentioning that in Israel 'Abd al-Nasir was depicted as a despot, rather than as one of the post-World War II African leaders who pursued the struggle for decolonization. The soldier is indifferent to the kerchief as an intimate possession of its owner, or as a popular platform for sharing anti-imperial sentiment through photography.[17]

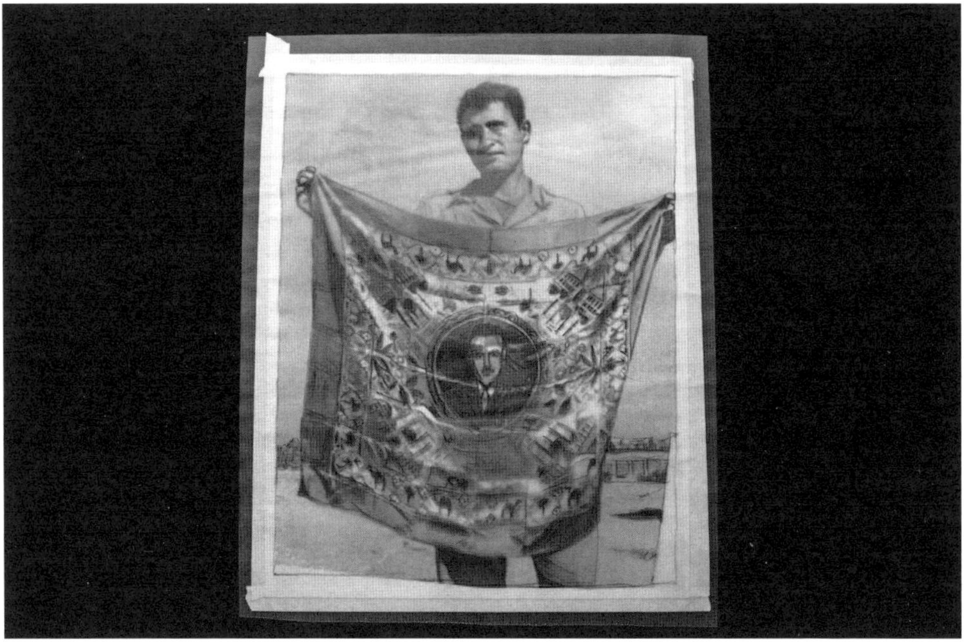

Fig. 7 Unshowable photograph, "A paratrooper holding a kerchief with the picture of Jamal 'Abd al-Nasir, Al Sab'ha Mission, Operation Volcano," November 2, 1955, from NIA

Like many looted Palestinian items, the photo-kerchief was not appropriated in the imperial manner that recognizes the value of the looted item and thereby enriches its national patrimony. Rather, it was reduced to its "content," devalued as a sign of a backward culture based on a leader's personality cult, and denied its particularities as a specific form of personalized photo-object. To this day, the destruction of decades of photographic activity in Palestine has not ceased to affect the conditions for the possibility of creating and researching photography in the entire region. Photographs taken in other places and times by Palestinians, with the intention of documenting the destruction unleashed by Israeli soldiers as they looted archives of documents and photographs, reaffirm this assumption regarding the way photographs are handled when looted.

Obviously, the looting and dispossession of Palestinians who were made "refugees" or "infiltrators" meant economic disaster for Palestinians and benefit for Israeli Jews. As regards culture, however, the law of communicating vessels did not hold in the same way. The massive ruination, destruction, and appropriation of the infrastructure of culture in Palestine in the late 1940s produced dispossession not only among Palestinians: what was lost was not exclusively Palestinian but common, as culture is often produced. Jews were also dispossessed of the cultural infrastructure of a mixed society of which they had been a part, as well as of their own past in Palestine, a past that became identified solely with Arabs, since Israel imposed itself as representative of the Jews and in opposition to Palestine.

This could not endure if Israel had not been invented as another manifestation of the same standardized political entity recognized, endorsed, and promoted by the international apparatuses of imperial nation-states, in whose maintenance the media participate. Otherwise, how else can it be explained that a violent resolution—the partition plan for Palestine, against the will of the majority of the local population—could be taken by an international body that was shaped as an imperial institution and implemented by a minority of Jews with much violence, and that a cohort of international photographers would capture the event with this imperial terminology? How could Magnum photographers such as David Seymour or Robert Capa depict the plunder of Palestine as the creation of a new state or world in which Jewish sovereignty could triumph? How was it that they could conflate the plight of the Palestinians with the difficulties encountered by the migrant Jews, who at that point were made guardians of the new sovereignty? Misled by the documentary protocols that they were using, and thus becoming implicated in what was misleading about them, acting as if lived worlds were reducible to their real-estate components and nation-building campaigns, these photographers dismissed the plight of the indigenous population as well as the destruction of the common. Differences between situations were blurred in such a way that perpetrators could be depicted as victims or law enforcers, even though they were responsible for the destruction of the existing world and the plight of others.

This might be referred to as a momentary blindness of 1948, if it had not endured and been reproduced in the coming years in a way that solidified the outcome of violence as facts on the ground that the photographers were there to document. Here are a few photos taken in 1956 by Burt Glinn in already destroyed Palestine, the newly declared state of Israel. Even when they were shown seventy years later, they were displayed only with their minimalist original caption: "Palestinian Prisoners." Both the display and the caption take the imperial narrative for granted and assume that there is no harm in reiterating it, nor any need to question the authority of those who acquired their imperial rights and sovereignty against the Palestinians whom they expelled from their homes. These Palestinians are not "prisoners." In the photos taken in 1956 in Gaza, they are rather brutalized, either as they attempt to return to their homes or when the Israeli occupying forces invade their homes. Either way, the most important fact—their expulsion from their homeland, Palestine, six years earlier—is → Fig. 8

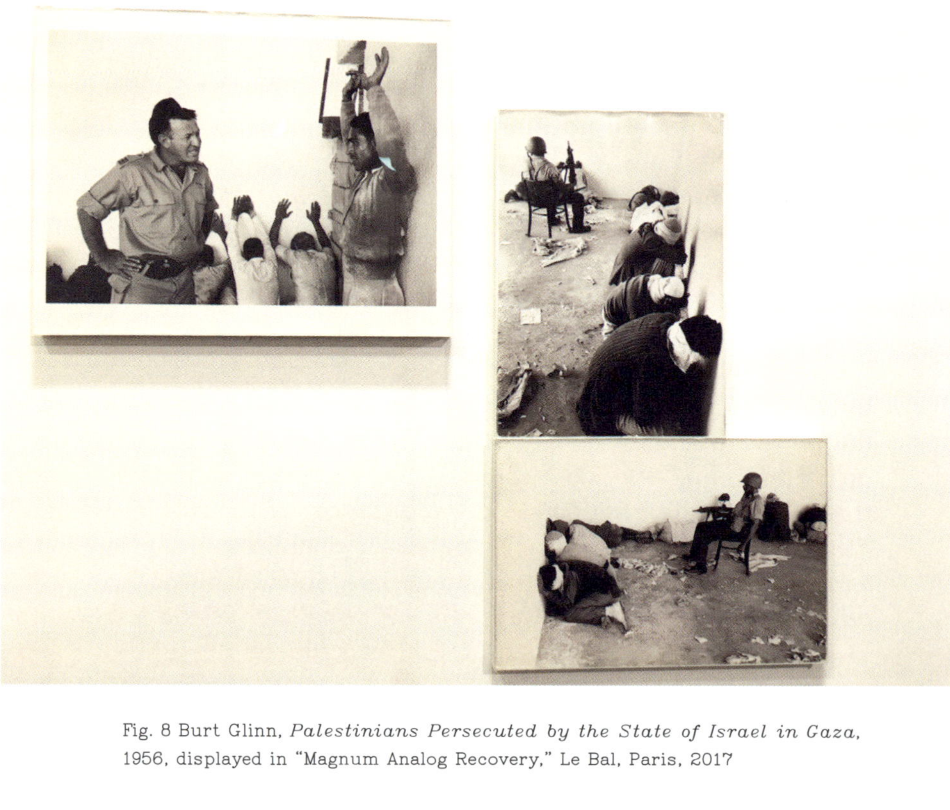

Fig. 8 Burt Glinn, *Palestinians Persecuted by the State of Israel in Gaza*, 1956, displayed in "Magnum Analog Recovery," Le Bal, Paris, 2017

completely removed from the context in such a way that, as they insist on their right to return to their homes, they are forced to embody incriminating imperial categories such as “infiltrator” or “intruder,” for which they are seized, blindfolded, thrown on the ground in torture-like positions, with their hands up for hours, feeling the proximity of guns directed at them by modern citizens, who are soldiers for short periods and who enjoy a set of imperial rights to keep them prisoners of these categories. They are made into the unacknowledged participants in such photographs: those whose spaces have been invaded through the exercise of imperial rights so that their images can continue to circulate, tagged with imperial categories that photographers often use as if they were spokespersons of imperial regimes. Contrary to certain rights that people enjoy within their communities, imperial rights do not emanate from the community of which people are members, on behalf of their membership, or for the sake of a shared world. On the contrary, such rights are derived from the invasion of others' communities and the destruction of the worlds in which those others enjoy certain rights.

Infiltrators cannot exist anywhere except in (Israeli) archives, and they cannot persist there unless Israeli Jews collaborate in their fabrication. In all other places where “infiltrators” might be looked for, their presence is short-lived. They are either killed and eliminated, or returned to their “proper” place—that is, refugee camps—where they stop being infiltrators but continue to reveal the illegitimacy of the Israeli regime. Hence, the study of the figure of the infiltrator cannot but be the study of his or her twin, the figure of the Israeli citizen, whose existence is predicated upon the infiltrator's existence. My companion and I experiment in studying the commons from outside the roles assigned to us by the same differential sovereign regime and through a plethora of other modalities of interactions than those prompted by these roles.

What was destroyed in the violence of the late 1940s was much more than any single photograph—even a photograph whose caption has been altered—could ever convey.[18] The year 1948 was the ruination of the non-partitioned space Arabs and Jews shared in Palestine, and the imposition of the logic of partition along national and ethnic lines as the condition of being there. Thus, each photograph that is taken in this space—once Palestine, now

Israel—instantiates this condition, even when no traces are perceptible within the borders of the photographic frame. Whenever a camera is held in this place, regardless of what the individual photographer seeks to capture, this condition is reproduced. This imperial imprint can be reconstructed from the limits of what can be seen, studied, or said, who can participate in the telling, and how far and how much these constraints can be pushed away. Hence, when this condition is transcended, the state acts virulently to bring things to their "right order."

Here is the time to return to the Great March of Return, and to ask why Palestinian journalists and photojournalists, wearing visible vests with the name of their profession on them, are overtly targeted by Israeli snipers. It is not what they might capture in their cameras that is the threat that has to be suppressed; it is rather the fact that they are completely disrespectful of the empire protocols regarding how to take photographs in imperial zones of violence. They are not there to take photographs of "Palestinians" as if they were a delineated object given to the photographers' eye from the point of view of those who forced them to be "the Palestinians" in this drama—that is, seen in their relation to the Israelis. The Palestinian photographers, themselves incarcerated with other Palestinians in Gaza, obliterate the distance expected from photojournalists, and perform a symbolic, affective, and physical proximity between themselves and those who, according to these protocols, are supposed to be their raw material. This is a proximity of people whose diverse interests do not pit them against one another, as they are expected to be by empire's protocols, but rather who ally with each other in care for a sustainable, shared world that empire and capital seek to prevent from existing. By overriding a variety of imperial and capitalist constitutive divides, they become the target for law enforcers and snipers, the proxies of the state. Palestinians participating in the Great March of Return contest the law of the nation-state erected in 1948 that made them intruders to and in their homeland. This is not another episode within the "Israeli-Palestinian conflict"—which is another imperial invention. It is the persistence of a non-imperial struggle against the imperial-capitalist enterprise of which the state of Israel is part and which should be understood on a global scale. It is a struggle against the many forms and structures of violence that imperial → Fig. 9

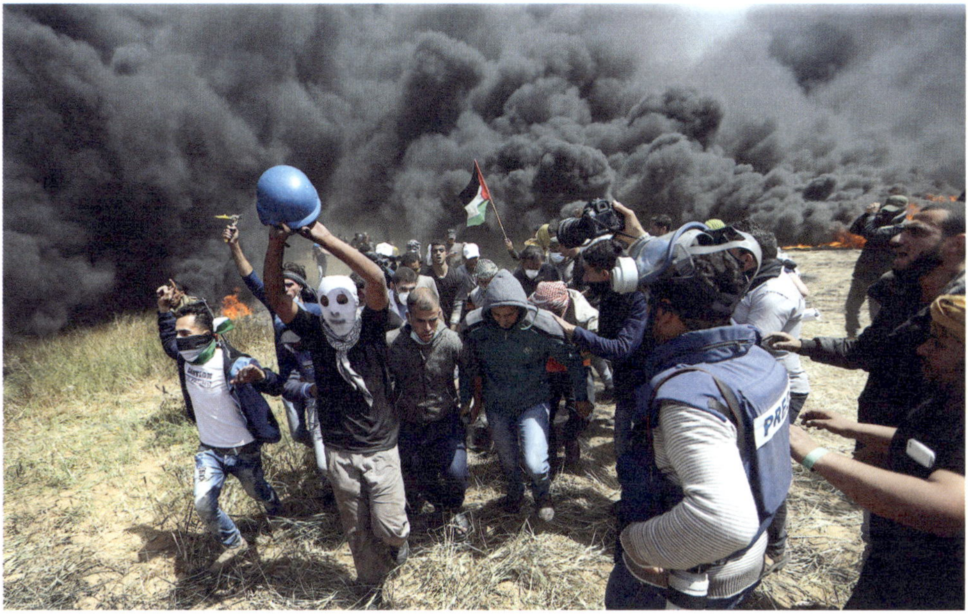

Fig. 9 Palestinian photojournalist Yasser Murtaja being evacuated after being shot by Israeli troops, the Great March of Return, April 6, 2018

states seek to naturalize as laws by virtue of their very existence. Within this context, it becomes clear that the large number of Palestinian journalists and photojournalists shot by Israeli snipers week after week since the beginning of the Great March of Return is not unrelated to the fact that these photographers act as part of their community, and are not delegates of an international media milieu; they pursue this profession out of affectionate proximity and commitment to their own community. In these images, in which they are seen being carried on stretchers by other members of the community, there is much of what the imperial state—the strong ally of imperial markets—is mandated to disallow.

1. Earlier and different versions of this essay were published as: Ariella Azoulay, “Photographic Conditions: Looting, Archives, and the Figure of the ‘Infiltrator,’” *Jerusalem Quarterly*, no. 61 (2015): 6-22; Ariella Azoulay, “The Imperial Condition of Photography in Palestine: Archives, Looting, and the Figure of the Infiltrator,” *Visual Anthropology Review* 33, no. 1 (spring 2017): 5-17.

2. On the document and the archive, see Ariella Azoulay, *Potential History* (London: Verso, 2019).

3. On the mass “repatriation” of millions in Europe after World War II, see Mark Mazower, *No Enchanted Palace: The End of Empire and the Ideological Origins of the United Nations* (Princeton, NJ: Princeton University Press, 2009).

4. On labor camps, see several photos in Ariella Azoulay, *From Palestine to Israel—Destruction and State Formation: A Photographic Record of Destruction and State Formation* (London: Pluto Press, 2011); Yazan Al-Saadi, “On Israel’s Little-Known Concentration and Labor Camps in 1948-1955,” *Al-Akhbar*, September 29, 2014, http://english.al-akhbar.com/node/21763.

5. To date, no research has been conducted on the reasons why those women either agreed or refused, nor has any investigation been made of the connection between their decision to leave and whether one of their loved ones had been slaughtered in Tantura.

6. For more on the images taken during this expulsion, see Azoulay, *From Palestine to Israel*.

7. On the Tantura expulsion and the conditions of research around it, see Ilan Pappé, “The Tantura Case in Israel: The Katz Research and Trial,” *Journal of Palestine Studies*, no. 3 (Spring 2001): 19-39.

8. Jacques Derrida, *Archive Fever: A Freudian Impression*, trans. Eric Prenowitz (Chicago: University of Chicago Press, 1996), 7.

9. Ibid., 2.

10. Ibid.

11. Ibid., 36.

12. Ibid.

13. Ibid.

14. Gish Amit, “Salvage or Plunder? Israel’s ‘Collection’ of Private Palestinian Libraries in West Jerusalem,” *Journal of Palestine Studies* 40, no. 4 (2011): 6-23; Aron Shai, “The Fate of Abandoned Arab Villages in Israel on the Eve of the Six-Day War and Its Immediate Aftermath,” *Cathedra*, no. 105 (2002): 151-70; Rona Sela, *Made Public: Palestinian Photographs in Military Archives in Israel* (Tel Aviv: Helena, 2009).

15. See “The Paratroopers 1948-1958,” http://www.202.org.il/Pages/tagmul/list.php, to which soldiers uploaded their photos from “retaliation operations” in the 1950s. I picked two of these photos to show the ubiquity of looting.

16. There are numerous variations of this type of photograph showing Arab leaders publicly disseminated as incriminating material. See some examples in Benjamin Gepner, ed., *Album Sinai: A Picture Story of the Sinai Campaign* (Tel Aviv: Ledory, 1957) (the book’s Hebrew title reads “war” rather than “campaign”).

17. A similar kerchief is stored in the Imperial War Museum, where its caption reads: “A patriotic and inspirational propaganda scarf produced in Egypt in 1956. It bears Nasser’s portrait and scenes of the improvements and prosperity he planned for Egypt,

including the Aswan High Dam." Scarf, Egyptian, Imperial War Museum, catalogue number 10001, http://www.iwm.org.uk/collections/item/object/30089765.

18. On the looting of a house in Jerusalem, see Banyan Nuwayhed Al-Hout, "Evenings in Upper Baq'a: Remembering Ajaj Nuwayed and Homes," *Jerusalem Quarterly*, no. 46 (Summer 2011): 15-22. On the looting of the archives of Ali Za'rur, see Dalia Karpel, "Negative-Positive" [in Hebrew], *Ha'Aretz*, April 9, 2008, http://www.haaretz.co.il/misc/1.1317383. On Khalil Raad, see Sela's catalogue of the exhibition at the Nahum Gutman Museum in Tel Aviv: Rona Sela, *Khalil Raad Photographs 1891-1948* (Tel Aviv: Nahum Gutman Museum and Helena, 2010). See also Vera Tamari, *Filastin qabl 1948: laysat mujarrad dhakira: Khalil Ra'd (1854-1957)* [Palestine before 1948: Not Just a Memory: Khalil Raad (1854-1957)] (Beirut: Institute for Palestine Studies, 2013), which is based on Lebanese archives.

NECROPOLIS
Walking through a List of Deaths
Arkadi Zaides

Arkadi Zaides is a choreographer and performer who was born in the Soviet Union in 1979. He immigrated to Israel at an early age and in recent years has been based in France. As an artist, he deals with the ways in which political and social contexts affect bodily movements and gestures, and his work is a manifestation of how the term "choreography" has been expanded in recent years: it is no longer necessarily tied to subjectivist bodily expression, and accordingly its tools are no longer predetermined by or limited to dance, but rather may be used for analysis as well as activism. Zaides is specifically interested in the notion of the border, which he explores both literally (focusing on specific geographical border areas, and identifying a particular choreography that emerges in these spaces) and metaphorically (exposing different types of discourse and apparatus at work in relation to the figure of "the other"). In his stage and video works, Zaides focuses on documentary choreography. While documentary theater is usually text-based, reiterating verbatim the reality from which it is taken, Zaides, through the use of documentary footage, focuses on movement, highlighting the choreography that occurs in the social sphere, while observing, analyzing, and intervening in it as part of his artistic work. The "application of the verbatim to the sphere of movement demands substantial modifications to the theatrical model from which it stems," writes Frédéric Pouillaude.[1] As in documentary theater, Zaides's choreography also contains evidence, be it documents, existing archives, or documentary or archival footage. These materials are not points of departure or inspiration: they remain present in the final work, but they are also tampered and interfered with, altered, and modified in order to highlight their physical and choreographic qualities. The artistic research is conceptualized and realized through a collective process, including experts from various related domains.

It is usually extended over a long period of time and includes an analysis of the chosen document(s), interviews with those involved in their production and documentation, and the establishment of an archive for the project itself, as well as dramaturgy and aesthetics derived from these documents. The performance is then a culmination of all these aspects, placing the body and choreography (in its most expansive sense) as key attention points.

The following essay is the result of an intensive series of discussions conducted between Arkadi Zaides, dramaturge Igor Dobričić, and choreographer and researcher Emma Gioia during the working process for a stage project entitled *Necropolis*.[2]

In Europe after World War II, there were massive efforts to search for missing soldiers and citizens, many of which remained unresolved for decades. Only in the early 1990s, after Gorbachev's perestroika, were the Russian archives opened, finally allowing access to information about millions of German prisoners of war who had been previously untraceable. Since 2004, the German Red Cross has digitized two million prisoner files belonging to missing German soldiers and civilians from Russian military archives to create a database with personal information and details about their fates.[3] Germany has not been the only country to conduct such efforts. Approximately thirteen thousand Finnish soldiers went missing on Soviet territory during World War II. Following an agreement between Finland and the Russian Federation, in 1992 there began a search funded by the Finnish Ministry of Education and the Association for the Memorialization of Casualties of War. This search led to the location and repatriation of the remains of about a thousand soldiers. The forensic investigation included anthropological and mitochondrial DNA analyses of bone samples collected from soldiers and reference samples from putative maternal relatives.[4]

In the same vein, the Spanish Association for the Recovery of Historical Memory was founded in 2000 following a meeting of a small group of people at the site of one of the Spanish Civil War's bloodiest civilian massacres. More than two hundred thousand men and women were killed in extrajudicial executions as well as in prisons and concentration camps during and after the war. This organization's goal is to collect verbal and written testimonies and to excavate and identify bodies, which were often dumped in mass graves during Franco's dictatorship. Since its foundation, volunteers have dug up over 150 mass graves throughout Spain, establishing the identity of more than 1,400 exhumed bodies.[5]

More recently, following the end of the civil war in Yugoslavia (1991–2001), about forty thousand persons were reported missing as a result of the fighting. This led to the establishment of organizations such as the United Nations War Crimes Tribunal (2002), as well as legislation such as the Law on Missing Persons

(2004),[6] all in an effort to ensure the right of the missing to be sought for and identified, and to uphold the rights of the deceased's families during such search processes.[7] Mass-scale forensic investigations were conducted, including DNA sampling from relatives of missing persons, and matching to thousands of bodies retrieved from mass graves. Following this evidence, twenty-four years of investigations and prosecutions delivered 161 high-profile indictments. Ninety individuals have been sentenced for genocide, crimes against humanity, and additional crimes.

All the aforementioned serve to demonstrate the increasing progress made in recent decades regarding the proper handling of casualties of armed conflicts, forced disappearances, and other forms of violence in Europe. These processes are the result of years of labor on the part of human rights and humanitarian organizations, state institutions, activists, and families of the deceased. However, in recent years, this progress has been challenged by the flawed handling of deaths that take place on the shores of and inside the European Union. These are the deaths of "noncitizens" that occur outside of the protection of the nation as a result of the "refugee crisis" (or "crisis for refugees," as Gurminder K. Bhambra more aptly calls it to remove any doubt as to who is actually suffering).[8] These fleeing individuals find themselves devoid of rights, not only during their lives, but also after death. Forensic procedures essential to the future identification of these dead and missing persons are carried out improperly, and many bodies are buried without any documentation.

NATIONLESS AND NAMELESS, EVEN AFTER DEATH

In her discussion of "the right to have rights" in her 1951 book *The Origins of Totalitarianism*, Hannah Arendt was concerned with the direct link between the formulation of human rights and the fact that these rights were to be preserved in the context of the nation-state. According to Arendt, as long as these two concepts are linked, there will always be people who are left stateless and thus lacking rights: "We became aware of the existence of a right to have rights [...] and a right to belong to some kind of organized community, only when millions of people emerged who had lost and could not regain these rights because of the new global political situation."[9] By contrast with forced disappearances in Yugoslavia or Spain, there are many diverse reasons for the current mass migration into Europe, ranging from war and conflict to poverty, climate change, and persecution based on one's political beliefs or sexual orientation. The fact that some of these missing persons are classified as "voluntary" refugees—in contrast with those forced to disappear by military or totalitarian regimes—makes it harder to address them as victims of crime and therefore as demanding that necessary measures be taken. The structural reasons leading to these migrations (civil war, authoritarian regimes, etc.) fall less easily within the existing international treaties that hold European states accountable for such losses. These ambiguous circumstances make it very convenient for European countries to avoid ethical responsibility. As a result, the motivation to establish the identities of these deceased migrants—the very same migrants that Europe tries so desperately to keep out of its territory—as well as any sense of responsibility is diminished. Even upon death, one cannot escape the paradox at the heart of the territorially based sovereign-state system that Arendt addressed. She argued that "only with a completely organized humanity could the loss of home and political status become identical with expulsion from humanity altogether."[10]

For over a quarter of a century, UNITED for Intercultural Action, a network of hundreds of anti-racist organizations from all around Europe, has been compiling a list of refugees and migrants who lost their lives on their way to Europe. As of June 2020, the list contains information on 40,555 deaths, spanning sixty-nine pages densely filled with a long table, each row registering one death or group of related deaths—sometimes hundreds. The table breaks each death down into six columns: the date of the reported death(s); the number of bodies found in that specific case (from one person to 1,050 persons in the deadliest case reported); the deceased's name, gender, and age; their origin; the cause of death (drowning, suicide, police violence, poor access to medical care, etc.); and the source(s) that reported the case. Although the list dates back to 1993, over 90 percent of the deaths listed occurred after 2013. And it contains only those whose deaths have been reported. The toll in all is certainly much higher.[11] When scrolling through the many pages of the list, one cannot ignore the fact that row by row, under the "name" column, the entry "N.N." is repeated, standing for "*nomen nescio*," which is Latin for "name unknown." Consequently, the age, gender, and origins of these deceased are also absent from the list. A closer look reveals that only a very small percent of the dead are mentioned by name, leaving the vast majority without identifying details.

THE RIGHT TO BE ANALYZED AND INSTITUTIONALIZED IS NOT A GIVEN

In modern-day European countries, when a dead body is found, a standardized institutional procedure is launched. Pathologists and forensic experts are deployed to collect medical and biological data from bodies and from living relatives in order to enable identification. However, this procedure has not been followed for most of the victims of the current crisis for refugees at the gates of Europe. "The humanitarian community recognizes that proper handling of the dead is a key component in disaster response,"[12] nevertheless, the majority of migrants' bodies are insufficiently processed, rendering their future identification impossible. As more deaths occur and the list continues to grow, Europe's extreme neglect of this reality becomes clear, as it denies victims the most basic of human dignities. As the area of science able to establish the identity of a person, forensics also plays an important role in claiming a person's humanity. The right to legality, to inclusion and protection under the law, and one's ability to become a subject of forensic investigation and subsequently to be properly registered and buried, are linked to the ways in which bodies are represented, and also to how they are aestheticized, imagined, and given agency. This dynamic between visibility and invisibility, anonymity and identity, or affirmation and disempowerment has implications that are highly political.

When active withdrawal, neglect, and invisibilization become official procedure with regard to the community of dead migrants, any proper forensic registration of these bodies becomes a form of *counter-forensics*—as Thomas Keenan calls it—that proposes a mode of resistance to the status quo. "To dig," Keenan writes, "is to climb into the grave with the dead, to share a space with them, and to confront the fact of their death, not in order to undo what has happened (that cannot be done) but to transform their silence and disappearance into names, stories, and claims."[13] The attempts at counter-forensics applied to those documented in UNITED's list are made partly by isolated initiatives on the part of scientists and humanitarian organizations. Among them is Dr. Pavlos Pavlidis from Democritus University Hospital in Alexandroupoli. After being retrieved from the nearby Evros River, which is one of the main inland routes between Turkey and Greece, bodies in varying states of decomposition arrive in plastic bags at Pavlidis's laboratory. Sometimes the corpses are stored, refrigerated for months until all other avenues of investigation are exhausted. If the deceased's name and origin are impossible to determine, the numbered bodies are buried after the collection of DNA. In his office, Pavlidis keeps hundreds of items found on the bodies. These are often the only leads in the investigation. Yet another important figure who has committed herself to the proper and dignified documentation of the community of dead migrants is Cristina Cattaneo. In her laboratory at the University of Milan, this forensic pathologist and anthropologist investigates some of the most lethal cases that have occurred in the Mediterranean. Along with a team of researchers and volunteers, Cattaneo set out to collect postmortem evidence from and complete genetic profiles for hundreds of dead migrants. One case investigated by Cattaneo took place on April 19, 2015, when an overcrowded boat carrying over a thousand migrants from Libya to Europe sank to the bottom of the sea as a result of a collision with a Portuguese ship that was trying to help. A year later, the Italian navy used a complicated pulley system to raise the wreck to the surface. The hundreds of decomposed bodies were so tightly compressed under the deck that it took Cattaneo and her team several years to separate them.

Yet the aforementioned examples are like needles in a haystack. The vast majority of dead bodies are not retrieved from the sea, and most that are, are buried witout proper documentation. It seems almost as if proper forensic investigation is for the fortunate, while those who are not so lucky are left unaccounted for, their corpses buried without any investigation of where they came from or who they were. This mass grave scenario resonates with other moments in history and other geopolitical realities. A profoundly morbid reality related to injustice is thus overlooked, and a mass crime is not thoroughly investigated. Moreover, thousands of family members of these dead migrants are kept in a cruel limbo, as their missing relatives are officially neither dead nor alive. Until they are proven, with no grave site for relatives to attend and no death certificate to show to the authorities, thousands of stories of disappearance cannot achieve closure.

ARTISTS' RESPONSES
Formulating Civilian Responsibility toward the Nameless Dead

In *Return to the Postcolony: Specters of Colonialism in Contemporary Art* (2013), T. J. Demos follows the work of five contemporary artists who embark on a kind of "reverse migration" and "return to the postcolony to seek answers to urgent questions regarding the causes and histories behind the desires of multitudes to travel northwards."[14] Demos acknowledges a "fundamental spectro-ontology—or birthplace of ghosts—of the postcolony," claiming that "the colonial past still haunts us because it is a past that has not really past."[15] In order to "acknowledge the ghosts, to open up the repressed histories, to admit the colonial present, and to commence this politics of memory in partnership with the dead in struggle,"[16] it seems one need not travel far. By attempting to document all the people who lose their lives on their way to Europe, UNITED's list points to the deadly outcomes of the migration movement northward to which Demos refers. The mass of decomposed bodies and body parts at the bottom of the Mediterranean, inside Europe or on its shores, tells the story of a collective whose ghost hovers over the territory.

Several artists have already engaged with UNITED's list. Turkish artist Banu Cennetoğlu, for example, has been working with the list since 2007. Collaborating with curators, artists, and institutions, she has distributed updated versions of the list to newspapers as well as in public spaces such as billboards and transportation networks in cities including Berlin, Istanbul, Basel, and Athens. In mid-July 2018, as a result of a collaboration between Cennetoğlu and the Liverpool Biennial of Contemporary Art, the list was installed on a 280-meter blackboard on a central city street.

Two weeks after the opening of the biennial, the list was torn down by unknown vandals. The list was then reinstalled by the organizers but was repeatedly damaged until guards were hired to secure the site. The vandals were never found. In his 2019 lecture "Against Empathy: The Case for Rational Compassion," Paul Bloom argues that we should abandon empathy and acknowledge that our emotions "can lead us astray" when we relate to the suffering of others.[17] For him, empathy is like "a spotlight, it zooms you in on people you are then more likely to help. But like a spotlight we can point it at the wrong places and like a spotlight it is insensitive to numbers."[18] Paul Slovic, an expert on the effect of numbers and statistics on empathy (or the lack thereof), similarly argues that the response to two people in danger is not twice the response to one, because with the mere addition of one person we already begin to lose empathy.[19] One can only speculate that even if those who vandalized Cennetoğlu's installation might have shown empathy in the presence of a single "other," perhaps the way the list was displayed, handled, and presented to the larger public played a role in the set of emotions it produced.

When we discovered it in June 2018, the list and the community of the dead it documents became our obsession. We asked ourselves: How do we as artists, as citizens, respond to the mass deaths taking place around us? How are we to position ourselves and take responsibility? Thinking about all these bodies as a mostly unidentified collective scattered throughout Europe and in the surrounding sea, we began to wonder: What kind of gesture, even symbolic, could acknowledge this vast community of people? How could we collect, archive, and use evidence? Inspired by strategies of counter-forensics, we wondered how the list could be further investigated as a body of data, and what practice could be articulated that would resonate with this process of dealing with the remains, with the evidence—in this case, relating directly to dead bodies.

Members of the research group Forensic Architecture apply different forensic practices and produce documents that counter official state narratives. Its members—architects, software developers, filmmakers, investigative journalists, artists, scientists, and lawyers—not only investigate various state and corporate acts of violence, human rights violations, and environmental destruction, but are also constantly occupied with how to communicate their findings to a wider audience. They use public forums such as international courtrooms, parliamentary inquiries, United Nations (UN) assemblies, citizens' tribunals, truth commissions as well as seminars, publications, and exhibitions in art and cultural institutions to share their findings and to make their research processes transparent to viewers.[20] Through various multidisciplinary mediums such as participatory workshops, exhibitions, and installations, Forensic Architecture invites audiences to become acquainted with the process of counter-forensic research. This sharing of various investigation strategies as well as their findings democratizes the field of forensics.

Influenced by this, we returned to that mass grave that is the list of deaths, with the question of how we could conduct an investigation that would give a body to this highly abstracted database while simultaneously constructing a performance event that would not only provide the spectator with information but also question their own implication in this catastrophe. What mediums could be used to confront ourselves with the excluded, the undocumented, those who are not alive in all extreme senses of the word—physically and bureaucratically? How could we make the theatrical stage a place where the invisible (or those rendered invisible) become visible? By confronting the dichotomy between the dead and the living through a documentary approach to the contemporary geopolitical reality of migration, we began to imagine an immersive theatrical and choreographic experience that would allow spectators to feel literally implicated, and hopefully to recover their own sense of accountability. We thought of an experience that would allow spectators to "get closer" to individual deaths as well as to reveal a more complex structure, a place, a territory: an architecture of death we began to call *Necropolis*.

IMAGINING NECROPOLIS
Rationale and Methodology

The title of the project ostensibly refers to an ancient term for a burial ground: *necropolis*, the city of the dead. On a symbolic level, it strives to reactivate the archetype of an invisible, suppressed "community of the dead" that challenges and obligates us as a community of the living. Furthermore, it appropriates the literal effectiveness of the mythological imagination that Necropolis conjures up as a topos—a concrete metaphysical space. As a city, it is not a specific location but a meta-structure—the cemetery of cemeteries—that casts its shadow over the contemporary history and geography of Europe. Like the corpses buried in it, the city of the dead obviously has no body other than the body of data, an ever-expanding archive of what is meticulously extracted from the rotting remains of its dead. This growing database defines the layout of Necropolis, stretching in all directions across the space-time continuum, interconnecting the mythologies, histories, geographies, and anatomies of thousands of people. Without giving it much attention, Europe's citizens are slowly surrounded by all those who were not admitted, who are physical corpses of people, who are ghosts that are not taken into account. These dead also evoke the concept of "the other," that part by which one is haunted and which one excludes. During the artistic process, we strived to get closer to individual deaths mentioned on the list and to find more information regarding their whereabouts. We were asked to lead a series of short workshops in Stockholm, each with a different group of participants. We spent several hours with each group collectively investigating one specific case of death that had occurred in Stockholm and its surroundings, which we extracted from the list. Using personal computers and cell phones, participants collected information from the Internet related to these individual deaths. Several cases were thus somehow reopened, revealing in more detail the stories and narratives of the deceased. The physical proximity of the cases to the actual location of the workshop brought the list and the phenomenon it documents closer to the participants, who were unaware that such deaths took place in their city. The search through fragmented and unorganized scraps of information (newspaper articles, official police reports, human rights organization reports) unearthed the structural violence leading to those deaths.

But a question continued to haunt us, the same question we believe also weighs on the minds of thousands of relatives of the deceased on UNITED's list: Where is the body? Where are the actual remains of all these bodies? In what physical space may these individuals, this entire community of dead migrants, be grieved, mourned, and paid their last respects? In her lecture "Bodies That Still Matter," Judith Butler questions why some populations are regarded as more "grievable" than others. "To grieve another is to stand in relation to that other. It is a social relation, one between people, but," she points out, "it is also one that is mediated by cultural and political modes of representation." For her, "depending on the public sphere in which the loss takes place it can be registered with great lamentation, great sorrow or, it can be dismissed or covered over as if it were no loss." Butler argues that when populations are eradicated in war or other forms of violence, when these deaths could have been avoided, "the public acknowledgment of loss is crucial to the act of protest."[21] In addition to this acknowledgment, the space of personal and collective grieving requires a geographical location—a physical space where one can visit and perform rituals in accordance with cultural norms.

At a later residency, at Pact Zollverein Artists' Center in Essen, Germany, we further focused our search to resonate with the aforementioned necessity for a physical location of mourning. After an extensive online investigation regarding several deaths that occurred in the Ruhr area near the location of our residency, we focused on one article that specifically pointed out a cemetery where a twenty-three-year-old refugee from Sudan named Emanuel Thomas Tout was buried. Tout died in 1993 from injuries as a result of attempted suicide at a detention center in the small town of Herne. The article mentioned a memorial ceremony that had taken place in a cemetery ten years after his death. Upon discovering the name of the cemetery in which Tout was buried, we decided to visit his grave. The journey to the cemetery took several hours. When we arrived, we asked local personnel, who helped us to find the exact location of the grave by looking at hand-drawn plans pulled from their archives. One of the workers could remember Tout's funeral about twenty-five years previously, as well as the small memorial service of which we had read, which took place ten years later. "This was a famous case, the first of its kind in the region," he noted. "It stirred a lot of public debate, something that would not happen today," he added.

BUILDING NECROPOLIS
The Procedure

Visiting a cemetery always evokes a particular set of emotions. Visiting the grave of someone one is investigating but does not know personally is even more peculiar. Walking toward the actual place where the body was buried is a very disturbing experience. A person who until that moment has been just a name on a list, sometimes only a data entry or a statistic in a long list of over thirty-six thousand, now gradually gains a physical location. Arriving at the grave of Emanuel Thomas Tout, we each made a gesture of respect. We also decided to register the coordinates of the grave's location by measuring its longitude and latitude on our cell phones. We then made a short video documenting the walk from the cemetery gate to the grave, holding the smartphone in front of us as we walked. Since then, we have been continuously documenting the locations of graves in the vicinity of any place where we arrive, gradually mapping our Necropolis.

Deeper inside Europe, most of the graves of migrants and asylum seekers who have lost their lives are identified, as in the case of Emanuel Thomas Tout's grave. These individuals have already been registered and processed through border systems that determine their names and identities. But the vast majority of the casualties mentioned on UNITED's list died at sea, and the graves of the retrieved ones are usually unidentified. Most are located in the three main gateways into Europe: southern Spain, Italy, and Greece. Our first encounter with this aspect of the catastrophe was made possible due to a connection with Giorgia Mirto, a researcher and activist based in Sicily. Since 2011, Mirto has devoted herself to the issue of missing migrants and deaths at the borders, and she currently holds an updated archive of "border death" casualties buried in Italy. Most of the cemeteries in Sicily have graves of dead migrants, often hundreds at the same location. On our first visit to Sicily, we visited seven cemeteries in a week, and identified almost six hundred graves out of what Mirto estimates are approximately three thousand on the island.

After collecting data in different cemeteries, we return to our workspace and enter the coordinates taken at the graves into Google Earth. From the image of planet Earth floating in space, we can gradually zoom into this virtual representation of geography until we recognize the cemeteries we have visited, and then into the paths we have walked while searching for the graves, to discover the particular architecture of the graveyard from above. We can zoom further into the exact points where the graves are located, and hover above them. We also have the video documentation of our walks toward the graves, allowing us to get even closer to them from an eye-level perspective.

Google Earth and Google Maps are technologies primarily associated with the acceleration of mobility. Using them allows us to orient ourselves and find our way almost anywhere on the globe. Many migrants and asylum seekers also use these platforms to orient themselves during their journeys. But platforms such as Google Earth and Google Maps are also the direct successors of maps, aerial photography, and other surveillance devices developed to support military operations and territorial control. They originated at the time of European colonial projects—the same projects whose contemporary victims are documented on UNITED's list. These platforms carry within them the history of racialization and dehumanization. Our intention when inserting the coordinates of the migrants' and asylum seekers' graves is to hijack those platforms with information about the ultimate immobility—the deaths of those whose patterns of movement are both marked and produced as a disruption, a danger, delinquency.

Donna Haraway calls "for politics and epistemologies of location, positioning, and situating, where partiality and not universality is the condition of being heard to make rational knowledge claims. These are claims on people's lives; the view from a body, always a complex, contradictory, structuring and structured body, versus the view from above, from nowhere, from simplicity."[22] Our visit to the cemetery and our walk toward the grave, as well as being a respectful gesture to each grave identified, which was just part of a big and abstracted database mere moments before, strives to articulate an embodied investigation as Haraway proposes. Moreover, the entanglement and confrontation of these two perspectives—the "gaze from above" with its colonial roots, and the embodied knowledge proposed by Haraway—are crucial, and pave the way toward a liminal space that interrelates the geographies, mythologies, histories, movements, and anatomies of individuals who lost their lives on the way to Europe.

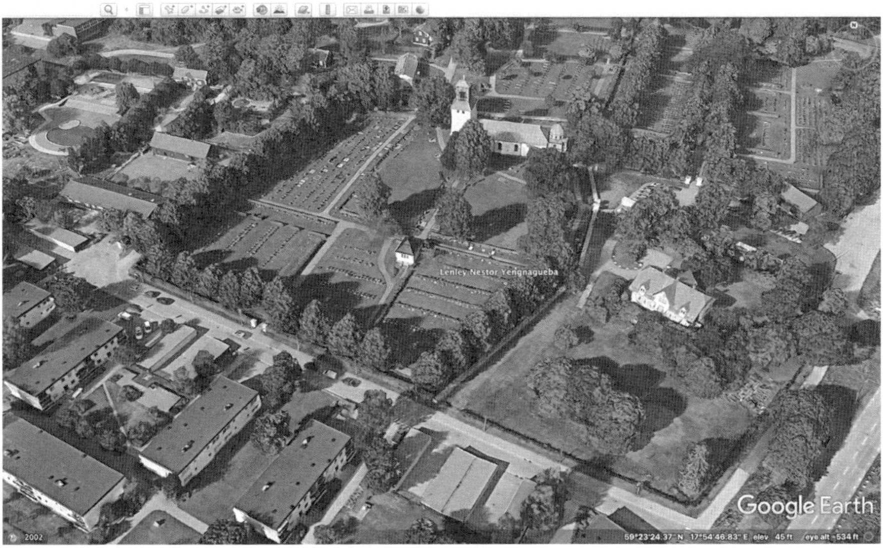

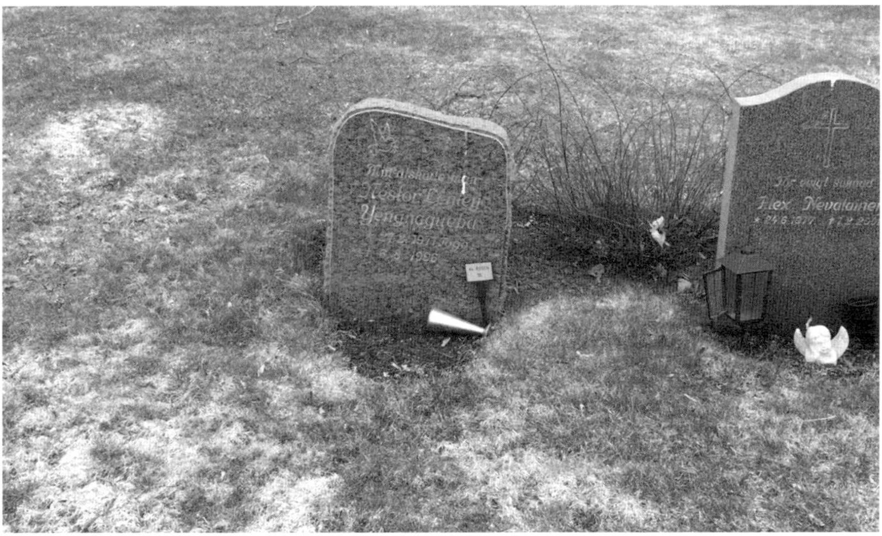

Found dead **06/08/1996**
Name, gender, age **Lenley Nestor Yengnagueba (M, 25)**
Region of origin **Togo**
Cause of death **Jumped out of a window of his home in Stockholm (SE) after immigration police rang the doorbell**
Source **Svenska Dagbladet/Dagens Nyheter/FARR**
Grave location search **Sunniva Vikor Egenes, Benjamin Pohlig, Arkadi Zaides**
Grave localization **Gabriel Smeets, Arkadi Zaides**

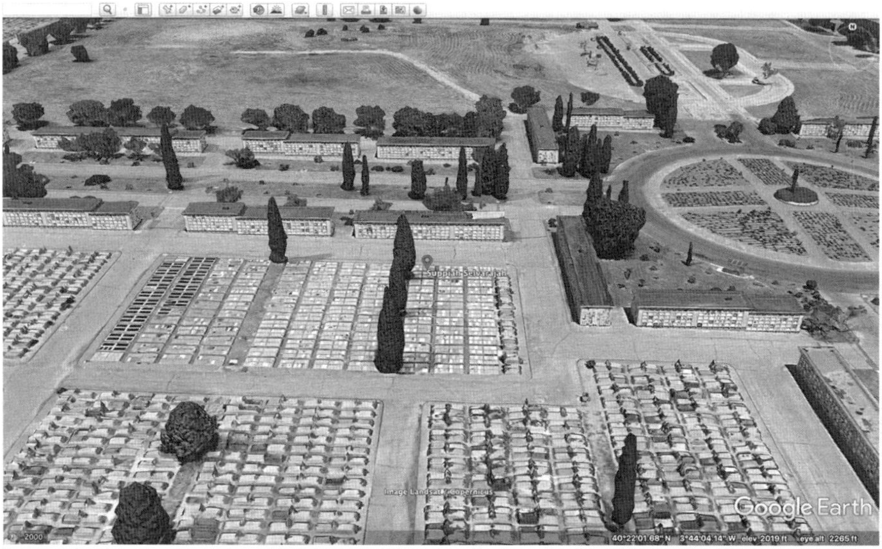

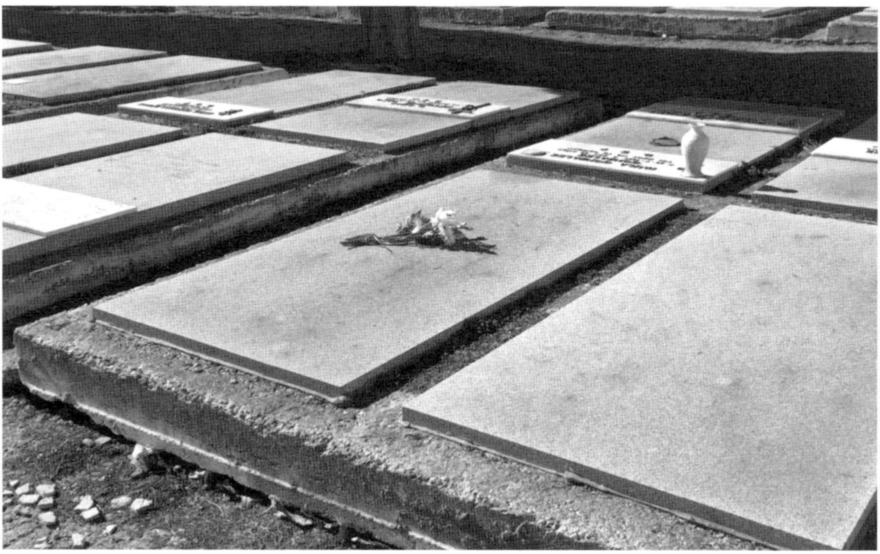

Found dead **14/06/1995**
Name, gender, age **Suppiah Selvarajah (M, 31)**
Region of origin **Sri Lanka**
Cause of death **Suffocated during a fire at his shanty in Madrid (ES)**
Source **Egin/DiarioVasco**
Grave location search **Simge Gücük, Julia Asperska**
Grave localization **Arkadi Zaides**

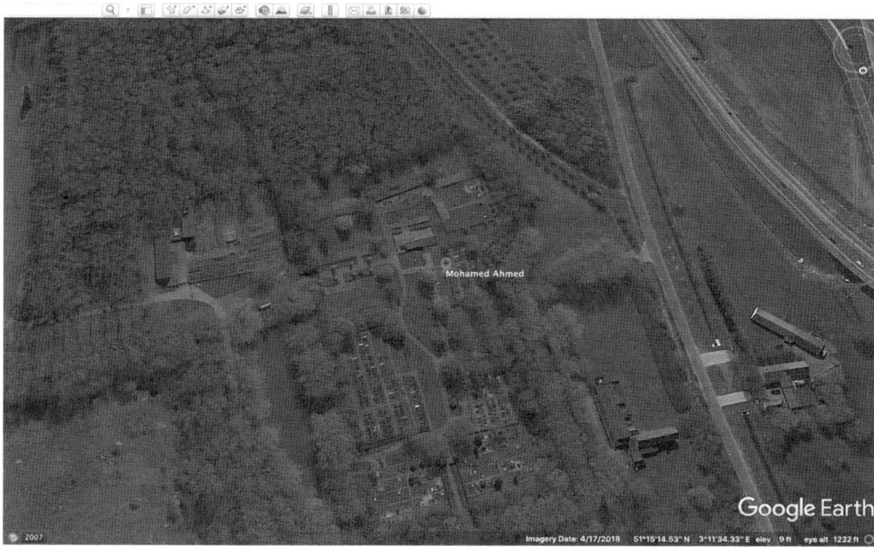

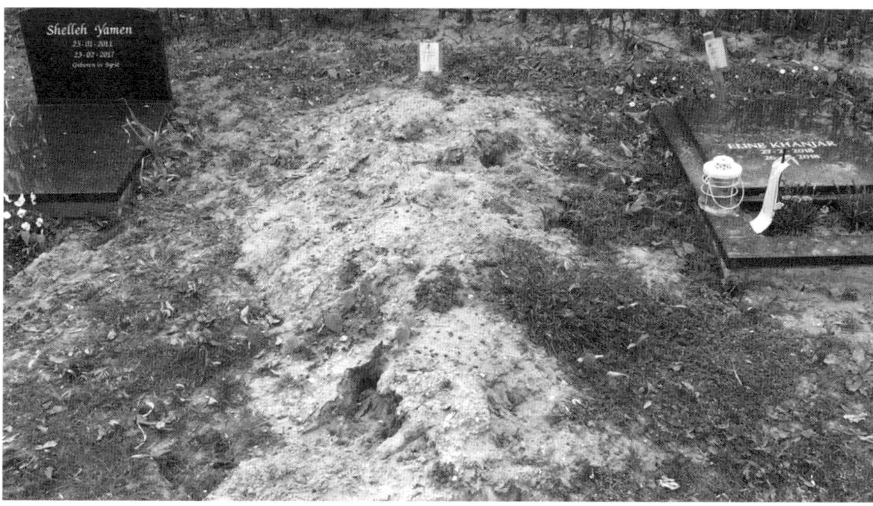

Found dead **29/01/2018**

Name, gender, age **Mohamed Ahmed (M, 39/40)**

Region of origin **Ethiopia**

Cause of death **Killed by a passing vehicle while escaping from the police next to Jabbeke (BE)**

Source **KW**

Grave location search **Myriam Van Imschoot**

Grave localization **Myriam Van Imschoot, Joris Van Imschoot, Doreen Kutzke, Arkadi Zaides**

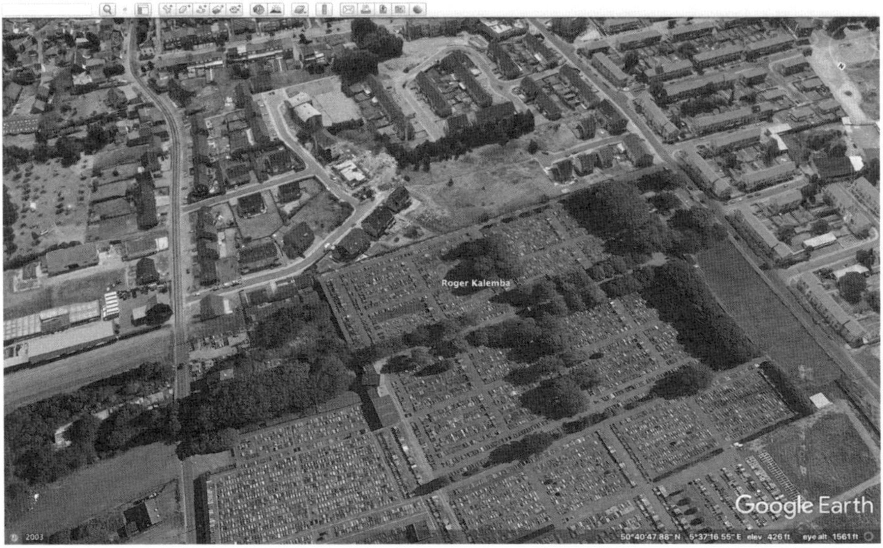

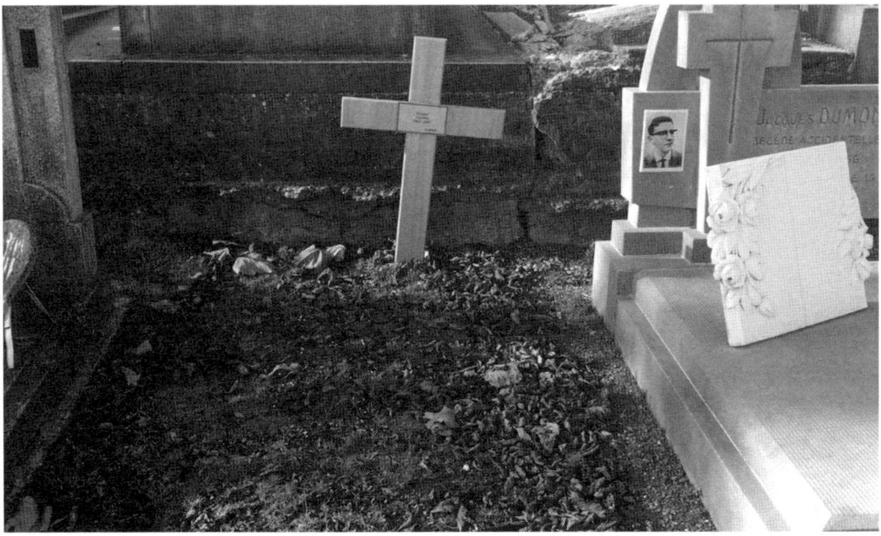

Found dead **19/12/2015**
Name, gender, age **Roger Kalemba (M, 50)**
Region of origin **Congo**
Cause of death **Commited suicide in a detention center Vottem (BE) the evening before his second deportation attempt**
Source **JRS - B News**
Grave location search **Emma Gioia**
Grave localization **Emma Gioia, Igor Dobričić, Arkadi Zaides**

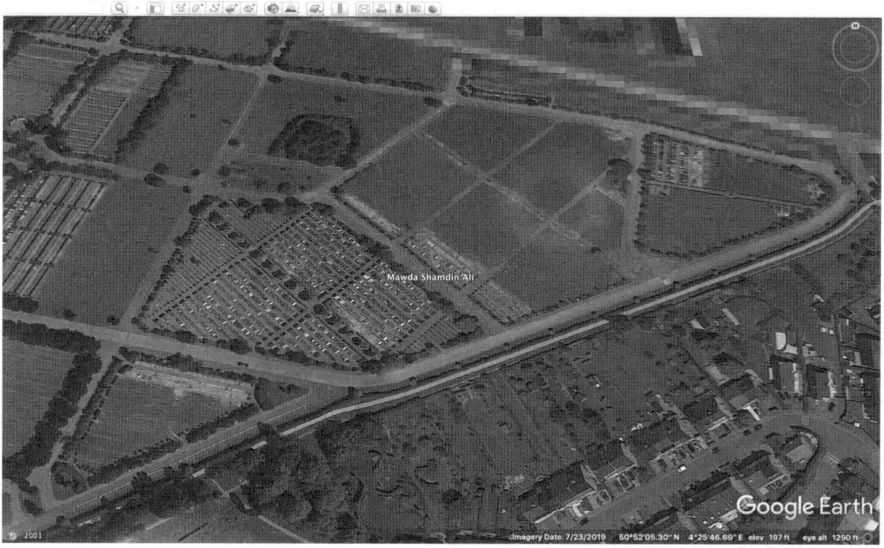

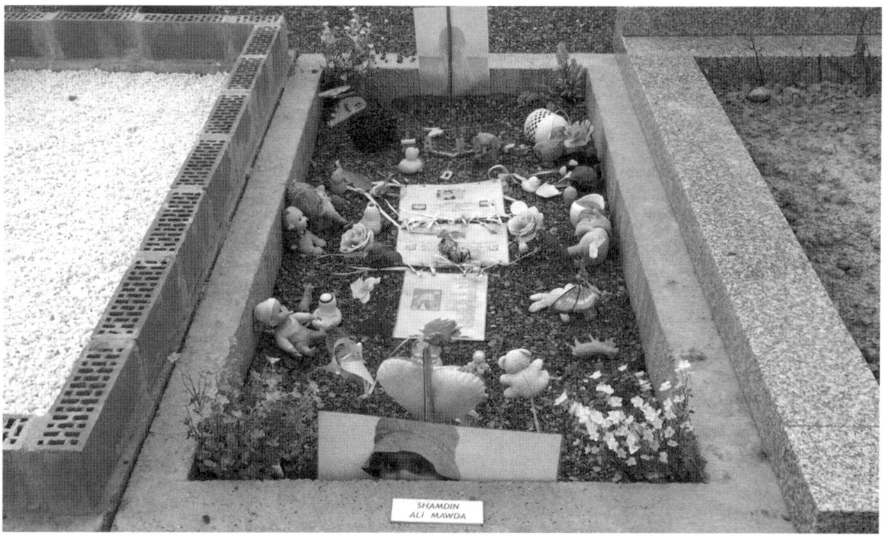

Found dead **17/05/2018**
Name, gender, age **Mawda Shamdin Ali (F, 2)**
Region of origin **Iraq**
Cause of death **Kurd, killed by runaway police bullet near Mons (BE) in wild pursuit of a migrant vehicle headed for the UK**
Source **AD/RTBF/RTLbe/DH/Sputnik/IOMZambia/EastAfrican**
Grave location search **Arkadi Zaides**
Grave localization **Myriam Van Imschoot, Sarah Leo, Arkadi Zaides**

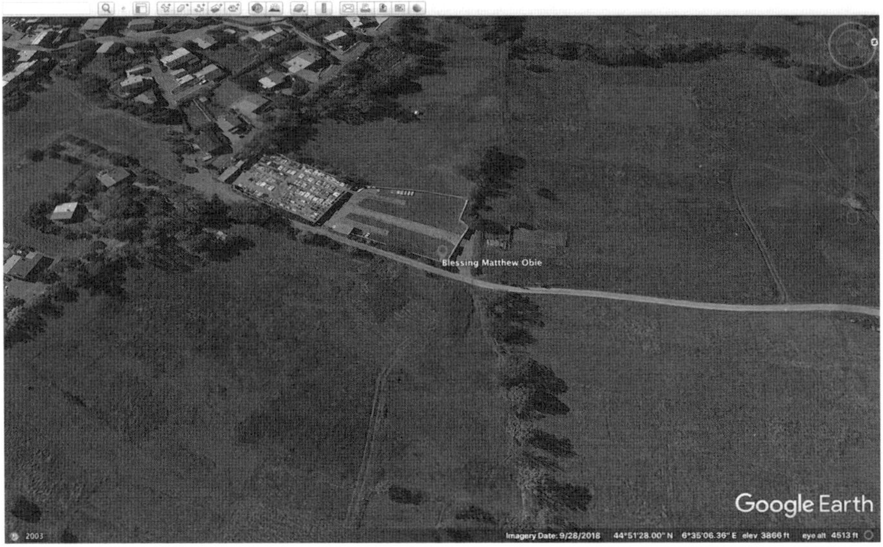

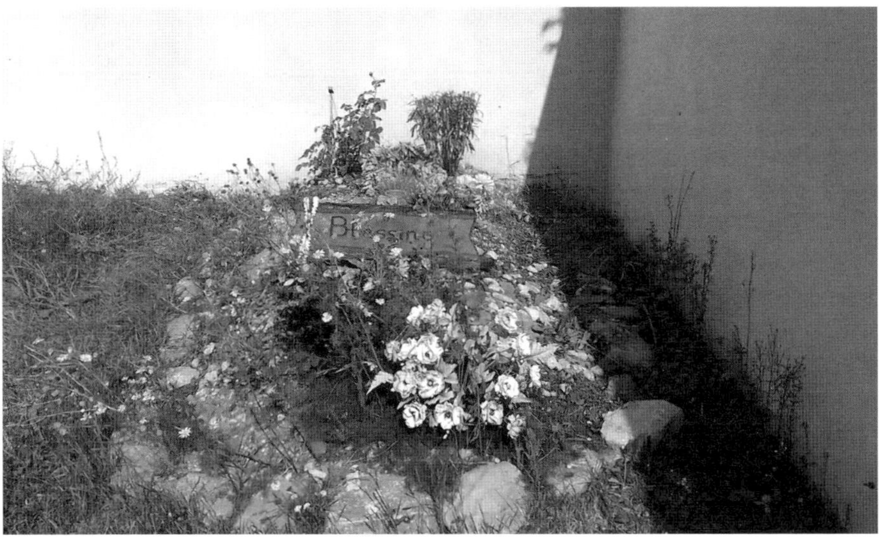

Found dead **07/05/2018**
Name, gender, age **Blessing Matthew Obie (F, 21)**
Region of origin **Nigeria**
Cause of death **Drowned in Durance river near Briançon (Alps, French/ Italian border) while fleeing the police**
Source **Vivre/CDS/Francetvinfo/20MFR/IOM/DICI/Liberation**
Grave location search **Yari Stilo**
Grave localization **Yari Stilo**

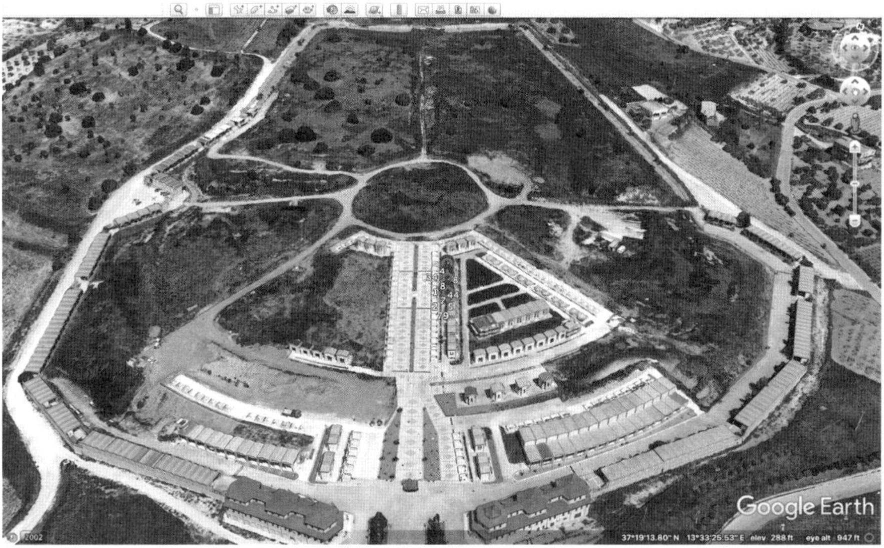

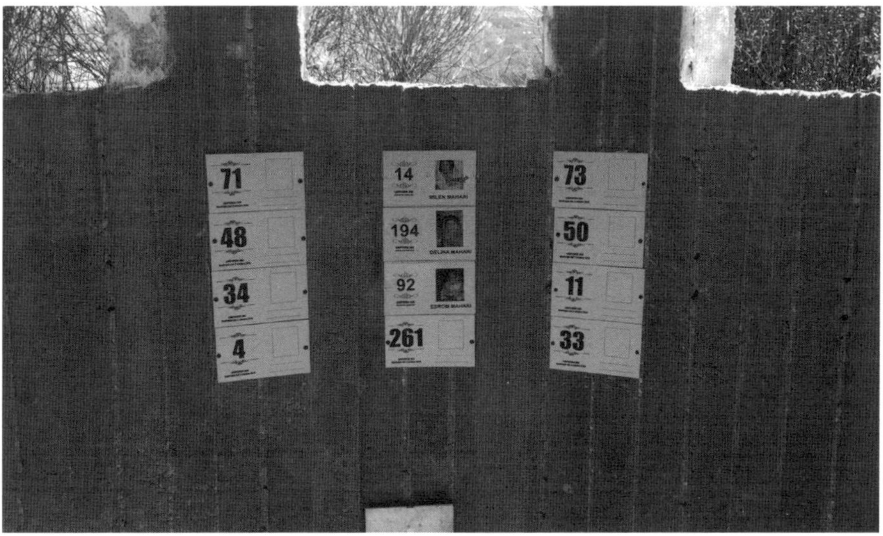

Found dead **03/10/2013**
Name, gender, age **N.N.**
Region of origin **Africa**
Cause of death **365 drowned after a boat from Libya caught fire and sank off the coast of Lampedusa (IT); 155 rescued**
Source **VK/NRC/ANP/AiN/Presse/NYTimes/BBC/Guardian**
Grave location search **Giorgia Mirto**
Grave localization **Arkadi Zaides**

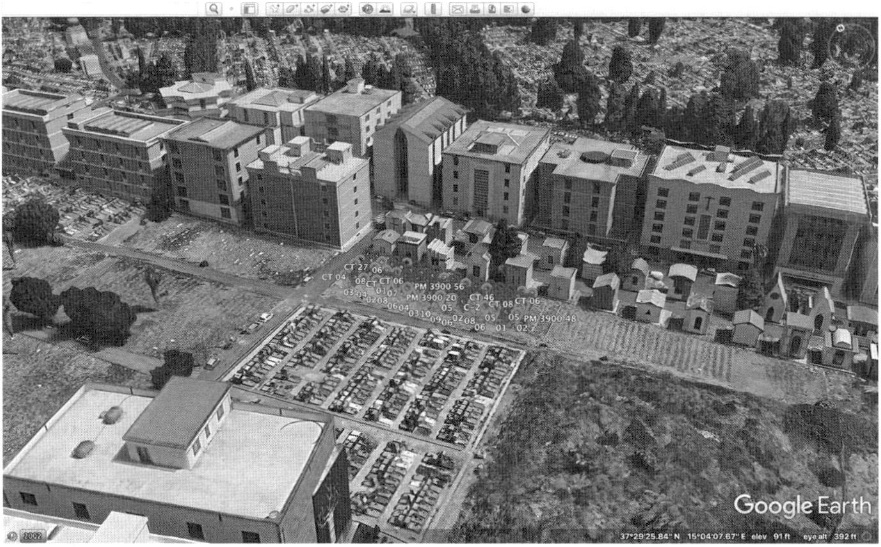

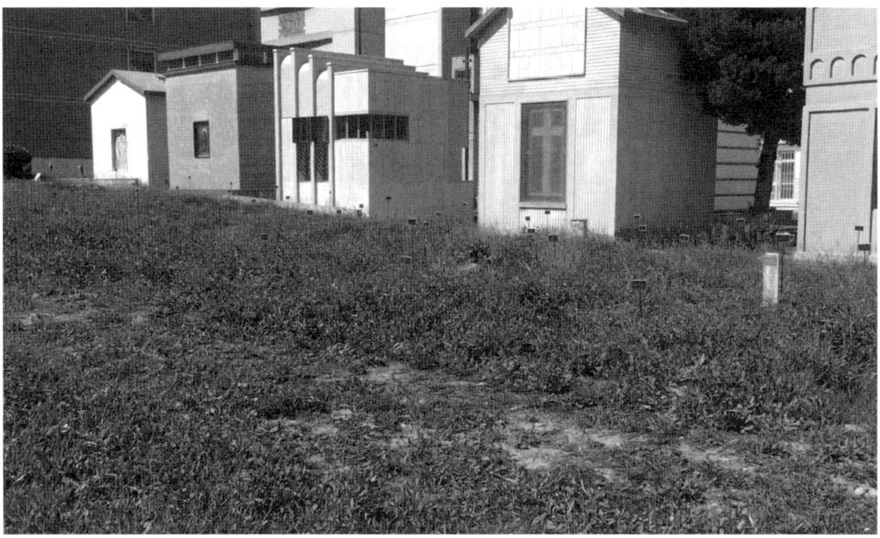

Found dead **Two hundred and twenty-two bodies located at Cimitero Monumentale di Catania, Sicily, Italy. Up to six bodies are buried in each tomb.**
Name, gender, age **N.N.**
Region of origin **Various**
Cause of death **Various**
Grave location search **Giorgia Mirto**
Grave localization **Arkadi Zaides**

NECROPOLIS AS PERFORMANCE
Activating the Virtual Space

The performance to come uses a rather monastic setup. A huge projection screen covers the back of the stage. A long table is placed at the front of the stage, as if to cut the space in two, creating a border between the audience and the large void of the stage, which is left empty. The table is full of technical equipment including computers as well as sound, light, and video-operating devices. An audio introduction accompanied by text on the screen invites the audience to enter the city of the dead: Necropolis. Two operators enter the stage and silently sit at the table, their backs to the audience. Using Google Earth projected onto the large screen, they first zoom into the location of the theater. The operators then zoom out to reveal a mark similar to those that indicate one's destination when one uses Google Maps. The operators zoom in toward the mark, which turns out to be a grave at a cemetery. They zoom out to reveal many more red marks, which form a complex architecture. Some of the marks are accompanied by names; others only have numbers. The operators continue to zoom in and out, to and from cemeteries and tombs, creating a virtual visual journey, until they reach the shores of Europe where the land meets the Mediterranean, and they hover over hundreds of graves marked on the shores.

The two performers are seated, facing the same direction as the audience—all gaze at the screens. The action of scrolling through data and geographical terrain via a digital platform, and the repetitive action of zooming in and out, is reminiscent of actions that often take place in surveillance control rooms, thus resonating with surveillance practices to which the deceased may have been subjected while still alive. It emphasizes and replicates the divide between those who research and study and those who are studied, perhaps against their will. "How things are ordered racially by way of surveillance," writes Simone Browne, "most often upholds negating strategies that first accompanied European colonial expansion and transatlantic slavery that sought to structure social relations and institutions in ways that privilege whiteness."[23] Browne uses the term "dark surveillance" in order to "situate the tactics employed to render one's self out of sight" and as an "imaginative place from which to mobilize a critique of racializing surveillance."[24] The ethical implications of the performed/watched procedure is thus brought forward, highlighting the unbridgeable gap between the collective that have the privilege to watch from a distance, to analyze and investigate, and the collective that lost their lives on the way toward the very territory from within which they are watched.

Whenever the application zooms in on a grave, additional information appears on the screen, revealing the exact coordinates of that location, the name (if known) of the person buried there, and the date and cause of death. At times there is a video capturing the walk from the cemetery gate toward that grave. The camera is held in front of the body at chest level, making it impossible to determine who holds it. It is a simple, silent walk toward a grave, toward many different graves at many different locations, always at the same pace, performed as if attempting to connect all these individual cases through one single repetitive gesture. While UNITED's list links all the cases by embedding them in one abstract document, these walks attempt to connect them through a gesture—a choreographic one. A series of such walks conveys an embodied practice to the spectators, and also alludes to the thousands of graves that are yet to be located—to the thousands of walks that are still to be performed.

THE FUTURE OF NECROPOLIS
The Invitation

We are mapping the invisible city of the dead—Necropolis—that consists of the marked and unmarked graves of the refugees who did not manage to reach their final destinations in Europe alive. To this end we use a list compiled by the UNITED network, containing tens of thousands of migrant deaths. We scan the list to identify the places where deaths occurred in proximity to our current location. Using the names and any other information available and relevant to the particular local case, we begin online research in an attempt to identify the exact burial location. If online research is not enough, we contact local institutions (city hall archives, detention centers, nongovernmental organizations, local cemeteries, etc.) that might help us to obtain information about a specific case. If our research yields results, we visit the location where the body is buried. Once at the exact location of the grave in question, we identify its geographical coordinates by using Google Maps on our smartphones. If several graves are found at the same location, we measure the coordinates of each grave. We then take a photo of the grave and register all its information. Using the video camera on a smartphone, we also document the walk from the gate of the cemetery to the grave. Finally, when back at our workspace, we enter the graves' coordinates into Google Earth and mark the grave on the map, linking all traces of our research to it (articles, URLs, photos, videos, and maps). This process has resulted in the gradual construction of Necropolis. The cornerstones of this city are the graves of thousands of migrants still to be found and located.

We strive to locate the graves of all those on the list. As we are a very small team, we invite friends and colleagues to carry out the same procedure and expand the architecture of the city of the dead. This is our invitation to you.

How can you join our search?

- Contact us, mentioning your interest in partaking in the search and specifying the location(s) where you would like to conduct it.

- You receive information related to the death cases that occurred in the area, taken from the UNITED list.

- You launch online research in an effort to identify the exact location(s) where one or several deceased are buried. If online research is not sufficient, you contact local institutions (city halls, archives, NGOs, detention centers, local cemeteries) that might provide information about the specific case(s).

- If your research yields results, you visit the location(s) where the body(ies) has (have) been disposed of.

- Once at the exact location of the grave, you identify its geographical coordinates with your smartphone. If several graves are found, you register the coordinates of each grave.

- Holding your smartphone horizontally at chest level, you film your way while walking from the entrance of the cemetery to the identified grave(s).

- You send us all the gathered information. After adding it to our database a new location in the city of the dead will be established.

The Necropolis team
arkadi.zaides@gmail.com

1. Frédéric Pouillaude, "Dance as Documentary: Conflictual Images in the Choreographic Mirror (On *Archive* by Arkadi Zaides)," *Dance Research Journal* 48 (2016): 19.

2. Thanks to Solveig Gade, Daniela Agostinho, Sandra Noeth, Alix de Morant, and Frédéric Pouillaude for their feedback and guidance during the writing process of this essay.

3. "Files from Moscow," Deutsches Rotes Kreuz, https://www.drk-suchdienst.de/en/services/second-world-war/projects/files-former-ussr.

4. "Repatriation and Identification of Finnish World War II Soldiers," NCBI The National Center for Biotechnology Information, https://www.ncbi.nlm.nih.gov/pmc/articles/PMC2080560/.

5. "What Is the Association for the Recovery of Historical Memory (ARMH)," La Asociación para la Recuperación de la Memoria Histórica (ARMH), https://memoriahistorica.org.es/who-are-we/.

6. The Law on Missing Persons created in 2004 "establishes the principles for improving the tracing process, the definition of a missing person, the method of managing the central records, realization of social and other rights of family members of missing persons, and other issues related to tracing missing persons from/in Bosnia and Herzegovina" or the Missing Persons Institute of Bosnia and Herzegovina (MPI) that has an obligation to find missing persons without discrimination and establish the Central Record of the Missing Persons (CEN), thereby restoring dignity to victims and responding to their families, and contributing to the satisfaction of justice and the implementation of the reconciliation process.

7. The ICRC (The International Committee of the Red Cross) Policy Paper with recommendations to policy-makers in cases of missing migrants acknowledges the specific needs of families of missing migrants including the need to "lift any specific administrative and legal barriers that families of missing migrants may face in the exercise of their rights, or in accessing existing services and benefits, including clarifying the legal status of a "missing person" in the national legal framework, or ensuring that the existing legal framework on missing persons covers the situation of families of missing migrants."

8. Gurminder K. Bhambra, "The Current Crisis of Europe: Refugees, Colonialism, and the Limits of Cosmopolitanism," *European Law Journal* 23, no. 5 (2017): 399.

9. Hannah Arendt, *The Origins of Totalitarianism* (New York: Schocken Books, 2004), 376.

10. Ibid., 377.

11. According to an estimate by a spokesperson for the International Committee of the Red Cross in an interview with our team, the number of victims would probably double if one were to take into account everyone whose body has not been found and who is therefore not included on the current list.

12. *Management of Dead Bodies after Disasters: A Field Manual for First Responders* (Washington, DC: PAHO, 2016), 3.

13. Thomas Keenan, "Counter-Forensics and Photography," *Grey Room*, no. 55 (2014): 73.

14. T. J. Demos, *Return to the Postcolony: Spectres of Colonialism in Contemporary Art* (Berlin: Sternberg Press, 2013), 10.

15. Ibid., 12.

16. Ibid., 10.

17. Paul Bloom, “Against Empathy: The Case of Rational Compassion” (lecture, December 19, 2016), https://www.youtube.com/watch?v=yhCGmDJQRpc&t=18s.

18. Ibid.

19. Thanks to Mushon Zer-Aviv for referring me to Bloom's and Slovic's work.

20. “About Agency,” Forensic Architecture, https://forensic-architecture.org/about/agency.

21. Judith Butler, “Bodies That Still Matter” (lecture, University of Tokyo, December 8, 2018), https://www.youtube.com/watch?v=xiG0w1nf0sU&feature=emb_title.

22. Donna Haraway, “Situated Knowledges: The Science Question in Feminism and the Privilege of Partial Perspective,” *Feminist Studies* 14, no. 3 (1988): 589.

23. Simone Browne, *Dark Matters: On the Surveillance of Blackness* (Durham, NC: Duke University Press, 2015), 17.

24. Ibid., 21.

FORENSIC (IM)PROBABILITIES
Entering Schrödinger's Box with Rabih Mroué and Hito Steyerl

Solveig Gade

In his seminal 2003 book *State of Exception*, Italian philosopher Giorgio Agamben argues that a main ingredient in the so-called War on Terror was the Bush administration's launching of a state of exception, a condition that implied the suspension of the juridical order and thereby allowed the United States government to detain suspected "enemy combatants" on an indefinite basis and without trial. However, Agamben explains, the suspension of a norm does not mean its abolition. Instead, it means the implementation of a space in which the norm may apply but not be effectuated, while decisions that are not legally sanctioned are brought into force. The state of exception, then, creates a space that at one and the same time is located inside and outside the juridical order. "In truth," Agamben posits, "the state of exception is neither external nor internal to the juridical order, and the problem of defining it concerns precisely a threshold or a zone of indifference, where inside and outside do not exclude each other but rather blur with each other."[1]

The blurring between *nomos* and *anomy*, legal right and pure violence, identified by Agamben in 2005 in relation to the War on Terror has since been taken to new levels with the spread of remote digital warfare.[2] Take, for instance, the instrument of former US President Barack Obama's official anti-terrorist doctrine: the drone. As French philosopher Grégoire Chamayou argues, drone warfare breaks with the modern idea of war as an endeavor based on the idea of fronts and opposing battle lines squaring up to each other. Representing instead a condition of globalized, militarized manhunt, and taking place in both zones of war and zones officially at peace, drone warfare, according to Chamayou, creates intense confusion around geographical, ontological, ethical, and legal-political categories. "Within what legal frameworks do drone strikes take place today?" he asks, and he goes on: "Where the US is concerned, it is impossible to say. Everything is blurred."[3]

This blurriness or uncertainty with respect to legal-political categories, and regarding who can be held responsible for which decisions, has become exacerbated by the increasing use of machine learning and algorithmic calculations, which has been brought by securitization and preemptive warfare, and which to an ever greater degree plays itself out across mundane and military spheres.[4] Indeed, as researcher and artist Susan Schuppli notes, in an era when the front lines are moving into spaces of computation, and when "algorithms execute and pixels cover up a crime,"[5] warfare increasingly takes place in digital spaces of abstraction that are inaccessible to the public, or for that matter to human perception.

Throughout recent years, a number of cultural workers and activists have sought to counter the withdrawal of contemporary warfare from public perception by investigating and presenting to the public a range of contested cases. An exemplary and much celebrated case in point is the interdisciplinary research agency Forensic Architecture, headed by architect Eyal Weizman and based at Goldsmiths, University of London. Affiliated with scholars and artists (including Schuppli), Forensic Architecture collaborates with and undertakes architectural and media research on behalf of various international prosecutors and human rights organizations. Alongside its presentations in political and judicial contexts, Forensic Architecture's investigations are often shown in artistic and cultural venues. Indeed, within the past decade or so, the group has become something of a superstar in the art world, and its activist practice of digging up and presenting material that testifies to war crimes and human rights violations has been widely celebrated by both critics and curators.[6] Rather tellingly, when Forensic Architecture was nominated for the 2018 Turner Prize, it was the group's "citizen-led evidence gathering," its collaboration with "communities affected by acts of social and political violence," and the fact that its work had led to "military, parliamentary and UN inquiries" that were emphasized by the Turner committee.[7] The group's aesthetic translation of this "evidence-gathering," however, was not foregrounded. Nor was the fact that in reality Forensic Architecture has rarely won any of the inquiries or cases in which it has been involved.[8]

While I do not hold this against Forensic Architecture, I do want to question the discourses within the art world that tend to base their notion of "evidence" on a much too straightforward and ultimately positivist definition. I also want to question the way in which the discursive sphere of art sometimes comes close to being reduced to an unambiguous showground for the presentation of such evidence. To this end, I will perform a close reading of, and try to think with, the 2012 lecture performance *Probable Title: Zero Probability* by Lebanese performance artist Rabih Mroué and German-Japanese media artist and scholar Hito Steyerl. Throughout the discussion I will draw on the definition of "forensics" and the notion of evidence offered by Weizman and Thomas Keenan, director of the human rights program at Bard College. Likewise, I will take inspiration from French philosopher Jacques Rancière's idea of the politics of aesthetics. More precisely, combining Keenan and Weizman's concept of the forum with Rancière's notion of the entanglement of aesthetics and politics, I will argue that while one of art's central characteristics is that it does not succumb to the logics that prevail outside of the sphere of art, it still offers a deeply and essentially political space in the sense that it provides a public site for discussing the conditions of the possibility of politics.

BONES MAKE GREAT WITNESSES

Associated with the late nineteenth century's development of new methods for merging photography with measurements and calculations, forensic science was initially associated with techniques used by the police to investigate crime.[9] However, as Weizman and Keenan posit in *Mengele's Skull: The Advent of a Forensic Aesthetics* (2012), since the unearthing in Brazil in 1985 of the remains of the Nazi war criminal Josef Mengele, forensic analysis has played an increasingly important role in investigations of war crimes and human rights violations.[10] Indeed, marked by the excavation of mass graves in the wake of the Srebrenica massacre in Bosnia and Herzegovina as well as the Rwandan genocide, a distinct forensic turn could be said to have taken place across international law and human environmental science. Sometimes at the expense of human testimony, material objects such as bones found in mass graves have increasingly been used in court as evidence of the crimes under investigation.[11] As the pioneering forensic anthropologist Clyde Snow, who headed the Mengele investigation, famously remarked: "Bones make good witnesses. Although they speak softly, they never lie and they never forget."[12]

However, Weizman and Keenan warn against simply replacing faith in the human witness with faith in material remains. Instead of arguing for a clear-cut distinction between "the human witness" and "the material witness," they contend that just as the testimony of the human witness may be faulty and subject to probability and margins of error, so may the material witness. They counter Snow: "Because [material objects] do not speak for themselves, there is a need for a translation, mediation, or interpretation between the 'language of things' and that of people."[13] Accordingly, Weizman and Keenan posit that forensics comprises a triangle of three interrelated elements: a contested object, a mediator, and a forum.[14] The "mediator" refers to the expert witness or scientist who interprets and claims to speak on behalf of the "contested object," that is, the material remains. The "forum" designates the public arena within which this procedure unfolds.

In the foreword to the 2014 book *Forensis*, Weizman distinguishes firmly between police forensics, which according to him should be understood as a disciplinary tool intended to affirm the power of the state, and what he terms *forensis* or "critical forensics," which aims to challenge received forensic practices. Whereas the former could be said to rely on the notion that facts and evidence are able to provide a scientifically approved account of truth, the latter pays just as much attention to the nontransparent processes that determine when something is assigned the status of evidence in the courtroom and when it is not. To return to the triangle of forum, mediator, and contested object, within critical forensics the forum might thus be conceived of as the site where evidence is presented to the public, but also and no less importantly where the political processes of evidence-making are foregrounded and exposed to critical investigation. As Weizman puts it: "Forensis [...] introduces both the production of evidence and the querying of the practice of evidence making."[15] Drawing on a broad understanding of aesthetics as that which is concerned with perceptions and the senses, Weizman and Keenan further argue that it is both an aesthetic and a political affair when something is allowed to appear as evidence within the forum.[16]

This way of understanding aesthetics as intertwined with politics can be related to Rancière's conception of aesthetics and his notion of the "distribution of the sensible." According to Rancière, the distribution of the sensible can be seen as the overall law that implicitly organizes rules and modes of perception within a given community. Thus, the distribution of the sensible sets divisions within that which presents itself to the senses: between what is visible and invisible, what is audible and inaudible, what can be said, thought, and done, and what cannot.[17] Politics, in Rancière's account, can thus be seen as an attempt to *redistribute* the given distribution of the sensible: "Politics revolves around what is seen and what can be said about it, around who has the ability to see and the talent to speak, around the properties of spaces and the possibilities of time."[18] Seen against this background, Weizman and Keenan's notion of the forum as a site for negotiating the status of contested objects can be said to involve a struggle over the distribution of the sensible, over what presents itself to the senses and is, within a specific political context, granted status as evidence.

Informed by these reflections, I will now turn to Mroué and Steyerl's lecture performance *Probable Title: Zero Probability*. While the work does not deal with the forms of digital or algorithmic warfare mentioned at the outset of this article, it does engage with how to approach the concept of evidence when (1) the contested objects in question are not acknowledged and therefore not rendered available to human perception, and (2) the war crime under scrutiny has not left behind any material objects.

MISSING PEOPLE

In their joint lecture performance, Mroué and Steyerl focus on war crimes and missing people. Steyerl engages with the alleged massacre of a group of fighters from the Kurdistan's Workers' Party (PKK) by the Turkish military in Kurdistan in 1998. To the best of her knowledge, her beloved friend from her teenage years, Andrea Wolf, lost her life in this clash between the PKK and Turkish

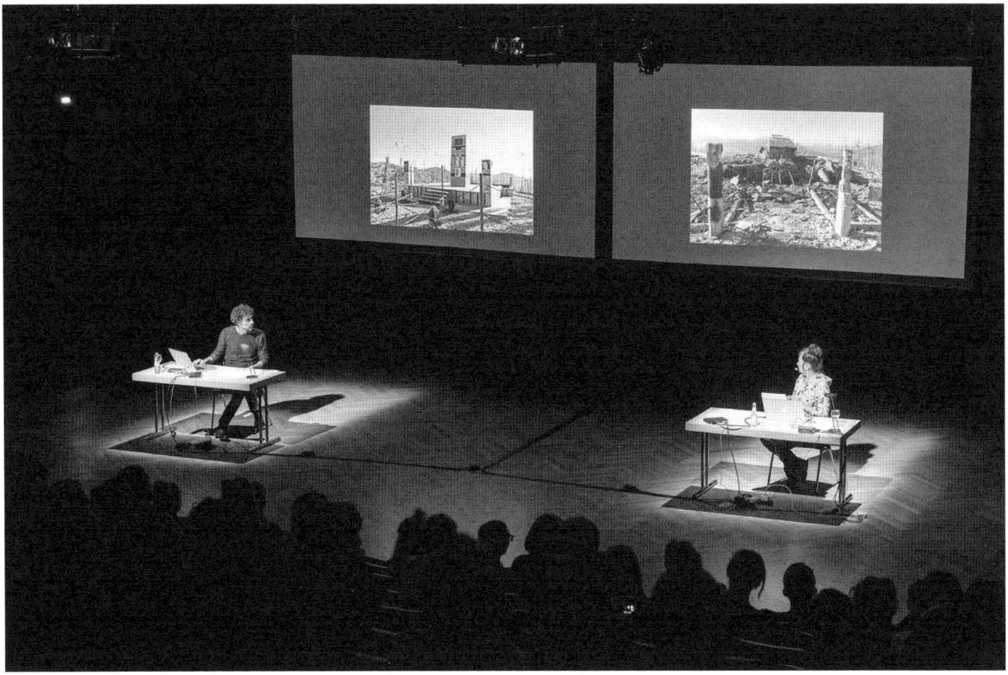

Fig. 1 Rabih Mroué and Hito Steyerl, *Probable Title: Zero Probability*, Bundeskunsthalle, Bonn, 2018

forces. Mroué, for his part, is preoccupied with the Lebanese Civil War (1975–1990), in the shadow of which he grew up. An estimated seventeen thousand people were disappeared during the civil strife.

Seated in a black box with their respective laptops at two identical tables in front of two screens divided by a one-meter slit, Mroué and Steyerl take turns delivering their accounts while projecting images and video onto the screens. The lecture opens with the question: "What is probability?" In an attempt to answer this question, Steyerl shows a short film in which she tosses a coin into the air and states that the probability of its coming down as either heads or tails is fifty-fifty. However, the coin does not come down at all, even though the probability of this happening is zero. Steyerl then suggests that it may have disappeared into the edit between the takes of the film—"the space of zero probability," as she terms it: "This space is teeming with one 100 percent improbable events. [...] The space of zero probability is not only able to swallow coins. It swallows all sorts of objects. Whole buildings and even whole landscapes. Lots of people have disappeared into this space, which is just slightly beyond the edges of representation. In other words, *it is the space of the missing*."[19] Relating the notion of the space of zero probability to contexts of war and conflict, specifically the Lebanese Civil War and the clash in Kurdistan, Mroué and Steyerl set out to unravel the logic of this impossible yet existent space, and the ontological status of those trapped within it. While Steyerl seeks to enter the space of zero probability by juxtaposing two incompatible versions of the same event, Mroué speculatively imagines how two incompatible accounts might meet in a state of indeterminacy. Let us begin with Steyerl's way of proceeding.

NO BONES, NO IMAGES, NO WAR

Steyerl suggests that we think about the space of zero probability by comparing it to a cinematic edit. Expanding on the cinematic metaphor, we might relate the idea of the edit to Judith Butler's concept of visual framing, unfolded in her 2009 book *Frames of War: When Is Life Grievable?*. Writing on Western media's portrayal of the twenty-first-century wars in Iraq and Afghanistan, Butler notes that operations of visual framing have strategically been pursued in order to establish a certain field of perceptible reality in which some human lives have been left outside the frame, *disappeared* as it were, whereas others have been allowed to appear.[20] Heavily influencing our perceptual and sensory apparatus, and in turn what we can hear, see, and apprehend as life—and also whether that life is worth grieving or not—such operations of framing are deeply political, and could be said to be expressive of Rancière's notion of the distribution of the sensible.

Steyerl approaches the contested question of whether Turkish military forces did or did not massacre a group of PKK fighters in northern Kurdistan in 1998 by juxtaposing two mutually exclusive framings of the event. To begin with, she shows the audience an excerpt from her film *November* (2004), in which we get to see a young Hito Steyerl together with her teenage friend Andrea Wolf. In the last scene of the film, Wolf literally disappears from the visual frame; Steyerl explains that the next time she saw her friend,

Wolf had been inserted into the visual frame of a martyr poster that paid tribute to her for her support of the Kurdish cause. Indeed, in the years since the clash, Wolf has become somewhat of an icon of socialist internationalism, not only in Kurdistan but also in Germany, where she has been memorialized in books, posters, ceremonies, and street demonstrations organized by radical German leftist and activists.[21] Having joined the PKK's women's brigade in Kurdistan in the mid-1990s, Wolf lost her life in 1998 together with forty other female PKK fighters in a clash with the Turkish military. Allegedly, Wolf and her allies were first taken prisoners, then tortured and executed, and finally abandoned in a mass grave. In 2013, following a Turkish human rights organization's discovery of what it claimed was the mass grave, a monumental tomb was erected in the Van region and named after Wolf.[22] To date, however, neither the Turkish nor the German authorities have investigated the case as a war crime, even though in 2010 the European Court of Human Rights found the Turkish government guilty of systematically preventing any clarification of what had taken place after the clash between Turkish military forces and the PKK.[23]

In *Probable Title*, Steyerl documents how, assuming the role of a forensic anthropologist, she ventured into the site of the alleged crime. While explaining her investigation, she projects images onto the screens that show her conducting an interview inside the mass grave with an anonymous person who claims to be an eye-witness to the massacre. In addition, a series of close-ups presents various objects that Steyerl asserts she found on the site. The objects include 7.62-millimeter and 20-millimeter G3 ammunition cases, as well as what looks like a bone from a human body. In the lecture, Steyerl presents her discoveries in a matter-of-fact manner that urges the audience to consider them as evidence, or "material witnesses," of a war crime neglected by both the German and the Turkish governments. As Steyerl wryly states: "The Turkish and German states claim that it is impossible to know what happened there [...]. Also if this was possible one would find out that nothing unlawful had ever happened there, especially not the war crimes described by witnesses, which are doubly impossible."[24]

The contrast between the official Turkish and German framings of the event and the framing represented by the activist and leftist groups is aptly illustrated by the two screens behind Steyerl. Whereas on the right-hand screen, we watch images documenting Steyerl's visit to the site, as well as the material objects she claims to have found there, we read on the left-hand screen that there is:

> No destroyed cave
> No battle
> No G3 7.62 mm ammunition cases
> No G3 20 mm ammunition cases
> No bodies
> No bullets
> No bones
> No images
> No war

Apparently, everything has disappeared into the space of zero probability! By juxtaposing the two contradictory accounts, Steyerl can be said to reveal the exclusionary operations of framing that are persistently conducted by political elites in order to confirm a certain distribution of the sensible. On the other hand, by inserting onto the right-hand screen images of objects whose existence is denied on the left-hand screen, she seeks to make not only the contested objects or evidence but also the lives of the PKK fighters reappear to public perception.

However, on closer inspection, Steyerl does not come across as the trustworthy forensic anthropologist or expert witness who faithfully and objectively translates the language of things into the language of people. On the contrary, the ways in which she subtly shifts between different roles—spanning from a woman in search of her much-loved teenage friend, to a dedicated amateur forensic anthropologist, to a highly sophisticated filmmaker capable of manipulating the audience's perception through her mastery of technical means—suggest an ambiguous approach to the idea of the forensic expert witness. Moreover, how can we, the audience, be sure that Steyerl is not lying when she claims that the projected photographs show her in the mass grave of the PKK fighters? And how do we know for sure that she did not place the objects she presents as evidence there herself? What Steyerl can be said to point toward, in other words, is the importance of the *performance* of the mediator, and her/his ability to get the audience to buy into her/his presentation of evidence. If we recall Weizman and Keenan's point about the forum as the site for the *construction* rather than presentation of facts, evidence, and truth, Steyerl can thus be said to propose that what is accepted as evidence does not only have to do with the given political context or realm of visibility in which the forum is located. It also relies on the performance of the mediator and her/his ability to manipulate the senses of the audience.

INSIDE SCHRÖDINGER'S BOX

By contrast with Steyerl's juxtaposition of two mutually exclusive framings of the same event, Mroué imagines how incompatible accounts can intersect in a state of indeterminacy. According to Lebanese historian Fawwaz Traboulsi, ever since the official end of the Civil War, the Lebanese state has systematically pursued a "policy of amnesia" in order to prevent the unleashing of new conflicts between the country's formerly conflicting parties.[25] Consequently, the fates of the many thousands of people who were forcibly disappeared during the war have not been investigated; nor have these people been officially confirmed dead. This in turn has left the missing in an uncanny state—a state of zero probability—in which they are suspended between life and death. In Mroué's words: "Most of the Lebanese people don't want to talk about it. Complete denial or total amnesia. It is as if the 17,000 people don't exist."[26]

In an attempt to counter this denial, and to grasp the ambiguous status of the missing, Mroué turns to quantum theory, specifically the thought experiment known as "Schrödinger's cat," conceived by Austrian physicist Erwin Schrödinger in 1935. Schrödinger created the experiment to show the absurdity of the so-called Copenhagen interpretation of quantum physics when applied to everyday objects and macroscopic terms. Simply put, the Copenhagen interpretation states that it is only upon observation that an object in a physical system comes to assume one exclusive state instead of several coexisting states. Schrödinger's scenario presents a cat, some radioactive material, a Geiger counter, and a flask of poison, all placed inside a sealed box. The amount of radioactive material should be so small that the probability that

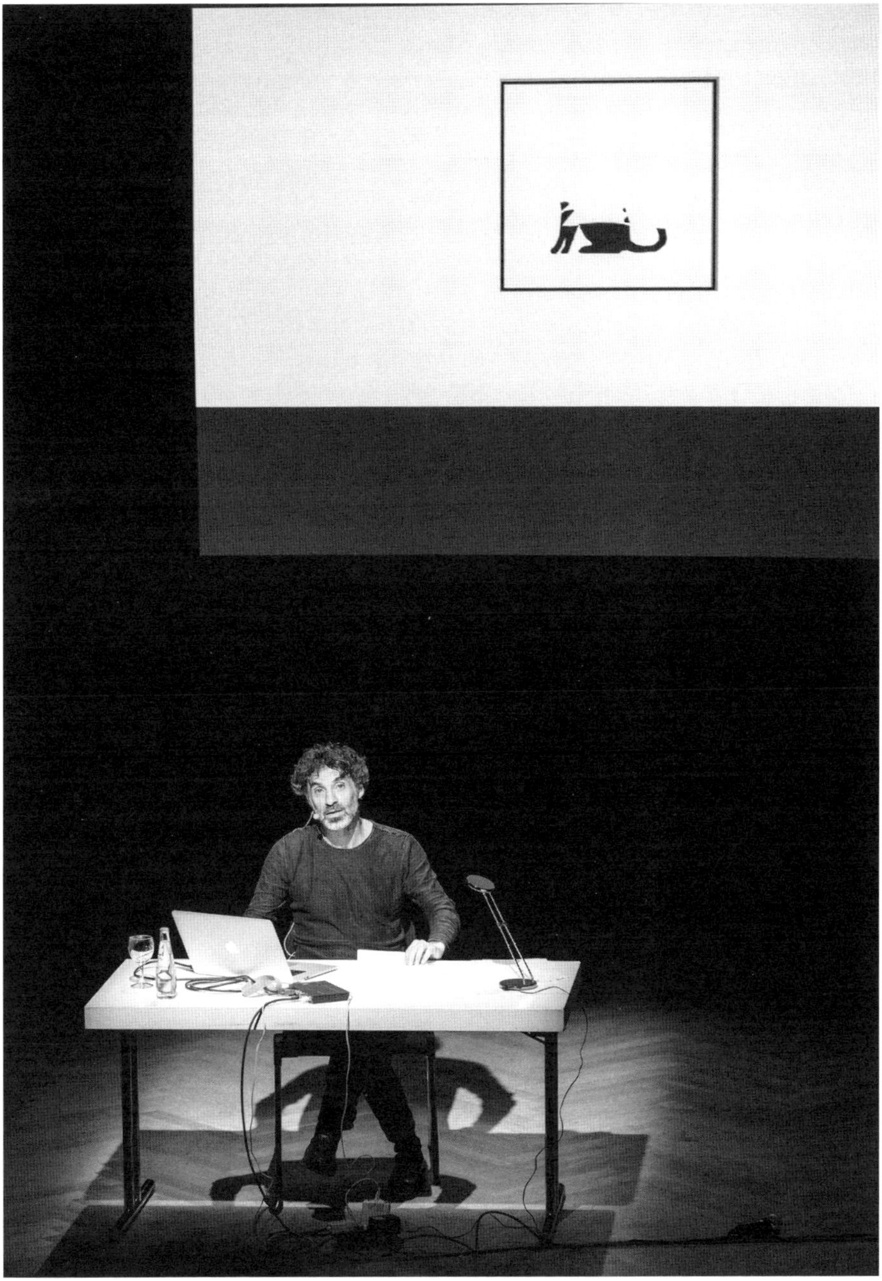

Fig. 2 Rabih Mroué and Hito Steyerl, *Probable Title: Zero Probability*, Bundeskunsthalle, Bonn, 2018

the Geiger counter will register it within the course of one hour is only 50 percent. If it does so, the poison will be unleashed from the flask and kill the cat. Schrödinger now suggests that only an hour later, when we open the box and observe the cat, the latter assumes the status of being *either* dead *or* alive. By contrast, inside the sealed box, where the cat is not exposed to the human gaze, it may find itself in state of *superposition*. In other words, inside the box, a living and a dead version of the same cat may feature and have become *entangled* with one another.

In the lecture, Mroué applies this thought experiment to a popular Beirut nightclub B018. While explaining the club to the audience, he projects a number of illustrative photographs and architectural drawings onto the screens. Built after the end of the war, the nightclub is said to be located on top of a mass grave.[27] It only opens at midnight, and allegedly the marble tables and wooden benches that furnish it are designed to resemble tombs and coffins. Once an hour the rooftop opens for a few seconds, after which it seals the club off again. Within this rather uncanny setting, Mroué reports, a bartender once complained that the bouncers had let in too many people. However, when asked to count the number of admitted guests, the bouncer on duty only counted 389, whereas the bartender counted 653 persons. This anecdote leads Mroué to speculate whether the nightclub can indeed be regarded as some kind of Schrödinger's box in which the dead and the living meet and get entangled. "Is it possible," he asks, "that the living meet with the dead in this club? They dance together? They drink together and before daybreak everyone goes back to his or her own world?"[28]

Mroué does not have any evidence to hand that can point to the mass grave allegedly buried underneath the club. He does not possess a material witness in the form of an ammunition case or a human bone. The images from B018 that he shows to the audience do not disclose anything unusual, such as ghostly appearances or the like. In fact, all he has are rumors of a mass grave, the anecdote about the bartender, and the officially unacknowledged truth that seventeen thousand people were forcibly disappeared during the Civil War. The contested objects that Mroué has at his disposal, in other words, are immaterial and intangible. They would never be accepted as evidence in the

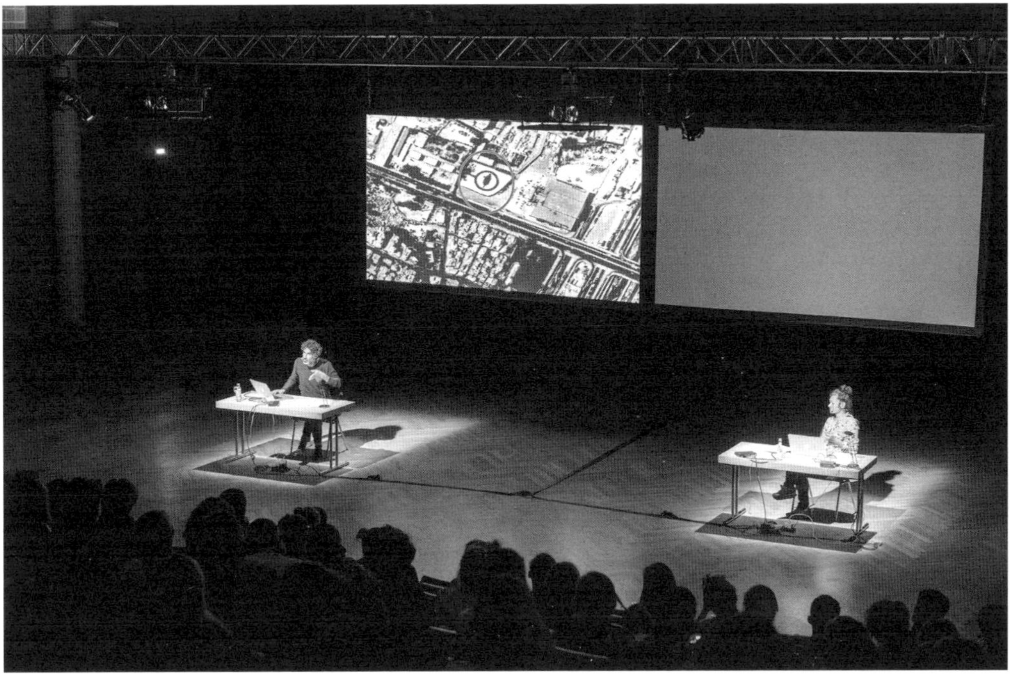

Fig. 3 Rabih Mroué and Hito Steyerl, *Probable Title: Zero Probability*, Bundeskunsthalle, Bonn, 2018

courtroom if the case of the seventeen thousand missing were ever to make it to court in Lebanon. But then again, Mroué does not really seem to be interested in succumbing to the usual procedures of the courtroom, or in investigating how those who are now underground might have died. Rather, he sets out to pursue the implications of speculatively applying Schrödinger's thought experiment to the fate of those who went missing during the Lebanese Civil War.

French philosopher Jacques Derrida's concept of the ghost might help us to better understand the ambiguous ontological status of the missing. As part of the hauntology he develops in *Specters of Marx* (1993), Derrida proposes that the figure of the ghost is well suited for undoing the idea of ontology understood as self-sufficient, self-identical presence. Occupying a liminal position between presence and non-presence, materiality and non-materiality, life and death, the specter cannot be identified as either dead or alive. Instead, it is positioned in a state of indeterminacy. Positing the specter as being, in a broader sense, the radical figure for "the other," Derrida calls on us to be receptive when addressed by it. Indeed, we must "learn to live *with* ghosts [...]. To live otherwise, and better."[29] Laden with ethical implications, not only regarding the (forgotten, unseen, excluded) other but also regarding all that is excluded from the depository of the sanctioned, acknowledged past, Derrida's hauntology ultimately constitutes "a politics of memory, of inheritance, and of generations."[30]

Mroué could be said to call on us to be receptive to the figure of the ghost. Even though it may not provide us with material objects that would later serve as evidence, the sheer fact of our being attentive to the broken, hardly discernible language of the ghost may help us to move beyond the policy of amnesia pursued by the Lebanese government. Importantly, though, and in consistency with his other works, the ghost that Mroué envisages is not filled with hatred or mourning.[31] On the contrary, it is a lighthearted ghost. It is a ghost that dances and drinks in B018 every night. More than just having fun, however, this gesture could be interpreted as a way of breaking away from the identity of someone who was tortured, mutilated, and disgraced. The lightheartedness and dancing of the ghost, in other words, can be seen as an act of resistance to what happened to those ditched in the mass grave. Likewise, the ghost's insistence on *coming back*, and its entangling itself with the living, could be construed as a way of stubbornly reminding the living of its existence, even though many of them might prefer to forget about the Civil War and the missing.

UNDOING IDENTITY THROUGH RECOMBINATION

The idea of the critical potential, attached to the indeterminate, ambiguous status of the ghost, is unfolded further by both Mroué and Steyerl in the last part of the lecture performance. Here they point out that because it is a widespread practice in war crimes to mutilate and dismember corpses, the commingling of human remains is a common occurrence in mass graves. In effect, one of the main objectives of the forensic anthropologist is to determine the identity of the victims by analyzing and, as it were, putting the remains of the deceased back in order. Along the same lines, Weizman and Keenan note that unlike the detective chief inspector, the forensic anthropologist does not ask: "What happened? How did you die?" Instead, s/he asks: "Who are you?"[32] However, rather than the gestures of either dismembering bodies or reassembling human bones, Mroué and Steyerl suggest a third approach: recombination. This approach centers on the combination of human remains in ways that go beyond the threshold of life and death. Linking back to Mroué's suggestion that we view B018 as a kind of Schrödinger's box, Steyerl phrases it thus: "What happens if the collages of bones and living people turn into assemblies—or why not, groups of dancers? [...] What if this is the counter-shot to the cutting down and dismembering of bodies: to assemble and recombine and to generate bodies that are not created by history and heritage, but that rather stumble out of nightclubs without really remembering how they got there in the first place?"[33] Apart from pointing to the perhaps liberating and even critical potential of imagining the indeterminate space between life and death as associated with dance and festivity, this line of thought invites us to think about modes of being that are not bound to or determined by preconceived categories of identity or heritage. The invitation should be seen in light of the fact that within contexts of war and conflict, the question of identity is typically linked to issues of ethnic, religious, or political belonging, and in turn is used strategically to wage war on those who do not fit into the identity categories in question.

By contrast, Mroué and Steyerl's notion of recombination urges us to think about identity as a multiplicity—as being in a state of superposition and entanglement—rather than as something that is predetermined, fixed, and homogeneous. To accept this invitation would amount to a challenge, however temporary, of the politically given distributions of the sensible that relegate us to either this or that identity and decide whether someone is worth grieving or not.

THE POTENTIAL OF UNCERTAINTY

The markers of contemporary warfare include states' and governments' ever more refined operations in spaces defined by uncertainty, as well as the blurring of *nomos* and *anomy*, legal right and pure violence, war and peace. In an essay on the state of missing people, Hito Steyerl argues that the strategic pursuit of indeterminacy, in terms of the legal status of disappeared persons, became a standard feature of various forms of government in the last part of the twentieth century. Linking back to Schrödinger, she argues: “Schrödinger’s innocent if eccentric quantum state of indeterminacy was echoed in political laboratories of sovereignty. Here, gaping political limbos were created in which law and exception blurred in deadly superposition, transforming certain death into a matter of probability.”[34]

In recent years numerous artists, cultural workers, and curators have responded to this “policy of indeterminacy” by turning to and welcoming a forensic fact-seeking approach. In an attempt to, as it were, make warfare reaccessible to human perception, they have assumed the role of expert witnesses determined to provide the public with *hard evidence* of war crimes and crimes against humanity. However, even though the practice of Forensic Architecture is often used as a prime reference for such endeavors, the deployed definition of evidence contrasts starkly with Weizman and Keenan’s definition in that it hinges on an ultimately positivist notion of evidence as indisputable facts. In a world flooded with manipulated digital data, “alternative facts,” and the strategic use of images as weapons, this notion appears ever more problematic.[35] When artistic practices predominantly view the art space as a showground for the presentation of facts and evidence, they run the risk of dispensing with the potential for ambiguity, untranslatability, and non-instrumentality, which has been associated with artistic practice since the late eighteenth century. However, while the aesthetic sphere offers a space that is not governed by the same logics of evidence and accountability as, say, the courtroom, I am not trying to make a case here for a modernist conception of the autonomy of art. Rather, following Rancière’s lead, I would argue that aesthetics and politics are deeply entangled with each other, but that art may offer a space that allows us to observe and negotiate the constant and mutually troubling relationship between art and politics.

Mroué and Steyerl offer an instructive example of how artistic practice may reappropriate the aforementioned indeterminacy and turn it into a critical tool by insisting on its potential, rather than succumbing to a realist idea of facts and evidence. For this purpose, they turn first to a forensic approach. But on closer inspection, it turns out that it is not so much the presentation of indisputable facts and material witnesses that constitutes the linchpin. Instead, what is emphasized is the importance of the mediator's performance and his/her ability to persuade the audience of his/her interpretation of the contested objects in question. At the same time, however, Steyerl is by no means engaging in a postmodernist relativism that would dispense with the idea of reality or the occurrence of crimes against humanity. The images Steyerl presents do point back to a reality. But more than the motif or *content* of the images, what is crucial is the *conditions* to which they testify: the politically shaped conditions that render invisible the possible evidence of an assault on forty female PKK fighters.[36]

In addition to making us attend to the overall frames—the distribution of the sensible—which could be said to guide the way we perceive the world around us, I contend that another crucial aspect of the lecture performance is its insistence on the utopian aspect of indeterminacy and superposition. As argued above, the notion of recombination suggests a way of thinking and being that goes beyond existing categories of identification and possession. This in turn makes it possible to imagine that inside the *boîte de nuit* known as B018, both the dead and the living may feature in entangled constellations that break radically with the identity-based thinking that prevails outside the club. However, in order to break with identity-thinking based on ethnic, religious, or political affiliations, one needs to turn to radically different logics and patterns of thinking than those that currently exist. As Mroué somewhat ironically puts it, commenting on his own attempt to calculate the possible number of recombinations between the living and the dead in B018: "Something was driving me to go further, although I know that the logic was not really solid. But who cares. I'm not a scientist and no one will take our talk into account."[37] Obviously, Mroué's observation should not be seen as an excuse for artists to engage with complex matters with a lazy-minded attitude. Rather, it suggests that because the sphere of art is not subject to the same logics as either the courtroom or science, it allows a certain degree of freedom, which in turn allows us to distance ourselves from the often deeply exclusionary logics and knowledge regimes to which we usually conform. Remembering Keenan and Weizman's notion of the forum, we may thus think of the art sphere as a deeply and essentially political space in the sense that it provides a public site for discussing the conditions of the possibility of politics. Accordingly, within the space of art we may learn to attend to voices and sights—such as those belonging to missing people—deemed improbable or downright nonexistent within the prevailing political regimes of thinking, doing, and perceiving.

Therefore, it is no coincidence that Mroué and Steyerl, who throughout most of the lecture have performed the roles of trustworthy, matter-of-fact *mediators*, end by staging a highly improbable event. Seeking to perform "a still dance in which dancers would be in a continuous move," they walk toward each other onstage and then leave the room via two different exits.[38] Concurrently, they are doubled on the screens in a prerecorded film, where we see them walking toward each other and then suddenly disappearing into the slit between the two screens. Mimicking the coin tossed by Steyerl at the beginning of the performance, they thus finally enter and disappear themselves into the space of zero probability that has preoccupied them throughout the lecture.

In conclusion, then, Mroué and Steyerl's lecture performance could be said to transform the performance space into a Schrödinger's box characterized by indeterminacy and improbability. By combining disparate elements such as visual notes from forensic fieldwork, martyr posters, architectural drawings, probability calculations, anecdotes, quantum physics, and thought experiments, it creates an ephemeral archive where the missing cannot be identified by means of bones or any other kind of "indisputable evidence," but are instead conjured up in the fugitive space of the performance. In this sense, the performance space created by *Probable Title* assumes the role of a public forum in which the audience is invited simultaneously to observe the construction of evidence, to commemorate those who went missing as a result of war and conflict, and finally to imagine modes of thinking and doing that break with ruling distributions of the sensible.

1. Giorgio Agamben, *State of Exception*, trans. Kevin Attell (Chicago: University of Chicago Press, 2005), 23.

2. The suspension of the law is, of course, not a new phenomenon. In Agamben's account, it is closely linked to the figure of the sovereign—he who can declare a state of exception—and can be traced back to the *iustitium* of Roman law. Ibid., 41-51.

3. Grégoire Chamayou, *A Theory of the Drone*, trans. Janet Lloyd (New York: New Press, 2015), 167.

4. Louise Amoore, "Algorithmic War: Everyday Geographies of the War on Terror," *Antipode: A Radical Journal of Geography* 41, no. 1 (2009): 49-69; Louise Amoore and Rita Raley, "Securing with Algorithms: Knowledge, Decision, Sovereignty," *Security Dialogue* 48, no. 1 (2017): 3-10; Lauren Wilcox, "Embodying Algorithmic War: Gender, Race, and the Posthuman in Drone Warfare," *Security Dialogue* 48, no. 1 (2017): 11-28.

5. Susan Schuppli, "Media as Conflict Zones," abstract for lecture presented at the (W)archives seminar held at the University of Copenhagen, August 21-22, 2017.

6. To name but a few examples from the past five years, Forensic Architecture's investigations have been presented at prestigious arts institutions and biennials such as the Whitney Biennial, New York (2019), Institute of Contemporary Arts, London (2018), documenta 14, Kassel (2017), Museo Universitario Arte Contemporanéo, Mexico City (2017), Museu d'Art Contemporani de Barcelona (2017), and Haus der Kulturen der Welt, Berlin (2014).

7. "Forensic Architecture," Exhibitions and Events, Tate Modern, https://www.tate.org.uk/whats-on/tate-britain/exhibition/turner-prize-2018/forensic-architecture.

8. At a masterclass given at the University of Copenhagen in November 2018, Thomas Keenan pointed this out in relation to Forensic Architecture's nomination for the Turner Prize. See also Ellen Mara De Wachter, "'I'd Rather Lose Prizes and Win Cases': An Interview with Eyal Weizman of Turner Prize-Nominated Forensic Architecture," *frieze*, May 2, 2018, https://frieze.com/article/id-rather-lose-prizes-and-win-cases-interview-eyal-weizman-turner-prize-nominated-forensic.

9. Luce Lebart, "Metric Photography of Crime Scenes," in *Images of Conviction: The Construction of Visual Evidence*, ed. Diane Durfour (Paris: Le Bal, 2015), 19.

10. Eyal Weizman and Thomas Keenan, *Mengele's Skull: The Advent of a Forensic Aesthetics* (Berlin: Sternberg Press, 2012).

11. According to Weizman and Keenan, during the "era of the witness," epitomized by the trial of Adolf Eichmann in 1961, the oral testimony of survivors and first-hand witnesses was assigned decisive weight and credibility. In the forensic era, however, material remains have gained increasing importance in war crimes investigations. Ibid., 11.

12. Clyde Snow in ibid., 66.

13. Weizman and Keenan, *Mengele's Skull*, 28.

14. Derived from the Latin forensis, the word "forensics" refers, Weizman and Keenan argue, to the "forum," and thus to the practices and skills of making an argument before a gathering, whether legal or political. Ibid., 28.

15. Eyal Weizman, "Introduction: Forensis," in *Forensis: The Architecture of Public Truth*, ed. Forensic Architecture (Berlin: Sternberg Press, 2014), 12.

16. Weizman and Keenan, *Mengele's Skull*, 66-67.

17. Jacques Rancière, *The Politics of Aesthetics: The Distribution of the Sensible*, trans. Gabriel Rockhill (London: Continuum, 2004), 13.

18. Ibid.

19. Rabih Mroué and Hito Steyerl, "Probable Title: Zero Probability" (unpublished script, 2012), my emphasis. I watched the lecture performance first in Berlin in March 2016 and again in Copenhagen in August 2017. The artists kindly provided me with a copy of the unpublished script.

20. Judith Butler, *Frames of War: When Is Life Grievable?* (London: Verso, 2009), 64-65.

21. Michael Rothberg, "Remembering Ronahi, Remembering Internationalism," *Days and Memory*, March 8, 2015, https://hgmsblog.weebly.com/blog/remembering-ronahi-remembering-internationalism.

22. Ibid.

23. Nilay Vadar, "German Sociologist Found in Mass Grave in Van," *Bianet*, June 17, 2011, https://bianet.org/english/minorities/130811-german-sociologist-found-in-mass-grave-in-van.

24. Hito Steyerl, *The Wretched of the Screen* (Berlin: Sternberg Press, 2012), 14.

25. Fawwaz Traboulsi, *Off the Wall: Political Posters of the Lebanese Civil War* (London: I. B. Tauris, 2009), xvii-xxi.

26. Mroué and Steyerl, "Probable Title," 13.

27. Opened in 1998, B018 is allegedly built on top of a mass grave located in an industrial district in north-eastern Beirut. Previously a camp first for Armenians and then for Palestinian refugees as well as southern Lebanese, Kurds, and Syrians fleeing unemployment, the site became the place of a massacre conducted in 1976 by militiamen of the Christian Lebanese Forces. Victims of the massacre are believed to lie buried in a mass grave erected on the lot. See Suzanne Cotter, "Beirut Unbound," *Out of Beirut*, no. 3 (2006): 29.

28. Mroué and Steyerl, "Probable Title," 19.

29. Jacques Derrida, *Specters of Marx: The State of the Debt, the Work of Mourning and the New International*, trans. Peggy Kamuf (New York: Routledge, 1994), xviii.

30. Ibid.

31. See Solveig Gade, "Learning to Live with Ghosts in the Aftermath of War: On Documentary Strategies in Rabih Mroué's *How Nancy Wished Everything Was an April Fool's Joke*," *Journal of War and Culture Studies* 8, no 4 (2015): 328-46.

32. Weizman and Keenan, *Mengele's Skull*, 17-18.

33. Mroué and Steyerl, "Probable Title," 35.

34. Steyerl, *Wretched of the Screen*, 150.

35. See Solveig Gade, "The Promise of the Index in Contemporary Documentary Performance," *Nordic Journal of Aesthetics*, nos. 55-56 (2018): 41-64; W. J. T. Mitchell, *Cloning Terror: The War of Images, 9/11 to the Present* (Chicago: University of Chicago Press, 2011); Roger Nathan, *Image Warfare in the War on Terror* (London: Palgrave Macmillan, 2013).

36. Steyerl refers to such imagery as "poor images." For more on the concept, see Steyerl, *Wretched of the Screen*, 31-45.

37. Mroué and Steyerl, "Probable Title," 21.

38. Ibid., 37.

TRANSITIONAL WHAT? Perspectives from Syrian Videographers on YouTube Takedowns and the "Video as Evidence" Ecology

Dima Saber

Stockholm, February 2018.[1]

—What is the problem we are trying to solve?
—The takedowns.
—The takedowns? Or YouTube's content moderation policies?
—Or who is speaking to YouTube about content moderation?
—All of the above.

In 2018, I helped to convene a roundtable at Stockholm University to discuss the repercussions of YouTube's machine learning algorithms and content moderation policies for the preservation and sustainability of eyewitness video from Syria.[2] The roundtable included key individuals and organizations working at the intersections of journalism, online literacy, law, political advocacy, and human rights, with representatives from the Syrian Archive, Witness, Amnesty International, the UC Berkeley Human Rights Center, Meedan, and Bellingcat. It was an opportunity to bring all these stakeholders together to get a better sense of what was *really* at stake as a result of YouTube's content moderation policies, and specifically its "automated flagging of extremist content."[3] The aim of the roundtable was to map out ways in which civil society organizations could:

- self-organize by setting up open communication channels to avoid duplicating efforts;
- build a common front to communicate with YouTube and other corporate social media platforms and get a better understanding of their content moderation policies;

- discuss a collective strategy to curate and preserve "at-risk" eyewitness video content from Syria, thus reemphasizing its value as a vital source for the documentation of human rights violations.

In addition to playing the role of "facilitators"—by bringing all these stakeholders together—we academics involved in these conversations benefited in two ways. First, we realized the need to set up a formal research network that could potentially further support such gatherings, with funding from an independent research body or council. Second, we were able to get a better understanding of the roles and mandates of each stakeholder within what we refer to as the "YouTube Syrian Image Ecology Map." At the heart of this ecology map is the Syrian Archive, a "Syrian-led collective of human rights activists dedicated to curating visual documentation relating to human rights violations and other crimes committed by all sides during the conflict in Syria, with the goal of creating an evidence-based database for reporting, advocacy, and accountability purposes."[4] → Fig. 1

Sandra Ristovska's work on eyewitness video,[5] and her analysis of the points of convergence between human rights collectives, activists, corporate social media platforms, and legal, intergovernmental, and policy stakeholders working in the fields of human rights documentation and investigation, is of particular interest to me here, and to the argument my essay attempts to make.[6] Ristovska highlights the role of the Syrian Archive as a mediator between those who create content and those who help to publicize, legitimize, and defend human rights claims. She writes: "[The] Syrian Archive takes on a mediating function: it brokers between eyewitness videos and the discursive publics forming around them because it develops the methodology through which visual information attains prominence, meaning, and relevance across institutional and legal contexts."[7] The ecology map, which we produced partly as a result of the Stockholm roundtable, does in fact account for some of these points of convergence, notably in terms of the key intermediary role that the Syrian Archive plays today between Syrian videographers on the ground and the legal, human rights, and policy stakeholders who make use of this content, either as part of their everyday practice or for its potential evidentiary value within local and international judicial contexts.

I currently sit on the advisory board of Mnemonics, the civil society organization that manages both the Syrian Archive and the Yemeni Archive. This position—and my relationship with the Mnemonics founders, which goes back to 2011, when the Arab uprisings were just starting to spread across the Middle East and North Africa (MENA) region—has offered me an insider look into the everyday practice of the archive team, as well as the opportunity to connect with and interview many of the eyewitness video creators whose voices form the basis of this essay.

But first, a word on commercial content moderation and how it relates to the issue of YouTube takedowns within the context of the Syrian war. Sarah T. Roberts's recently published work on content moderation on social media platforms does a great job of mapping out ways in which the Internet is now a "site of control, surveillance intervention, and circulation of information as a commodity."[8] She argues that a discussion of the nature and potential of the contemporary Internet can only be complete if it takes into account "the processes by which certain content created by users is allowed to remain visible and other content removed."[9] She highlights the cruciality of getting a better understanding of who makes those decisions, how they are made, and whom they benefit. All these questions around the political economy of the contemporary internet and the current threats to the sustainability of eyewitness videos from Syria were at the heart of the discussions we started in Stockholm.

According to participants in the roundtable, there have been reports of online content from the MENA region getting flagged and removed from corporate social media platforms since 2011, but the wave of deletions particularly intensified in summer 2017, when Google (which owns YouTube) announced four steps it was taking "to fight terrorism online."[10] Thousands of individual videos and channels were flagged for potential violations of the terms of service, with little or no warning, resulting in thirty-three million videos being removed in 2018, which amounts to roughly ninety thousand per day, according to an article published in May 2019 by the Electronic Frontier Foundation, Witness, and the Syrian Archive.[11]

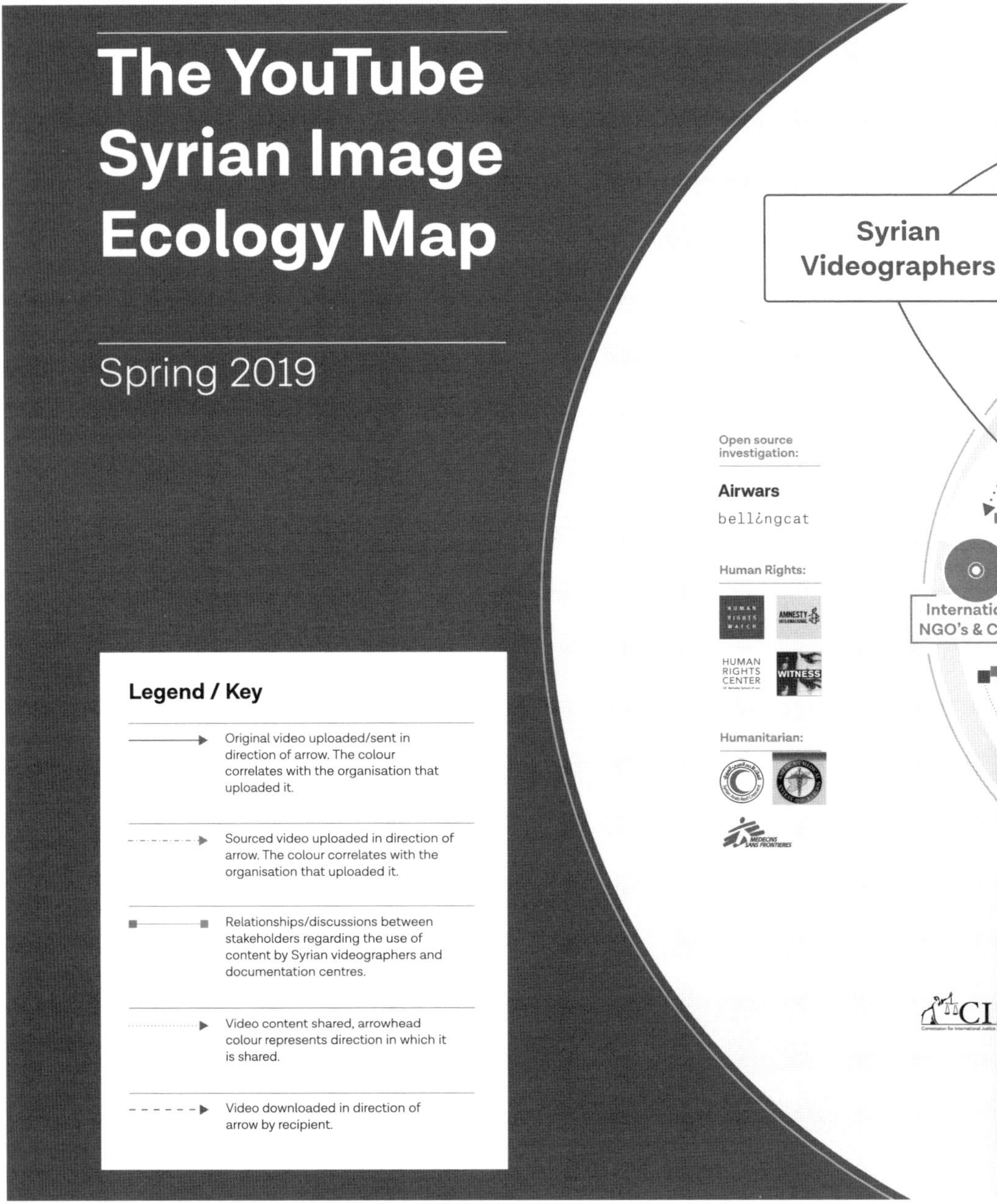

Fig. 1 YouTube Syrian Image Ecology Map. This map was developed with advice from the Syrian Archive team, including Hadi el-Khatib, Jeff Deutch, and Abdul Rahman al-Jaloud. Design by Kipp Jones (WildIlk).

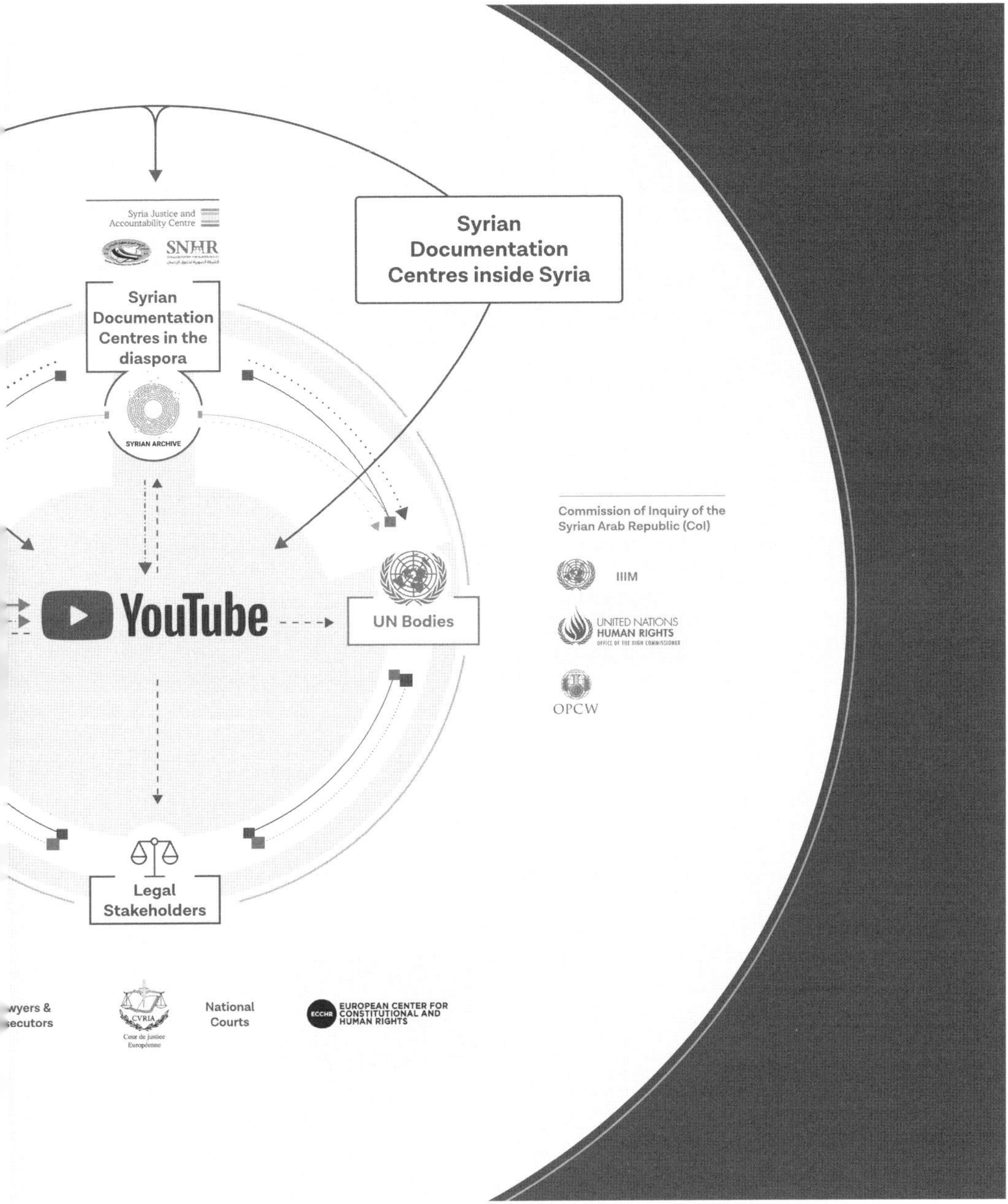
Syria Justice and Accountability Centre
SNHR
Syrian Documentation Centres in the diaspora
Syrian Documentation Centres inside Syria
SYRIAN ARCHIVE
YouTube
UN Bodies
Commission of Inquiry of the Syrian Arab Republic (CoI)
IIIM
UNITED NATIONS HUMAN RIGHTS
OFFICE OF THE HIGH COMMISSIONER
OPCW
Legal Stakeholders
wyers &
ecutors
CVRIA
Cour de justice Européenne
National Courts
ECCHR
EUROPEAN CENTER FOR CONSTITUTIONAL AND HUMAN RIGHTS

Mainstream media, civil society, academics, historians, activists, and archivists all wrote and spoke at length[12] about the effects of these mass deletions on the viable documentation of human rights abuses during the Syrian war, and their undermining of transitional justice[13] and postwar accountability efforts. Most of these articles quoted the stakeholders who were at our Stockholm roundtable, and all recognized the important work civil society organizations and collectives such as the Syrian Archive are doing in this regard.[14]

But one voice appeared to be missing from these public debates and discussions: that of the videographers themselves—the eyewitnesses who shot the video content and uploaded it to YouTube and other social media platforms.[15] As Ristovska recognizes of her work "Human Rights Collectives as Visual Experts," most of the academic and nonacademic literature on this issue has focused on the institutional, legal, and political advocacy environments within which this video content circulates, rather than on the videographers and witnesses who produced the material in the first place.[16] It is specifically this "gap" that my essay aims to address, by focusing predominantly on the perspectives of Syrian content creators who have been documenting the uprising and war since 2011 from a number of Syrian towns.

This essay is based on perspectives from fifteen interviews with Syrian videographers from Damascus, Homs, Hama, Aleppo, Daraa, Ghouta, Raqqa, and Deir Ezzour (some interviewees were interviewed more than once).[17] The interviews all took place in Arabic (except one) via Skype, WhatsApp, or Google Hangouts, between October 2018 and June 2019.[18] Some of the videographers included here are still documenting the uprising-war in Syria, mainly in Daraa, Hama, Al-Lataminah, and Idlib, and their names have been changed for security reasons.[19] The sample includes videographers who (a) operate as individual image-makers, (b) helped to set up or work as part of activist groups or media centers, (c) helped to set up or work as part of Local Coordination Committees, or (d) were embedded with the Free Syrian Army or other rebel battalions to document the conflict as it unfolded. This research does not include any pro-government views or perspectives, as this would have complicated the sampling criteria. The interviewees were aged between twenty-one and sixty-five; the youngest was thirteen years old when he shot his first videos of the protests in Raqqa on his mobile phone on his way to school in 2011.

The interviews included questions about purpose (why they had started to document the revolution), on value (why they thought their archive was important today, and how they hoped it would be used in the future), and on practice (how and where they archived their pictures and videos, and how they described their relationship with and use of YouTube and other corporate social media platforms). After giving a brief presentation of their motivations and the reasons for their documenting the revolution and war, my chapter argues that some of the concepts used by Western-based legal, intergovernmental, policy, and human rights stakeholders—such as "transitional justice," "postwar accountability," and "video as evidence of human rights violations"—are not concepts the videographers themselves identify with, use, or see value in. Furthermore, there is a discrepancy between the narratives of those who have left Syria and those who are still inside. This chapter argues that videographers in the diaspora have internalized the paradigms of the Western-centric institutional human rights matrix and now make use of its concepts and themes to speak of the value of their archives, while those who are still inside Syria have retained a community-centered, affective, and personalized narrative of their experience and the value they see in their archives today.

WHY WE ARCHIVE
Perspectives on Archival Value from inside and outside Syria

Filming for an "Imagined Community"

Archival scholar Terry Cook argues that the role of the archivist has shifted over the past century, from "passive curator to active appraiser to societal mediator to community facilitator."[20] While I do not necessarily agree with Cook's initial conception of archiving as a "passive" endeavor, his four shifting paradigms of the archival process might apply to vernacular content creation within the context of the Syrian uprising-war.

When asked why and for what audiences they had started to document the uprising, most of the Syrian videographers I spoke to said it had been first and foremost for Syrians in other cities:

> First, we wanted to show Syrians in other cities that this is really what is happening, so we take advantage of the digital world we live in. Everyone has Face [Facebook], everyone watches YouTube, etc. So we thought we might be able to get the message across much faster. [...] So when the protests started in 2011, we first started to record videos so we show people what is happening, people who are here I mean, who live in Syria, to motivate them, and encourage them to take part in the protests. (Hassan Abou Nooh, Talbiseh Media Office, interview, November 2018)

Building on Cook's shifting paradigms, one could argue that new information and communication technologies and the democratization of image production and dissemination have enabled Syrian activists to "create records to bind their communities together and foster their group identities."[21] Thus it was not international mainstream media or global public opinion that were first targeted by the footage Syrian videographers uploaded to YouTube and other corporate social media platforms, but their fellow Syrians in cities where protests had already started, especially those still under the control of the Assad regime. This focus on the Syrian community calls to mind Benedict Anderson's *Imagined Communities* (1983) and the "overarching comradeship of belonging" that brings together people of the same community or nation, irrespective of whether they have ever met or known each other, since "in the mind of each lives the image of their communion":[22]

> The revolution brought Syrian cities together, yes. I for example didn't know much about Idlib, I hadn't visited Idlib much. I never thought I'd ever go there. The revolution made me visit every town and every village in the Idlib governorate [...]. When I went back in 2018, I enjoyed so much being in every place where there had been protests in Idlib [...]. Even if there were no protests happening then, the feeling that I was in the same squares where the protests once happened was indescribable [...]. If it wasn't from these videos, if the young people of the revolution hadn't worked and documented

> all the protests, and showed us the squares of freedom and allowed us to hear the voices of the revolutionaries, we wouldn't have been able to know so much about other Syrian towns. (Roqayya Abbadi, Deir Ezzour, interview, March 2019)

This view was echoed by Abdel Majid El-Khatib, who had started documenting the protests in Raqqa when he was thirteen years old. He fled his hometown for Aleppo ten days after the Islamic State made it into the Caliphate's headquarters. When asked which of all the videos he had shot was the most important to him and why, he said:

> Of course, if you want me to talk from a sentimental point of view it is in 2012, in the days of the protests, when people took on the streets, when my generation, the school kids, took on the streets and began to feel they truly existed [...]. There were moments where, you know, it is about the feeling of belonging, which later on you discover were insignificant [laughs], but back then it was a very important thing, that one is discovering oneself for the first time and is feeling things for the first time, and also experiencing for the first time a sense of belonging [...]. Not only belonging to a specific town. Syria, for example, and this is the memory of a child I'm telling you about, I had absolutely no feelings toward this country, for me Syria was synonymous with the flag salutation we had to do in school every morning, but after 2011 the revolution gave us a lot, it introduced us to our country and its towns, to the fact that it was the cradle of many cultures and civilizations [...], that we were people who deserved to live well because we were good people. (Abdel Majid el-Khatib, Raqqa/Aleppo, interview, March 2019)

Testimonial, Evidential, and Historical Value

One of the main questions this work is concerned with is that of value. In addition to exploring the Syrian videographers' motivations for documenting the conflict, I was interested in understanding why they thought their footage was important and therefore worth preserving. Based on the discussions I had with them, it appears to me that the value of their eyewitness content is threefold: testimonial, evidential, and historical.[23]

In "Evidence of Me," archival scholar Sue McKemmish argues that record-keeping is a "kind of witnessing": "On a personal level it is a way of evidencing and memorializing our lives—our existence, our activities and experiences, our relationships with others, our identity, our 'place' in the world."[24] The testimonial value of their footage as "evidence of me," and by extension as "evidence of us," was common to all the discussions I had with Syrian videographers, both inside and outside of Syria: they all saw it as a personal record that attested to an important period of their lives, and to their personal experiences of the Syrian uprising:

> Half of the media office people died documenting and collecting this archive. Our whole life is in this archive. Our youth. Most of them died in their twenties and thirties. That is why this archive is important. So it doesn't really matter to us whether this archive gets used in court, or as evidence for whatever. None of this will bring the dead back. It is important because it is the only record of the best years of our lives. (Hassan Abou Nooh, Talbiseh Media Office, interview, November 2018)

Tragically, then, what this crowdsourced video content conveys is what was lost: the loss of so many lives, and the destruction of one's city, country, and belongings. As Abou Nooh put it: "We owe it to those who lost their lives documenting the uprising to preserve and defend this archive" (interview, November 2018). An important value of this crowdsourced footage lies in the fact that it is the last available record and testimony of some people, places, and things that have been destroyed by the war, and the fact that YouTube's content moderation policies today threaten its preservation and sustainability is both infuriating and disheartening to the videographers who risked their lives collecting it. This also makes the work of organizations such as the Syrian Archive all the more important.

Beyond the testimonial and affective value of their crowdsourced footage, and its rootedness in the needs and aspirations of their own locality and community, the Syrian videographers I interviewed also saw it as the only available counter-narrative to state regime propaganda. News reports broadcast by state-run and private mainstream outlets such as Syria TV, Al-Ekhbariya, Addounia TV, and the Syrian Arab News Agency locally, and RT and ANNA-News internationally, all discredited the social movement, either labeling the protests fake news or attributing them to "foreign interference" in Syria's internal affairs.[25] The crowdsourced content produced by Syrian videographers on the ground thus acquired important evidential value—"this (and not state propaganda) is what is happening in Syria"—and historical value—"we must remember, and the world must remember, that this happened in Syria." The latter is especially important given Syrians' experience in the 1980s of the Hama massacre, of which no tangible traces remain today apart from the memories of those who experienced and/or recounted it. Moreover, given the current balance of power, and as Bashar al-Assad seems to be reestablishing himself as the rightful president on the international scene, the videographers' footage has acquired new evidential value: "If we stop documenting, then he will have won the war" (Mohamed,* Ghouta/Idlib, interview, December 2018). Mohamed Fares al-Maghrebi of Step News Agency said the same: "Assad hasn't won yet. Our news agency will last beyond the revolution. [...] If we do stop documenting, then he will have won" (interview, October 2018).

In the absence of any mainstream media to cover the conflict, videographers and citizen journalists operating inside Syria stepped in to fill the information vacuum,[26] and they see themselves as the last custodians of this narrative of the 2011 revolution:

> I embedded myself with the Free Syrian Army and the revolutionaries to document the liberation of several towns. Of course as an independent civilian, but I took part in armed invasions to document the liberation [...]. For example, when the regime was talking about victories in suburbs of Hama, when they invaded and we called it the "Russian invasion of Hama," an army officer went on TV to talk about the regime's victory. A few days later, I went to exactly the same location, and I made a report that I uploaded to YouTube. Every time the regime spoke about making victories in a location, I'd go there to show that the revolutionaries were still in control of the area, and to expose the regime's lies [...]. All these videos are still available on YouTube as evidence for the world to see. (Mahmoud,* Al-Lataminah, interview, December 2018)

TRANSITIONAL WHAT?
Nowness vs. Postwar Accountability

In her analysis of the rise of eyewitness video and its implications for human rights, Sandra Ristovska explains that visual information has recently gained a new level of legitimacy as a key evidentiary tool for a better understanding of human rights concerns.[27] Within this framework, eyewitness video content produced by Syrian videographers since the beginning of the uprising in 2011 and uploaded to corporate social media platforms has become an important tool to track and document human rights violations by the Syrian regime and other parties involved in the conflict, to the extent that it has actually become the only channel through which political advocacy claims are made visible and human rights violations assessed. When YouTube's new content moderation policies put this video content "at risk," mainstream media and the legal, policy, and human rights stakeholders all saw this as a serious threat to transitional justice and accountability efforts in the context of the Syrian war.[28] I wanted to investigate whether the Syrian videographers who had shot and collated this content thought the same.

Mahmoud* is over sixty years old. I first interviewed him in December 2018, and I have been in conversation with him since. His house in Al-Lataminah, a northern town in the Hama governorate, was hit by mortars and partly destroyed in May 2019. His family fled to a refugee camp, but he stayed behind. He started documenting the revolution in the early days: "The videos I made were very short then," he told me, "no more than one minute each." Then the first military invasions started. He uploaded his first video to YouTube in April 2012 after a regime air strike killed forty-nine civilians. At the time of writing, he is in Al-Lataminah, documenting what he still calls the Syrian revolution.

When I asked him if he thought his footage could be used in transitional justice efforts,[29] to help to bring the Syrian people together after the war has ended, he said: "Transitional what? Our lives, issues, and priorities are all confined in this present moment" (interviews and personal communications, December 2018 to June 2019). The closest English translation I can think of for the Arabic *'aniyya* is "nowness." It was not that he was unable to project himself into the future; rather, he just wanted us to focus my conversations with him on the present moment, since what was happening then was all that mattered to him.

Connected to this focus on the present moment and this unwillingness to think of their videos' potential *after* the war has ended, most of the Syria-based videographers I interviewed expressed a profound disinterest in concepts such as "transitional justice," "video as evidence," or "postwar accountability":

> When it comes to hope, I don't have any hope in the international community. Those who allowed him [Bashar Al-Assad] to use chemical weapons against his people when he did it won't hold him accountable for it years from now. (Mohamed,* Ghouta/Idlib, interview, November 2018)

> For us, it was our duty to document, as an attempt to stop the massacres and to stop the killing [...]. Now whether it'll actually affect the regime and be used to take the regime to court, well, I don't think so, I mean the footage won't have this influence, I mean, not in the future [...]. If it were to happen, we would be more than happy, I mean if the regime were to be convicted for every crime they committed, but do I think the work we did will make this happen in the future? To be frank, in my opinion, it won't, it will be very hard. (Mahmoud,* Al-Lataminah, interview, December 2018)

This distrust of any form of transitional justice was the result of years of disappointments, which had progressively fed into a complete disinterest in international judicial systems: as the Syrian videographers continued to risk their lives to document the daily atrocities they witnessed, no serious measures were taken to stop the killing. Eight years later, the value of this footage as primary forensic evidence for the investigation of human rights violations—which, as I described at the beginning of this chapter, is the main argument underpinning the outcry by legal and human rights stakeholders against YouTube's takedowns—is not necessarily what the videographers inside Syria concern themselves with today:

> Let me go back to this idea I was telling you about, about people watching him kill his people live on TV and how they won't hold

him accountable years later. The chemical massacre that took place in Ghouta in 2013—all the countries were closely following, via satellite, every military activity in Syria, right? Great. So how is it even possible that five years after the massacre, they still say things like "the Syrian regime might be responsible for the chemical attack in Eastern Ghouta and for the killing of fifteen hundred people with chemical weapons"? Five years later, they still can't confirm for sure [...]. All right, where is the accountability? No one is holding anyone accountable. (Mohamed,* Ghouta/Idlib, interview, November 2018)

Instead, they speak about their footage in very personal terms. As Cook writes, "archives are constructed memories about the past, about history, heritage, and culture, about personal roots and familial connections, and about who we are as human beings; as such, they offer glimpses into our common humanity":[30]

Interviewer: Of all the videos you took, which one do you think is the most important?

Interviewee: A video report I made about a little girl from Sahel el-Ghab who was blind. Her dad was arrested by the regime, and her mother had left her and got married. She was thirteen years old and had two younger brothers whom she took care of. She also took care of her elderly grandparents. After I did a report about her, a humanitarian organization came and helped her and her family. Their situation has greatly improved as a result. This is the most important one. (Abed,* Hama, interview, April 2019)

Interviewee: A video I made in 2015 about a ten-year-old girl who had lost her legs during the war, and because of the video I made, I was able to connect her to an organization which helped her. (Achkar,* Hama, interview, April 2019)

Abou Douma* is twenty-six years old. He was one of the people who helped set up a Local Coordination Committee in Daraa, the town where the protests started in March 2011. Although he currently lives in Germany, he still shares Mohamed's and Mahmoud's distrust of the international legal system:

> Of course I hope this footage gets used to hold to account those who were responsible for what happened in Syria [...]. But I don't believe it will happen, because that's what we're used to in the Middle East. War criminals never pay for their crimes. Look at Mubarak in Egypt and Ben Ali in Tunisia. Only in Libya he was held to account, but it didn't happen that way. There should have been a proper trial. But maybe it's because Libyans knew that if they left it to court, he'd be acquitted like Mubarak, I don't know. I don't think they will ever be held to account, no. (Abou Douma,* interview, March 2018)

For Abou Douma there is a difference in how people think about accountability and justice if they are inside Syria or outside. It also depends on when they left, and where they went: "If someone is experiencing the events first-hand from the inside, it is completely different from how they look at them when they leave. Your way of thinking is different. In my opinion, you're more likely to be able to see the bigger picture when you're out of the war zone" (Abou Douma,* interview, March 2018).

Findings from my interviews confirm his reading. I present below perspectives from two Syrian archivists based in Turkey and Europe respectively who for a few years now have been working in more organized and institutionalized settings. They are both able to see beyond the current destruction and war, and their depictions of the value of eyewitness content coming out of Syria are much closer to those of legal, human rights, and political advocacy groups based in the West. What my essay argues is that Syrian visual content creators based in the diaspora—the citizen journalists, archivists, photographers, videographers, and filmmakers, whether working in an individual capacity or as part of a collective, who fled the war zones for more secure places—have internalized, adopted, and adapted the paradigms of the Western-centric institutional human rights matrix, and now make use of its concepts and themes to speak of the value and potential of their records.

Ahmed Ramadan started documenting the uprising in 2011 when he was in Damascus. He then moved to Deir Ezzour, where he covered the frontline battles until 2014, when his father was killed by the Islamic State. Later he fled to Turkey and started working through the media collective Al-Furat Post (formerly Deir Ezzour Is

Slaughtered Silently). Since then his work has focused on archives. He helped to set up the Al-Furat Anti-Violence and Terrorism Center, which focuses on sustainable development, women, children, and "most importantly, the trial of war criminals in Syria." I asked him if he thought the footage he had been collecting might one day be used as evidence to hold criminals to account:

> Of course I do. There are now so many people working in a serious way on this. In France, in Switzerland, and they have asked me for a copy of my archive, and I said if it comes to Bashar al-Assad's regime I'm willing to give you anything you want. Just give me a link, and I'll upload it. This is a real and serious issue now, journalists and lawyers are all working on this. (Ahmed Ramadan, Deir Ezzour/Turkey, interview, March 2018)

He did say he expected the process to take a long time, depending on the priorities of the world's Great Powers, but that it was bound to happen: "These videos are very important, not only for international courts now, but for future generations maybe a hundred years from now. There are countries that committed war crimes and are now paying the price maybe two hundred, three hundred, or even four hundred years later [...]. So in my opinion this issue isn't going anywhere and it will not be forgotten" (Ahmed Ramadan, interview, March 2018).

This view was shared by Artino, a freelance Syrian war photographer currently based in Europe. He covered the chemical attack on Eastern Ghouta for Reuters; then when things became too overwhelming and risky, he fled with his family to Brussels, where he is still trying to build a life that is not haunted by what he calls the "trauma of the images of death." He does not necessarily believe in transitional justice, but he does believe in the power of Syrian eyewitnesses to push for these images to bring about justice:

> Since I started taking pictures of Syria and the revolution [...], I was hoping that my pictures are used to put him to trial, to face his crimes [...]. I was always thinking of the picture which stopped the war in Vietnam. I would look at the picture and say, when will my pictures do this? [...] There are moments where you lose hope and get overwhelmed [...], but once you see how a lot of people

> are doing a great job, even within ten years or twenty years, it will take long, but still if we say no, there will be no justice and it is hard, then dictators like Bashar would get away with it. Even if he dies, to be honest we need to continue with this to bring justice to these families, even if it is the grand-grandchild of this guy who got killed in jail, I need to make sure justice will come to this child [...]. The first time I was thinking about this idea of transitional justice and citizenship, it was in 2011. Then in 2013 it changed, since the time that the regime used chemical weapons on us. Since I saw that many people getting killed in front of me [...], I lost my feeling about justice. Still until now I don't believe in this, I don't believe in the whole Brussels thing, because if we leave it to them they won't do anything, they will just continue their job [...]. They will have more meetings. It will go to Geneva one hundred. But it is us, our duty to do something about this. (Artino, Eastern Ghouta, interview in English, February 2019)

In her exploration of the relationship between individual archives and collective experience, Sue McKemmish writes that archivists often think of the value their personal records might have for other people, and that "society has constructed systems and regimes to carry personal archives beyond the boundaries of an individual life so it fulfils its role of transforming 'evidence of *me*' into 'evidence of *us*.'"[31] This power of personal records to effect a shift from individual to collective experience is particularly relevant to the value attributed by Artino and the other Syrian videographers I spoke with to their own eyewitness content. Indeed, a red thread that ran through all the conversations I had with videographers, both inside Syria and in the diaspora, was collective memory and national identity, and the importance of these records for preserving the history of the uprising-war for generations to come. Moreover, throughout all my discussions with the videographers, the idea of justice kept recurring—not necessarily judiciary justice as human rights stakeholders define it, but social justice, as Abdul Rahman Jaloud put it:

> For our right to understand what happened and remember it a few years from now: this in itself is what justice is, not legal justice against a person or a regime, but justice as the right of a population

> to know what war is, to learn from this experience, so people can talk to each other rather than kill each other. (Abdul Rahman Jaloud, personal communication, November 2018)

My research has found that despite its unreliability, YouTube remains the main host of crowdsourced Syrian video content today. As Tarleton Gillespie shows, YouTube has been very effective in positioning itself as the champion of user-generated content, as a "place from which to speak and be heard," a free platform to "empower everyone to speak [...], lifting us all up, evenly."[32] Sarah T. Roberts also alludes to this "myth of unfettered possibility for democratic free expression" on social media platforms such as YouTube.[33] She does so while emphasizing the discrepancy between YouTube's promise (with its "Broadcast Yourself" slogan) of "unidirectional, direct user-to-platform-to-dissemination media creation opportunities" and its commercial content moderation processes, which complicate and directly contradict the notion that corporate social media platforms are free-speech zones.[34]

In fact, many of the Syrian videographers I spoke to never expected YouTube to play the role of gatekeeper; they thought "it would [always] be a mere facilitator, supporter, host."[35] They even believed this to such an extent that they used YouTube as their own memory, as Wassim el-Homsi told me in an interview in March 2019: "I didn't keep offline copies of my videos, because during that period, as I told you, I'd upload what I shot to YouTube and delete it [from my camera, phone, and laptop]. I was convinced that YouTube was like my memory, so everything that was on YouTube was going to stay on YouTube." Except that it was not, as his experience subsequently revealed:

> I have my own YouTube channel, it is still online. But in June 2012 there were about a thousand videos on my channel, in one night they all disappeared; everything that was on YouTube disappeared, and instead a video of Bashar al-Assad appeared on my channel. In one night, all of a sudden. First I thought the Internet wasn't working because I couldn't access my channel, then it opened, and I found a video of Bashar al-Assad, and songs, and all [...] I lost all of those videos [...]. Bottom line is what you lose from YouTube, you never get back. (Wassim al-Homsi, Homs, interview, March 2019)

Another finding from my ongoing discussions with Syrian videographers that I have not addressed in this chapter concerns the ways in which their archival practice is shaped by YouTube itself—that is, by the platform's usability and interface design. This calls to mind the concept of "activist-technology entanglement," a useful framework to explore how the uses and practices of activists and social change advocates are paradoxically shaped by corporate-owned software platforms.[36] The Syrian videographers' archival practice was formed progressively over the years; while at the beginning of the uprising they used different software (such as Google Drive, Skype chat rooms, and e-mail) and hardware (such as flash and external hard drives) to store their content, YouTube slowly became their go-to platform, because it offered a free and relatively easy-to-use service that they at first thought was sustainable and reliable.

Shea, Notley, and Burgess suggest that negotiations and compromises must be made between regulators, technology producers, and activists in order to attend to the unavoidable frictions caused by activist-technology entanglements.[37] However, my findings reflect a total lack of clarity, and imbalanced communication:

- The Syrian videographers still do not have a clear sense of what triggers the flagging and removal of their videos and channels, or, more importantly, how to avoid it or what to do when it actually happens. According to my research, this is a space where civil society organizations should focus their efforts and make an important contribution, whether through the provision of training or by running targeted awareness-raising campaigns.

- There are no direct communications between YouTube and any of the videographers on the ground, which makes the work of "brokers" and "mediators" such as the Syrian Archive, the Syrian Observatory for Human Rights, and other documentation centers in the diaspora (described in Figure 1) all the more important. My research also shows that international nongovernmental and civil society organizations working on open-source investigations (such as Bellingcat) and human rights advocacy efforts (such as Human Rights Watch, Witness, Amnesty International, and the UC Berkeley Human Rights Center) have taken on a mediator role between

YouTube and the Syrian documentation centers, in most cases without having any contact with videographers on the ground. This multilayering of relationships between videographers, human rights collectives based in the West, and corporate social media platforms is undermining efforts to address the issue of takedowns as swiftly and efficiently as is needed today. Nondisclosure agreements that YouTube, Facebook, and other corporate platforms require from the parties they are working with add yet another layer of complication to an already tangled ecology.

- Finally, the Syrian videographers on the ground have lost all trust in YouTube since the waves of deletions started, yet they still rely on it as the main online host of their video content in the absence of any free, reliable alternatives. This is another space where my research shows civil society organizations could play a significant role.

That being said, and in an attempt to nuance the rising concerns over YouTube's "interference" with the history of the Syrian uprising and war, I would like to end this essay with a few thoughts on what was lost and what still remains of the footage shot in Syria since 2011.

It is true that thousands of videos were uploaded to YouTube and were lost as a result of various content moderation strategies (both human-led and automated). It is also true that some of this content included vital documentation of human rights abuses, which might now be lost forever. All this is particularly damaging for the videos and channels whose owners were either killed or are currently in jail; in the absence of the authors, it becomes very hard to know what content is being removed, and almost impossible to get YouTube to put it back online (based on conversations with the Syrian Archive team).

It is also true that some of the content is being deleted by the users themselves, and in fact an important part of solving the issue of online takedowns is to understand the different types of deletions.

Finally, it is particularly true that the biggest loss involves what was left behind in Syria when activists and videographers had to flee and could not bring their cameras, laptops, or hard drives with them for security reasons. This was the case with most of those who fled central towns and cities and had to pass through a number of checkpoints to get to the border, because "getting caught with a hard drive containing footage of protests was the ultimate crime and could cost people their lives" (Zeina Armanazi, Aleppo, interview, March 2018).

But what is also true—and is often ignored by legal, human rights, and political advocacy groups, as well as by mainstream media—is that the history of the Syrian uprising and war is not only on YouTube; a very important part of it is right here, in Europe and the West,[38] whether on external hard drives that were smuggled out,[39] or in the memories of all those who fled:

> To be honest, I don't think YouTube is important at all. It was important in a specific moment in time, when the videos first came out and people saw them, but I don't think any of these videos would be used in court, because they've been edited, logos have been added to them. Most of the original footage still exists, and this is what matters and what could be later used in court [...]. In the Erbine Local Coordination Committee we only uploaded about twenty-five percent of the videos we shot in total. Even the pictures, if there are one hundred thousand pictures online, we have at least a million other pictures offline. (Abdel Sattar Charaf, Eastern Ghouta, interview, March 2019)

Some of the material is stuck in Syria, but a lot made it out of the country. Far from trying to downplay the effects of YouTube's takedowns on the preservation of the digital history of the Syrian war, this chapter makes the case for including videographers themselves in debates and discussions about the value of their content. No one knows this archive better than those who shot it, and unless the eyewitnesses themselves are brought into the ongoing debates about the value, usage, and sustainability of eyewitness video content from Syria, there will be no hope for transitional justice, or for postwar accountability.

1. This essay was written as part of the "Resistance-by-Recording" project based at the Department of Media Studies, Stockholm University. The research was made possible by Riksbankens Jubileumsfond, reference no. P14-0562:1.

2. The roundtable was organized as part of the "Resistance-by-Recording" project, with funding from the Department of Media Studies, Stockholm University.

3. Electronic Frontier Foundation, Witness, and Syrian Archive, "Caught in the Net: The Impact of 'Extremist' Speech Regulations on Human Rights Content," https://www.eff.org/wp/caught-net-impact-extremist-speech-regulations-human-rights-content.

4. The Syrian Archive, https://syrianarchive.org/en.

5. Sandra Ristovska, "Strategic Witnessing in an Age of Video Activism," *Media, Culture and Society* 37, no. 7 (2016): 1034-47.

6. Sandra Ristovska, "Human Rights Collectives as Visual Experts: The Case of Syrian Archive," *Visual Communication* 18, no. 3 (2019): 15.

7. Ibid., 10.

8. Sarah T. Roberts, *Behind the Screen: Content Moderation in the Shadows of Social Media* (New Haven, CT: Yale University Press, 2019), 6.

9. Ibid., 27.

10. "Four Steps We're Taking Today to Fight Terrorism Online," Google Europe, https://www.blog.google/around-the-globe/google-europe/four-steps-were-taking-today-fight-online-terror/.

11. Electronic Frontier Foundation, Witness, and Syrian Archive, "Caught in the Net."

12. Hundreds of articles have been published by mainstream media on the issue. See for example, among many others, Armin Rosen, "Erasing History: YouTube's Deletion of Syria War Videos Concerns Human Rights Groups," *Fast Company*, March 7, 2018, https://www.fastcompany.com/40540411/erasing-history-youtubes-deletion-of-syria-war-videos-concerns-human-rights-groups; Dia Kayyali and Raja Althaibani, "Vital Human Rights Evidence in Syria is Disappearing from YouTube," *Witness*, 2018, https://blog.witness.org/2017/08/vital-human-rights-evidence-syria-disappearing-youtube/; Kate O'Flaherty, "YouTube Keeps Deleting Evidence of Syrian Chemical Weapon Attacks," *Wired*, June 26, 2018, https://www.wired.co.uk/article/chemical-weapons-in-syria-youtube-algorithm-delete-video; Malachy Browne, "YouTube Removes Videos Showing Atrocities in Syria, " *New York Times*, August 22, 2017, https://www.nytimes.com/2017/08/22/world/middleeast/syria-youtube-videos-isis.html; Alexander J Martin, "YouTube Deleted Syrian War Crime Evidence," *Sky News*, August 15, 2017, https://news.sky.com/story/youtube-deleted-syrian-war-crime-evidence-10989430.

13. See Joshka Ivanka Wessels, "YouTube and the Role of Digital Video for Transitional Justice in Syria," *Politik* 19, no. 4 (2016), https://doi.org/10.7146/politik.v19i4.27634.

14. See Jeff Deutch and Hadi Habal. "The Syrian Archive: A Methodological Case Study of Open-Source Investigation of State Crime Using Video Evidence from Social Media Platforms," *State Crime Journal* 7, no. 1 (2018): 46-76.

15. Arguably, another voice that is also missing from these debates is that of the "invisible content moderators," who often work, as Sarah T. Roberts puts it, in very difficult conditions through queues of digital content to sort user-generated material "into either

the acceptable or the rejected pile." Roberts, *Behind the Screen*, 34. Roberts explains that issues of scale aside, the vast majority of video and image content uploaded to social media platforms in fact still requires human intervention to be properly screened and flagged for deletion.

16. Ristovska, "Human Rights Collectives as Visual Experts."

17. These interviews were made possible thanks to a collaboration with one of the Syrian Archive's cofounders, Abdul Rahman al-Jaloud, with whom I have been working since 2017. The connection with key Syrian videographers, some of whom are still operating in war zones, would not have happened without the advice and support of al-Jaloud, who has built long-standing relationships with activists and archivists on the ground, and who recommended me to them so that meaningful conversations became possible.

18. The sampling criteria and interview questions were developed as part of the "Resistance-by-Recording" project. All the interviews were undertaken by the author.

19. The names that have been changed are marked with asterisks.

20. Terry Cook, "Evidence, Memory, Identity, and Community: Four Shifting Archival Paradigms," *Archival Science*, no. 13 (2013): 95.

21. Ibid., 113.

22. Benedict Anderson, *Imagined Communities: Reflections on the Origin and Spread of Nationalism* (London: Verso, 2006), 19-21.

23. An important distinction is worth highlighting here between "evidential" and "evidentiary." As I describe later in the essay, the latter is a theme that underpins the institutional narrative of key human rights stakeholders when it comes to highlighting the value of eyewitness video content from Syria.

24. Sue McKemmish, "Evidence of Me," *Archives and Manuscripts* 45, no. 3 (1996): 175.

25. See Al-Ekhbariya, "Important clarification," April 25, 2011, https://www.youtube.com/watch?v=vNPrw6mVgTE; Addounia, "Media mis-information," May 9, 2012, https://www.youtube.com/watch?v=5MrvtNtjpJM; RT, "Bashar al-Assad in an exclusive interview with RT," November 10, 2019, https://www.youtube.com/watch?v=SXQcsLHXsW4&feature=youtu.be&t=499.

26. See Melissa Wall and Sahar El-Zahed, "Syrian Citizen Journalism," *Digital Journalism* 3, no. 5 (2015): 720-36.

27. Sandra Ristovska, "The Rise of Eyewitness Video and Its Implications for Human Rights: Conceptual and Methodological Approaches," *Journal of Human Rights* 15, no. 3 (2016): 347-60.

28. Rosen, "Erasing History."

29. See Andrieu Kora, "Transitional Justice: A New Discipline in Human Rights," https://www.sciencespo.fr/mass-violence-war-massacre-resistance/fr/document/transitional-justice-new-discipline-human-rights-0.

30. Cook, "Evidence, Memory, Identity, and Community," 101.

31. McKemmish, "Evidence of Me," 181.

32. Tarleton Gillespie, "The Politics of 'Platforms,'" *New Media and Society* 12, no. 3 (2010): 352.

33. Roberts, *Behind the Screen*, 27.

34. Ibid., 71.

35. Gillespie, "The Politics of 'Platforms,'" 353.

36. Pip Shea, Tanya Notley, Jean Burgess, and Su Ballard, "Editorial," *Fibreculture Journal*, no. 26 (2015): 1-7.

37. Ibid., 5.

38. On the value and importance of "refugee archives," see Dima Saber and Paul Long, "Refugee Writing, Refugee History: Locating the Refugee Archive in the Making of a History of the Syrian War," in *Refugee Imaginaries: Research across the Humanities*, ed. Emma Cox et al. (Edinburgh: Edinburgh University Press, 2019), 444-62.

39. See Dima Saber and Paul Long, "'I Will Not Leave, My Freedom Is More Precious Than My Blood': From Affect to Precarity—Crowd-Sourced Citizen Archives as Memories of the Syrian War," *Archives and Records* 1, no. 38 (2017): 80-99.

BIOGRAPHIES

DANIELA AGOSTINHO is a visual culture theorist and an independent curator. She is Assistant Professor in the Department of Arts and Cultural Studies, University of Copenhagen. She currently leads the project *Archival Encounters* through a fellowship from the Novo Nordisk Foundation. Her research interests include cultural theories, visual and digital culture, artistic research, postcolonial studies, and transnational feminist theories. She is co-editor of *Uncertain Archives: Critical Keywords for Big Data*, with Nanna Bonde Thylstrup, Annie Ring, Catherine D'Ignazio, and Kristin Veel (MIT Press, 2021), and *The Uncertain Image*, with Ulrik Ekman, Nanna Bonde Thylstrup, and Kristin Veel (Routledge, 2019), and the author of numerous articles in journals such as *Philosophy of Photography*, *Surveillance & Society*, and *Senses & Society*.

HEBA Y. AMIN is an Egyptian visual artist, researcher, and lecturer based in Berlin. She is the co-founder of the Black Athena Collective, the curator of visual art for the *Mizna* journal, and one of the artists behind the subversive graffiti action on the set of the television series *Homeland*, which received worldwide media attention. Amin has had recent exhibitions at the 10th Berlin Biennale, 15th Istanbul Biennale, MAXXI Rome, Künstlerhaus Bethanien Berlin, Kalmar Art Museum Sweden, La Villette Paris, FACT Liverpool, Kunsthalle Wien, the Museum of Modern Art in Warsaw, the Kunstverein in Hamburg, Berlin Berlinale 9th Forum Expanded Exhibition, and the IV Moscow International Biennale for Young Art.

ARIELLA AZOULAY is Professor of Comparative Literature and Modern Culture and Media, Brown University, and an independent curator and filmmaker. She is the author of numerous publications, including *Potential History: Unlearning Imperialism* (2019), *Civil Imagination: A Political Ontology of Photography* (2011), *From Palestine to Israel: A Photographic Record of Destruction and State Formation, 1947-1950* (2011), *The Civil Contract of Photography* (2008), and *Death's Showcase: The Power of Image in Contemporary Democracy* (2001). Azoulay was formerly professor of visual culture and contemporary philosophy at the Program for Culture and Interpretation, Bar Ilan University. In recent years, Azoulay has produced several documentary films that address different aspects of the history of Israel and Palestine.

SVEA BRAEUNERT is DAAD Visiting Associate Professor in German Studies and Film and Media Studies at the University of Cincinnati. Her research interests include visual and digital culture, photography, time-based media, and memory studies. She is the author of a book on left-wing terrorism in German art, *Gespenstergeschichten: Der linke Terrorismus der RAF und die Künste* (Kadmos, 2015), and coauthor and co-curator of *To See Without Being Seen: Contemporary Art and Drone Warfare* (University of Chicago Press, 2016).

ANTHONY DOWNEY is Professor of Visual Culture in the Middle East and North Africa, Birmingham City University. He is the recipient of an AHRC

Global Challenges Research Fund (to develop a four-year project on education provision in conflict zones), and he sits on the editorial boards of *Third Text* and *Digital War*. He is the series editor for Research/Practice (Sternberg Press, 2019). Recent and upcoming publications include *Unbearable States: Digital Media, Cultural Activism and Human Rights* (forthcoming, 2021); *Critique in Practice: Renzo Martens' "Episode III: Enjoy Poverty"* (Sternberg Press, 2019); *Don't Shrink Me to the Size of a Bullet: The Works of Hiwa K* (Verlag der Buchhandlung Walther König, 2017); and *Future Imperfect: Contemporary Art Practices and Cultural Institutions in the Middle East* (Sternberg Press, 2016).

SOPHIE DYER is a London-based researcher and designer who specializes in visual, open source, and human-rights-based investigations. She currently works with Amnesty International's Crisis Response Programme in the Evidence Lab. She is a founding member of the Feminist Open Source Investigations Group and is one half of the citizen sensing project Open Weather. From September 2017 to April 2019, she was a Senior Researcher and Advocacy Officer at the civilian casualty monitor Airwars. Beyond Airwars, she has worked freelance with Forensic Architecture, among others. Dyer studied visual communication at the Glasgow School of Art before completing a master's degree at the Centre for Research Architecture at Goldsmiths, University of London. She sits on the *Journal of Digital War* editorial board.

ANDERS ENGBERG-PEDERSEN is Professor of Comparative Literature in the Department for the Study of Culture, University of Southern Denmark. He writes and teaches in the fields of eighteenth-to-twenty-first-century literature (German, French, Russian, Scandinavian) with a particular focus on war; the history and poetics of knowledge; cartography; and intersections of literature and philosophy. He is the author of *Empire of Chance: The Napoleonic Wars and the Disorder of Things* (Harvard University Press, 2015) and editor of the volumes *Literature and Cartography: Theories, Histories, Genres* (MIT Press, 2017) and *Visualizing War: Emotions, Technologies, Communities* (Routledge, 2017). He currently directs two collective research projects on warfare and aesthetics (funded by the Carlsberg Foundation and the Velux Foundations), and is at work on a book titled *Military Aesthetics: Technology, Experience, and Late Modern War*. He also serves as an editor of Prisms: Humanities and War, a book series with MIT Press.

SOLVEIG GADE is a theater and performance scholar and dramaturge. She is Associate Professor in the Department of Arts and Cultural Studies, University of Copenhagen. Her research centers on experimental and post-dramatic strategies in contemporary theater and performance and the ways in which these strategies respond to their surrounding political contexts. She served as a playwright at the Royal Danish Theater (2008–2014). From 2019 to 2020 she was a professor at the Danish National School for Performing Arts. In her current research project, she focuses on war and conflict in the post-9/11 era as depicted in contemporary documentary performance, dance, and visual art. Selected journals in which her research has appeared include *Performance Research*, *TDR: The Drama Review*, *Nordic Theater Studies*, *Nordic Journal of Aesthetics*, and *The Journal of War and Culture Studies*.

CRISTIÁN GÓMEZ-MOYA is a researcher, editor, artist, and curator. He is head of the program in Visual and Media Studies in the Faculty of Architecture and Urban Studies, University of Chile. His research is concerned with visuality, documents, and archives at the intersection of art and politics. He holds a PhD in Art History and Theory from the University of Barcelona. He was a visiting lecturer at the Center for Latin American and Caribbean Studies, New York University (2013); the Hemispheric Institute, New York University (2010 and 2013); and the Instituto de Cooperación Catalán-Iberoamericano. He was coordinator of the project *Human Rights/Copy Rights* (Vicerrectoría de Investigación y Desarrollo,

Museo de Arte Contemporáneo, Universidad de Chile, 2011-2012). He is a member of the network Conceptualismos del Sur, the research project *Archivos/Museos/Modernidades* (Museo Nacional Centro de Arte Reina Sofía), and co-founder of the research platform Tristestópicos. He is the author of the book *Derechos de mirada: Arte y visualidad en los archivos desclasificados* (Editorial Palinodia, 2012).

SOFIE LEBECH is a Danish director, performer, and author. She is Associate Professor at Malmö Theatre Academy and holds a PhD in Theatre and Performance Studies from the University of Copenhagen. Her artistic practice is research-based, and she writes, performs, and stages with a focus on reenactment, documentary strategies, and the meeting between fiction and reality. Since 2003 she has made numerous performances, research projects, site-specific interventions, and installations. Her works include *This if for Her* (2017), *Precarious Life* (2014), winner of the Danish Arts Foundation's 2014 award, *VI (WE)* (2014), *Invisible Visible* (2013), and *Walk in Cairo* (2012).

KATHRIN MAURER is Professor of Humanities and Technology and leader of the Center for Humanities and Technology at the University of Southern Denmark (SDU). Her research interests include surveillance technology, drones, German literature, visual culture, and aesthetic theory. She has published *Visualizing the Past: The Power of the Image in German Historicism* (De Gruyter, 2013) and *Visualizing War: Emotions, Technologies, Communities* (Routledge, 2018) as well as numerous articles in journals such as *New German Critique* and *Media, War, and Conflict*. She is also a Senior Fellow at the Danish Institute for Advanced Study at SDU and the recipient of a research grant from the Alexander von Humboldt Foundation.

KEVIN MCSORLEY is Senior Lecturer in Sociology at the Open University, UK. His research explores transformations in violence, warfare, and militarism, particularly through the lens of the body and sensory experience. His research projects *War and the Body* and *Sensing War* have produced agenda-setting events, networks, and publications. He is the editor of *War and the Body: Militarisation, Practice and Experience* (Routledge, 2015) and author of numerous articles on the lived experiences of war and the afterlives of conflict, militarism and physical culture, the militarization of sensation, drone warfare, and torture.

DIMA SABER is a Reader in Media and Cultural Studies, Birmingham City University. Her research is focused on media depictions of conflict in postwar and post-revolution contexts and on the role of archival records in identity-building processes. She is responsible for leading and delivering projects in citizen journalism in the North Africa Western Asia region (NAWA), exploring ways digital literacy can foster social impact and enhance the work of political activists in post-revolution and conflict countries such as Lebanon, Egypt, Syria, Yemen, and Palestine. Her publications include work on the mnemonic potential of crowd-sourced archives of the Syrian war; on the role of vernacular archives in the constitution of a history of the Syrian conflict; on Hezbollah and IS video-game productions, and on Al Jazeera's coverage of the July 2006 war. She is a board member of the Syrian Archive, the Yemen Archive, and the MENA Design Research Centre.

NANNA BONDE THYLSTRUP is Associate Professor of Digital Media and Communication at Copenhagen Business School. Her research and teaching focus on aspects of datafication, technology, and culture. She is particularly interested in how digitization and datafication are changing cultures and social and material relations. She is the author of *The Politics of Mass Digitization* (MIT Press, 2019) and co-editor of *Uncertain Archives: Critical Keywords for Big Data* (MIT Press, 2021). She has written numerous articles and essays on infrastructures of forgetting and remembering, gendered epistemologies in digital infrastructures, archival affects, small media, content moderation and care, reuse ethics, environmental media, and data waste.

ORAIB TOUKAN is an artist and scholar. She holds a PhD in Fine Arts from Oxford University, Ruskin School of Art. Until fall 2015, she was head of the Arts Division and Media Studies program at Bard College at Al Quds University, Palestine, and was visiting faculty at the International Academy of Fine Arts in Ramallah. Toukan is author of *Sundry Modernism: Materials for a Study of Palestinian Modernism* (Sternberg Press, 2017) and the essay-film *When Things Occur* (2016). Recent exhibitions at institutions including the Asia Pacific Triennial, the Mori Art Museum, Akademie der Künste, Berlin, Heidelberger Kunstverein, Qalandia International, the Centre for Contemporary Art Glasgow, and the 11th Istanbul Biennale. Her writings have appeared in a number of publications, collected works, and biennial readers.

SARAH TUCK is a Lecturer at HDK-Valand - Academy of Art and Design, University of Gothenburg, and Head of Unit, Craft and Fine Art. Her principal research interests lie in the relationship between photography, history, politics, and cultural memory. Recently her work has explored the uses of drone technologies in surveillance, war, and protest, supported by a collaborative initiative of the Hasselblad Center and Valand Academy in partnership with Nicosia Municipal Arts Centre, Nicosia, Cyprus, and the Zahoor Ul Akhlaq Gallery in Lahore, Pakistan. In 2015 she published *After the Agreement: Contemporary Photography in Northern Ireland*, a curated research project funded by the Arts & Humanities Research Council UK, which considers the affective meanings of photographs in the sociopolitical context of "post-conflict" in Northern Ireland. Her work has traversed a wide range of situated practice, including community development, post-conflict processes, and institutional networks where questions of agency, knowledge production, and representation have always been central.

KRISTIN VEEL is Associate Professor at the Department of Arts and Cultural Studies, University of Copenhagen. Her research engages with the impact of digital technology and datafication on the contemporary cultural imagination, with a particular interest in invisibilities, uncertainties, overload, and the gigantic. Her most recent book, coauthored with Henriette Steiner, is *Tower to Tower: Gigantism in Architecture and Digital Culture* (MIT Press, 2020). She is co-editor of *Uncertain Archives: Critical Keywords for Big Data*, with Nanna Bonde Thylstrup, Daniela Agostinho, Catherine D'Ignazio, and Annie Ring (MIT Press, 2021) and *Invisibility Studies: Surveillance, Transparency and the Hidden in Contemporary Culture*, with Henriette Steiner and Annie Ring (Peter Lang, 2015).

LOUISE WOLTHERS, PhD, is Head of Research and Curator at the Hasselblad Foundation, Gothenburg. She has conducted research and curated exhibitions at institutions such as the National Museum of Photography and the National Gallery of Denmark. She has co-edited publications such as *Lost and Found: Queerying the Archive* (2009) and contributed to numerous academic journals and books on photography, visual culture, and contemporary art. She coordinated the research project *WATCHED! Surveillance, Art and Photography* (publication and touring exhibition, 2016-2017). Recent articles include "Monitoring the Margins: Street Views of Sex Workers" (in *Photography & Society*, 2017) and "Seeing Through Scandinavian Exceptionalism: Tina Enghoff's Photography" (*Journal of European Studies*, 2017).

ARKADI ZAIDES is an Israeli independent choreographer and visual artist of Belarusian origin, currently living in France. In Israel, he performed in several companies, such as the Batsheva Dance Company, and the Yasmeen Godder Dance Group, before embarking on an independent career in 2004. He obtained a master's degree from the AHK Academy of Theater and Dance in Amsterdam. His performances and installations have been presented in numerous dance and theater festivals, museums, and galleries across Europe, North and South America, and Asia. Over the years he has curated projects such as *New Dance Project* (2010-2011) with choreographer

Anat Danieli, *Moves Without Borders* (2012-2015), and *Violence of Inscriptions* (2015-2018) with the scholar, curator, and dramaturge Sandra Noeth. The latter gathered artists, thinkers, and human-rights activists to negotiate the role of the body in producing, maintaining, legitimizing, representing, and aestheticizing structural violence. He is a recipient of numerous prizes, among them the Emile Zola Prize for Performing Arts, awarded to Zaides for demonstrating engagement in human-rights issues.

AIMÉE ZITO LEMA is a Dutch-Argentinian visual artist who in her praxis engages with issues revolving around social memory through personal narratives placed within broader historical contexts. She works with a variety of media, ranging from photography to sculptural installations, performance art, and the moving image. Born in Amsterdam and raised in Buenos Aires, she began her studies at the Buenos Aires University of Fine Arts and later graduated from the Gerrit Rietveld Academie, Amsterdam. She holds a master's degree in Artistic Research from the Royal Academy of Art in the Hague and was Artist-in-Residence at the Rijksakademie van beeldende Kunsten, Amsterdam. Her work has been displayed at Centro Cultural de la Memoria Haroldo Conti, Buenos Aires, 2020; Hangzhou Triennial of Fiber Art, 2019; the Eye Filmmuseum, Amsterdam, 2019; the Gulbenkian Museum, Lisbon, 2018; Kunsthall Trondheim, 2017; MACBA, Barcelona, 2017; the 11th Gwangju Biennale, 2016; Kunstmuseum Bonn, and the Centre Pompidou, Paris, 2016, among other venues. Zito Lema lives and works in Amsterdam.

IMAGE CREDITS

63 Fig. 1 - Johannes Kepler, *Die Astrologie des Johannes Kepler: Eine Auswahl aus seinen Schriften*, ed. Heinz Artur Strauss and Sigrid Strauss-Kloebe (Munich: Oldenbourg, 1926), 185.

68 Fig. 2 - Det Kongelige Bibliotek.

72 Fig. 3 - Johann Christian Ludwig Hellwig, *Das Kriegsspiel—ein Versuch die Wahrheit verschiedener Regeln der Kriegskunst in einem unterhaltenden Spiele anschaulich zu machen* (Braunschweig: bei Karl Reichard, 1803). Forsvarets Bibliotek.

75 Fig. 4 - John Prados, *The Rise and Decline of the Third Reich*, 3rd ed. (Baltimore: Avalon Hill Game Company, 1974). Private photo. Courtesy of John Prados.

84 Fig. 1 - Property of University of Chile. Photographic negative, 1957. Management of Municipal Works Archive, 1976.

95 Fig. 2 - Photograph, 1976. Registry of Lands, Mines, and Industrial Properties in Santiago. Santiago de Chile, 2019.

96-97 Figs. 3, 4 - Photograph, 1980. Property Register, Registry of Lands, Mines, and Industrial Properties of Santiago. Santiago de Chile, 2019.

99-100 Figs. 5, 6 - Photograph, 1957. Annals of 1957. Central Archive Andrés Bello. Santiago de Chile, 2019.

103 Figs. 7, 8, 9 - Cerrillos Archive Project Team, Santiago de Chile, 2019.

104 Figs. 10, 11, 12 - Cerrillos Archive Project Team, Santiago de Chile, 2019.

106 Figs. 13, 14 - Cerrillos Archive Project Team, Santiago de Chile, 2019.

130 Fig. 1 - Courtesy of the artist; Metro Pictures, New York; Altman Siegel, San Francisco.

146-47 Fig. 1 - Courtesy of Haitham Mossad.

154-57 Figs. 2, 3 - Courtesy of the artist.

159 Fig. 4 - Courtesy of the artist.

166-67 Fig. 1 - Courtesy of the artist.

170-71 Fig. 2 - Courtesy of Hasselblad Foundation and Valand Academy.

172-73 Fig. 3 - Courtesy of the artist.

174-75 Fig. 4 - Courtesy of the artist.

178 Fig. 5 - Courtesy of the artist.

179 Fig. 6 - Courtesy of the artist.

180-81 Fig. 7 - Courtesy of the artist.

184-85 Fig. 8 - Courtesy of the artist.

186-87 Fig. 9 - Courtesy of the artist, Photographers' Gallery, and NOME Gallery.

272-79 Archive images: Argentina Archivo General de la Nación Dpto. Doc. Fotográficos.

280-83 Exhibition shots from *The Subversive Body* (2016), installation with inkjet print photographs on paper, wooden structures/tables. Documentation of exhibition at Wilfried Lentz, Rotterdam, 2016. Photo: Sander van Wettum. Courtesy of the artist and Wilfried Lentz, Rotterdam.

286-87 Fig. 1 - Photo: Søren Meisner.

298-99 Fig. 2 - Photo: Søren Meisner.

310 Fig. 1 - Courtesy of the Non-Imperial Archive.

311 Fig. 2 - Courtesy of the Non-Imperial Archive.

314 Fig. 3 - Courtesy of the Non-Imperial Archive.

324 Fig. 4 - Courtesy of the Non-Imperial Archive.

326 Fig. 5 - Courtesy of the Non-Imperial Archive.

327 Fig. 6 - Courtesy of the Non-Imperial Archive.

328 Fig. 7 - Courtesy of the Non-Imperial Archive.

330 Fig. 8 - Photography by the author.

333 Fig. 9 - Photo: Ibraheem Abu Mustafa/ Reuters/Ritzau Scanpix.

351-58 Courtesy of the artist.

370 Fig. 1 - Photo: David Ehrtl © Kunst- und Ausstellungshalle der Bundesrepublik Deutschland GmbH.

375 Fig. 2 - Photo: David Ehrtl © Kunst- und Ausstellungshalle der Bundesrepublik Deutschland GmbH.

377 Fig. 3 - Photo: David Ehrtl © Kunst- und Ausstellungshalle der Bundesrepublik Deutschland GmbH.

388-89 Fig. 1 - Designed by Kipp Jones (WildIlk).

Cover Courtesy of the artist.

(W)ARCHIVES
Archival Imaginaries, War,
and Contemporary Art

PUBLISHED BY
Sternberg Press

EDITORS
Daniela Agostinho
Solveig Gade
Nanna Bonde Thylstrup
Kristin Veel

COPYEDITOR
Merl Storr

DESIGN
ATLAS Projectos

TYPEFACES
Hershey-Noailles under SIL Open Font License 1.1. A collection of vector fonts developed ca. 1967 by Dr. Allen Vincent Hershey at the Naval Weapons Laboratory, US Navy, originally designed to be rendered using vectors on early cathode-ray tube displays. Decomposing curves to connect straight lines allowed Hershey to produce complex typographic designs.

Digitized and expanded by Luuse (Brussels) for the visual identity of Centre d'Art Villa Noailles, adding Handles, *Italic*, Old French, and Times Simplex, among other variations, to preexisting Roman Simplex and Roman Complex.

PAPER
Arena Natural Rough 120g/m² wood-free, OBA free
Favini Remake Sand 250g/m², including
40% recycled pulp and 25% leather by-product

PRINTING AND BINDING
Gráfica Maiadouro, Maia, Portugal

DISTRIBUTION
The MIT Press
Art Data
Les presses du réel

ISBN 978-3-95679-456-8
N° D.L. / L.D. no. 477743/20

Sternberg Press
Caroline Schneider
Karl-Marx-Allee 78
D-10243 Berlin
www.sternberg-press.com

DANMARKS FRIE FORSKNINGSFOND
INDEPENDENT RESEARCH FUND DENMARK

NY CARLSBERG FONDET
NEW CARLSBERG FOUNDATION

CARLSBERG FOUNDATION

ACKNOWLEDGMENTS
This publication was made possible by generous support from the Independent Research Fund Denmark, the Carlsberg Foundation, and the NY Carlsberg Foundation.

The editors would also like to thank Sayuri Alsman, Max Bach, Nisrine Boukhari, Mariam Ghani, Amr Hatem, Ekaterina Kalinina, Sajid Khan, Nuno da Luz, Margarida Mendes, Rabih Mroué, Gonçalo Sena, Susan Schuppli, Hito Steyerl, and Leah Whitman-Salkin.